Cambridge Introductions to Music
Opera

What is opera and how does it work? How has this dramatic form developed, and what is its relevance in the modern world? Perfect for music students and opera-goers, this introductory guide addresses these questions and many more, exploring opera as a complete theatrical experience. Organised chronologically, and avoiding technical musical terminology, the book clearly demonstrates how opera reflected and reacted to changes in the world around it. A special feature of the volume is the inclusion of over a hundred illustrative tables. These provide a detailed, easy-to-follow analysis of arias, scenes and acts; visual guides to historical movements; and chronologies relating to genres and individual composers' works. Overall, the book fosters an understanding of opera as a living form as it encounters and uses material from an ever-expanding repertoire in time, place and culture.

ROBERT CANNON created the first ever degree in Opera Studies, validated by the University of Manchester for Rose Bruford College. He now works as an independent lecturer, music critic and writer.

Cambridge Introductions to Music

'Cambridge University Press is to be congratulated for formulating the idea of an "Introductions to Music" series.' Nicholas Jones, *The Musical Times*

Each book in this series focuses on a topic fundamental to the study of music at undergraduate and graduate level. The introductions will also appeal to readers who want to broaden their understanding of the music they enjoy.

- Contain textboxes which highlight and summarise key information
- Provide helpful guidance on specialised musical terminology
- Thorough guides to further reading assist the reader in investigating the topic in more depth

Books in the series

Gregorian Chant   David Hiley

Music Technology   Julio D'Escrivan

Opera   Robert Cannon

Serialism   Arnold Whittall

The Sonata   Thomas Schmidt-Beste

The Song Cycle   Laura Tunbridge

Cambridge Introductions to Music
Opera

ROBERT CANNON

CAMBRIDGE
UNIVERSITY PRESS

CAMBRIDGE UNIVERSITY PRESS
Cambridge, New York, Melbourne, Madrid, Cape Town,
Singapore, São Paulo, Delhi, Tokyo, Mexico City

Cambridge University Press
The Edinburgh Building, Cambridge CB2 8RU, UK

Published in the United States of America by Cambridge University Press, New York

www.cambridge.org
Information on this title: www.cambridge.org/9780521746472

First published 2012

Printed in the United Kingdom at the University Press, Cambridge

A catalogue record for this publication is available from the British Library

Library of Congress Cataloguing in Publication data
Cannon, Robert, 1947–
Opera / Robert Cannon.
    p.   cm. – (Cambridge introductions to music)
Includes bibliographical references and index.
ISBN 978-0-521-76302-8 (hardback)
1. Opera.   I. Title.
ML1700.C195   2012
782.1 – dc23   2011041744

ISBN 978-0-521-76302-8 Hardback
ISBN 978-0-521-74647-2 Paperback

For Edmonde

Wer ein holdes Weib errungen
Stimm' in unsern Jubel ein!
Nie wird es zu hoch besungen,
Rettern des Gatten sein.
(*Fidelio*, act II Finale)

Contents

Appendixes

Tables

Introduction

It demands as much effort on the listener's part as the other two corners of the
triangle, this holy triangle of composer, performer and listener.

(Benjamin Britten, in Kildea, 2000: 261)

The impulse to combine words, music and action has existed from the very beginning
of drama. Indeed, musical drama mainly preceded the purely spoken, which immediately begs the question: where does opera begin? One simple but useful answer is at
the point where people called their works 'operas' (or its equivalent). But to do this
gives the impression of opera coming from nowhere, born fully formed, like Athena.
Looking further back than the Florentine *Camerata* suggests the multifarious nature
of musical theatre, the range of its potential and priorities.

Opera has never ceased to grow and change – often quite radically. This book
is an attempt to describe and show the development of the many different things
that 'opera' can be. It is not a history, but its organisation is broadly chronological since opera developed in a very conscious way across Europe. It is essential to
remember that specific composers and operas are included as examples of particular
aspects of operatic development and not as studies in their own right even in those
chapters devoted to a single individual (Wagner in Chapter 10 and the section of
Chapter 8 on Verdi). This remains true in the later chapters (16, 17) which address
specific examples of modern and contemporary opera exploring, often in the composers' own words, their ideas about what opera is and how it works in social and aesthetic terms. In all cases, composers and works have been chosen that an opera-goer
might reasonably have been able to actually see and all of which have been recorded.

There is, then, a strong sense of linear development, but there is also an emphasis
on how quite different types of opera coexisted, each demanding a different aesthetic
response. Thus, while there is a study of the line between Metastasian *opera seria*,
the 'internal' reforms of Rameau and Jommelli and the more radical 'reforms' of
Gluck, it is essential not to adopt an evolutionary attitude and simply see opera
progressing towards Gluck or Wagner and discarding its preceding achievements.
The operas of Lully, Handel, Rameau and Traetta, let alone those of Rossini, Wagner,
Offenbach, Berg and Adams, each have their own qualities and strengths. Each needs

to be understood in its own right while also seeing how they grew out of what came before and then led to something different.

To appreciate this requires understanding how operas work. The book is, therefore, designed to uncover the mechanisms, the working parts of opera, by looking at its major periods and exponents. This is complicated because opera combines the 'abstract' nature of music with the concrete nature of words and stage settings. As a result its development combines many things and depends upon changes beyond its own artistic world. At different points it is necessary to look away from opera to the wider aesthetic, social, political and cultural context. Only by doing this is it often possible to understand how and why the music, libretto, dramaturgy or staging changed.

The book is aimed at two complementary readerships. The student of music who needs a basis for approaching this very particular and complex musical application, and the person who is already familiar with opera and wants to know more than is provided by a history or synopses. It assumes a basic knowledge of the chronology of opera; access to a good guide such as Kobbé or *The New Grove Dictionary of Opera* for synopses; an elementary awareness of musical terms such as melody, harmony, rhythm and modulation. Its aim is to enable the reader to

- develop a clear chronological through-line, but centred on change rather than evolutionary 'progress'
- understand the many different ways in which opera and its forms work
- appreciate the formative role of opera's major exponents
- see how opera and its development reflected and reacted to changes in the world around it.

While the book may be used as a point of reference for particular periods or even composers, it is designed to be read as a whole, developing an aesthetic for opera, the terms for analysing it and the language for discussing it.

Two features are designed to help the reader gain a sense of context and the movements of which opera was a part. These are series of tables and four generic chapters.

The tables offer visual guides to the complex relationships explored in the text. Charts of this kind can falsify relationships by making them look simpler, more direct or less ambiguous than they really were. Nevertheless they are used here as frameworks within which ideas and interconnections can be studied. There are four main kinds:

1 Schematic representations of historical (social, cultural, political) movements and events (Table 7.1).
2 Chronologies relating to a genre or a composer's work (Table 8.9).

3 Structural analysis of acts or scenes (Table 10.4).
4 Detailed analysis of a selected passage (Table 8.12). These are designed to be
   followed with a score or aurally, and parallel the libretto with a commentary on
   the music and drama. The translations are literal so as to follow each line unit of
   text.

The date given for an opera is generally that of the premiere, but where a composer's development is concerned the date of composition is given if this is substantially different from the first performance.

The book is organised in three parts, each dealing with a key phase in opera:
part I, the seventeenth and eighteenth centuries; part II, the nineteenth century;
part III, the twentieth and twenty-first centuries. The four generic chapters (6, 12,
15, 18) deal with topics that arise from the particular concerns of a part but which
also apply across the whole book. They are primarily meant to help focus a series of
questions about opera as a living form as it encounters and uses material from an
ever-expanding repertoire in time, place and culture.

This book covers a wide range of material and would not have been possible
without the interest, help and advice of many people. Chief among these I should
especially like to thank my wonderful, sympathetic and witty editor, Victoria Cooper,
my forbearing and unfailingly supportive wife Edmonde, the scholar and opera-lover
Michael Downes and my hard-working 'lay' reader Julia Edwards.

Part I

The seventeenth and eighteenth centuries

Chapter 1

Pre-operatic forms

Opera is a dramatic form whose primary language is music. A successful opera must work both musically and dramatically; to understand opera means understanding both elements, and how they interact. This is what makes the study of opera fascinating: it requires us to keep two art forms in balance to create a third. The challenge of opera lies in the potential conflict between these elements, each of which has its own priorities and structures. In some periods it has been dominated by the music – Handel or Rossini, while in others it is the drama that dominates – Gluck or Berg. But the opposition is a false one. It is never a matter of domination, but of the balance that is appropriate to what the composer is trying to achieve and the meaning he or she wants to create.

To define opera as 'a dramatic form whose primary language is music' is very broad – as it has to be if it is going to accommodate works as different as *Aida*, *The Mikado* and *Lulu*, let alone have the potential for coping with *West Side Story* or *The Phantom of the Opera*. A broad definition is useful, moreover, because it can help to avoid generic traps. Thinking about opera can be restricted by and to those works that were consciously written as and called 'operas' or one of the many variants of the word. Wagner used the term 'music drama' precisely because he had defined 'opera' to his own satisfaction and decided that what he was creating was different: 'The history of opera, since Rossini, is at bottom nothing else but the history of operatic melody' (Goldman and Sprinchorn, 1970: 107).

Pre-opera: Greek drama

The history of opera proper begins at the turn of the sixteenth century. But there are many examples of musico-dramatic works earlier than that, reaching back through the mediaeval period to the Greeks. These are of interest because they show the strong impulse to create works that combine music and drama, and because they help develop and test the criteria that are needed for the enormous variety of performance types that make up 'the opera'.

The Greek theatre made significant use of music, played, sung and danced. The term *strophe*, one of the divisions of the choral ode, means a 'turn', indicating part of the choreography, and the word *orchestra* means 'dancing place'. How the music was used, in what way and for which elements (soloists, chorus) is uncertain, although it seems unlikely that it was through-sung. What seems clear is that while the plays used music to heighten, emphasise and ritualise certain moments, it was an accompaniment rather than an integral part of the action. Despite later fascination with the Greek theatre and its performance, there was no direct continuity from the Greeks, and their influence only reappeared with the academic interest of the late fifteenth century.

Pre-opera: mediaeval music theatre (liturgical, sacred and secular drama)

The mediaeval drama, in its different forms, also made extensive use of music. In the twelfth-century *Herodes* one instruction reads:

> Tunc demum surgentes [Pastores] *cantent* intra se: Transeamus usque Bethlehem.

> Then let the (shepherds), arising, *sing* among themselves: *Let us now go unto Bethlehem* (emphasis added).

In the later *Second Shepherds' Play*, there is evidence that the audience would have been familiar with musical terms:

> II pastor: Say, what was his song? Hard ye not how he craykd it?
>   Thre brefes to a long?
> III pastor: Ye, mary, he hakt it.
>   Was no crochett wrong.   (Happé, 1975: 291)

From about 1000 there developed a considerable body of dramatic works in which music played a major part. Some have spoken passages, others are set throughout. Broadly, these fall into three main groups, all of which were contemporary with one another (Table 1.1).

The Mass itself is often seen as a theatrical event accompanied by music. However by at least the tenth century the liturgy was expanded to include consciously the-atrical, sung episodes. The first narrative chosen was the visit of the three Marys to the tomb (*Sepulchrum*) beginning with the *Quem quaeritis?* (Whom seek ye?) which naturally called for a response between participants:

> While the third responsary is being sung, let the remaining three [brethren] follow . . . in the manner of seeking something . . . These things are done in

Table 1.1 *Mediaeval dramatic forms*

Liturgical Drama	Sacred Drama (Created outside the church)	Secular Drama
Dramatic episodes written as part of the liturgy	Plays dramatising sacred themes and episodes (Biblical, Saints' lives, etc.)	Plays with non-sacred subjects
▼	▼	▼
Quem quaeritis? *Les Trois Maries*	Mystery Play cycles *Ordo Virtutum* *Ludus Danielis*	*Jeu de Robin et de Marion*

imitation of the angel seated on the monument, and of the women coming with spices to anoint the body of Jesus. When therefore that one seated shall see the three . . . let him begin in a dulcet voice of medium pitch to sing: *Whom seek ye in the sepulchre, O followers of Christ?*   (J.Q. Adams, 2008: 9)

The liturgical dramas dramatise Biblical events as part of the church service. Starting from the *Quem quaeritis*, these became increasingly complex. A particularly fine late example is the early fourteenth-century *Les Trois Maries* from Origny-Sainte-Benoîte. The musical form is monodic chant which, while very beautiful, makes little if any differentiation between the characters of the Maries, the Merchant, the Angels, etc. However there is a truly dramatic moment as Mary Magdalene encounters Christ, portraying her sense of loss and mystical rapture at the '*Noli me tangere*'. The text contains clear stage directions:

Our Lord says:	*Marie!*
Marie Magdalene says at the foot of Our Lord:	*Raboni!*
and stays thus until Our Lord has sung:	*Do not touch me. I am not yet ascended unto my Father.* (*Les Trois Maries*)

To what extent the music is dramatic, as distinct from part of a dramatic moment, is a moot point.

The sacred drama is a dramatisation of Biblical episodes, saints' lives, or moral tales, but not as part of the liturgy. They are sacred, moral entertainments. The earliest extant example is Hildegard of Bingen's twelfth-century morality *Ordo Virtutum* (Order of the virtues), a battle between Good and Evil for the human soul. Like *Les Trois Maries* the music is monodic chant, but there is also spoken text – since the Devil was denied divine harmony. Like *Les Trois Maries* the plainchant does not vary with the narrative. But the conflict inherent in the text implies dramatic performance as do the stage directions in the early thirteenth-century *Ludus Danielis*. Unlike *Les Trois Maries*, this consists of a series of distinct melodies interspersed with plainchant. In the episode of the Writing on the Wall, Belshazzar is instructed '*stupefactus clamabit*' (he will cry out in amazement), which must have at least affected the singing.

By contrast, Adam de la Halle's late thirteenth-century *Le Jeu de Robin et de Marion* is a purely secular drama. It combines a boisterous folk play for the common people with a pastoral, depicting the life of (idealised) shepherds. The music consists of secular forms: chansons, motets and rondeaux which alternate with comic, vernacular dialogue to produce something very like the later *Singspiel*.

Le Jeu de Robin et de Marion comes closer to the modern idea of opera than any of the other pieces so far. On the other hand Olivier Messiaen's *Saint François d'Assise*, Virgil Thomson's *Four Saints in Three Acts*, or Philip Glass' *Satyagraha* are, perhaps, closer to *Les Trois Maries* or the *Ordo Virtutum* than *Le Nozze di Figaro* or *Tosca* in the relatively distanced way in which the action and music relate to one another. This means that any simple ideas of what opera is are challenged as soon as the lyric theatre is considered seriously. The danger is always to look for a single definition by which to determine if any musico-dramatic piece is or is not an opera. To do so is always likely to create false oppositions. Any definition has to be as inclusive as possible, a basis for analysing the multitude of ways in which words and music have worked together. In these examples the music accompanies the flow of the dialogue and action, but neither characterises nor comments, it is not a positive dramatic voice.

Mannerism and the growth of overtly expressive music

It often seems extraordinary that, from the very start, something as complex as opera should have been able to produce masterpieces that are part of the mainstream repertoire. More than this: the objectives and problems of the first opera composers set an agenda that remains fundamental. One reason is that, although opera proper was created around the year 1600, the elements it drew on, both secular and sacred, were already highly sophisticated. These included a range of vocal forms; texts written to be set to music and independent poetry; and a variety of dramatic forms. Significantly for one aspect of the way opera was to develop, almost all operated within courtly or state circles, under the patronage of educated men and women who wanted to use the arts to promote their prestige.

The range of musical and performance activities was enormous, some of which are indicated in Table 1.2. Music for its own sake included settings of texts as solo songs and madrigals, often to words by major literary figures such as Petrarch.

Table 1.2 *Performance types and activities of the late Renaissance*

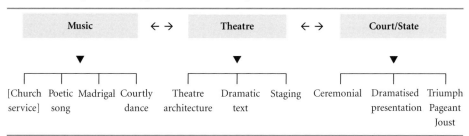

Music	← →	Theatre	← →	Court/State
▼		▼		▼
[Church service] Poetic song Madrigal Courtly dance		Theatre architecture Dramatic text Staging		Ceremonial Dramatised presentation Triumph Pageant Joust

Court and diplomatic functions – welcoming ambassadors and visiting nobility, the celebration of anniversaries and special events – all included music, all of which informed, and was informed by, the rapid growth of theatre, its dramaturgy, texts and scenography.

The work of the three 'founding fathers' of the opera was grounded in this increasingly secular culture. Peri wrote twenty-one dramatic works as well as songs including settings of Petrarch and Michelangelo. Caccini's work includes four dramatic pieces, three of which are operas, and two collections of madrigals and songs. Monteverdi composed nineteen dramatic works and over two hundred secular songs and madrigals in addition to his sacred works. Perhaps it is significant that the dramatic opening of the *Vespers* is an adaptation of the first music of his opera *Orfeo*.

One way of understanding how the new cultural trends affected music, is to place it in the context of other contemporary arts:

1590	Buontalenti	Belvedere of the Pitti Palace, Florence
1595	Carracci	Gallery of the Palazzo Farnese, Rome
1597	Caravaggio	*The Calling of Saint Matthew*
1598	Peri	*Dafne*
1600	Peri	*Euridice*
1602	Caccini	*Le nuove musiche*
1603	Maderno	Facade of Santa Susanna, Rome
1607	Monteverdi	*Orfeo*
1610	Monteverdi	*Vespro della Beata Vergine*
1611	Rubens	*The Descent from the Cross*

The late sixteenth and early seventeenth centuries are a period of transition between the High Renaissance and the Baroque. Its art and architecture have a resonance of their own in what is called the Mannerist style. There is greater flamboyance and sense of individuality than in the Renaissance, but greater classical restraint than later in the Baroque. In Maderno's facade of Santa Susanna of 1603, there is a broadly classical structure: a triangulated pediment and symmetrically placed classical columns. But these are used to far richer, more dramatic effect than in a classical building. The pediment at the top echoes another over the door; the columns are doubled up, creating an interplay of light and shade; the niche above the door is deeply recessed and detailed. The whole is designed to have an effect – to be dramatic. This is typical of the Mannerist style in a period when the belief and optimism of the Renaissance proper was beginning to decline. As it did so, religious art was increasingly called upon to *dramatise* the faith. In a later development, as faith waned further, so the Baroque would *theatricalise* it.

Added to this is an increasing sense of the human. In Caravaggio's work there is an intense sense of precise atmosphere – detailed location, time of day, lighting, costume – with the characters caught at a particular moment. *The Calling of Saint Matthew* shows the tax gatherer seated at a table counting money while Christ is hardly visible, wrapped in his cloak with his face turned away. It is the man behind him, pointing to Matthew, who is emphasised. The viewer is shown where to look by the dramatic diagonal shaft of light that passes beneath the window and fixes the future saint who is quite unaware that his life is about to be changed forever. This is a recognisable world with real people in it construed as immediate drama. It is this immediacy and reality of sensation that informs the songs and madrigals of the period and will underpin the opera when it begins. Monteverdi's 'Ah, dolente partita' from *Il quarto libro de' madrigali* of 1603 (the year of Santa Susanna) explores and expresses intense human feeling in just such a way, imitating the sighs and sorrows of the lover and turning them into music.

The text of Monteverdi's 'Ah, dolente partita' comes from Guarini's *Il Pastor Fido*, the most famous pastoral drama of the period. The pastoral, derived from Theocritus and Virgil, invokes an idealised world of shepherds and shepherdesses and became one of the most popular literary dramatic forms of the time. Significantly it provided the basis for the first Renaissance piece of music theatre: Poliziano's *La Fabula di Orfeo*. Poliziano was a classical scholar and humanist poet in the Medici circle. He also worked in other courts and in 1480 was asked to write a play for the political double marriage of Chiara Gonzaga to Gilbert de Montpensier and Isabella d'Este to Francesco Gonzaga:

> I was asked for the fable of Orpheus ... which I wrote in the space of two days, during continuous tumult, in the vulgar style so that the spectators might better understand it.

The result was a pastoral drama with sung and spoken text and instrumental interludes.[1] After the instrumental *Introdotto* there is a prologue followed by eight scenes divided by seven instrumental *Intromesse*. The music has not survived. However it seems that extant music was fitted to the words and subsequently local music may have been adapted wherever it was performed. The text consists of a series of solos and choruses using a range of rhyme schemes and strophic forms. The solos are often of considerable length, parallel to Poliziano's Greek dramatic models. They are fully characterised and, as in a play, there is no verbal repetition. The one exception is Aristaeus' *canzona* 'Udite, selve, mie dolce parole' (Hear, woods, my sweet words), where the character is asked to 'sing'.

There are three significant things here for the development of early opera. First, Poliziano was asked to write in the classical style, but wrote original drama rather than a translation or version of an extant classical play. The second is the emphasis on the 'vulgar' (vernacular) 'so that the spectators might better understand it'. Finally, the score consisted of a series of melodious arias. The last in particular has implications for the way in which the dramatic and musical austerity of the *Camerata* gave way to more 'entertaining' forms so quickly after it arrived in Rome and then Venice.

Orazio Vecchi's *L'Amfiparnaso* of 1594 is a rather strange piece, offering an alternative direction. This is a narrative in which all the roles are sung as four- or five-part madrigals. The characters and plot are typical of the *Commedia dell'arte*, a popular tradition that would later make its own contribution to the development of opera. Although a performance of *L'Amfiparnaso* would not be 'acted', its characterisation and narrative make it genuinely dramatic. In act I, scene i, Pedrolino tries to attract Hortensia's attention on behalf of his master, the elderly Pantalone; despite the choral format, the action and characters are clearly characterised.

Italy: the *Intermedii*

In 1589 a complex entertainment was mounted to celebrate the marriage in Florence of Ferdinando I de' Medici and Christine de Lorraine. This consisted of six *Intermedii* that were performed between the acts of a light comedy, *La pellegrina* (The pilgrim lady). However the *Intermedii* themselves were intensely serious. Each is a through-composed musical drama lasting between 12 (*Intermedio II*) and 30 (*Intermedio VI*) minutes, whose purpose was to glorify the newly wed rulers. The theme is derived from sixteenth-century Neo-Platonism: harmony and its earthly analogue, music, which the new sovereigns will establish on earth.[2] However, this is not a continuous narrative nor are the personae or chorus individualised. What the *Intermedii* do offer, however, is almost all the component parts of which opera will be made:

- There is an integral relationship between the dramaturgy, music and staging. The latter was magnificent, employing mechanical ingenuity and superb design, something that would become a major feature of opera.[3]
- They are high-minded, using classical motifs with a conscious emphasis on philosophical and humanist ideas.

Table 1.3 *Musical types employed in the pre-opera*

Choral		Solo Voice		Instrumental	
Motet	Madrigal	Song	Declamation/ Recitative	Dance	Sinfonia Ritornello

- The intellectual scenario was possible because they were performed for the court and a (presumed) educated audience.
- They contain a wide range of musical types, including madrigals, strophic song, declamation/recitative, narrative ballet, dances, and orchestral sections – *sinfonie* and *ritornelli.*
- There is a range of solos, including the rhetorical opening by Harmony, the drama of the Sorceress' invocation in *Intermedio iv*, and Arion's expressive solo in *Intermedio v.*

This level of sophistication transferred directly to the first operas, as did the different vocal forms. This is not surprising since Caccini and Peri were two of the composers of the *Intermedii.* However, while Caccini and Peri were masters of the tuneful, strophic solo song, neither the *Intermedii* nor the opera use this other than where the character is required to 'sing'. This is significant, because the strophic song, with its dominant (repeated) melody, becomes so fundamental to later opera where its potential and limitations become crucial to the whole debate about the function of music in opera (Table 1.3).

Strophic song

Strophic song is the setting of a series of *strophes* or verses, each with a clear metrical and rhyme scheme which dictate the rhythm and melodic structure. For example, Peri's setting of Rinuccini's 'Tra le donne onde' (Among the women who are honoured) consists of eight *strophes*, each with the same complex interplay of rhymes and metre. The central column shows the number of syllables:

Tra le donne onde s'onora	8	Among the women where are honoured
Arno e Flora	4	Arno and Flora
Di belezze e d'honestate	8	With beauty and honesty
Nobil Mus' a dir m'inspira	8	Noble Muse inspire me to tell
Su la lira	4	On the lyre
Il bel fior d'ogni beltate:	8	The lovely flower of all beauty:

Table 1.4 *Renaissance theatrical forms using music*

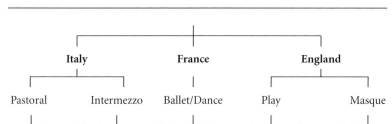

The short, bouncing second and fifth lines are an invitation to syncopation, contrasting with the elongated, repeated metre of the first, third, fourth and last lines. By contrast, his lament 'Uccidimi, dolore' (Kill me, suffering) consists of eight unrhymed sections, in lines of varying length, beginning:

Uccidimi, dolore,	7	Kill me, suffering,
e qui mi veggia	5	and here may he see,
L'idolo mio spietato	7	my pitiless idol,
Per soverchio martire	7	by crushing torture
Innanzi a lui morire.	7	before him, my death.

The metre does not impose itself and there is no rhyme; the long-breathed paragraph delays the climax on the word 'morire' (to die). This prosodic freedom allowed Peri to reflect the inherent crescendo towards the last words. It also means that he could write without the constraint of fixed melody.

'Uccidimi, dolore' is a particular kind of declamatory song, the popular lament, the musical equivalent of the emotional, psychologically real moments that Caravaggio and Salvator Rosa, for example, painted. It also allows the singer to demonstrate their full dramatic and vocal range. It is this kind of flexible solo writing that dominates the *Intermedii* and the first operas. A particularly strong example is Arion's lament in *Intermedio v*, written by Peri for himself. Dramatic impulse, the demands of text and character, are priorities. Only later, under commercial pressure, would strophic, melodic writing come to dominate.

France and England

In France and England parallel forms developed as part of the same courtly world. In both, native forms were combined with Italian imports to create new ones (Table 1.4).

The French equivalent of the Italian *Camerata* was the (more formal) *Académie de Poésie et de Musique*, founded in 1570, which had a major interest in the relationship between music and words, in particular within metrical verse forms. At the same time France had a performance tradition in courtly ballet and it is out of this that the first quasi-opera, *Circé ou Le Balet Comique de la Royne*, developed. Significantly, although the music and words are both by Frenchmen, it is almost always attributed to its Italian 'producer', Catherine de' Medici's dancing master, Baldassare di Belgiojoso – later Baltasar da Beaujoyeulx.

Circé consists of three *intermèdes*, but unlike the Florentine *Intermedii* these form a single narrative. There is also a far greater emphasis on dance – something that came to characterise French opera. The solo writing consists of a small amount of rather stately recitative, while the *chants* and *chansons* are more formal and less expressive than their Italian equivalents. This partly reflects the tight verse forms which limit the music's flexibility. Much of the drama resides in the dialogue and, above all, the spectacle, so that the music accompanies rather than dramatises.

Similarly in England, the masque, which had developed during the sixteenth century, became a full-scale theatrical form by the beginning of the seventeenth. Scenically it drew on the wonders of Italian staging which Inigo Jones had seen and which became a major feature of the performances. Like the *Intermedio* and the French court ballet, the masque combined dance, song, choral and instrumental music with the spoken word, but with a much greater dramatic sense. In Ben Jonson and Inigo Jones' *The Masque of Oberon*[4] the music is also more varied than in *Circé*, ranging from the *catch* 'Buzz, quoth the blue fly', through the lute song 'Nay, nay, you must not stay' to the contemplative 'Now my cunning lady, Moon'.

The basic elements of opera are present in each of these works. But what is missing is a genuine sense of drama with the music, words and action together delineating character, emotion and situation. In true opera the music is an integral part of the dramatic language, working from *inside* the action and the characters. It is the ability to do this that marks the divide between these early proto-operatic forms and the opera itself.

Chapter 2

First operatic forms

The impulse to draw these elements together to create the opera itself was provided by the Florentine *Camerata*, a loose assembly of musicians, artists and poets who were concerned with the performance of Greek drama and music. A great deal of theoretical writing had come down from the classical period, but none of it offered a basis for practical performance, especially frustrating because of the known close relationship between Greek music and the drama. This became central to the debate as to how these admired plays might be performed as part of the Renaissance revival of the classical arts.

The *stile rappresentativo*

Several members of the *Camerata* were involved in *La pellegrina*, among them Peri, Caccini and their patron Giovanni de' Bardi. In a letter, de' Bardi's son Pietro later related how Vincenzo Galilei (the mathematician's father) 'was the first to let us hear singing in *stile rappresentativo* . . . Accordingly he let us hear the lament of Count Ugolino, from Dante', and goes on to say that Caccini and then Peri experimented with the new style and that Peri 'together with Giulio [Caccini] sweetened this style and made it capable of moving the affections in a rare manner . . . The first poem to be sung on the stage in *stile rappresentativo* was the *Story of Daphne* by Signor Ottavio Rinuccini, set to music by Peri . . . I was left speechless' (Strunk, 1998: 523 5). The first experiments with the *stile rappresentativo* were in the form of the lament followed by a full-scale dramatisation of the legend of Daphne. Like Poliziano, despite their admiration for the classics, these men chose not to set extant classical plays with their own vernacular texts. This was a modern, experimental medium.

In 1600, Peri published his second opera, *Euridice*, and in the 'Preface' explained what he – and others in the *Camerata* – had attempted:

> it pleased the Signori Jacopo Corsi and Ottavio Rinuccini that I . . . should set to music the tale of Daphne . . . to make a simple trial of what the song of our age could do. Whence, seeing that it was a question of dramatic poetry

and that, therefore, one should imitate in song a person speaking... I considered that that type of voice assigned to singing by the Ancients which they called 'diastematic' (as it were, sustained and suspended) could at times speed up and take an intermediate path between the suspended and slow movements of song and the fluent, rapid ones of speech, and thus suit my intention.

(Strunk, 1998: 659–62)

Peri is describing a kind of vocal writing that would bring out the emotional and expressive content of the words. From the beginning, the question of the kind of music that should be used for the opera was a major concern, and has remained so for composers for whom the opera was above all a dramatic form. Both Peri and Caccini wrote attractive, melodious songs. But in the opera where, as in the drama, a speech develops from moment to moment, line to line, a repeated melody would make that kind of flexibility impossible. The challenge, therefore, was to write music that would be effective and a real presence while not drawing attention to itself as a separate element. The problem is illustrated in scene ii of Peri's *Euridice* where Orfeo laments his beloved's death in 'Non piango e non sospiro' (I neither weep nor sigh). The music certainly dictates the pace: the change, marked 'più agitato' (bar 433) at 'O mio core, o mia speme, o pace, o vita!' (O my heart, my hope, O peace, O life) is appropriately dramatic. Key words are emphasised effectively: 'cara' in the second line; 'non *posso*' at the end of the third; 'cadavero' in the fourth (emphasis added). But as music, it is not interesting. The 'intermediate path between the suspended and slow movements of song and the fluent, rapid ones of speech' seems little more than a guide to an actor rather than an expressive medium for the actor-singer. What was needed was music that could support the text without subordinating the words, but at the same time *adding* to the drama as a positive presence. Successfully done, this would give real life to the *stile rappresentativo*.

Aria, arioso, recitative, singers

In one sense the *stile rappresentativo* represents the ideal relationship between words and music. But very quickly opera began to incorporate other musical forms. Monteverdi's *Orfeo* uses melodic song as well as the madrigal for the choruses which divide its five acts. The texts of both *Euridice* and *Orfeo* were modelled on the Renaissance understanding of Greek drama: a prologue announcing the theme, followed by a sequence of five *episodes*, separated by choruses in which bystanders commented on the action. The chorus could take part in the episodes but, again, as observers rather than advancing the action (Table 2.1).[1]

Unlike *Euridice*, *Orfeo* also incorporates instrumental elements: the *sinfonia* and *ritornello*. The *ritornello* forms part of the repetitive structure of the strophic solo

Table 2.1 *Musical forms used in early opera*

Chorus		Solo Vocal		Instrumental	
Strophic song	Madrigal	Strophic song	Declamation	Dance Ritornello	Sinfonia
		Aria ← → Arioso	Recitative		

song or chorus; the *sinfonia* is closer to the overture or prelude. The second act of *Orfeo* opens with a *sinfonia* followed by an eleven-verse strophic song with each verse separated by *ritornelli*. As the word implies, the *ritornello* is the 'return' or repeat of the introductory orchestral section. It could also be choreographed, and as such plays a major part in the development of opera in France.

The kind of strophic writing at the opening of Orfeo's act iv 'Quale onor di te fia degno?' (What honour is worthy of thee?), soon become formalised as the *aria*. Although the word has a range of early uses, it almost always implies a tune-based solo passage. Self-contained melody is by its nature separated from the surrounding declamation, so that the aria quickly came to be a (potentially) free-standing element.

The declamatory writing is of two kinds. An example of the first is the messenger's 'speech' in act ii. This is much closer to the kind of music Peri composed for his *Euridice*. It is highly flexible, designed to carry the text forward and gives the singer the basis for dramatic expression. In itself, it has little musical shape or interest. Once opera left the serious environment of the *Camerata*, the tension between this kind of writing and (popular) melody rapidly led to the 'diastematic' being relegated to what will be called 'recitative' (*recitativo*).

Standing in between *aria* and *recitativo* is a kind of semi-aria: the *arioso*. This is lyrical but freer than the strophic *aria* and more dramatic than *recitativo*. Its lyrical style grew out of the lament tradition with its wide-ranging flexibility. It became the staple of Monteverdi's operatic style and is one of his major contributions to opera. *Orfeo*'s act i 'Rosa del ciel, vita del mondo' (Rose of the heavens, life of the world), is a rapturous apostrophe to Euridice. The combination of lyrical musical interest and dramatic flexibility ensures while that the music is rich, full of character and musically interesting it never interrupts the flow of the drama.

First and second practice

In 1605 Monteverdi published his *Fifth book of madrigals* and prefaced it with a 'Letter' in which he referred to *The second practice, or, the perfection of modern music.*

In 1607 his brother wrote a commentary on the 'Letter', explaining what the term meant: 'By First Practice he understands the one that turns on the perfection of the harmony, that is, the one that considers the harmony not commanded, but commanding, and not the servant, but the mistress of the words... By Second Practice... he understands the one that turns on the perfection of the "melody," that is, the one that considers harmony commanded, not commanding and makes the words the mistress of the harmony' (Strunk, 1998: 536–44).

In act II of *Orfeo*, at the same moment as in Peri's *Euridice*, the hero reacts to the news of his beloved's death. Monteverdi's setting is deceptively simple. The first line consists of three phrases:

> 'Tu se' morta, mia vita, ed io respiro?'
> Thou art dead, my life, and I am breathing?

But he sets it as:

Tu se' morta,	Thou art dead,
se' morta mia vita,	art dead my life,
ed io respiro?	and I am breathing?

The opening 'se' morta' is tragic, but its repetition becomes the expression of Orfeo's horror – how can he still live and breathe? The final note rises unexpectedly to emphasise the shock of the final line. He does the same with:

Tu se' da me partita	Thou art departed from me
Per mai più non tornare, ed io rimango?	never more to return and I remain?

which become

Tu se' da me partita	Thou art departed from me
se' da me partita mai piu	art departed from me never more
mai più non tornare ed io rimango!	never more to return and I remain!

Monteverdi builds the pressure as what has happened, and what the character is thinking, grow in his mind. He does this through repetition but also the flexible tempo, and the simple but effective chordal accompaniment. This creates a beautiful sequence, a melodic line that is expressive, supporting the character's development, but never drawing attention away from the words which remain 'the mistress of the harmony'.

Monteverdi is adept at manipulating the musical forms themselves as part of his dramatic expression. In act II he inverts the expected sequence of declamation followed by melody. The scene begins with a Sinfonia followed by Orfeo, the Second Shepherd and the Chorus in a sequence of eleven verses alternating with *ritornelli* culminating with the Second Shepherd proclaiming the universal happiness of the day. At this point the flow of melody is abruptly broken by the Messenger as he announces Euridice's death in austere, declamatory tones. The *musical* effect is brutally dramatic.

Because Orfeo was a musician, this allowed composers to make a feature of 'song' as one of the musical elements. At the opening of act I the Second Shepherd invokes 'cantiam, pastori' (let us sing, shepherds), but the music continues in the declamatory style. Instead Monteverdi reserves his richest melodic invention for special purposes. In act IV Orfeo leads Euridice back to the upper world. He starts by 'singing', but as the drama develops, he changes from the carefree melody of the first three verses and their *ritornelli* to the pensive *arioso* 'Ma mentre io canto, ohimè, chi m'assicura/Che'ella mi segua?' (But while I sing, alas, who assures me/That she is following me?). Ironically, as the tension rises at 'Ma che temi, mio core?' (But what do you fear, my heart?), he uses *recitativo* as he turns to reassure himself that Euridice is still there – and so loses her. In this sequence from strophic melody through *arioso* to dramatic *stile rappresentativo*, the forms themselves are an essential part of the expression and experience of the drama.

Rome and Venice: entertainment and commerce

Peri's and Caccini's work was written for Florence, underpinned by the intellectual atmosphere of the *Camerata*. Similarly Monteverdi's *Orfeo* was created in Mantua for the art- and antiquary-loving Gonzagas. All this had changed by the time Monteverdi wrote his last operas for Venice. By then, opera had moved out of the *Camerata*'s rarefied ambit and developed under new conditions, first in Rome and Venice, and then France, Germany and England (Table 2.2).

The first new sphere of influence was Rome where, because of the Church's antipathy, opera was only possible by reflecting the ethos of the Counter Reformation. The result was edifying titles such as Cavalieri's 1600 *Rappresentatione di Anima e di Corpo* (Representation of the Soul and the Body), Kapsberger's 1622 *Apotheosis sive Consecratio SS. Ignatii et Francisci Xaveri*, Landi's 1632 *Sant'Alessio* and later Marazzoli's 1656 *La Vita Humana* (Human Life). Despite this, the Church had a vital effect on the development of opera, in particular the role of soloists. The Church's ban on women in services included choristers. High parts were taken by pre-pubescent boys whose short career span meant that a longer-term solution was needed. The result was the castrato voice which would dominate opera in the seventeenth and eighteenth centuries, other than in France. In addition, the opera provided new artistic and financial opportunities for the large number of highly trained singers in the Roman choirs. As they took advantage of this, vying with one another and gathering supporters, a 'star system' developed.

Table 2.2 *Early operatic forms: tragedy and mixed (comedy and tragedy)*

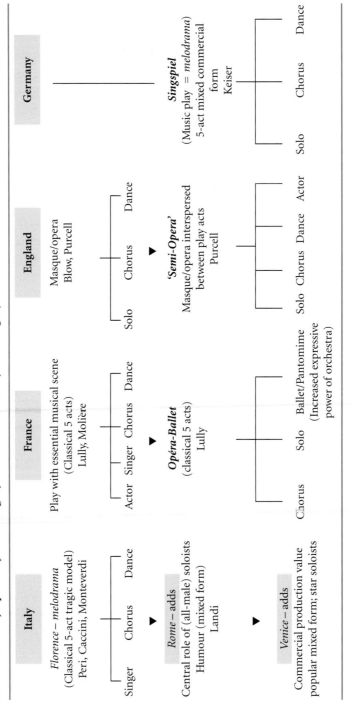

Italy	France	England	Germany
Florence – melodrama (Classical 5-act tragic model) Peri, Caccini, Monteverdi	Play with essential musical scene (Classical 5 acts) Lully, Molière	Masque/opera Blow, Purcell	
Singer Chorus Dance	Actor Singer Chorus Dance	Solo Chorus Dance	
▶ *Rome – adds* Central role of (all-male) soloists Humour (mixed form) Landi	▶ *Opéra-Ballet* (classical 5 acts) Lully	▶ *'Semi-Opera'* Masque/opera interspersed between play acts Purcell	*Singspiel* (Music play = *melodrama*) 5-act mixed commercial form Keiser
▶ *Venice – adds* Commercial production value popular mixed form; star soloists	Chorus Solo Ballet/Pantomime (Increased expressive power of orchestra)	Solo Chorus Dance Actor	Solo Chorus Dance

The sumptuous and highly competitive ethos of Roman opera also affected the overall structure. Opportunities were required for scenographic display and both the dramaturgy and music began to shift to accommodate these new values. Landi's *Sant'Alessio* became one of the most famous operas of its period. Despite its serious subject it is the first to include humorous passages, such as act i, scene iii, where two pages fail to recognise the saint and tease him.[2] It also contains several exciting scene changes, including a vista of Rome, Hell (complete with hell-fire), Heaven and a great deal of flying.

Monteverdi in Venice (*L'incoronazione di Poppea*)

These tendencies greatly increased once opera moved into the commercial world of Venice where the first public theatre, the Teatro San Cassiano or Teatro Tron, opened in 1637. With the exception of a few other commercial centres such as Hamburg and London, almost all opera in the seventeenth and eighteenth centuries was intended for the court and designed to promote its self-image. Free of these constraints, Venetian commercial opera developed a broader range designed to please a pay-ing audience, one of whose criteria was straightforward entertainment. The result was:

- A disregard for the restriction of the Aristotelian unities and, in particular the separation of tragic and comic genres. Significantly, many of the first singers of opera were recruited from *Commedia dell'arte* troupes who combined acting, singing and dance. The mixture of the serious, sentimental and comic would have come quite naturally to them.[3]
- The opening up of the dramaturgical structure, which allowed for numerous changes of location and scenery as well as the introduction of magical and spec-tacular effects. The result was that texts were increasingly designed to incorporate this, affecting plot and characters.
- Stars became increasingly attractive to audiences. As a result, texts were struc-tured so that they could have prominent scenes of different emotional and musical kinds, with the music frequently tailored to particular singers and their abilities.
- The aria became increasingly important as a vehicle for attractive melody and star performance.
- The economics of commercial opera meant that the orchestra was usually small, with an emphasis on chamber, sometimes solo, scoring and with very rare use of a chorus.

Monteverdi's last opera, *L'incoronazione di Poppea* (1642), was written for Venice and is in many respects quite different from *Orfeo*:

- Most obviously, *Orfeo* runs for under 2 hours, while *Poppea* fills a whole evening.
- The classical five acts have been abandoned for three acts divided into scenes with changing locations.[4]
- Where the characters in *Orfeo* remain idealised types, in *Poppea* they are fully realised human beings with individual problems and traits.
- Unlike the classically rigorous *Orfeo*, *Poppea* includes comedy. Act I, scene II between the two despondent guards sets the tone – realistic, wistful, angry and humorous; the ambiguous role of the nurse Arnalta, cast as an alto, stands somewhere between Juliet's nurse and the standard *confidante*.

Poppea's score is more complex than *Orfeo*'s. It consists of *aria*, *arioso* and *recitativo*, but so integrated that much of the time it is difficult to hear where one ends and the other begins. This is in part due to Monteverdi's ease in handling his medium; but it is also because the music is so completely attuned to the nuances of character and action, as in the act I, scene iii extended dialogue between Poppea and Nerone (Table 2.3).

Poppea's libretto is more nuanced than *Orfeo*'s, taking the audience on a complex journey through a morally challenging world. It mixes high tragedy, pathos, sentiment and sardonic humour in a fluid sequence that presents conflicting views of the same emotions and actions. It is precisely this integrated quality that allows Monteverdi to create an equally flexible score, in which forms – *aria*, *arioso*, characterised *recitativo* – merge into one another to create a musico-dramatic whole.

Cavalli (*Giasone*)

Poppea could only have been written in a republic. Busenello's libretto is a condemnation of tyranny: of Love's tyranny over Fortune and Virtue, Poppea and Nerone; and of its main characters' selfishness as they seek erotic gratification. In this sense, *Poppea* is as serious a work as the *Camerata* could have wished, which makes it atypical of Venetian opera as it shifted towards a more commercial, sheerly entertaining art form. The major exponent of this is Cavalli who, significantly, was involved in theatre management and finance as well as composition. His *Giasone*, the most popular opera across Europe for almost half a century, shows exactly how opera was changing.

The libretto, apparently on a classical theme, is a confection that bears almost no relationship to the Jason myths. Instead it is constructed to allow for a number of new emphases. Scenic variety and effects are essential, as Table 2.4 shows, where the sequence is designed less as an essential of the plot than to provide the audience with a series of visual delights.

Table 2.3 L'incoronazione di Poppea: *act i, scene iii*

15	Poppea: Signor, deh, non partire! My Lord, oh, do not part!'	Sensuous *arioso* culminating in the self-dramatising:
32	Ahi, perir, ahi mancar quest'alma sento Ah, to perish, ah, I feel my soul would die	
38	Nerone: La nobilità de' nascimenti tuoi The nobility of your birth	Nerone replies in prosaic recitative
53	Vanne, vanne – Go, go	Monteverdi uses short melodic phrases to create what are really brief arias, by repeating lines for the sake of musical form, to create incisive moments of deeply felt pleading.
68	In un sospir – With a sigh that comes	
94	Poppea: Signor, sempre mi vedi – My lord, you ever see me	
120	Nerone: Adorati miei rai – My adorable eyes	Recitative but so expressive that it sounds like *arioso*, reflecting and enhancing his continued emotions
130	Poppea: Che di voce si amara a un solo accento ahi, perir, ahi mancar quest'alma sento! From such a bitter voice a single note Ah, to perish, ah, I feel my soul would die	through the repetition of Poppea's lines and Nerone's response and ornamentation
153	Poppea: Tornerai? – Will you return?	Finally the moving and witty passage in which Poppea simply repeats her challenge that eventually seduces Nerone into the final passionate sequence of 'Addio's.

Attractive as this must have been, it exposes the results of Venice's commercial pressures. The librettist has created a plot whose real function is to accommodate a number of novel scenes, many of which are irrelevant to the main action. In act i, scene v, Orestes, queen Isifile's *confidant*, complains of his arduous duties. The scene initially continues the action, but then becomes an interpolated comic interlude. The focus is Demo, Egeo's stammering dwarf. The role was probably written for a singer who specialised in this kind of part. Demo has an aria written in a popular style ('Son gobbo, son Demo' – I am a hunchback, I am Demo). After a comic recitative quarrel, a mock-heroic series of pardons culminates in Demo's satirical description of himself as a warrior ('Grande? Se mi vedessi' – Noble? If you could see me).

Demo is an example of the growing cult of the solo singers who needed vehicles in which they could display their musical and dramatic ability. His aria 'Son gobbo'

Table 2.4 Giasone: *the scenic structure*

Act/Scene		Location
Prologue		Seashore with a view of the Island of Colchis
I	i–xii	Garden with a small palace
	xiii	Countryside with huts at the mouth of the Ibero
	xiv	Medea's magic chamber (with incantations)
II	i–ii	Countryside with huts
	iii–vii	Keep of the fortress of the Golden Fleece
	viii	The cave of Aeolus
	ix	A demolished harbour. Storm at sea
	x	Storm at sea
	xi	Soldiers and sailors disembarked from the *Argo*
III	i–v	A flowery glade
	vi–viii	Countryside with huts
	ix–xv	The valley of the Orseno
	xvi	Deserted place with ruins

is also typically melodious, and *Giasone* is notable for its attractive arias and duets such as the scene for Medea and Giasone act III, scene ii, 'Sotto il tremolo ciel' (Beneath the trembling heavens). This begins with a languorous recitative that leads into the lyrical duet itself, similar to the last duet of *Poppea*. Melody, drama and star vehicle are combined in Medea's outstanding and influential incantation scene in act I, scene xiv, where she summons the spirits of the underworld, 'Dell'antro magico' (From the ancient cave). This long passage is dramatically and musically complex, moving through *arioso*, *aria* and *recitativo*:

- It begins with a darkly coloured instrumental introduction, a *sinfonia* designed to paint the scene;
- In the first vocal section the melody is heavily accented, emphasised by the pounding bass, creating a sense of concentration, dire thoughts and dark arts;
- Suddenly the music erupts in an *arioso* which is then unexpectedly interrupted for a soft, reflective moment at 'L'amoroso desio ch'l cor mi stimula' (The amorous desire that stimulates my heart) before the outpouring of vitriol continues, until
- The brief aria-like 'Orridi demoni' – a mere three lines, then
- Further imprecation, until
- The rhythmic, quasi-aria of four lines 'Dalla sabbia/Di Cocito' (From the sands of Cocytus), and finally
- Simple recitative for the last two lines that precede the Chorus.

This is hugely dramatic, but less credible than anything in *Orfeo* or *Poppea*. This is a star vehicle in which music, scenography and solo performance create maximum effect. Commercial activity demanded those elements that could attract audiences and sustain investment in the theatre buildings and sets which could be added to stock and used for later productions. By contrast, far less money was spent on the two potentially expensive items of chorus and orchestra. Cavalli's orchestra is small, with a variety of instruments but rarely more than one to a part. Where a larger vocal impact was needed – for jubilation or public mourning – the characters themselves joined together in chorus.

The impact of commercial pressures was considerable, drawing opera away from the austere world of the *Camerata*. One history of opera is the struggle between a purist vision of a high-minded, moral force, and a popular tendency towards melody, production values, star casting and entertainment. The reforms of Gluck and Wagner were designed to address just this problem. But with these changes also came not simply adulteration but the creation of distinct genres with their own criteria, each demanding its own critical criteria.

France: the rule of Lully (*Armide*)

Just as in Venice, French opera was moulded by its performance conditions. Although French opera had a commercial aspect it always echoed the taste and aspirations of Versailles, where it was designed as part of the elevation and conscious glorification of the monarchy. This had begun with Louis XIII under the guidance of Cardinal Richelieu, and was accelerated by their successors, Cardinal Mazarin and Louis XIV. The Italian-born Mazarin (Mazzarino) turned to his native culture to find ways of achieving this, in 1664 inviting the greatest architect of the age, Bernini, to Paris to redesign the Louvre. Italian opera, including Cavalli's *Egisto* and *Xerse*, had been performed in France since 1645 and in 1659 he commissioned an opera from Cavalli to celebrate the marriage of Louis XIV and Maria Theresa of Spain. As opera became more established, the native emphasis on ballet helped create a particularly French operatic form. As early as 1654 Carlo Caproli's *Le nozze di Peleo e di Teti* had been structured to include ballet.

The dominant French composer of opera was to be another Italian, Giovanni Battista Lulli – Jean-Baptiste Lully. His first full opera, *Cadmus et Hermione*, only appeared in 1673, but this had been preceded by work in dramatic genres that helped form his own style and established the aesthetic of French opera up into the late eighteenth century. These included ballets, *entrées* and the *Comédies-ballets* of which twelve were collaborations with Molière. Each included substantial musical elements. In *Le Bourgeois Gentilhomme* of 1670, each of the five acts ends with a ballet, several of which include solo and ensemble singing. However, unlike the *Intermedii* of *La pellegrina* these are integral to the action and the *Cérémonie Turque* in act IV is the climax of the drama. Lully's work with Molière crucially helped him develop his feel for the French language and to understand the dramatic needs of the drama/libretto.

Louis XIV used the classical as the model for his personal and political image. Reflecting this, the French arts were increasingly dominated by a classical aesthetic. This especially affected architecture and the theatre as the most public of the arts. Of Racine's thirteen plays, five are reworking of Greek originals and four have classical subjects. This is reflected in Lully's operas which:

- adopt the five-act classical structure and never mix the comic and serious;
- include substantial dance episodes, but always as part of the action;
- emphasise the importance of the libretto, as both action and literary text;
- invoke a sense of classical propriety, although the opera, unlike the theatre, was encouraged to use Italian-style scenography including scenic effects and marvels (Table 2.5).

Unlike Venice, the courtly performance conditions also meant that resources were available for large orchestral forces, a chorus and a *corps de ballet*. What remained the same was the requirement for dramatic structures that would include all these elements. *Armide* (1686), shows how the Lullian opera deploys vocal, balletic, orchestral and scenographic resources. Within this, Lully developed a musical style which was suited to the French language and prosody, making highly flexible use of both *récitatif* and *arioso*. In addition, influenced by the theatre, and unlike the Venetian opera, all of this is welded into a dramatically cogent whole.

The size and quality of Lully's orchestra allowed him to develop his instrumental writing beyond anything possible in Italy. The *ritournelles* and *prélude*s in many cases play a significant part in creating the visual and emotional scene. Act II, scene iii is set beside a stream with sweet-smelling flowers and gentle breezes. The *Prélude* depicts this with a long flowing line of gently rising and falling quavers which continues into the following *air*. As Renaud enters the music itself becomes an enchantment. In his *air de sommeil* (sleep aria), 'Plus j'observe ces lieux' (The more I see this place), the gently rippling music of the *Prélude* hypnotises him with its own and the scene's beauty. The lyrical line is flexible, closer to an *arioso* than an *air*, and avoids an obvious melody that might distract from the dramatic moment.

In act II, scene iv a spell is cast over Renaud by demons disguised as shepherds and shepherdesses. Its mixture of dance, song and chorus derive from the older Pastoral *intermède*, but here given a dramatic function. Within a clear, very formal structure Lully writes some of his most exquisite music: the *Prélude* and following

Table 2.5 Armide: *spectacle, dance/ballet and orchestral music*

		Scenic elements (italics)	Dance/ballet	Orchestral
Prologue				Overture
		La Gloire	Entrée, Menuet, Gavotte en Rondeau	
		La Sagesse	Entrée, Menuet I, Menuet II	
		Choeur		Overture (reprise)
Act 1	Scene i			Ritournelle
	Scene ii			
	Scene iii	*The Peoples of the Kingdom of Damascus manifest in dance and song the joy they feel at the power the beauty of their Princess has exercised on the knights in Godfrey's camp*		
			March – Monologue	
			Rondeau – Solo and chorus	
			Sarabande – Solo and chorus – Sarabande	
	Scene iv		March (reprise)	
Act 2	Scenes i			
	Scene ii			Prélude
	Scene iii			Prélude – ends
				Prélude (reprise)
	Scene iv	Solo Naiad		Prélude
		Chorus		
		The Demons, in the shape of Nymphs, Shepherds and Shepherdesses, cast a spell over Rinaldo as he sleeps and garland him with flowers		
			Air 1 – Air 2	
		Chorus	Air 2 – Air 1	
		Chorus		
	Scene v			
Act 3	Scenes i – iii			
	Scene iv	*Hate emerges from Hell, accompanied by Furies Cruelty, Vengeance, Rage and the Passions attendant upon Hate*		
				Prélude
		Hate – Hate and chorus –		
		The attendants of Hate eagerly break and burn Love's weapons		
		Hate and his attendants	Air	
		Hate, Armida, Hate	Air (reprise)	

(*cont.*)

Table 2.5 (*cont.*)

			Scenic elements (italics)	Dance/ballet	Orchestral
Act 4	Scene i			Ends with Air	
	Scene ii		Chorus	Gavotte – Canaries	
			Chorus	Air	
			Scene continues		
	Scenes iii				Prélude
	Scene iv			Air (reprise)	
Act 5	Scene i				Ritournelle – Passacaille
	Scene ii				Passacaille (reprise)
	Scene iii				Prélude
	Scenes iv–v		The demons destroy the enchanted Palace. Exit Armide upon a flying chariot		

chorus, the two contrasting *airs* of the ballets and the Heroic Shepherdess' two *airs* (Table 2.6).

Other scenes call for different writing. Scene v is an extended solo for Armide as she tries to kill Renaud. This became one of the most celebrated scenes in early French opera. It is highly dramatic as contradictory emotions – hate and love – rage for control. Initially Lully does not use melody, which he reserves for the resolution. The bulk of the scene is an expressive and volatile declamatory recitative, shifting with Armide's passions. Only when her violent hatred has been forced to submit to her love for Renaud is melody introduced, in the final section 'Venez, venez' (Come, come) as she calls on her demons to waft her away 'au bout de l'Univers' (to the ends of the universe). The French opera continued to exploit the musical and dramatic correlation between recitative and aria. In Italy, the development remained musically dominated, leading to the formalisation of the *da capo aria* that left the recitative with little musical interest.

Germany (Keiser's *Croesus*)

In Germany, a commercial theatre was established in Hamburg in 1678. The leading figure was Reinhard Keiser who, like Cavalli, was both composer and manager. As in Venice the result was opera designed to appeal to a middle-class, paying audience and Keiser's operas are notable for their variety of musical forms, singing roles and sheer attraction.

Table 2.6 Armide: *act II, scene iv*

A	B	C	B	C	A
Orchestral Prélude, Chorus	Ballet: Air 1	Heroic Shepherdess: air	Ballet: Air 2	Heroic Shepherdess: air	Orchestral Prélude, Chorus
Naiad: air					

Table 2.7 Croesus: *act I, scene ix*

A	B		C	
Alternating verses then duet	Alternating verses	Alternating verses	Alternating verses	Trio
Clerida / Elmira	Eliates / Clerida	Clerida / Orsanes	Orsanes / Elmira	Clerida, Eliates, Orsanes
Elmira loves/is loved by Atis	Eliates rejected by Clerida	Clerida rejected by Orsanes		

The full title of *Croesus*, shows a mixture of quasi-classical education and good moral sentiment designed to appeal to a merchant audience: *A true story of the mutability of the worldly glory and wealth of the proud deposed and reinstated Croesus.* The narrative combines a broad classical framework derived from Herodotus with comic and erotic elements. As in *Giasone* there is a succession of varied locations and the range of forms, learned from Italy, has been arranged to create an attractive product. For example:

- coloratura *da capo aria*: Elmira's act i, scene v, 'Er erweckt in meinem Herzen' (He awakes in my heart);
- popular strophic *arietta*: Elmira and Trigesta's duet in act i, scene ii, 'Empfinden gleiche Schmerzen' (To feel the same sorrows);
- comic *recitative* and *aria*: Elcius' act i, scene xi, 'Hört, wie die Eulen (Hear how owls)/'Liebes-Schmerzen' (Love's ache).

Like Cavalli's stammering Demo, *Croesus* uses novelties, such as the dumb Atis who can only 'speak' through dumb-show interpreted by his servant Elcius.

Keiser makes expressive use of both musical figures and individual instruments. In act i, scene ix four lovers meet, three of whose love is rejected by the object of their affection. For this, Keiser writes two duets, with contrasting melodies, followed by a trio in which the three rejected lovers join in a comment on love. The music is consistently interesting, while the dramatic contrast at each 'Ich kann nicht' (I cannot) is both amusing and affecting (Table 2.7).

Even more than in Cavalli, recitative is restricted to 'action', with the aria increasingly becoming the main object of both dramatic and musical attraction. This tendency will dominate operatic development from now on, until it is challenged in the great moments of 'reform'.

Chapter 3

Formalisation

By the middle of the seventeenth century opera had established itself, moving between the worlds of the commercial, popular opera of Venice or Hamburg and that of the court. The commercial world enjoyed the mixed genre combining comedy and tragedy, a growing star system and a developing audience. By contrast, the courtly world continued to demand classically based plots, high moral purpose and restraint. Musically, too, a series of tensions developed as the attractions of the melodious aria increasingly relegated the monodic, diastematic writing of Peri and Caccini to those passages where information was needed to carry the action forward. Conversely, the aria increasingly became the centre of musical attention while its dramaturgical function contracted. As these two elements became more distinct, opera potentially became a mere vehicle for the aria. France alone withstood these tendencies, here opera continued to develop as a genuinely dramatic form. The direct link between royal/state encouragement of the arts and their centralised control, was established through the *Académies*.[1] These were designed to ensure that the arts fulfilled their role in enhancing the nation's prestige. From 1661 onwards Louis XIV embarked on a series of military and diplomatic offensives that gave France a leading role in the political life of Europe.[2] The success of the monarchy, its brilliant display in the arts and its Europe-wide political authority, made the king the paradigm for rulers and France their cultural model.

Towards *opera seria:* first stage – Apostolo Zeno

Significantly, the Italian return to the original seriousness of opera was inspired by French criticism, and the initial response came from writers. The result was the codification of opera and a formalisation of its elements, including the music, which established the dominant form of the late seventeenth and eighteenth centuries, the *opera seria* (serious opera).[3] Opera was to be 'cleansed' of the comedy, mangled adaptations of the classics and wilful scenic excesses of works such as *Giasone* and *Croesus*.

The first 'reformer' was the scholar, antiquary, poet and dramatist Apostolo Zeno. In 1710 he founded *Il Giornale de' Letterati d'Italia* (*The Journal of Italian Letters*) in an attempt to set Italian literature on a more 'regular' – i.e. French classical – basis. This parallelled the work of the contemporary *Accademia degli Animosi* (Academy of the Brave), modelled on the French *Académies*, which was concerned with the restoration of 'good taste' in the arts generally and specifically the quality of the libretto. In particular the *Accademia* strove to resist the demands of mere popular taste. In 1709 Zeno was employed by the Hapsburg claimants to the Spanish throne. They required an opera that would demonstrate their qualities as monarchs who understood their role as servants of the state, and who respected law and virtue. Zeno wrote two libretti, each with a single subject, no comedy or spectacle, and all attention focused on the (classical) hero who represented his patron. Nine years later he was invited to become the Court Poet in Vienna. Imperial patronage freed him from commercial, populist constraints. The libretti he produced:

- came closer to the (so-called) Aristotelian unities of time, place and action;
- developed coherent characterisation;
- developed the *liaison de scène*, turning a myriad of separate scenes whose logic was dictated by the need for entertaining contrast into a smooth flow of logical narrative;
- increasingly eliminated the comic;
- turned for his subjects to history rather than myth, although drawn from a wide field that included Greece and Rome, China, Persia, India and Scandinavia.

The objective of these libretti was the moral education of the audience within an enlightened but absolutist political structure. The central virtue this celebrated was the exercise of clemency. While the monarch knew precisely what his (errant) subjects truly deserved, he also understood how best to apply justice in the interests of social and political harmony, Plato's highest social virtue. In Zeno's libretti, therefore, *pathos* (true feeling) was substituted for the potentially destructive emotion of terror, so that whatever the struggle, his operas were resolved in the *fine lieto* (happy ending), restoring harmony.

Zeno's libretti were quickly appreciated and, like those of his successor, Metastasio, were set many times, although they were almost always altered to suit the composer and his practical needs. This could involve either changing the poetic text or reshaping the drama itself depending on the:

- number, kinds and demands of singers available;
- particular audience and its expectations;
- requirements of the patron;
- occasion for which it was being written;

- predilections of the composer: perhaps a desire to write illustrative (storm or pastoral) music or specific kinds of aria to display emotions such as rage, love or sorrow.

Zeno's *Griselda* used a libretto probably written in 1701 and first set by Pollarolo. It was then altered for a string of composers:

G. Bononcini	The King's Theatre, London, 1722. The plot remained the same, but the text was rewritten. One character (Corrado) was cut and three of the principles were renamed.
Vivaldi	The Teatro San Samuele, Venice, 1735. The text was revised by Goldoni, reducing the number of arias and duets from thirty-nine to nineteen. Several of the arias were rewritten as simile arias to provide Vivaldi with the opportunity to write descriptive music. Others were added to fill out the character of Griselda, played by Anna Girò, a limited singer but fine actress.
A. Scarlatti	Teatro Capranica, Rome, 1721, for a semi-private performance commissioned by Prince Ruspoli. Text was added and parts cut completely, so that little of the detail of the original plot remained. All the major characters were then set for castrati (including Griselda) (Strohm, 1997: 33ff.).

Scarlatti's remodelled *La Griselda* is not yet fully formed *opera seria*. However, it shows the impact of Zeno's reforms, ordering the narrative and developing a structure within which the music becomes equally formalised:

- Structurally it consists of three acts divided into a number of scenes with four locations in act I and three in each of acts II and III.
- The *liaisons de scène* mean that characters overlap as they enter and exit, never leaving the stage empty, and themselves become the logic of the dramatic action.
- The action has a single narrative line, uninterrupted by comic interpolation.
- The only scenic events (the disembarkation in act I, scene vi and the hunt in act II, scene x) are both required by the narrative.
- The story, while not historical, has a worthy literary source in Boccaccio's *Decameron*.
- The last scene shows king Gualtiero displaying clemency, wisdom, love and human feeling as Griselda is welcomed back by her loving(!) husband, Ottone and the guilty populace are pardoned.

The *da capo* aria

Scarlatti's *La Griselda* consists of a series of scenes, in the majority of which a recitative is followed by a *da capo* aria.[4] These share the same structure: an ABA form where, after the B section, the performer returns to the A section and sings *da capo* (from the head/top).[5] The dramatic implications of this repetition are problematic – or were felt to be so by the end of the eighteenth century and were one of the major stumbling blocks for appreciation of the *opera seria* into modern times. In the *da capo* aria the text consists of two contrasting, or complementary, short verses (usually two or four lines each). Most of the *da capo* arias in *La Griselda* are of the most straightforward kind, such as Roberto's aria in act I, scene vi. The text is a quatrain, rhyming abab (Table 3.1a).

Tables 3.1a La Griselda: *act I, scene vi,* da capo *aria structure*

Rhyme	Text	Setting	Translation
a1 b1	Come presto nel porto crudele Il mio fato mi volle guidar.	A	How fast to the cruel port My fate wished to guide me
a2 b2	Quando altrove le stanche mie vele Nembo irato doveva portar.	B	Whereas elsewhere my tired sails The angry clouds should bear me.

Within this there are repetitions and orchestral *ritornelli*. Typically, at each repetition there are differences, mainly of ornamentation, so that the whole becomes as in Table 3.1b.

Table 3.1b La Griselda: *act I, scene vi,* da capo *aria structure, with ornamentation*

Main sections		A				B			A – *da capo repeat*			
Musical repeats	Rit	A	Rit	A	Rit	B	B	Rit	A	Rit	A	Rit
Text and repeats		a1, b1		a1, b1		b2, b2	b1, b2		a1, b1		a1, b1	

This is an 'entrance aria', designed to allow the singer to make his or her mark – as both a character and a performer. It has complex ornamentation, with extended passages at bars 49–60 and 86–98. However, although this forthright music is appropriate to the character's indignation, it is neither psychologically nor emotionally revealing. The repetition does not seem to matter: it is a formal announcement of the character.

However, elsewhere the *da capo* form can be effective in creating a genuine dramatic and psychological moment, as in Griselda's 'Mi rivedi, O selva ombrosa' (You see me again, O shady forest) that opens act II. Gluck later mocked the *da capo* form, asking how a character can start somewhere (A), develop his or her thought (B) – and then go back to the beginning again! But it doesn't have to be seen like that:

- A: Griselda wistfully locates herself, rejected and exiled to the forest from which she had been plucked.
- B: she turns with a simple openness to her old surroundings, although well aware that she is no longer the person she once was.
- *da capo* (A), she returns to the present, her exile, to which, as the repetition itself suggests, she is now resigned.

The repetition makes dramatic and personal sense. In Scarlatti's tender setting, the character expresses resigned abandonment with neither self-pity nor anger; the orchestra alone tells us what is happening within this long-suffering, uncomplaining heart, with its repeated sobbing figure of a rising dotted semiquaver and demi-semiquaver. Both the verbal and musical material with which Scarlatti works are highly structured: formal in their prosody and musical repetition. Yet from this it is quite possible to create not just a moving aria, but a moment pregnant with feeling, meaning and a real sense of personal situation. Indeed, the essence of the baroque world is that, despite the formality of structures such as the *da capo* aria, there should be genuine meaning and emotional expression.

Music and emotion

The emotions were to be stirred, but within reason. Aristotle's *Poetics* provided the basis for this aesthetic of what might be called 'emotional decorum'. The objective was 'by means of pity and fear' to bring about 'the purgation of such emotions' (Aristotle, 1970: 39). The seventeenth century understood these (much-debated) words to mean that, by having such emotions aroused and then expended in the artificial world of the theatre, the audience were able to leave prepared for balanced and rational conduct in society.

This was the personal and social function of art; but how was it to be reconciled with aesthetic pleasure? How could the tragic be 'enjoyed'? What kind of material and effects were appropriate to serious, but entertaining, art? This was the context within which the seventeenth and eighteenth centuries debated, and tried to understand, the power of art: how it worked, how it could or should be controlled, what it *was*. A major concern was the relationship between the imagination and the emotions, music's ability to evoke in a way that can move and excite. How did art do this? Was the result real or illusory? And was such stimulation – private and public – healthy or perhaps dangerous? In 1702 the French churchman, historian and – significantly – physician, Abbé François Raguenet wrote: 'If a storm, or rage, is to be described in a symphony, [the Italians'] notes give us so natural an idea of it, that our soul can hardly receive a stronger impression from the reality than they do from the description . . . the imagination, the senses, the soul, the body itself are all betray'd into a general transport' [Strunk, 1998: 676]. The idea of art as the direct expression of feeling is baldly stated in *The complete music director*, by the composer, performer and music historian Johann Mattheson, a colleague and friend of both Keiser and Handel: 'since the true goal of all melody can only be a type of diversion of the hearing through which the passions of the soul are stirred, no one will accomplish this goal who is not intent upon it, who is not himself moved' (Strunk, 1998: 698).

Sentiment and rhetoric

Music was therefore understood – and expected – to be expressive. But this seems to make the *da capo* aria all the more difficult to accept judged by romantic examples. In Philip II's 'Ella giammai m'amò' (She never loved me)[6] or Wotan's 'Als junger Liebe Lust mir verblich' (When young love's force waned within me)[7] character is revealed and developed. They are journeys for both character and audience, because the nineteenth century understood the world through individual development. The dramas of Ibsen and Chekhov, Verdi and Wagner, focus on character and use the kind of dramatic structure in which it is most fully revealed.

For the eighteenth century, the truth of the world lay in a series of actions conditioned by a rational universe rather than a series of hidden, inner (psychological) states The aria was therefore expected to expose a particular state of mind at a particular moment. An individual would feel and react quite differently depending on their situation – and to that extent might appear to be a 'different' person, as Metastasio explained:

> I believe that a person may act differently in different situations without inconsistency of character. Timanthes, is a valiant young man, subject to the emotions of youth, though naturally reasonable, and furnished by education with maxims suitable to persons of his rank. When assaulted by passion, he is impetuous, violent and inconsiderate. But when he has time to reflect, or any object present, reminds him of his duty, he is just, moderate, and rational. (Kimbell, 1991: 195)

As a result, an aria can certainly be dramatic but will always be conditioned by, and expressive of, character within the narrative moment. Its function is to engage the audience in that moment and its dominant sentiment.[8]

Like a persuasive speech, art was seen as a kind of rhetoric, the art of persuasion. The parallel is made explicit by the musician and teacher Heinrich Koch: 'Certain more or less noticeable resting points for the mind are generally necessary in speech and thus also in the products of those fine arts which attain their goal through speech, namely poetry and rhetoric, if the subject that they present is to be comprehensible. Such resting points for the mind are just as necessary in melody if it is to affect

Table 3.2 *Quintilian's rhetorical structure as applied to the* da capo *aria*

Introductio	Arousal of listeners' interest		Orchestral *ritornello*
Narratio	Principal theme of speech	A i	Statement of main theme
Argumentatio	Defence of thesis against the opposition	A ii	Development of main theme
Confutatio	Confutation of the opponent's arguments	B	Change of tempo, key, melody and words
Confirmatio	Resumption and expansion of original argument to convince	A	Repetition and ornamentation of first theme
Conclusio	Final plea		Cadenza

our feelings' (Strunk, 1998: 778). Spoken rhetoric therefore provided a potential model for understanding the impact of music. The discovery in 1416 of Quintilian's *Institutio Oratoria* provided a major text for the teaching of rhetoric and for analysing how other arts, in particular music, worked. His model for the ideal speech could be translated into the structure of the *da capo* aria (Table 3.2).

Handel (*Rinaldo*)

The intellectual circles of the Earls of Chandos and Burlington, within which Handel moved, would have understood this relationship between rhetoric and artistic intention and form, which shows how the intrinsic formality of the *da capo* aria could become a powerful tool for affecting an audience. In *Rinaldo*, the opera with which Handel introduced himself to London, the *da capo* aria is designed not just as a single unit, but often as part of larger musical and dramatic structures. Act I ends with a sequence of three scenes (vii–ix) all focused on Rinaldo's reaction to Almirena's abduction (Table 3.3a).[9]

Together, these three scenes form a single dramatic unit. They take the hero and the audience from despair to resolution, but do so through a series of distinct moments. Each aria is the expression of a single state of mind or reflection that, in itself, does not contribute to the forward thrust of the action. Instead, each dwells upon a particular sentiment: loss, despair, resolution. In each case, too, the *da capo* form confirms the abiding state of mind through its return to the first section; and it is precisely this – confirmation rather than forward movement – that each aria is designed to establish (Table 3.3b).

Far from being a *merely* formal structure, and indeed a hindrance to expression, in the hands of a major composer the form itself becomes part of the drama. At the

Table 3.3a Rinaldo: *act I, scenes vii–ix, formal musical structure*

vii	Recitative:	Armida, Almirena, Rinaldo		Armida struggles to take Almirena from Rinaldo
	Prelude			Almirena and Armida disappear in the magic cloud
	Aria:	Rinaldo	'Cara sposa'	Rinaldo's despair and defiance
viii	Recitative:	Goffredo, Eustazio, Rinaldo		Why does Rinaldo not act?
	Aria	Rinaldo	'Cor ingrato'	Rinaldo wonders at himself and tells himself to act as he should
	Recitative:	Rinaldo, Goffredo, Eustazio		All three are amazed by what has happened
ix	Recitative	Rinaldo		(Prompted by Eustazio's example) Rinaldo determines to act
	Aria	Rinaldo	'Venti, turbini, prestate'	'Winds, whirlwinds, lend Rinaldo your strength'

same time, the *da capo* aria, and other formalities of the *opera seria*, could produce a formulaic response. In part this was the result of the most thoroughgoing attempt to return the opera to its roots and provide it with a serious literary model by Zeno's successor, Metastasio.

Opera seria: second stage (Pietro Metastasio)

In 1729 Metastasio succeeded Zeno as Caesarean court poet at Vienna. Between then and 1782 he wrote twenty-eight libretti and thirty-two *Feste, Azioni* and *Componimenti*. He belonged to the reformative Arcadian Academy which included Scarlatti, whose aim was to purify opera, modelled as closely as possible on the French theatre. Racine and Corneille, rather than Lully or Quinault, were its ideals. Metastasio's indebtedness (and modesty) is clear in a letter of 1761:

> [I am] unworthy of the second praise which you have been so obliging as to bestow upon me, of having ingeniously and with wonderful art adapted French tragedies to the Italian stage; at least I can venture to say with truth, that this is what I never intended. Having perused the best dramatic productions of other countries, I always meant to write originally. And if the circumscribed condition of our natures or a memory . . . has suggested to me beauties which I had read before upon similar occasions; supposing I was the inventor of them, I had taken the credit to myself.   (Kimbel, 1991: 185)

Table 3.3b Rinaldo: *act I, scenes vii–ix*

Scene vii	Recitative between Armida, Rinaldo and Almirena	
Prelude	*Rinaldo and Armida draw their swords, and prepare to attack each other; in the mean time a Rock rises from under Ground full of dreadful Monsters, and covering Armida and Almirena, carries them away.* [Rinaldo collapses]	
Aria A section	3/4 *Largo* Ritornello	a lyrical line in which pairs of quavers gently throb before
	Cara sposa – Dear bride	the voice enters with a sustained melody centred on the rhythm of the opening words 'Cārǎ spōsā'.[1]
		The phrases to which the repeated words are sung (bars 12–14, 28–29, 38–40, 46–49) are all different, so that the A section (12–71) becomes a series of interrupted thoughts. Clearly, Rinaldo can do nothing but repeat his love for Almirena
B section	*Allegro* Dell vostr'Erebo sull'ara From your altar in Erebus	The B section then breaks into 4/4, marked *allegro*, in which Rinaldo defies the evil sprits who have taken his beloved. It is a single outburst whose rapid semi-quavers end in
	O spirti rei – You evil spirits	a two-bar unaccompanied cadenza on the words 'caro sposa'
A: *da capo*	Cara sposa – Dear bride	But at this point Rinaldo can still do nothing but mourn, exclaim but not act. It seems appropriate that after his brief, but useless outburst, he relapses into the opening, dominant state of emotional torpor.
Scene viii	Recitative: Goffredo is amazed at the hero's paralysis; Rinaldo replies that he has been so stricken 'That scarce my tongue can utter what I feel'.	
Aria A section	*Adagio* E flat minor	The aria sees him beginning to return to his senses and realise what he must do. It is very dark and accompanied by the continuo instruments alone, further deepening the sense of isolated grief.
	Cor ingrato – Poor heart	Rinaldo still dwells on his own feelings. Where 'Cara sposa' moved from *adagio* to *allegro*, here

(*cont.*)

Table 3.3b (*cont.*)

B section	*Presto* Ma se stupido – rassembri But if you seem senseless	the B section is a *presto*. Rinaldo looks at his numbed state and demands that the fury burning within him arouse him to action. The music is rapid and florid, with three long runs (bars 14–15, 17–18, 21–22), before
A: *da capo*	Cor ingrato – poor heart	returning to the A section. Rinaldo is still 'numbed' but now aware of what he must do.
	Recitative: Goffredo urges Rinaldo to visit the Magician who will enable them to recover Almirena.	
Scene ix	**Recitative: Alone, Rinaldo is inspired by Goffredo's ray of hope and, more importantly, as a result of the passage from 'Cara sposa' to 'Cor ingrato', knows what he now has to do.**	
Aria A section	*Allegro*	In the last aria Rinaldo is finally able to resolve his personal feelings and simply act. The *allegro* continues through the B section emphasising both as part of the same thought.
	Ritornello	Unlike the continuo accompaniment of 'Cor ingrato' the accompaniment is oboes and strings with solo violin and oboe; the mood is bright, expansive and resolved. The ritornello itself has a cadenza at its centre for the two solo instruments (10–12) emphasising virtuosity – so often an analogue for heroic resolve.
	Venti, turbini Ye winds, the rapid race of air	Rinaldo opens with a three-bar cadence (18–20) calling for winds and whirlwinds to lend wings to his feet,
B section	Ciell, numi　Heavens, gods	the B section, still *allegro* simply adds a request for the gods to strengthen him before
A section	Venti, turbini Ye winds, the rapid race of air	confirming his opening resolve.

1. ¯ = long, stressed syllable.
˘ = short, unstressed syllable.

Libretto

Metastasio's reforms both strengthened and added further restrictions to Zeno's work. The libretto was required to aim at simplicity, naturalness, dignity and instruction, as well as being good literature. In terms of content:

- Plot was required to conform fully to the (presumed) Aristotelian unities stipulating a single action, a time-scale of one day, and a single location or close proximity of locations, and
- to maintain the focus of the drama, there should be no more than eight characters.
- As a moral vehicle, the concern was with what *should*, rather than what actually *does*, happen. The tragic ending was considered 'uncivilised' and counter to the Prince's ability to resolve all problems, so that pathos rather than horror were to be aimed at.
- Similarly, only natural phenomena such as storms were permissible. Magic, wonders and supernatural events were banished, as was the ballet as a mere *divertissement* and distraction from the serious dramatic intention.

In matters of form:

- The number of arias was reduced to between twenty and thirty, all in *da capo* form with only one duet and few (usually ceremonial) choruses.
- Normally, each scene consisted of a recitative followed by an aria and the character's exit. However the exit could be prevented, so that the disruption of the form was an analogue for the dramatic moment.
- The acts balanced the private and public worlds. Usually act i took place in relative privacy, act ii was normally set in public, with act iii moving towards public resolution.
- Characters usually assembled by the middle of acts i and ii, and then gradually dispersed, often leaving a single character on stage (as distinct from later romantic dramaturgy in which acts often have large-scale climactic endings) (Table 3.4, p. 44).

Practicalities

Libretti were now increasingly subject to two quite different priorities. The first was the formal requirements of the Metastasian ideal, while the second was the demands of the singers. The result was a set of generally accepted 'rules' to which every librettist and composer had to conform, or simply find his work rejected out of hand. The practical implications were broadly:

Table 3.4 *Zeno, Metastasio and the formalisation of the* opera seria

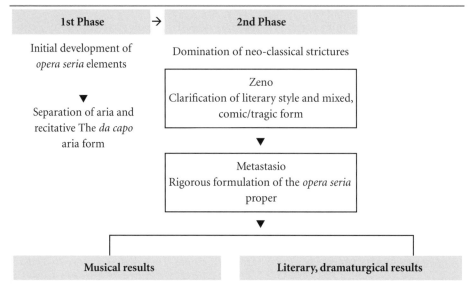

1st Phase →	2nd Phase
Initial development of *opera seria* elements	Domination of neo-classical strictures
▼	**Zeno** Clarification of literary style and mixed, comic/tragic form
Separation of aria and recitative The *da capo* aria form	▼
	Metastasio Rigorous formulation of the *opera seria* proper

Musical results	**Literary, dramaturgical results**
– Primacy of words obviates anything other than the solo voice (duets as alternating voices) – The solo aria is restricted to the *da capo* form – Most music restricted to noble characters and sentiments – Order of arias determined by character's and singer's rank rather than narrative – Music expressive but bound by the decorum of courtly convention	The hieratic Metastasian libretto automatically determined the dramaturgy, musical sequence and meaning of the *opera seria*: 1 Modified use of 'classical' dramatic form to reflect the demands and self-image of the courtly world leading to: – Subjects restricted to classical or other noble characters and material – Rigid exclusion of comic and low characters – Insistence on the *fine lieto* – harmonious ending 2 Libretto structured to reflect the precedence of the courtly world leads to: – Fixed order of characters and singers – Allocation, number and position of scenes and arias according to rank of character (and singer) – Insistence on the stage never being empty determines the sequence of entrances, confrontations and exits – and therefore the dramatic structure

- five or six arias, placed at the most effective points (entrance, dramatic exit) for the two main roles;
- three or four arias each for the secondary couple;
- one or two arias (at most) for supporting roles – fathers, advisers, confidants, etc.

Table 3.5 Rinaldo: *roles and casting, 1711 and 1731*

	1711	1731
Rinaldo	Castrato mezzo soprano (Nicolini)	Castrato mezzo soprano (Senesino)
Almirena	Soprano	Soprano
Armida	Soprano	Contralto
Goffredo	Castrato contralto	Tenor
Eustazio	Castrato contralto	Cut
Mago	Castrato contralto	Bass
Argante	Bass	Contralto
Araldo	Tenor	Bass

The impact of this can be seen in *Rinaldo*. In part this is interesting precisely because Handel only set three Metastasio (highly adapted) libretti,[10] probably turning to him, albeit in adaptation, as his libretti started to become fashionable in the late 1720s.

Despite its proliferation of scenic locations and effects, the cast is restricted to seven main characters. The arias and duets are allocated according to the importance of the role but also the specific singer. In addition (as with *La Griselda*), standard practice meant that when any opera was revived, changes were demanded to accommodate new casting and any other economic or social circumstances. New arias might be required, with others transposed and some roles cut, with consequent alterations to the libretto. *Rinaldo* was premiered in 1711 and then revived in 1712/13, 1714, 1717 and, with the most radical changes in 1731 to enable more economical production demands and satisfy the demands of the new star, Senesino (Table 3.5).

Musically, the 1731 score used ten numbers from 1711 unchanged, eleven were transposed, seven were revised and five numbers were reallocated. In addition, two numbers were newly composed and eight were borrowed from other works.[11] The role of Eustazio was cut altogether. All of this required changes not only to the sung text but to the production and stage directions. Table 3.6 shows how the characters had their quotient of arias (and duets) allotted according to the importance of the role. But this should not disguise the fact that this in itself directly reflected the star rating of the actual singers. If the totals at the head of each column make it look like a league table, that is precisely how both singers and their followers would have seen it.

Metastasio's clarification of the libretto thus had the unexpected result of enhancing the role of the singer as the central attraction. At the same time, it diminished production values. In Metastasio's own printing of *Alessandro nell'Indie*[12] stage directions are minimal:

Table 3.6 Rinaldo: *1711 distribution of arias and duets*

Act	Scene	Rinaldo 8 (+ 2 × D)	Eustazio 5	Goffredo 5	Armida 4 (+ 2 × D)	Almirena 4 (+ 1 × D)	Argante 3	Mago 1	Sirene 1	Donna 0	Araldo 0
I	i	A		A		A					
	ii		A								
	iii			A			A				
	iv						A				
	v				A A						
	vi	D		Duet		D A					
	vii	A									
	viii	A	A								
	ix	A									
II	i	A	A	A							
	iii		A								
	iv			A		A	A				
	vi	D	Duet		D						
	vii	A									
	viii								Duet		
	ix				R A A						
III	ii							A			
	iv	A		A							
	vi				D	Duet	D				
	vii					A					
	viii		A								
	ix	A									
	x			A							
	xiii				Coro						

Note: A = Aria, D = Duet, R = Recitativo accompagnato.

Act II   Royal apartments
Act III   Portico of the royal gardens.   (Metastasio, 1761)

Directorial indications are confined to footnotes even though these include vital indications of who is speaking to whom without which much of the text is incomprehensible. Clearly the intention was to create a 'pure' literary text.

By contrast, *Rinaldo* is far more complex in every respect. The difference is not simply one of literary convention, but of the whole style of the work. *Rinaldo* was intended to amaze its audience and was designed by Handel and the manager/playwright Aaron Hill to 'frame some Dramma, that, by different Passions, might afford the Musick scope to vary and display its Excellence, and fill the Eye with more delightful Prospects, so at once to give Two Senses equal Pleasure' (Hogwood, 1984: 63). A selection of the stage indications for act I of *Rinaldo* (1711) shows the extent to which this aim was realised:

Act I	i	*The city of Jerusalem besieg'd. A prospect of the walls. And a Gate on the plainest side of the Town. Part of the Christian Camp on the right side of the stage.*
	iii	Argante from the City, drawn through the Gate in a Triumphal Charriot, the Horses white and led by arm'd Blackamoors. He comes forward attended by a great Number of Horse and Foot Guard . . . [13]
	v	Armida in the air, in a Charriot drawn by two huge Dragons, out of whose mouth issue Fire and Smoke.
	[Later]	The Chariot being descended, The Dragons rush forward, and draw her toward Argante . . . [14]
	vi	*A delightful Grove in which the Birds are heard to sing, and seen flying up and down among the trees.*
	vii	[Rinaldo and Armida] have drawn their Swords, and are making at each other, when a black Cloud descends, all fill'd with dreadful Monsters spitting Fire and Smoke on every side. The Cloud covers Almirena and Armida, and carries 'em up swiftly into the Air, leaving in their Place, two frightful Furies, who having grinn'd at, and mock'd Rinaldo, sink down and disappear.

To Metastasio, *Rinaldo* would have been a travesty of what true opera was about. Instead of a clear action that fixed the audience's attention on its noble and heroic theme, *Rinaldo* is dramaturgically diffuse, relies on magical powers, scenographic machinery and visual effects. He would have considered all this a distraction from the serious consideration of character, action and their consequences. Far closer to his ideal was Graun's *Cesare e Cleopatra* (1742) which took into consideration all aspects of opera as court entertainment and political statement. In this context the arbiter of taste – often the Prince himself – was involved in, and in extreme cases dictated, the subject, text and even the music. The physical presentation of opera emphasised these conditions. The audience was in full light,[15] and could therefore see one another and be seen by the authority. Whoever's court it was would be seated in a dominant position; indeed, the notion of perspective scenery compounded the centrality of the ruler. The seat that commanded the world also commanded the (only) perfect view of its representation in the world on stage.

This is explicit in Graun's career and work when he became Royal Kapellmeister to Frederick the Great in 1740. Frederick, famous as both flautist and military despot, clearly loved music – but as it suited his taste and needs. As his Kapellmeister, Graun wrote at his patron's behest more precisely than perhaps any other composer has done. In the opera, Frederick controlled the choice of subject, libretto, casting, production and music. There are examples of Graun recomposing arias two or three times before Frederick was satisfied.

Graun's *Cesare e Cleopatra* was written for the sumptuous opening of the Berlin Royal Opera House (Unter den Linden in Berlin). It is typical of the full-blown *opera seria*.[16] It consists of a series of coupled recitatives and *da capo* arias, with one duet (in act iii, scene xi), and two choruses that open and close the opera. The drama shows Caesar overcoming the irrationality of love, hatred and the desire for revenge, to reach an equilibrium as a humane, but self-controlled ruler. In each number a single emotion is displayed rather than explored, carefully contained within the convention of the *da capo* form and the social demands for decorum and self-control:

i.vi	In 'Quel che lontano', Caesar meditates on the fact that absence makes the heart grow fonder. Despite attractive writing and a delicate flute line in the *ritornelli*, it is less an outpouring of passion than a decorous acknowledgement of an emotion.
i.viii	Cleopatra's 'Tra le procelle assorto' (While deep in the tempest) is a telling contrast. The tempo and, above all, use of florid runs, create a more convincing picture of a character in emotional tumult: something quite inappropriate for the ruler himself. i.viii implies that Cleopatra will need to be contained if she is to become a royal consort.
iii.i	Affected by treachery, Caesar rages 'Voglio strage, e sangue voglio' (I want slaughter, I want blood). The aria is fiery: its tempo and the leaps in the melody and vocal line are accentuated by interjections from the lower strings either on single notes or semi-quaver figures.
iii.viii	Caesar has readjusted himself. In 'Sentir che me chiama' (To hear myself called), the music is stately and decorous save for the two lines 'Che barbaro affanno/È questo per me!' (What base distress/ Is this for me!). Notably, while this consists of the two usual stanzas (quatrains A and B) two lines are added to the first quatrain, as though Caesar's anger has briefly spilled over. Graun mirrors this as the two extra lines break the formal musical pattern.
iii.xi	The (love) duet 'Ecco mio ben l'istante' (The moment has come, my love) is, again, controlled – beautiful but stately. It expresses consonance through the (unusual) intertwining of voices.

The paradox is, that while Metastasio's stipulations succeeded in bringing opera back to a purer musico-dramatic form, the very clarity and narrowness of his aesthetic all too easily become merely formulaic. Combined with the reduction in scenic and dramatic variety, this potentially undermined opera's appeal and vitality. To overcome this required either an artist who could afford to challenge convention, or a radical change in the social and political context of opera.

Chapter 4

Reform: the reintegration of elements

The reaction against *opera seria* was so strong that the critique of contemporaries such as Gluck and Calzabigi was later taken at face value. As late as 1965 the revised edition of *The Oxford Companion to Music* was still explaining that

> [there] lived and worked, during the first half of the eighteenth century, some of the greatest composers of the whole history of opera . . . but not one of their operas has any place in the operatic repertory now . . . chiefly . . . from the excessive formality of their treatment. It is just possible that the world may come to take pleasure again in these one-time favourites, but the greater probability is that they will merely continue to be revived occasionally for the interest of historically-minded connoisseurs.
>
> (Scholes, 1965: 711)

The masters of *opera seria* were able to inhabit the form and create works that stand up in modern production. The root problem was not, therefore the formality *per se*, but the social and political world that it reflected. This was compounded by the fact that the main reformers, Zeno and Metastasio, were both literary figures for whom opera's essential language, music, was neither a priority nor their expertise. For them, the opera was squarely based on the libretto. The result was a literary structure, within which a place had to be found for the music, the virtually universal *da capo* aria. Divorced from carrying the narrative, the *da capo* aria became increasingly self-standing. This was exploited by singers as they came to dominate productions, insisting on opportunities for vocal display and inserting favourite arias into whatever opera they performed – the so-called 'portmanteau' arias with which they toured from one opera house to another. Ultimately this led to the 'pasticcio', whole operas made up of well-received arias/tunes from any number of works.[1]

By the latter part of the century these abuses had become sufficiently well known to be (half-)satirised by Goldoni when he described his first attempt to write a libretto. On presenting it to the manager he was gently taken aside and told:

> If you were in France, you might take the trouble to please the public; but here, you must begin by pleasing the performers; you have to satisfy the composer of the music; you have to consult the scene painter; there are rules for everything,

50

and it would be a crime against true dramaturgy if one dared offend them, if one failed to observe them.

Listen, he continued; I am going to show you some of these rules, which are immutable, and which you do not know.

The three principal characters in the drama must sing five arias each; two in the first act, two in the second, and one in the third. The performers of the second rank can only have three, and the other roles must be content with one or two at the most. The author of the words must provide the composer with the various opportunities which allow nuances of light and shade in the music, and take care that two melancholy arias do not follow one another; it is necessary to arrange, with the same care, the bravura arias, the action arias, the arias of the secondary characters as well as the minuets, and the rondeaux.

Above all, it is most necessary to take care to give neither the passionate nor the bravura arias or the rondeaux to the secondary characters; these poor people must be content with whatever they are given, and it is forbidden to honour them.

(Goldoni, 1992: 128–9)

Finally, because the music of the recitative was – of necessity – less complex and musically interesting than that of the aria, the latter attracted all the attention, leaving the recitative as a necessary evil, as the French Ambassador de Brosses reported: 'Chess is marvellously well adapted to filling in the monotony of the recitatives, and the arias are equally good for interrupting a too assiduous concentration on chess' (Grout, 2003: 222).

Algarotti's 1755 *Saggio Sopra l'Opera in Musica* is an historical critique of modern opera; in it, he discusses a number of 'abuses', prefaced by the assertion that 'it is impossible to preserve [the arts] from decay and in the unimpaired enjoyment of their constitutional vigour without making them revert from time to time to their original principles . . . No art now appears to stand so much in need [of having this] put in practice as that of music' (Strunk, 1998: 914).

His main criticisms are that

- The composer has usurped the overall power in opera, 'contracting all the views of pleasing to his department alone'.
- 'The twin sisters, poetry and music, no longer go hand in hand.'
- The recitative 'as it is wont to be the most noisy part of an opera, so it is the least attended to . . . It seems as though our musical composers were of the opinion that the recitative is not of consequence . . . But the ancient masters thought in quite a different manner.'
- 'Brilliant passages' should only be used 'where the words are expressive of passion or movement', and the 'repeating of words . . . that are made for the sake of sound

merely are devoid of meaning and prove intolerable to a judicious ear' (Strunk, 1998: 914).

Differing aspects of reform

Many composers sought to address this. However, while some, such as Jommelli and Traetta tried to make the *opera seria* and above all the *da capo* aria work better ('internal' reforms), others including Benda and Gluck, developed radically different approaches ('radical' reforms). All these worked within a small circle dominated by Vienna, Paris and some of the smaller but artistically notable German and Italian courts. Common influences were Rameau who was equally concerned with the restrictions of the Lullian model in France, as well as major developments in ballet (Table 4.1).

Parallel advances were being made in the ballet. Jean-Georges Noverre choreographed Jommelli's pastorale *Il trionfo d'amore* and later several of Gluck's operas in Vienna and Paris. Noverre developed, if he did not actually invent, the *ballet d'action*, the first real attempt to turn the ballet into a dramatic form. In his *Lettres sur la Danse et sur les Ballets*, he explained that he required scores that were 'written to fit each phrase and thought' to create dance drawn from all the arts in which 'all of these elements should be combined with poetry and imagination' (Clarke and Crisp, 1973: 29). Gasparo Angiolini, Noverre's great rival, was equally committed to ballet as a dramatic medium. Like Noverre, he worked with Gluck, first choreographing his ballet *Don Juan* and then the ballet sequences in *Orfeo ed Euridice*. He also choreographed two of Traetta's operas. This circle of influences was completed by Marco Coltellini, whom Calzabigi considered his successor and who wrote the libretto for Traetta's *Antigona* and in 1765 prepared *Telemaco* for Gluck.

Neo-classical ideals

These men were influenced by many of the ideals that had inspired the *Camerata*. At this moment of crisis in opera, they turned to the Greek drama again, reflecting the wider neo-classical movement. This grew out of the opening up of Greece in the 1750s when, for the first time since the decline of the Eastern Empire, significant numbers of Europeans began to explore the Turkish-held lands of Greece and its Asia Minor extension.[2] For the first time, Europeans saw the art of Greece as distinct from a generalised sense of 'Antiquity' – which turned out to have been the art of Rome. The result was a considerable shock. Goethe's reaction to the temples at Paestum was typical:

Table 4.1 *Approaches to the reform of opera/opera seria*

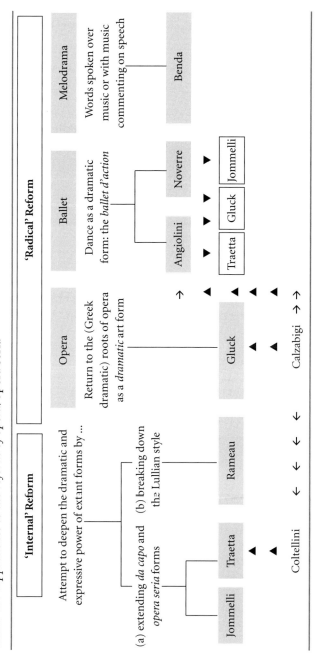

> At first they excited nothing but stupefaction. I found myself in a world which was completely strange to me . . . But I pulled myself together, remembered the history of art, thought of the age with which this architecture was in harmony, called up images in my mind of the austere style of sculpture – and in less than an hour I found myself reconciled to them and even thanking my guardian angel for having allowed me to see these well-preserved remains with my own eyes. (Goethe, 23 March 1787)

Suddenly the work of the Renaissance was understood as, at best, an adaptation of the Roman: not Homer, but Virgil translated into Italian. Neo-classicism now aspired to return to the purity of Athens or the early Roman Republic. In painting, sculpture and architecture it dismissed what it saw as the flippant, merely ornamental way in which both the Baroque and Rococo had treated the classical. Where Boucher, for example, uses classical subjects for decorative and erotic purposes without any regard for the classical itself, David projects the world of the heroic, austere Roman Republic as a moral and political as well as aesthetic ideal. Similarly, Handel's *Partenope* bears little relationship to its supposed sources and is, instead, an elegant comedy of the sexes. By contrast, Gluck's *Alceste* carries all the weight and moral seriousness of its Greek source.

At the same time there was a broad realisation that reform was needed whether based on classical principles or not, as Diderot explained:

> Truth, goodness and beauty have their claims . . . Anything not bearing their stamp is admired for a time, but in the end you yawn . . . The reign of nature is quietly coming in, and that of my trinity, against which the gates of hell shall not prevail: truth, which is the father begets goodness, which is the son, whence proceeds the beautiful which is the holy ghost. (Strunk, 1998: 927)

This was the spirit that encouraged composers to try to recover the dramatic credibility of opera. It meant either re-examining the conventions that had developed, or dispensing with them altogether.

Internal reform

Rameau (*Hippolyte et Aricie*)

Although 'reform' usually meant reform of the abuses of Italian opera, in France, too, change was wanted. French opera had always been carefully constructed as drama, drawing on the theatre of Racine and Corneille. It had not needed Metastasio to correct lapses in dramaturgy or quality of text. But, like the *opera seria*, it had become increasingly rigid, tied to Lully as the indispensable model and standard. From the 1730s onwards a new energy was introduced by Rameau. His operas were important not just in their own right but because his printed scores became a source of inspiration for artistic circles in Germany, Italy and Austria where formative composers such as Jommelli, Traetta and Gluck worked.

French operas were strictly categorised and Rameau wrote in most of the available forms so that his innovations in the great *Tragédies en musique* grew out of a practical experience of French opera in all its variety (Table 4.2).

Table 4.2 *French operatic forms as used by Rameau*

Tragédie en musique	6	'Serious' opera – **Hippolyte et Aricie; Castor et Pollux; Dardanus; Zoroastre; Linus; Les Boréades**
Comédie-lyrique	2	'High comedy' in opera
Opéra-ballet	7	Balanced mixture of (serious) opera and ballet
Comédie-ballet	1	Balanced mixture of high comedy and ballet
Acte de ballet	9	Short version of the *opéra-ballet*
Pastorale héroïque	4	Arcadian opera with mythical heroic characters
Pastorale	1	Arcadian, purely pastoral, opera

In fact, Rameau retained all the formal, external features of the Lullian opera, but informed them with a new flexiblity. Elements flow into, interrupt and cross over one another, creating larger units that are driven by the characters and their dramatic situation. To enable this, Rameau developed

- a greatly enhanced, expressive use of the orchestra and solo instruments
- vocal writing that is always focused on the demands of the text, with no vocal display for its own sake
- a continuum between *recitativo*, *arioso* and *aria* proper
- complete integration of the chorus and ballets within the action.

All this was evident in his first Tragédie, *Hippolyte et Aricie* (1733). Act IV, scenes iii and iv show Rameau's variety and integration of musical elements. He weaves music and words together in a tightly organised unit including all the usual forms of dance, *airs* and *récitatives*, but gives them a new dramatic coherence: a series of twenty-five highly varied elements welded into a flowing dramatic whole (Table 4.3).

Rameau was also an important theorist. In his *Traité de l'Harmonie* he explains how an opera composer should work: 'A good musician should surrender himself to all the characters he wishes to portray . . . He must declaim the text well, at least to himself, and must feel when and to what degree the voice should rise or fall, so that he may shape his melody, harmony, modulation and movement accordingly' (Strunk, 1998: 696). The results are evident in the all-important confrontation between Phèdre and Hippolyte in act III, scene iii. It shows Rameau's incisive handling

Table 4.3 Hippolyte et Aricie: *act IV, scenes iii and iv*

Act IV, Scene iii		
200	Chorus	Divided between full and small chorus
279		*Premier air en rondeau pour les chasseurs et chasseresses*
332		*Deuxième air en rondeau pour les chasseurs et chasseresses*
360		Choeur des chasseurs et chasseresses – including solo lines
387	Orchestra	*Premier menuet* based on a hunting motif
411		*Deuxième menuet en rondeau* for oboe and bassoon, making a very rustic, simple effect.
433		*Bruit de mer et vents* marked *Vite*, shift from C major to B♭ major, change to duple time. Strings play a series of repeated demi-semiquavers with a short, rising, wind-like figure for flutes at the end of the bar that increases by one note each time
448	Chorus	Chorus breaks in with its exclamation first of alarm 'Quel bruit! Quels vents!' followed by horror as the sea monster appears and then an impassioned appeal to Diane
462	Hippolyte	Duple time as Hippolyte faces the monster – Aricie tries to stop him
460		*Hippolyte advances on the monster in his chariot*
464	Aricie	Common time. Rising and falling figure of eight semiquavers in the strings as Aricie exclaims at the struggle between Hippolyte and the monster.
467		Aricie quails at the sight. The strings alternate between two figures
467/8		*The monster, wounded by Hippolyte, covers him in smoke*
471	Chorus	Throbbing semiquavers in the strings as Aricie despairs of Diane. The chorus cry out to the goddess
474		*Everything finally vanishes, and nothing is seen but the chariot*
474		*Récitatif*: Aricie begins to faint
476		*Lent*: over tied quavers with crochets as Aricie swoons
483	Chorus	The chorus sing in parallel, exclaiming at the loss of Hippolyte.

Table 4.3 (*cont.*)

Act iv, Scene iv		
489	Phèdre	*Air avec choeur des chasseurs et chasseresses* Duple time. Phèdre, unaccompanied, asks what the cry is that she has heard
451	Chorus	The chorus, again in parallel, explains that Hippolyte is no more
493	Phèdre	Start of Phèdre's monologue. Tempo shifts between 2/4, 3/4 (494) and 4/4 (497). Dynamics marked *fort, doux*
498	Chorus	3/4 The chorus recounts what happened
506	Phèdre	*Basse continue* alone as Phèdre realises the truth, and then
514		2/4 Continuo and strings: she understands her own guilt
559	Chorus	The chorus, again in parallel, repeats their statement from 451 that Hippolyte is no more

of dialogue, with all the elements stripped down to their musical essentials. It consists of 150 bars divided between five formal elements. The first three and the last are only accompanied by the *basse continue*, while Hippolyte's *Air* has a small string accompaniment, emphasising the scene's musical and dramatic continuity (Table 4.4).

Table 4.4 Hippolyte et Aricie: *act iii, scene iii*

56	Récitatif en dialogue	Hippolyte and Phèdre	Basse continue
107	Duo (vivement)		
153	Récitatif en dialogue		
168	Air (vivement)	Hippolyte	Strings
180	Récitatif en dialogue	Hippolyte and Phèdre	Basse continue

The dramatic expressiveness produced by Rameau's musical integration, flexible orchestral and harmonic resourcefulness made his operas a model for composers who wished to explore and reinvigorate their own operatic traditions.

Jommelli and Traetta

Just as Rameau reformed from within the Lullian model, so the reforms of Jommelli and Traetta were made from within the *opera seria*. Five elements characterise their work:

- new approaches to the *da capo* aria, making it either more emotionally expressive through extension (Jommelli) or more responsive to the text (Traetta)
- use of ensemble writing (duet, trio, quartet)
- introduction of the chorus (Traetta)
- richer use of the orchestra
- wider use of *recitativo accompagnato,* often dissolving the distinction between recitative and aria.

Jommelli was a significant orchestral as well as operatic composer and he used his symphonic grasp to expand the *da capo* aria, increasing its scope and expressiveness. While it remained self-standing, it became a more articulated dramatic entity. In his 1763 *Didone Abbandonata,* his third setting of Metastasio's libretto, Aeneas' act III, scene vi aria 'A trionfar mi chiama' (I am called to triumph) extends to just under ten minutes.[3] About to abandon Dido, Aeneas celebrates his change from lover to warrior. This is a musically complex piece. It consists of an A section in two parts, divided by the *ritornello* and in which the second A is considerably varied. The result is an eight-part structure: *ritornello,* Ai, *ritornello,* Aii, *ritornello,* B, a further varied A, *ritornello*/coda (Table 4.5).

Aeneas's character is strongly projected through the aria's musical complexity itself, but the words remain as limited by the formality of the repetition as in any *da capo* aria. Typically, most of the vocal line in the A sections is taken up with decoration, mainly on the significant word 'trionfar'. But however much the *da capo*

Table 4.5 Didone abbandonata*: act III, scene vi, 'A trionfar mi chiama'*

0.00–0.27	Ritornello	Ri	1 Moderate tempo	
0.27–1.05		Rii	2 Fast tempo	
1.05–2.30	A i		First quatrain	Dominated by ornamentation of 'trionfar'
2.30–2.44	Ritornello		2 Fast tempo	
2.44–3.14	A ii	a	First quatrain: lines 2 and 1	
3.14–4.24		b	First quatrain: line 3 'E già sopra'	New, dotted melody, mainly consisting of ornamentation
4.24–4.32	Ritornello			
4.32–5.00	B			
5.00–9.24	A repeat of i–ii			
9.24–9.33	Ritornello/coda			

structure is expanded it remains a limiting, musical, rather than a verbal or dramatic one. At the same time, the critic Christian Schubart reported that Jommelli 'studied his poet [and] improved on him often'. His acute response to text is evident in act III, scena ultima/xviii whose text looks like a standard recitative followed by an aria and orchestral coda. But here Jommelli creates an *arioso* of great dramatic power. There is no melody but instead, accompanied declamation ranging from violent despair to resignation, followed by a musical description of the fall of the city that fades into darkness – not unlike the scene endings in *Boris Godunov*.

Like Jommelli, Traetta reworked the *da capo* aria, but importantly reintroduced ensemble writing and the chorus. In 1758 at the Court of Parma, the intendant, Di Tilly, proposed a new approach to opera that would unite elements of the French *Tragédie lyrique* with Italian 'aria opera'. As with Jommelli at Stuttgart, Rameau's scores were a source of inspiration. Significantly, the librettist for Traetta's 1772 *Antigona* was Marco Coltellini, Calzabigi's pupil, who had prepared *Telemaco* for Gluck in 1765.

Where Jommelli expanded the traditional form of the *da capo* aria, Traetta inverted it and increasingly concentrated on the verbal text. In Antigona's act I aria 'D'una misera famiglia' (From a wretched family) she recounts the terrible history of Oedipus' children. But Traetta is keen to avoid the problem of the repeated text, and changes the internal structure of the *da capo* aria. The text of the A section consists of two quatrains (abbc, addc) linked by the two shared rhymes, a and c. These are sung right through without the expected repetition. The B section again consists of two quatrains (effe, ghhg), but it is here that the repetition occurs. The *da capo* then returns to the A *melody* as usual – but with new words. As a result there are two sets of repetition:

• the A melody in 1 and 3 but with new words in 3; and
• B in 2.

The effect is to bind the usual tripartite *da capo* musical structure together, allowing Antigona to dwell on her central plight (B) (Table 4.6).

Traetta also makes extensive use of the ensemble. The *Terzetto* in Act I starts with Antigona's riposte to Creon, 'Ah de' tuoi re, tiranno'. The trio that follows alternates solo lines with ensembles. Its rapidity precisely mirrors the energy of the argument, emphasised by the orchestra's continual interruption/punctuation. Finally, Traetta reintroduced the chorus, sanctioned by Greek classical precedent, and which brought a new major musical and dramatic dimension to the opera.

Table 4.6 Antigona: *act I, 'D'una misera famiglia'*

1	A	No textual repetition	abbc	addc	
2	B	Text repeated as in normal 'A' section	effe	ghhg	Repeat: effe
3	A	A's melody repeated but with new text	ijik		

Radical reform

Benda and Gluck

Benda

Jommelli and Traetta accepted the operatic forms they inherited and tried to breathe new life into them. But others rejected the *opera seria* completely. The first of these was the Bohemian Jiří (or Georg) Benda. Like Graun, he had worked for Frederick the Great, later becoming Kapellmeister to Duke Friederich III of Saxe-Gotha. There he encountered the important Seyler theatre troupe whose leading actress, Charlotte Koch, was to become something of a muse to him. Between 1765 and 1778 Benda wrote a series of operas;[4] but at the same time he also turned to the spoken drama and in 1778 wrote extended incidental music for *Macbeth*. The works for which he became best known were his four *melodramas*, two of which were inspired by Charlotte Koch.

The musical precedent for the melodrama was Rousseau's *Pygmalion*. Rousseau had successfully composed the pastoral comedy *Le Devin du Village*. But he became involved in the debate over the relative merits of French and Italian as languages for musical setting, deciding that 'there is neither measure not melody in French music, because the language is not capable of them' (*Lettre sur la Musique Française*, in Strunk, 1998: 908).

In 1770 he turned away from the sung word to write his melodrama *Pygmalion* in which music alternated with spoken text. Madame de Staël wrote: 'When words and music follow each other, both effects are increased; sometimes they are improved by not being harnessed together. Music expresses situations, words develop them. Music can take the portrayal of impulses beyond words; words can portray feelings that are too nuanced for music' (*Lettres sur Rousseau*, 1788, in Strunk, 1998: 981).

In Benda's *Medea* (1778), music is used in three ways.

- Most of the time music and speech *alternate*, with the music either reflecting on what has been said, creating a bridge to the next thought or sustaining the mood, while the actor pauses in thought.
- In the central passage of act I, Medea speaks *over* the music which enhances and lends pathos to her meditation.
- In act VI, the orchestra *illustrates* the storm followed by Medea's furious rush into the temple as she goes to kill her children.

The effect is dramatic and allows the text to be absolutely clear, neither obscured by the inherent problems of singing, nor abandoned for vocal display. While this is not an operatic form, it highlights the contemporary struggle to find a way of writing that was musical and properly dramatic, with due weight given to the libretto. The resolution to the problem lay, however, in another direction, one that sought to turn against everything that opera had become since it left the austere world of the Florentine *Camerata.*

Gluck: 'The poem is no more made for the music than the music for the poem'

Gluck was well placed to effect his reforms. He had written for most of the major opera houses and, like Rameau, had worked in most of the current operatic forms and was a master of the *opera seria* and *da capo aria* form. Table 4.7 shows the range of his compositions, including sixteen operas to libretti by Metastasio, three of them *after* the first reform opera, *Orfeo ed Eurydice.* In 1752 Gluck had settled in Vienna where he became Konzertmeister and then Kapellmeister to the Prince of Saxe-Hildburghausen. In this capacity he set several of Metastasio's libretti, but with recitatives by Count Durazzo, the Intendant of the Viennese Theatres. In 1761 Durazzo introduced Gluck to the choreographer Gasparo Angiolini and his future librettist, Raniero de' Calzabigi.

In 1761 Angiolini collaborated with Gluck (and most probably Calzabigi) on the *ballet d'action Don Juan, ou Le Festin de Pierre.* The musical characterisation is striking, ranging from the serenade (no. 3) to the startling finale (no. 31) described in the 'Programme': 'The demons tie him and throw him into the utter depths of hell, and from time to time one can see the eddying flames which devour him' (*Programme de Ballet de Don-Juan,* in Winter, 1974: 134). The rapid rising and falling strings with the brass sounding the note of doom over them is hugely effective and musically exciting, presaging the same moment in Mozart's *Don Giovanni* twenty-six years later. It was with the ballet that Gluck first started to compose – and perhaps consider – his new kind of musical theatre. At the same time Durazzo was reshaping the drama by employing a French theatre company, paralleling what was happening in so many courts and which had affected Jommelli, Traetta and Benda.

The year after *Don Juan* came the ground-breaking *Orfeo ed Euridice* (1762), but it was only in 1767, five years later, that Gluck finally abandoned the *opera seria* and its variants to devote himself completely to the 'reformed' opera. In 1765 he was still working with Metastasio, writing the delightful comic *serenata Il Parnaso Confuso.* Melpomene's 'In un mar che non ha sponde' (On a sea without a shore) shows Gluck's ability to write a typically florid *da capo* aria, in which the singer could 'display the agility of [her] fine voice in lengthy passage-work' – the very thing he was to complain of in the 'Preface' to *Alceste* two years later.

Gluck remains in some ways a controversial figure: his operas have never been popular. Whatever their pleasures he himself was clear that 'An opera such as *Alceste* is no entertainment, but a very serious occupation for whoever listens to it' (Howard, 1995: 147). What Gluck addressed – and this is why both Berlioz and Wagner

Table 4.7 *The range of Gluck's operatic genres*

1741–65

	Dramma Musicale	Festa Teatrale	Componimento Pastorale	Azione Teatrale	Serenata	Opéra-Comique	Ballet 1761–5	Prologue
1741–61	17 (12 by Metastasio)	2	1	*Le Cinesi* (Metastasio)	1	7	*Don Juan*	*Il Prologo*
1762				*Orfeo ed Euridice*				
1763–5	3 (2 by Metastasio, 1 by Coltellini) ▶			▶ ▶	1 *Il Parnaso Confuso* (Metastasio)		5	*Feste d'Apollo*

1767–81

	Dramma Musicale	Tragedia	Tragédie	Tragédie opéra	Drame lyrique	Drame héroïque	Opéra-ballet	Prologue
1767		*Alceste*		▶				
1769		▶		▶				
1770	*Paride ed Elena*	▶		▶				
1774		▶	*Iphigénie en Aulide*	*Orphée et Euridice*				
1775		▶			*Cythère assiégée*			
1776		↗ ↗	*Alceste*					
1777						*Armide*		
1779			*Iphigénie en Tauride* ▶				*Echo et Narcisse*	
1781			*Iphigenie auf Tauris*					

would later pay such attention to him – was not style and musical convention so much as the purpose of opera. Foremost was the drama. Words, character and situation were always his starting point. He echoes Rameau when he is reported as saying that: 'Before I begin, my greatest concern is to forget I am a musician. I even forget myself in order that I shall see only my characters. The attempt to do otherwise poisons all the Arts which aspire to the imitation of Nature' (Olivier de Corancez, in Howard, 1995: 245). This conditions the music, in which: 'the voice, the instruments, all the sounds, the very silences, must work towards a single aim, that of expression, and . . . the union between words and music must be so close that the poem is no more made for the music than the music for the poem' (Howard, 1995: 178).

Orfeo ed Euridice

Orfeo brought together four major personalities: Gluck himself, Calzabigi, Angiolini and the *castrato* Gaetano Guadagni who created Orfeo and of whom Calzabigi said '*Orfeo* went well, because we discovered Guadagni' (Howard, 1995: 57). The result was the first of the 'reform' operas. The collaboration itself was significant. It demonstrated the extent to which the reforms grew out of an emphasis on opera as a holistic dramatic medium in which all the performing arts were interdependent as they had been in the Greek theatre. In part this reflected the spirit of neo-classicism. But this was neither antiquarian nor revivalist, as he insisted: 'These old Greeks were men with one nose and a pair of eyes, just like us. We do not have to submit to their rules like servile peasants. On the contrary, we must throw off their clothes, break free of the chains they would bind us in, and seek to become original' (Howard, 1995: 153). Similarly iconoclastic, Calzabigi 'held that music, on whatever verses, was no more than skilful, studied, declamation, further enriched by the harmony of its accompaniments, and that therein lay the whole secret of composing excellent music for a drama' (Howard, 1995: 55).

The hallmarks of reform opera are all present in *Orfeo ed Euridice*:

- The Overture was designed as an integral part of the drama, setting the mood and scene, leading directly into the opening mourning
- The chorus plays an integral part, even though they are only observers, as in the Greek drama
- Similarly the ballet was integral to the action rather than a mere *divertissement*
- Although the score is divided between recitative, chorus, aria, etc. this is the first of Gluck's 'tragic operas manifesting total continuity, of which each part is intimately connected with every other, each enhancing and strengthening the rest, and working together reciprocally' (Arnaud, in Howard, 1995: 170).

- None of the arias is *da capo* and, while lyrical, only once is melody allowed to draw attention to itself at the point where Orpheus, the singer, breaks into the famous 'Che faro senza Euridice?'

All these points were formalised five years later, in the 'Dedication' to *Alceste*.

Alceste

The 'Dedication' was probably written by Calzabigi, but quite clearly represents Gluck's own views as repeatedly expressed in his letters and conversation. It is a manifesto for reform, divided here into six points to highlight its argument:

- "When I undertook to write the music for *Alceste*, I decided to strip it completely of all those abuses . . . which have for so long disfigured Italian opera."
- "I thought to restrict music to its true function of helping poetry to be expressive and to represent the situations of the plot, without interrupting the action or cooling its impetus with useless and unwanted ornaments."
- "I did not . . . want to hold up an actor in the white heat of dialogue to wait for a tedious ritornello, nor let him remain on a favourite vowel in the middle of a word, or display the agility of his fine voice in lengthy passage-work, nor let him wait while the orchestra gives him time to recover his breath for a cadenza."
- "I did not feel it my duty to skim quickly over the second part of an aria, which may well contain the most passionate and significant words . . . to accommodate a singer who wants to show in how many ways he can capriciously vary a passage, rather than ending the aria where its meaning ends."
- "I also considered that my greatest efforts should be concentrated on seeking a beautiful simplicity. I have avoided making a show of complexities at the expense of clarity; and I did not think it useful to invent novelties which were not genuinely required to express the situation and the emotions."
- "There is no convention that I have not willingly renounced in favour of the total effect." (Quotations from Howard, 1995: 84–5)

In *Alceste*, the closed musical forms and melody that characterise the *opera seria* were abandoned. Instead arias, recitatives, choruses and ensembles are woven together to create units dictated by the demands of the drama. Act 1, scene ii opens with the people in mourning. This is followed by a *scena* for Alceste which begins (bar 48) with a recitative that exemplifies Calzabigi's concept that 'music, on whatever verses, was no more than skilful, studied, declamation'. Rather than being musically neutral, however, the very simplicity expresses Alceste's pious resignation to fate. The form of the aria that follows is dictated by the changes, emotional heightening and developments that she undergoes. It is the emotional fragility of someone who has so far presented a noble and accepting face, but is in reality deeply troubled (Table 4.8).

Table 4.8 Alceste: *act I, scene ii, 'Io non chiedo, eterni dei'*

Aria for Alceste			
80–86 4/4 Moderato			Lyrical theme for oboe solo, which would normally be expected to be a *ritornello*; however, not only does it not return later, it is dropped as soon as the voice enters
87–95	Io non chiedo, eterni dèi Tutto il ciel per me sereno	I do not ask, eternal gods that all heaven be serene for me	Similarly, the lyrical and melodic character of the opening section, in which Alceste makes her modest demands of heaven, ceases as she begins to reveal her inner state.
96–112 3/4 Adagio	Ma il mio duol consoli almeno Qualche raggio di pietà [Last line repeated]	But at least allow my sorrow some ray of pity	The aria moves to her real, interior feelings as distinct from her serene public face. The music remains lyrical but without a sense of 'tune' and becomes increasingly declamatory. Gluck extends (rather than decorates) the word *raggio* (ray) as Alceste continues her appeal to the heavens.
113–129 4/4 Allegro	Non comprendi mali miei Né il terror che m'empie il petto. Chi di moglie il vivo affetto Chi di madre il cor non ha. [Last two lines repeated twice]	None understands my ills Nor the terror that fills my breast. Who, of a wife the living love, Who a mother's heart, has not.	The throbbing accompaniment increasingly reveals the twin poles of her *mali* (ills) and *terror* (love for her husband and fear for her children's future). The repetition of the last two lines, each with its own setting emphasises this.
Duet for Eumelo and Aspasia			
130–145 3/4 Andante	*Eumelo* Madre mia . . . *Aspasia* Bella madre . . .	My mother . . . Lovely mother . . .	The children's simple vocal line and harmony emphasise their innocence and creates a dramatic foil to Alceste's increasing emotionality.

(cont.)

Table 4.8 (*cont.*)

Aria for Aleste (continued)

146–155 4/4 Allegro	Cari figli, del diletto Sposo mio ritratti espressi.	Dear children, of my beloved Husband perfect portraits,	The music grows increasingly agitated, with repeated figures in the upper strings, as Aleste dwells on her children.
156–173	Freddo ho il sangue in ogni vena Se a voi penso, o figli amat. Ah, di me più sventurati Non vi renda il Fato almen?	My blood is cold in every vein If I think of you, loved children! Ah, more unfortunate than me May Fate at least not make you!	An insistent motif first heard in the strings (twice) and then (twice) in the vocal line seems to reflect her freezing blood. The motif is repeated for the second two lines.
173–188	Repeat of text at 113–129 but with new musical emphasis:		Aleste now returns to her own complaint, that no one understands her ills.
178	m'empie il petto	fills my breast	Her heart swells in a new figure, rising to high C.
183	chi di madre il cor non ha	who does not have a mother's heart	The central theme becomes a point of reference as Aleste sings in unison (marked *crescendo* and *tutti*) with the orchestra.
189	The aria leads directly into the chorus but with a change to Moderato and B♭, separating their expressions from Aleste's		

Alceste's aria 'Ombre, larve' in act I, scene v is both dramatic and begins by suggesting a memorable melody. The scene begins with a long accompanied recitative as Alceste resolves to sacrifice herself. Finally, she recognises that God/the gods move within her and that she will become an example for future wives. At this moment of triumph over her own weakness the orchestra enters and the key shifts to B flat. A gently throbbing figure announces Alceste's opening, musically striking motif as she addresses the gods with new-found resolution. It recurs three times, punctuating the aria, but despite its attractiveness it remains an isolated motif. Gluck stops the aria becoming melody-centred unlike Orfeo's 'Che faro'. Neither *da capo* nor *strophic*, its musical form is that of the character's inner struggle and falls into five dramatic sections (Table 4.9).

Finally, an example of how Gluck was able to integrate all the elements of a complex scene. Act III, scenes ii and iii is the moment of final parting for Alceste and Admeto as the Deities of the Underworld call for their due. This is a *dramatic* unity woven out of a sequence of moments, each of which responds to the psychological and dramatic growth of the character or event (Table 4.10).

Gluck was clear that his 'music will be fully effective only in the proper situation' (Howard, 1995: 156) and most trenchantly that his 'sole aim was to enter into the content and situation of the drama, and to seek to give expression to these' (Howard, 1995: 95). With this, he established a new attitude and criteria for opera. Like Wagner a hundred years later, this would split the world of opera, between those for whom it was essentially a dramatic form and those for whom it was primarily musical

Table 4.9 Alceste: *act I, scene v*

63–88	Andante	'Ombre, larve'	Alceste proudly refuses to ask for pity or mercy for what she is about to do
89–91	Moderato		In a more lyrical passage she again refuses to complain of her fate and prepares to exchange herself for the husband she is taking back from the gods
92–117	Andante	'Ombre, larve'	She asks the gods not to be offended by what she has dared to do
118–144	Allegro spirituoso		She feels an unknown force at work within her, greater than herself. This spirited, exultant passage ends with the only ornament in the aria (142)
145–162	Andante	'Ombre, larve'	Full of resolve, Alceste returns to her opening address to the gods, reaffirming that she requires neither pity nor mercy.

Table 4.10 Alceste: *act III, scenes ii and iii*

Act III, scene ii			
251	2/4, E♭ major *Andante.* Oboes and strings	The Deities call on Alceste to fulfil her vow	Oboes in minims over strings playing repeated semi-quavers. The chorus almost in a monotone – impassive and implacable.
275	4/4, C major Strings	Alceste suddenly becomes aware that the moment has come	The contrast with Alceste's final realisation of what she has committed herself to is striking. A speech-based recitative with semibreve accompaniment on the strings, but ending in perturbation with the strings in agitated semiquavers.
284	2/4, E♭ major, *Andante* Horns and strings	The Deities demand that Alceste come with them	Similar to 251, but with horns insisting over the strings.
289	4/4 Full orchestra	Admeto asks to be taken instead of Alceste	Admeto's music is marked *smaniando* (raving). Its long lyrical line sounds like Romantic Italian opera. It is an impassioned plea.
301		The Deities interject	The Deities' insistence is emphasised by constant triplets in the strings.
312		Admeto asks for a final embrace	Alternating quavers and quaver rests in the strings, like a faltering heart.
315		Alceste asks for a final embrace	
318		The Deities insist	Repeat of the music at 301.
330		Deities: 'Vieni!' – 'Come!' Admeto: 'Barbari!'	Held semibreves/minims.
332		The Deities lose patience	Repeated, insistent, agitated semiquavers.
336		Alceste's farewell	The music falters with the upper strings' rising figure.
Act III, scene iii			
1	*Tutta.* Full orchestra	Orchestra	The devastating return to the opening of the act I 'Intrada'.
15	Recitative	Voices, Evandro and Ismene confirm Alceste's death	Semibreves and minims accompany the sound of voices entering.
19			A trembling, pulsating *tremolando* figure.
25		Ismene and Evandro in their grief and abandon	The voices harmonise in thirds, sympathetically echoed in the upper strings but still *tremolando*.
34	*Lento.* Full orchestra	Mourning chorus	In parallel lines and simple harmony, the chorus mourns, each part singing on a single note creating great blocks of sound, until bar 42.

and (usually) melodious. Yet at the same time, Gluck's operatic and social sphere remained that of the court or its emulators. Above all, his classical subject matter and austerity beg the question as to whether his operas were the start of a new tradition or the end of an old one. The extent to which this was true is shown by looking at a complete alternative to the *opera seria* – the social, musical and dramatic tradition of the *opera buffa* and its revolutionary impact.

Chapter 5

Comedy and the 'real world'

Rameau, Jommelli and Traetta sought to reform opera as a received form. Gluck had taken this further, breaking the mould of *opera seria* completely. But none had changed its courtly ethos and antique subject-matter. To this extent, their reforms were limited to a better realisation of an art form rooted in the exigencies of the *ancien régime. Opera seria* would never break away from this. To do so required recognising a new social world with different priorities. The *opera buffa* took its themes, situations and characters from the increasingly important bourgeoisie and the lower classes and their social priorities, moral codes and aesthetic requirements. With this, realism and sentiment were introduced into the otherwise rarefied world of the opera which would help create new expectations of what opera was, as well as what its social and artistic functions were (Table 5.1).

Table 5.1 *The implications of comedy for the opera*

Dramaturgical implications			Musical implications
			Popular/strophic melody
Character humour Sentiment and romance	→	Realistic plot and character	→ Ensemble
Social comedy Satire	→	Range of classes	→ Character description
Farce	⇒	Comedic complication and resolution	→ Concerted structures

Realism and sentiment

This shift mirrored the changes in the composition of society. By the seventeenth century, trade had become a social force that challenged the supremacy of the landed aristocracy. With the growth of the middle class, wealth became separated from land: a merchant might not have an estate, but he did have coffers filled with gold. This led to an increasing emphasis on those areas of knowledge that trade needed: above all science, and its subsidiary elements – mathematics, economics, geography, astronomy and languages – which began to challenge the traditional focus of learning and high culture – religion, the arts and the classics. The result was a vocal, powerful section of society that wanted its own place in the political machinery that shaped its destiny. Out of this grew a new form, the novel, that used prose and the language of life to describe people and places as the middle class knew and valued them, and dealing with the themes that mattered to them – money, marriage and possessions. So, too, a new kind of theatre was needed, one that stood between high tragedy and traditional comedy: the *philosophe* Denis Diderot called it *le drame*.[1]

This was a 'middle ground' that paralleled the middle class and their emphasis on what one made for oneself rather than simply inherited, reflecting a work ethic, individual responsibility and self-reliance. These qualities found their ethical focus in the idea of private conscience. Theologically this was the Divine Spirit operating without recourse to the mediation of the (Catholic) priest. In practice, it derived from the individual's reaction to, and feelings about, the world. This is what the eighteenth century understood as 'sentiment': reaction and judgement based on conscience and made manifest through 'natural' feeling rather than reason alone.

These elements coincide in Richardson's *Pamela* with its subtitle *Virtue Rewarded*. Published in 1741, the novel showed how a young girl in service resisted her master's advances until he felt constrained to marry her. *Pamela* was quickly translated into French where it inspired Voltaire's *Nanine* and a number of dramatisations. Among them was Goldoni's *Pamela* and a series of other plays and libretti. The most popular of these was Piccinni's aptly titled *La buona figliuola* (The Good Daughter). Like Pamela, the heroine, Cecchina, (almost) suffers for her virtue but wins a noble hand at the end. The comic opera' would combine this concern with the things that really mattered to the emerging bourgeoisie.

The growing importance of comedy as a serious vehicle finds theoretical expression in Diderot. The *Encyclopedia*, published between 1751 and 1780, was designed to make all knowledge available to all men and challenge the (artificial) barriers of the *ancien régime*. Diderot's article on theatre explained the moral role of comedy. In the past there had been 'The misuse of comedy . . . to make the most serious professions appear ridiculous', but in the new world

> Comedy is much more suited than tragedy to present instructive scenes. Tragic events are outside the ordinary course of nature, whereas every day instances

occur where the successful outcome depends on good sense, on prudence, on moderation, on knowledge of the world, on decent behaviour, or on some particular virtue, and where the opposite of these qualities produces disorder and confusion . . . For all the scenes of human life, only the comic theatre can provide true models of good and evil, of a reasonable way of behaving and a foolish one.   (Diderot, in Dukore, 1974: 288)

Intermezzi and the *opera buffa*

Comic opera

The development of comic operatic forms is complex with two main roots, in the *intermezzo* and the *opera buffa*. Behind these lay the traditions of the *Intermedio* and *contrascene*, the growing use of comic characters and scenes within the mixed-genre opera.

Contrascene

From very early, opera had included humour, such as Landi's drunken Charon in *La morte d'Orfeo* and the misguided pages in *Sant Alessio*. Monteverdi's *L'incoronazione di Poppea* has a range of comedy, including the realistically weary guards and the ambiguous, self-seeking Arnalta. Dramaturgically these offer a contrast with, and often a deliberate counterpoint to, the dignity, high morality and seriousness of the rest of the action. Significantly all these characters are from the lower classes and converse about ordinary feelings and subjects. In the operas of Keiser and Cavalli specific sections of larger scenes were given over to comic characters, and an important feature was the use of melodic, often strophic, song derived from popular music. These episodes quickly became a feature in their own right called *contrascene* (counter-scenes). The next stage was to concentrate them in specific places: the ends of acts I and II and the middle of act III (rather than the end, which was reserved for the main plot resolution). Handel's semi-serious works such as *Serse* and *Semele* make a feature of them. Zeno and Metastasio's 'regularisation' ended this with the rigorous separation of the comic and tragic. However, while this banished such material from the *opera seria*, it did not diminish the public's desire for unpretentious opera that was melodious, undemanding and close to their own world. Nor did it please those singers – and composers – who specialised in the comic. Instead of disappearing, the *contrascene* took on a life of their own as the comic *intermezzo* (Table 5.2).

The comic *intermezzo*[3]

The comic *intermezzo* was essentially developed in Venice. The first known independent example is *Frappolone e Florinetta* of 1706, which set the agenda for the

Table 5.2 *Development of the* contrescene, *the* intermezzo *and* opera buffa

Opera		Intermedio
1609	Humorous scenes in Landi's *La morte d'Orfeo*	Tradition of separate entertainments between the acts of the drama and opera e.g. *La pellegrina*
1649	Humorous servants in Monteverdi's *Poppea* Satirical scenes in Cavalli's *Giasone*	
1670s →	Mixed serious and comic characters and scenes: Keiser, Handel	▼ Ongoing into nineteenth century

▼

Contrascene –

Servants/lower-class characters involving parody, humour – and sentiment → Eventually placed at end of acts I and II (where they lead into the *Intermezzi*) and middle of act III

c. 1700 The reforms of Zeno – and then Metastasio – enforce separation of the serious and comic

▼ ▼

Venice-centred Intermezzo 1700–50	Naples-centred *Opera buffa* 1707 →	*Opera seria*

c. 1709 Neapolitan dialect comedy   1736 Goldoni's reform of the spoken and lyric comedy

next fifty years. The *intermezzo* had to be economical: it was only an adjunct – however desirable – to the main *opera seria*. It used two singing characters, and sometimes a third who was generally silent. The characters are almost always the bourgeoisie and their servants with a plot that tends to revolve around the problems of love, frequently entrapment into marriage. This is the theme of two of the most famous: Telemann's *Pimpinone* and Pergolesi's *La serva padrona*. Each has a number of important features:

- the use of the *da capo* form which, in these miniature, middle-class pieces, has an ironic, comic effect;
- sprightly, often sprung melodic, lines with a strong popular appeal;
- incisive character writing, especially for the comic *basso* roles.

Telemann's *Pimpinone* was the fourteenth of his twenty-nine comic and serious operas. It was premiered in Hamburg in 1725, performed between the acts of

Handel's *Tamerlano*. The libretto is adapted from Albinoni's 1708 *Intermezzo* – in Germany called a *Zwischen-Spiele* – of the same name. The arias are in both Italian and German, as in Keiser's serious operas. Like an *opera seria* the score alternates recitatives with arias and – a major innovation – an increasing number of duets. All the arias are *da capo*, lighter and more overtly tuneful. For example, in Vespetta's opening 'Chi mi vuol, son cameriera' (Who wants me, I am a housemaid), the melody seems just right for a young girl offering her (domestic) services. But the full *da capo* treatment becomes tendentious and ironic, especially in the B section, where she tells us that she is 'bene . . . sincera, non ambisco/non pretendo' (decent . . . honest . . . I am not ambitious/I do not feign); the setting is weightier than either her status or honesty permit (Table 5.3).

Pimpinone's aria 'Ella mi vuol confondere' (She wants to confuse me) is again *da capo* with a greatly extended B section that runs to eleven libretto lines which Vespetta interrupts at one point. Again, a style that was appropriate for a Caesar is out of place here. Its pretension helps create Pimpinone's character and predicament: the old(er) man who should know better. It is the forerunner of the traditional comic *basso*: Rossini's Doctor Bartolo or Strauss' Baron Ochs. Perhaps the most overtly comic number is the penultimate duet in which the newly married couple face up to the horror of their situation. Pimpinone begins 'Wilde Hummel, böser Engel!' (Wild bee, savage angel), to which Vespetta responds 'Alter Hudler! Galgen-Schwengel!' (Ancient muddler! Dangling corpse!). The music is strongly rhythmic and animated, with the two voices singing against and over one another. The *intermezzo* ends as Vespetta affirms her ascendancy over her husband. Pimpinone's long bass notes form a miserable ground beneath Vespetta's sprightly, triumphant line.

The essence of the musical *comedy* here lies in the *opera seria*'s dominant form deployed in a trivial domestic situation. Its musical appeal lies in its lighter, more popular style of melody. In Pergolesi's 1733 *La serva padrona* the comic began to find a style of its own. Again there are two vocal characters and the narrative is essentially the same as *Pimpinone*, but the dramatic handling is more nuanced. There is genuine narrative development where *Pimpinone* is a straightforward contrast and conflict.

Most of the arias are again *da capo* but Pergolesi's musical characterisation is stronger than Telemann's. The humour lies less in the ironic use of the *da capo* aria than in the inherent musico-dramatic treatment. This is strongest in the writing for Uberto. His opening, 'Aspettare e non venire' (I wait and no one comes) has a structure whose sudden repetitions and emphasise reflect his bewilderment and

Table 5.3 La serva padrona: *'Chi mi vuol, son cameriera'*

| Ritornello | A | Ritornello | A with variants and ornament; | Lengthy B | Full A repeat |

frustration. The later ' Sempre in contrasti' (Always in contradictions) is *da capo*, but the constant repetitions of his short lines breaks the overall form down into a real character piece. His 'Sono imbrogliato' (I am trapped) similarly whirls him onwards in a spiral of muddle-headed confusion, a precise analogue for his predicament. Serpina's mock-sentimental 'A Serpina penserate' (You will think of Serpina) has a seductive melody that seduces both the audience and Uberto. However, it alternates between his pleading 4/4 *larghetto* and her 3/4 *allegro* asides, allowing her to use – and expose – a variety of moods as she wheedles her way around her victim.

In general, the comic opera offered a new kind of music: simpler, more obviously popular and tuneful. Crucially it was also written to ensure that the words were at all times clearly audible – otherwise the humour would have been lost. Perhaps even more significantly, it consistently drew characters together in genuine duets, where two characters, usually opposed in sentiment and desire, are either ironically given the same melodic material, or cut across one another with contrasted material. This was a new emphasis that would be enhanced by the greater dramatic potential of the full-scale *opera buffa*.

Naples and the *opera buffa*

From the sixteenth century Naples had been one of the major European musical centres. Its four conservatoires produced some of the greatest names in opera including Pergolesi, Jommelli, Traetta, Paisiello and Cimarosa, composers associated with both the serious and the comic opera. In 1701 the first known dialect play was performed in Naples, a comedy defined by its realistic language and lower-class characters. Six years later *La Cilla*, the first dialect opera, appeared. While this maintained the *intermezzo* style, it developed as a full-length comic opera. By 1718 Alessandro Scarlatti had written his comic masterpiece *Il trionfo dell'onore* and the *buffa* form had begun to spread throughout the peninsula and beyond.

However there was no real dramaturgical tradition for the new form to follow. One possibility was the *Commedia dell'arte*, which used music, song and dance.[4] The early comic opera combined its often extravagant, vulgar action with the farcical structure of the classical comedy (above all Plautus and Terence) from which the *Commedia* itself ultimately derived. Like the *intermezzi*, the characters and situations were from the middle and lower classes. Looking to the Neapolitan theatre, the libretti were written in dialect while, like the *intermezzi*, the music was more obviously popular and often with a local flavour. One result was to give the *opera buffa* a low reputation. By 1709 the critic Zambeccari was complaining that everyone in Naples was going to see a 'really disgusting piece' (Kimbell, 1991: 315) – a comic opera called *Patrò Calienno de la Costa*. Then, in the same way that the mixed serious opera had been reformed by Zeno and Metastasio, the *opera buffa* was charged with a new cultural force – and once again by a playwright.

The reform of Italian comedy

The development of the *opera buffa* coincided with the reform of the Italian theatre led by Goldoni. His aim was to change what he saw as the crude *Commedia dell'arte* and put in its place a refined comedy of manners that would reflect the finesse of Molière's language, characterisation and construction. The results, however, are closer to the sentimental comedies of Goldsmith and Sheridan. In 1736 Goldoni's theatrical producer asked him to write a comic libretto and he took the opportunity to refine the relatively crude *opera buffa* just as he had the comic drama. His influence was enormous. Altogether Goldoni wrote the libretti for eighteen *intermezzi*, eight *opere serie* (of which Vivaldi and Traetta each set one and Galuppi two) and fifty-two *opere buffe* (with thirteen set by Galuppi and others by Traetta, Scarlatti, Salieri, Piccini, Haydn and Paisiello).

Galuppi

Goldoni's impact can be judged by Galuppi's 1760 *L'amante di tutte* (The Lover of all Ladies). Although the libretto is by Galuppi's son Antonio, Goldoni's influence is evident in the way the narrative and characters are developed. Although the opera is a succession of recitatives and arias, this is lost in the lively complexity of the plot. Galuppi's score creates characters who are both comic and real, in their aspirations and emotions, which the score articulates using relatively complex structures. In Conte Eugenio's act II, scene vi 'Povero Conte Eugenio, adesso sì' (Now poor Count Eugenio, indeed), the philandering Count considers his strategic situation. He goes through a series of thoughts and emotions, which requires a shifting musical structure divided between five sections. The *recitativo accompagnato* itself is in four different moods followed by a pronouncedly sentimental arioso and a *recitativo secco* before the aria proper 'Se sapeste, o giovinottii' (If you knew, young fellows) (Table 5.4).

The cast contains several comedic types, each clearly defined by Galuppi:

- The pert servant girl, Dorina (in the tradition of Vespetta and Serpina). In act II, scene viii she ridicules the idea that she can be seduced by a handsome face (as her masters and mistresses have been). Her 'Quel bel soggetto/quel bel visetto' (This lovely person/this lovely face) is sprightly and attractive. Its pizzicato and flute accompaniment is engaging and, like her, sparkles and mocks.
- The pompous Marchese (derived from the tradition of the *miles gloriosus*). His act II, scene ii 'Figlio de Re Pepino' (The son of King Pepin) creates an overblown

Table 5.4 L'amante di tutte: *act ii, scene vi, 'Povero Conte Eugenio, adesso si'*

Orchestral introduction	Sprightly with pronounced melodic motif	
Recitativo accompagnato	Povero Conte Eugenio...	Punctuated by the orchestral motif
	Allor vedrei/Cadere a' piedi mie...	Andante
	Udrei mancar la delicata voce...	Allegro
	E dirmi sdegnosetta in tuon pietoso...	Andante
Arioso	Parmi d'udirla esangue...	Strong lyrical *arioso* writing
Recitativo secco	No no non voglio,...	
Aria	Se sapeste, o giovinotti,...	Moderato, jaunty. Sung through and repeated

figure as he recites his ridiculous lineage and turns himself into the type of the comic *basso*.

- The bored, unfaithful wife, Lucinda. In her act ii, scene iii 'Conoscerete un giorno' (One day you will know) she warns her husband that one day he will realise what he has lost by not trusting her. It is in three sections. First, two quatrains to a stately tempo and melody as she convinces Don Orazio of her sincerity; second, the tempo continues as, in an aside, she explains why she appears to be crying; and third, a change to a laughing *allegro* as she exclaims at her success.
- The Arlecchino-based trickster, Mingone. In act ii, scene i he begs for pardon in 'Perdonatemi, o signore' (Pardon me, signor). The aria is a stately *andante*, plain, open and evidently sincere, typical of this ambiguous type of the loveable rogue.

The *opera buffa*'s most significant formal innovation is the extended use of *ensemble*, ranging from extensive duets to the whole cast concerted finales that end each of the acts. The latter are not simply the equivalent of the choruses of rejoicing that end the *opera seria*. They are complex *actions* in which the characters are engaged, creating misunderstanding, confrontation and ultimate reconciliation, as well as comedy. This is done *through* the music, which plays its own part in the complication of the action. At this stage there is no over-arching musical development but, instead, a chain of sections building to the climax. But this still creates an explosive comedic energy that Rossini will later perfect. In the finale of act ii, scene x, the main characters assemble for a series of assignations, in the dark, with inevitable misunderstandings. They mis-match, talk and even kiss at cross-purposes. All five main characters take part in this continuous musical structure which consists of a series of *accompagnato*

Table 5.5 L'amante di tutte: *act ii, scene ix*

Aria	Conte Eugenio Conte/Mignone	Oh che tenebre
Aria	Conte Eugenio Conte/Mignone	Se mostrai d'amar
Duet	Conte/Mignone Lucinda/Don Orazio	Duet: Oh questa è bella
Aria	Lucinda	Dunque voi bel signorino

sections interspersed with brief, melodic arias and duets. The opening is set out in Table 5.5.

Unlike the two *intermezzi*, *L'amante di tutte* has no *da capo* arias. Instead there are melodious arias sung without repetition except as part of the character's thought or as a coda. The emphasis on popular melody will become one of the *opera buffa*'s most potent – and ambiguous – contributions to opera in general.

Piccini

In Piccini's *La buona figliuola* simple, sweet melody is a major feature. Goldoni's libretto is one of several pieces he drew from *Pamela*. Where the Galuppi is really an extended joke, *La buona figliuola* is more complicated and developed. Like all great comedy, it offers a vision of a world that can be healed. In *Pimpinone* and *La serva padrona*, foolish characters are simply mocked. In *La buona figliola* they struggle for the heroine's virtue and happiness. Ultimately, good and innocence triumph: as in Richardson's original, this is sentimental comedy. Its focal melodies are replete with feeling – sentiment – above all those for Cecchina herself, starting with the opening of act i as she welcomes the beauty of the morning ('Che piacer, che bel diletto' – How lovely, what delight). The high point is her *air de sommeil* in act ii, scene xii 'Vieni, il mio seno di duol ripieno' (Come to my breast, so full of sadness). This celebrated moment finds Cecchina alone and dejected. After a recitative in which she narrates her suffering, she sinks to the ground. Woodwind gently play over muted strings before her two opening lines, introducing a melody whose decorative extensions become the pleading and sighing of an exhausted heart. Although the text is only two lines, the aria is in three sections, as it slowly leads her into sleep. It is a moving moment of sentimental comedy: suffering that will be healed.

As in *L'amante di tutte*, each of the acts leads to a major ensemble of confusion – and resolution. The end of act ii (scene xiv) is especially complex and teeters on the brink of tragedy until the Marchese's 'Donne mie, non m'importa' (Ladies, I do not care). However the musical impetus is more deftly handled and sustained than in the Galuppi. Despite the succession of characters arguing in different combinations, there is an over-arching sense of direction that steadily builds until the Marchese dramatically intervenes and halts it; but at this stage of the opera it has to fall apart once more as the characters squabble with renewed vigour over his favours. The union of dramatic and musical structure makes this a real drama, informing its characters, from a range of classes, with genuine feeling. Piccinni's lightness of touch, combined with genuine sentiment, make the opera intensely human, allowing the *opera buffa* to rival the noble aspirations and classical subjects of the *opera seria*.

Mozart

These innovations changed the nature of opera itself, particularly affecting

- The emancipation from the courtly, class-bound restrictions of *opera seria* and moving towards a focus on the drama of recognisable people, comedic or otherwise. When Mozart agreed to set Metastasio's libretto for *La clemenza di Tito* he insisted that the libretto should be 'ridotta a vera opera' (reduced to a real opera) (Robbins Landon, 1988: 112).
- The potential for comedy as a profound form.
- The use of the ensemble. Mozart's two great *opere serie*, *Idomeneo* and *La clemenza di Tito*, make particular use of the ensemble to humanise what are otherwise typically hieratic, classical subjects.
- The increase in the range of music, from noble arias to popular melody.

The notion that Mozart is a 'classical' composer implies a sense of clarity and observation of form. But he is also close in spirit to the adventurous expressiveness of *Sturm und Drang*. In the operas in particular he breaks and remoulds form as required by the characters' emotions and their situation. The result is music that responds profoundly to both the structure and detail of his libretti. This is not surprising. Mozart was writing at the high point of opera reform. In 1778 he was in Mannheim where he heard the famous orchestra and mixed with singers and musicians who had performed the *opere serie* of Jommelli and Traetta as well as *opere buffe* by Galuppi and Piccinni. When he came to write *Idomeneo* in 1780–1 he would be working with many of the musicians he had met at the Mannheim court (Gutman, 2000: 383–406). Despite Leopold's later mistrust, Gluck, who admired *Die Entführung aus dem Serail* (The Abduction from the Seraglio) (Howard, 1995: 231) was a major influence: Mozart keenly attended the rehearsals for the German-language version of *Iphigenie auf Tauris* (Cairns, 2006: 83). Vital though the dramaturgy and poetry of the libretto were, it was the music that was the essential *language* of his operas. David Cairns believes that his experience of Gluck's operas underlay his belief that 'in an opera the poetry must be the handmaid of the music' (Cairns, 2006: 83). Mozart's description of Osmin's act I aria 'Solche hergelauf'ne Laffen' (Such a jumped-up puppy) in the *Entführung* shows how he understood the balance between text, character and music:

> Whether violent or not, the passions must never reach any degree of revulsion in their expression; music, even in the most ghastly situations, must never offend the ear, but, despite such circumstances, must give pleasure and thus remain music... as Osmin's rage gradually increases, there comes (just when the aria seems to be at an end) the allegro assai, which is in a totally different measure and in a different key; this is bound to be very effective. For just as a man in such a towering rage oversteps all the bounds of order, moderation and propriety, and completely forgets himself, so must the music too forget itself... I have gone from F (the key in which the aria is written), not into a remote key, but into a related one, not, however, into its nearest relative D minor, but into the more remote A minor.   (Anderson, 1990: 161–2)

Similarly, Mozart writes about Belmonte's act I aria 'O wie ängstlich, o wie feurig' with the same sense of priority:

> Let me now turn to Belmonte's aria in A major, 'O wie ängstlich, o wie feurig'. Would you like to know how I have expressed it – and even indicated his throbbing heart? By the two violins playing octaves. This is the favourite aria of all those who have heard it, and it is mine also. I wrote it expressly to suit Adamberger's voice. You feel the trembling – the faltering – you see how his throbbing breast begins to swell; this I have expressed by a crescendo. You hear the whispering and the sighing – which I have indicated by the first violins with mutes and a flute playing in unison.   (Anderson, 1990: 161–2)

The aria's form directly reflects the different stages of the text as Belmonte moves from emotional moment to moment. It falls into four sections: Belmonte's distress at seeing his beloved again, but at such a disadvantage; his physical pain; rapture as he recalls her voice; despair as he asks himself whether it was only a dream. But the aria is more fragmented than this would suggest. it is a series of acute moments (Table 5.6).

   As in Gluck, the musical structure is dictated by the dramatic development. But the requirement for 'the poetry [to] be the handmaid of the music' means that there is an emphasis on the music in its own right, and greater melodic content.

The balance of reason and feeling

It is precisely this melodic appeal which meant that until relatively recently Mozart was not taken seriously as a 'thinking' artist (Cairns, 2006: Prologue). He was considered to be essentially decorative and courtly:

Table 5.6 Die Entführung aus dem Serail: *act 1, no. 4*

4	Recitative ending .... Dich! (you!)	The *recitative* ends abruptly on the word 'Dich' which is left suspended between the end of the *recitative* and the start of the aria proper – which now starts just as abruptly.
5–8	O wie ängstlich, o wie feurig O how fearful, o how fiery	The aria begins with a strong rhythmic figure as Belmonte exclaims at his fear and ardour before
9–13	klopft mein ... Beats my ...	his heart pants with a pulsating figure echoed by the violins before going into
14–17	liebevolles hertz ... love-filled heart	the full (four-bar decoration) rapture of the word 'liebevolles'.
19–23	Und des Wiedersehens Zäh-re And the tears at seeing again lohnt der Trennung bangen ... Recompense for anxious parting	Belmonte's simple rising and falling figure suggests the tears he refers to in the sharp descending motif in the first violins before
24	Schmerz – Pain	his tone changes as the line ends in pain on the word 'Schmerz' with F in the cellos and violas, C in the violins.
25–27	Lines repeated	Belmonte's previous figure reappears, slowed down and stretched out as he reflects back on the original parting.
28–32	Schon zittr'ich und wanke I tremble, I falter schon zag ich und schwanke I hesitate, I shrink	A new figure, sharply rising and falling in the strings, suggests Belmonte's anxious breath. Then
33–39	es hebt sich die schwellende brust my heart beats and swells	over a strong rhythmic base (quavers in the violas and second violins, semiquavers in the cellos and rippling demi-semiquavers in the first violins) Belmonte sings a crescendo mirroring the emotional swelling of his breast.

> We know the Mozart of our fathers' time
> Was gay, rococo, sweet, but not sublime
> A Viennese Italian, that is changed
> Since music critics learned to feel 'estranged';
> Now it's the Germans he is classed amongst
> A Geist whose music was composed from angst.
>   (Auden, 1956)

The shift indicates a central feature of Mozart's achievement, above all in the operas with da Ponte: towards an essential ambiguity. These operas are the first in which the dramatic meaning has to be interpreted from the relationship between libretto and score. Whether *Don Giovanni* is actually an *opera buffa, Così fan tutte* a humane comedy or a mere if elaborate farce, are questions that are posed by the relationship between score and libretto. That ambiguity is typical of a world edging towards revolution and completely new realities.

The da Ponte operas (*Così fan tutte*)

Così is the most original of the operas Mozart wrote with da Ponte and, therefore, probably the most direct expression of their interests. Central to it is the eighteenth-century concern with the tension between reason and feeling. Using Love as its focus, it asks what reliance can be placed on either the feelings or pure reason, and ultimately how these can be brought into equilibrium. Despite this major theme, it has had an especially ambivalent reception history (Cairns, 2006: 181–3). Throughout the nineteenth and early twentieth centuries it was either ignored or rejected because of its so-called cynicism, although the sheer beauty and refinement of its music was always acknowledged. In 1952 the critic Gerhart von Westerman was still writing that 'However superficial the text and unreal the action, one must not forget that this is a farce in which everything is fun and laughter, without any deeper significance, though perhaps with a slight tinge of irony. Musically *Così fan tutte* is a masterly *opera buffa*. Thanks to Mozart's genius all the characteristics of the form of opera here achieve their final and most perfect fulfilment' (Westerman, 1973: 98).

As a comedy, the libretto provides an excellent narrative framework, filled with incidents (the march to war, the entry of the 'Albanians', the fake suicides, the magnetic treatment, the marriage and, of course, the dénouement). It also includes a variety of forms, especially ensembles ranging from duets to full chorus. An analysis of act 1 shows how different it is from the *opera seria*'s rigid alternation of recitative and (*da capo*) aria, while in act II only four of the thirteen numbers are arias (Table 5.7).

Table 5.7 *Così fan tutte: Act 1, sequence of numbers*

Scene	Number	Character
Scene i	No. 1 Terzetto	
	Recitativo	
	No. 2 Terzetto	
	Recitativo	
	No. 3 Terzetto	
Scene ii/iii	No. 4 Duetto	
	Recitativo	
	No. 5 Aria	Don Alfonso: 'Vorrei dir'
	Recitative	
Scene iv	No. 6 Quintetto	
	Recitativo	
	No. 7 Duettino	
	Recitativo	
Scene v	No. 8 Coro	
	Recitativo	
	Recitativo / No. 8a Quintetto	
	No. 9 Coro	
	Recitativo	
Scene vi	No. 10 Terzettino	
Scene vii	Recitativo	
Scene viii–ix	Recitativo	
	Recitativo	
	No. 11 Aria	Dorabella: 'Smanie implacabili'
	Recitativo	
Scene x	No. 12 Aria	Despina: 'In uomini!'
	Recitativo	
Scena xi	No. 13 Sestetto	
	Recitativo	
Scene xii	No. 14 Aria	Fiordiligi: 'Come scoglio'
	Recitativo	
	No. 15 Aria	Guglielmo: 'Non siate ritrosi'
	No. 16 Terzetto	
Scene xiii	Recitativo	
	No. 17 Aria	Ferrando: 'Un'aura amorosa'
	Recitativo	
Scene xiv–xvi	No. 18 Finale: Sestetto	

In fact, the essence of the opera lies in the tension between its solo arias and the ensembles as the individuals struggle to find their own truth. These ensembles are far more complex than Galuppi's or Piccinni's simple chains of numbers. They develop organically, as the music reflects the shifts and changes in each character as the drama develops. In act I, scene ii/iv the five main characters meet for the pretended departure. The libretto dramatises this with a straightforward contrast between the men's comic hesitation and bravado, the women's histrionics and Don Alfonso's ironic support. Mozart's score, however, makes the scene far more ambiguous and revealing:

- It lends genuine passion to the women's despair, while still suggesting that their overstatement implies a weakness that will later be exploited.
- The men are genuinely nervous as well as deliberately appearing to be tentative.
- Don Alfonso is ironic but less ironic than knowing.
- All five must be real enough in their overt statements to be able to enter the final quintet.

Overall, the passage falls into eight sections that increasingly expose their real feeling (Table 5.8).

Fiordiligi is the most conflicted character in the opera. More than her companion she genuinely falls in love with her Albanian suitor and then despairs as she realises how she has betrayed both herself and her original love. The *scena* is more complex – as she is herself. It begins with her *recitativo accompagnato* which is actually the climax of a long recitative passage for all six characters. This in itself is typical of Mozart's flexible approach to form, allowing musical shapes to emerge as the dramatic moment and characterisation require. One of the features of Mozart's writing is the extent to which these arias seem to have a central or over-riding melody which in fact consists of a series of short melodic fragments (Table 5.9).

The major, dramatic contrast with this masterpiece of self-deception is Fiordiligi's act II, scene vii aria 'Per pietà, ben mio, perdona' (For pity, my love, forgive), which alternates between her opening plea for forgiveness and her avowals of a renewed strength that will overcome weakness and temptation.

Like those of Rameau and Gluck, Mozart's operas span the full range of available types. At the end of his life, his last works included three radically different forms: *opera seria, opera buffa* and the *Singspiel*. But none of these conforms to the usual expectations; and within them musical forms, too, have been redefined, largely through their dramatic needs:

- The strophic, popular, melodic aria: Cherubino's 'Voi, che sapete', Don Giovanni's 'Deh, vieni alla finestra', Papageno's 'Ein Mädchen oder Weibchen' and Sarastro's 'O Isis und Osiris'.

Table 5.8 Così fan tutte: *act 1, scene ii/iv*, 'Sento oddio'

1–14	*Guglielmo* Sento, oddio, che questo piede è restio nel girle avante *Ferrando* Il mio labbro palpitante non può dette pronunziar	I feel, O God, that this foot Is unwilling to step before her My trembling lip Is unable to speak at all.	Ferrando and Guglielmo make a timid entrance. The music has the men on tiptoe, as each sings in brief, tentative fragments separated by alternate quavers in the strings and quaver rests. They are either ashamed, nervous of what will ensue, afraid of the damage they may do – or all three.
15–18	*Don Alfonso* Nei momenti più terribili sua virtù l'eroe palesa	In the most dreadful moments The hero displays his virtue	Don Alfonso mocks them – why? Does he think they are afraid to test their partners' virtue? Is he, as so many critics state, merely a mocking cynic? His music can be played in a number of ways. But there is nothing in it that suggests more wry reflection – rather than knowing irony or sarcasm.
18–30	*Fiordiligi, Dorabella* Or che abbiam la nuova intesa a voi resta a fare il meno; fate core, e entrambe in seno immergeteci l'acciar.	Now we have received the news there only remains a lesser deed; take heart, and in our breasts Plunge the steel.	The women, in harmony, demand that the men slay them. There is a serenity about the opening that is more beautiful than this demand might seem to require. We also note the little figure in the clarinets and oboes that sounds rather like gentle laughter.
30–35	*Ferrando, Guglielmo* Idol mio, la sorte incolpa se ti deggio abbandonar,	My idol, blame fate that I must abandon you.	Ferrando and Guglielmo now also sing in harmony, repeating the music of their opening section but set to different words. Heartened at the women's despair the men are emboldened and proceed by blaming fate: which is a lie.
36–39	*Dorabella* Ah no, no, non partirai *Fiordiligi* No, crudel, non te andrai *Dorabella* Voglio pria cavarmi il core *Fiordiligi* Pria ti vo' morire a piedi.	Ah no, no, you shall not part No, cruel one, you shall not go I want first to tear out my heart First I want to die at your feet.	Now the women seem to lose control in alternating outbursts, quite different from their previous, controlled passage. They abandon their neat harmony and ask, not for death, but for their lovers not to abandon them. The music is nobly tragic but obviously deeply felt.

(cont.)

Table 5.8 (*cont.*)

39	*Ferrando:* Cosa dici? *Guglielmo:* Te n'avvedi?	What do you say? Can't you see?	Ferrando and Guglielmo are impressed and ask Don Alfonso what he thinks. Their phrases, sung aside and *piano*, are a challenge to Don Alfonso. The men are satisfied.
39–46	*Don Alfonso* Salvo amico 'finem lauda'.	Steady, friend. 'Praise the end.'	Don Alfonso tells them to wait and see. There is no irony or humour in his phrase. Rather there is a clarity of purpose in the strings' figure between his phrases, the simple, repeated dotted semiquaver–quaver–crotchet on the same note, suggesting the realistic sobriety of his position.
47–64	*Tutti* Il destin così defrauda le speranze de' mortali. Ah, chi mai fra tanti mali chi mai può la vita amar?	This destiny defrauds The hopes of mortals. Ah, who ever among so many ills Who ever could love life?	All five now sing together, accusing fate for dashing mortal hope, ending with the text asking 'Chi mai può la vita amar?' (Who ever could love life?) The five take on a commentative, choric function. Their ensemble singing halts what has been a series of separate elements whose naivety, sincerity and posturing are all open to question. The passage ends with an absolute unity on the insistent repetition if the word 'Chi?' (Who?) Who is free from what life *is*? We note the sheer beauty of this passage. At the same time the music and words apply to each of them in their own way, but if Don Alfonso is truly a cynic it seems strange to find him allowed to participate in such 'sincere' music.
65–92	Repetition of bars 36–64		The pessimism or seriousness of the ensemble casts a shadow over the women's passionate outburst (repeated from bar 36.) It gives it a truth that we doubted earlier. The same is true of the exchange between the men: this is not gloating but Ferrando and Guglielmo's real delight – and Don Alfonso's realism.
92–108	Extension creating a coda to the repetition of bars 47–64 and ending *piano* with four-and-half bars in the orchestra		The passage almost fades away: there is a sadness at what has to be gone through to come to terms with the nature of the world. Here is the central text of the 'School for lovers.' The complexity of *Così fan tutte* is that the lovers have unquestioningly believed in the reliability of emotion; the men have been seduced because of this unthinking naivety into an artificial test – and Don Alfonso wants them not to learn that women are fickle, but that life demands something more than feeling – reason, too.

Table 5.9 Così fan tutte: act 1, scene iii/xi, 'Temerai! Sortite fuori... Come scoglio'

Recitativo: Fiordiligi wavers between the strident, tragic tones used earlier by Dorabella, and a more personal, genuine, emotion		
44–50	Temerai! Sortite fuori di questo loco e non profani l'alito infausto degl'infami detti nostro cor, nostro orecchio e nostri affetti!	Rash men, leave this place and let not the foul breath of your infamies profane our heart, our ears and affections!	In strident tone Fiordiligi dispatches the men. Her phrases are interspersed with forceful figures: a rising sequence of semiquavers and dotted quavers.
51–53	In van per voi, per gli altri invan si cerca le nostre alme sedur.	In vain for you, in vain for others, to try to seduce our souls.	This is accompanied by a held chord as she asserts the natural steadfastness to which she aspires.
54–59	L'intatta fede che per noi già si diede ai cari amanti	The intact faith that we have already spoken to our beloveds	A series of rising chords introduces a personal avowal of her pledged faith. The first violins repeat the previous semiquaver and dotted quaver but this time *legato* and *piano*, as if gently murmuring their sympathy/approval of her sentiment.
60	saprem loro serbar infino a morte, a dispetto del mondo e della sorte.	we know will be kept unto death, despite the world and Fate.	The rising chords of bar 54 are repeated as she turns from faith in her pledge to her beloved to the more dramatic claim that it will be kept in the face of death, the world and fate.
Aria: Andante maestoso		
1–2			The first two bars announce the ambivalence within Fiordiligi: a chord *forte* and then a portentous rising sequence of semiquaver and dotted quavers. But this is followed by a *piano* trill and an echoing rising sequence of much more straightforward quavers. It is as though the second figure deflates the rhetoric of the first.
3–10	Come scoglio immoto resta contro i venti e la tempesta,	As a rock remains unmoved Against the winds and the storm,	High drama as Fiordiligi's line reaches from B down to D, from lower C up to E and then down an octave and then from F down to B below the stave. Her effort to be the steadfast rock is clear – but the *piano* trill and a rising sequence of straightforward quavers seems to undercut it; not perhaps doubting her sincerity, but
11–14	la tempesta	the storm	as she reaches a high B above the stave, the sense of histrionics is made clear.

(cont.)

Table 5.9 (*cont.*)

	Allegro: The tempo now changes to a much brighter *Allegro* as Fiordiligi becomes more human, personal and realistic – but without ever abandoning her fidelity		
15–23	così ognor quest'alma è forte nella fede e nell'amor.	thus this soul remains strong in its faith and love.	The clarinet and bassoon lend warmth to this passage; the voice trips sympathetically in figures of tied quavers and semiquavers.
24–31	Con noi nacque quella face che ci piace e ci consola.	This torch was born in us Which both consoles and pleases.	Now the oboe and bassoon start an accompaniment in *legato* rising and falling quavers as Fiordiligi's line runs along in the delight of her love.
32–44	E potrà la morte sola far che cangi affetto il cor.	And death alone can Effect change within our heart.	As she reverts to self-dramatisation so the music returns to a portentous *seria* style. But at
45–53	far che cangi affetto il cor	Effect change within our heart	the emphasis on 'il cor' (the heart) the music softens, with a gently laughing figure in the oboes at bar 49.
54–58	The orchestra leads back to a variant of the opening with in a series of agitated semiquavers		
55–67	Come scoglio immoto resta contro i venti e la tempesta,	As a rock remains unmoved Against the winds and the storm,	This variant of the opening is equally forceful, but without the same strident leaps in the vocal line; instead, there is a new clarity that can bear decoration
68–78	così ognor quest'alma è forte nella fede e nell'amor.	thus this soul remains strong in its faith and love.	but, as the first time (bar 15) it once again softens into the music that accompanies the more personal third and fourth lines, then calms through 'nell'amor' (in love) marked *sfp* and coming to rest on the *piano*.

Più allegro: **The tempo changes again, although significantly this (varied) repetition of the first four lines does not revert from its *Allegro* to the *Andante maestoso* of the opening. Instead it continues, far more easily into *a Più allegro***

79–86	Rispettate, anime ingrate, questo esempio di costanza	The music climbs in a series of chords to create a triumphant assertion of constancy, repeated after the first line.
87–101	e una barbara speranza	The vocal line flows and, sure of herself, Fiordiligi dwells for seven bars (95–101) on the word 'speranza' (hope), laughing at the mere idea of some wretch even hoping to seduce her!
102–108	non vi renda audaci ancor!	In a new legato figure she sings assuredly, if darkly, of her position and
109–128		this is confirmed by a bar of rising triplets, again on clear chords which punctuate each repetition of the words of the last line. As she comes to the end of the aria Fiordiligi's vocal line lightens before (115), when she rises to a high B in a triumph of virtue.

- The virtuoso '*seria*' aria: including Fiordiligi's 'Come scoglio' and the Queen of the Night's arias.
- The choruses: these range from the (ironic) formality of the villagers in *Le nozze*'s 'Giovani liete' to the Enlightenment celebration of *Die Zauberflöte*'s 'Die Strahlen der Sonne'.
- The ensembles: these include the fragmented complexity of *Così*'s 'Sento, oddio' to the integration of 'Fortunato l'uom che prende'.
- The aria: this has been broken down into a sequence of dramatic units, as in 'Come scoglio'.

In each case, Mozart reworked, even redefined, standard forms – and, more important, standard expectations. In Monteverdi, Handel and Gluck the music mirrors the dramatic situation and its characters. In Mozart, this becomes far more complex – ambiguous and fragmentary. From now onwards it is not possible to understand any aspect of the opera – music, libretto, dramatic structure – separately. Mozart's age of growing social and political conflict is reflected in a completely new challenge to the opera and its creators.

Chapter 6

Authentic performance

> These days, period performance does not claim to be 'authentic' – if we play a Vivaldi opera, we do not reproduce the social situation of an 18th-century Venetian theatre. Our music is no more 'authentic' than that of modern-instrument performers, but we do know more about the music we play. I'm proud that modern performers now know that they can't play Vivaldi like Brahms.
>
> (Biondi, 2009: 16)

The idea of authentic performance has become a major concern in music, affecting an increasingly broad repertoire. But beyond the apparently simple notion of playing something as the composer wanted there are two quite different enterprises:

- The discovery, preparation and performance of older music that has not been part of the traditional repertoire.
- The creation of authoritative texts/scores as a basis for performance of these works, as well as many that have long been considered standard repertoire.

Underlying this are two ideas:

- That there is such a thing as an 'original' score or performance;
- That a single authoritative score/text and style can be ascertained as a basis for 'authentic' performance.

The idea of the 'original' is an area of debate in the study of all the arts. Beyond the philosophical implication, there is the recognition that each of them involves a confrontation between a work and an audience who come from different worlds. Even if the 'original' could be recreated – or one could return to it in time – it would still not be possible to receive it as its contemporaries had. The work, the 'original', would have become different (Table 6.1).

These concerns begin with the actual score. There may be a composer's autograph, but even this will not necessarily be the composer's definitive thoughts. Beyond this, the translation from score into print and then performance has always involved change. With something as complex as opera this is rarely

Table 6.1 *Transmission of text: tradition and authenticity*

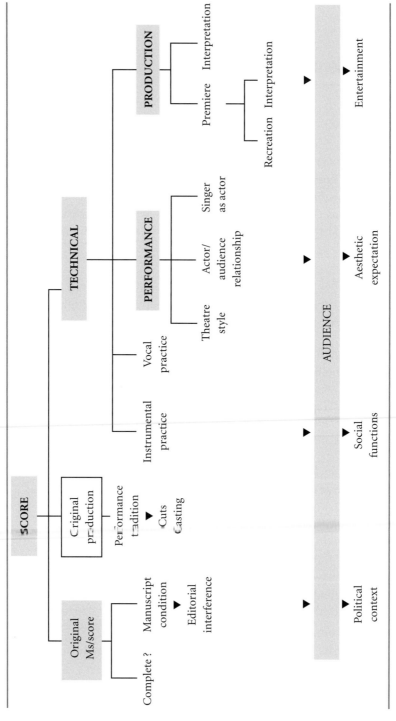

straightforward, even if the composer himself (or herself) is involved: so many elements may interpose, including the availability of singers and instruments, financial constraints and the social function. There is then likely to be a long process between the initial performance and modern times, involving alterations – some of which may be improvements – that constitute a 'tradition'. These will be the result of changes in performance practice, technical developments in production, changes in the layout and size of the theatre and shifts in audience expectation. Finally, any of these may be affected by social and political changes. It then becomes increasingly difficult to revert to the original score or way of performing, as musicians, especially singers, will have been trained in and learned the 'traditional' version. So, for example, it was never possible to get Boris Christoff, the greatest Boris Godunov of the post-war years, to learn the original Musorgsky score.

The early music revival

The growing concern with authentic performance started in the early years of the twentieth century with a new interest in 'early music'. This paralleled work in the theatre, where directors such as William Poel and Granville Barker realised that Shakespeare's plays needed to be understood as texts for the exposed Elizabethan stage and that modern production values undermined their essential dynamic. As composers of the Elizabethan and Restoration periods were investigated, it became obvious that this 'older' music required different techniques and instruments that were no longer available. Musicians such as the Dolmetsch family revived the viol consort, Wanda Landowska championed the harpsichord. Wind instruments followed. In the 1960s the world of mediaeval music was popularly opened out by musicians such as David Munrow who introduced a whole range of old instruments including shawms and gitterns. In the 1950s the world of the singer was changed with the rediscovery of the counter-tenor voice by Alfred Deller. In a very different area, the world of operatic *bel canto* roles was revived in the 1950s by singers such as Maria Callas and Joan Sutherland.

What was considered older music had been played in the past, but always arranged to suit contemporary taste. The argument was that modern audiences would not tolerate the old sounds and that had Bach or Monteverdi been alive today they would have taken advantage of the larger orchestras, technically improved instruments and so forth. Handel – above all *Messiah* – had long been performed by 'monster' choirs; in 1789 Mozart was commissioned to make his own reorchestration, and Thomas Beecham's version, complete with extended percussion and originally recorded in 1947, has been reissued on CD. There are still those who prefer a bigger – essentially nineteenth-century – orchestral/choral sound. It is fascinating to listen to other, previously obscure music, in versions such as Respighi's *Ancient airs and dances* or Tibor Serly's orchestrations of Gesualdo madrigals

Just as it is important to approach a production with the appropriate historical awareness, so an audience should be enabled to understand how that production has been derived. Monteverdi's *Orfeo* or *Poppea* at Drottningholm, Glyndbourne or the English National Opera have all been intended as quite different kinds of experience, ranging from 'authentic/period' performance, through social realism to modern symbolism or orientalisation. This chapter is concerned with the choices that lie behind any performance and which are integral to the audiences' experience. The concern with 'authenticity' in the literal sense is a major aspect of this, but it actually affects each performance.

The score

Almost all performances start with a score/text. Establishing reliable, critical editions is a vital scholarly activity no matter what the period:

- *Inaccuracies in the original (printing).* These are often due to the composer's hand-writing, compounded by the fact that whoever was responsible for the initial printing may have tried to 'improve' what he thought were mistakes or unaccept-able elements in the manuscript (harmonies, instrumentation). Janáček is a major example of this.
- *Initial staging.* In some cases cuts have been made before, during and after the first performance that the composer did not live to resolve: *Carmen* is a prime example. In addition, with *Carmen* this went as far as the later substitution of recitatives for the original spoken dialogue to make it suitable for performance at the Opéra rather than the less prestigious Opéra-Comique. That Bizet wanted spoken dialogue was ignored – and there are (star) singers who continue to insist on the 'grander', quite erroneous, version. In other cases a composer submitted to radical cuts, changes in dramaturgical shape and vocal casting in order to get the work into the repertoire, as with Gounod's *Mireille*. More complex are the composer's own revisions. Both the 1847 and 1863 versions of Musorgsky's *Boris Godunov* are masterpieces. Doing either means leaving out wonderful material. A version that includes everything was never sanctioned by the composer.
- *Later performing tradition.* This may involve traditional cuts, such as the last scene of *Lucia di Lammermoor*, so that the opera could end more 'dramatically' with Lucia's death. Similarly, Lucia's extended cadenza in the mad scene was written more than half a century later for Melba. On the other hand the use of the (very effective) glass harmonica in the same scene was written by Donizetti but may never have been used by him. What to do?

It is essential to know which of the several versions prepared by Rameau of his *Hippolyte et Aricie* has been chosen, and why. Or which version of Verdi's *Don Carlo/Carlos*. Should Wagner's *Der fliegende Holländer* be performed in its one- or three-act version? How should a performance of Puccini's *Turandot* end? The composer left it incomplete – which is how Toscanini performed it at the premiere. Puccini wanted Zandonai to complete it, but Alfano was commissioned although his ending has never been used as he wrote it (the so-called 'Alfano ending' is actually Toscanini's revision of it); there is now a new ending by Luciano Berio and the Chinese composer Hao Weiya has been asked to compose another. None of these responses has been considered satisfactory. Which is to be used and, as in all of these cases, why?

Technical elements

These include a number of issues that depend on knowledge – or lack of it – of the original performance conditions of the piece and how this relates to modern practicalities. Many involve the singer, some of which are explored more fully in Chapter 12. Some are very specific, and research has been able to clarify them – although decisions and choices still remain. Others are far more nebulous, although unavoidable.

Instruments and instrumentation

The *Avvertimento* to Emilio de' Cavalieri's *Rappresentatione di Anima et di Corpo* begins: 'In order to perform on the stage the present work, or other similar ones, and follow the instructions of Signor Emilio del Cavaliere [*sic*] ... it seems necessary that ...' (Cavalieri, 1970). Detailed instructions follow for singers, the instruments and how they were to be used. However, with many early operas, knowledge is far sketchier. In *Orfeo*, the instruments are listed – but with several omitted that are then needed; but in *Poppea* there are no indications of the orchestration at all. In these cases, whoever is responsible has to make informed guesses, however well researched. Consider the contrast between two recordings of the very earliest operas. Roberto De Caro's recording of Peri's *Euridice* uses a mixture of keyboard, wind and plucked instruments. He writes: 'In his Preface, Peri named only those few of his aristocratic or wellborn friends who took part in the first performance ... There must, however, have been other instruments in the small ensemble' (Caro, 1992). His sound is functional and rarely rises above the level of restrained accompaniment. By contrast, Nicolas Achten's recording of Caccini's *L'Euridice* uses keyboards and a range of plucked instruments, as he explains: 'we brought together the most important continuo instruments that were extant in Florence around 1600 – Caccini himself was able to play all of them' (Achten, 2008). The sound is dramatic and sonorous. The danger is to think that either is 'right' or sounds like the original performances. As always, what is needed is to know what choices have been made, and why.

The early music or original instrument 'movement' has changed thinking about older instruments as well as the way in which modern instruments were previously played: the kind of bow and bowing techniques used; brass instruments became valved over a period and some composers preferred the old sound; timpani were struck differently and different fabrics produced a different sound. This has resulted in a variety of approaches: orchestras made up of instruments built and played as they may originally have been; modern instruments played with an 'historically informed' approach; and resolutely modern sounds. In addition, there is the question of how instruments sound together – and, vitally, are balanced against singers. The challenge is, as always, to create an acceptable sound, albeit one that is imaginatively associated with another period:

> When Raymond Leppard brought *L'incoronazione* to modern light in his ground-breaking production at Glyndebourne in 1962, he argues that the score needed fleshing out with additional orchestral accompaniments and vocal embellishments. The result was to make it sound more like 'Real' opera. Nowadays, the tendency is to adopt a more restrained approach according to the conventional canons of early-music performance practice. But as a result *L'incoronazione* sounds less and less like an opera in the normal sense.   (Carter, 2008: 61)

Pitch and range

The entry on pitch in *Grove* baldly states that 'the oldest extant harpsichord tuning instructions (Aaron, 1523) suggests that the initial note, *C*, be placed at any pitch one might wish' (*Grove*, 1980, xiv: 779). Concert pitch has varied over the centuries and between countries. It is important not only because it affects the tone colour of a piece, but also the practicality of performance, especially for singers. While a stringed instrument can easily be tuned up or down, a voice cannot. While singers' parts can be written down to make them practicable, this affects their musical and dramatic impact. The most obviously problematic area is that of the *castrato* (see p. 389), but for all voices the choice of pitch does not simply affect particular notes, but the performance of florid passages in the Baroque, *coloratura* in the *bel canto* and the high *tessitura* demanded by a number of modern roles, such as Ariel in Thomas Adès' *The Tempest*.

This problem is, in a way, a peculiarly modern one. Earlier periods had no difficulty in making radical alterations when a role, originally conceived for one singer, was revived for another who had different qualities. Handel or Mozart thought nothing of either writing a new aria entirely, or making substantial changes to the original. The concern with 'authenticity' makes this impossible. Audiences want to hear what the composer 'intended'. The problem with this becomes clear when faced with a tantalising choice between two equally fine versions of an aria.

This is primarily an editorial matter, but one that every conductor faces, caught between scholarly rectitude and a more flexible aesthetic response, as Arthur Hutchings puts it in his notes to the 1964 Solti recording of *Orfeo ed Euridice*:

> Purists who say 'Stick to the original Vienna version and the Italian words' are now rarely heard, but at one time they sometimes had their way, knowing that they deprived audiences of some lovely items – the Dance of the Furies, the piece with the solo flute, just mentioned [in the Elysian Fields, act II], additional music at the entrance to Hades ... and the song for Euridice, *Cet asile aimable*, with choral refrains. It must be admitted that the pro-Vienna critics had one strong reason for their opinions – that, in arranging the part of Orpheus to suit a tenor, Gluck lost the more satisfactory sequence of keys, and controversy is never likely to end concerning the casting of the main character as a tenor or an alto.
>
> (Hutchings, 1964)

This is a sophisticated piece of writing at whose centre is the simple desire not to lose some of Gluck's loveliest music. The pursuit of 'authenticity' will always bring with it choices that are at the heart of opera – or any other art form – as a living experience.

The singer[1]

Singing manuals exist from the early sixteenth century, but whether these represent real practice, an ideal or a teacher's personal view – which may be conservative or 'advanced' – is often hard to tell. Certainly what they chart is how crucial aspects of singing have changed, including:

- Notions of what constitutes vocal beauty.
- How to use specific elements such as ornaments and *portamento*.
- Training for virtuosic display in cadenzas and other extemporised passages, involving both technique and taste.
- The relationship between the articulation of words and the physical demands of the music and voice production.
- The dramatic implication of the singer's role.

Much of this involves the changing balance between the technical and the expressive. Recordings going back to the 1880s show how very differently vocal sound was produced and enjoyed. In opera, this is complicated by questions of the relationship between beautiful sound, verbal clarity and drama. Maria Callas' fame rests less on the beauty of sound than her dramatic intensity. This goes beyond matters of technique, but technique is essential if the singer is to achieve what he or she intends or what is expected of them. It is also a major concern for those whose priority is vocal beauty – which in some periods has been the composers' as well as the audiences' main interest. How singers are taught – which can be conservative or advanced according to the teacher's attitude and their understanding of the differences between the styles of different periods – is vital. But this in itself generates a number of challenges:

- In an age that is historically aware and can therefore require singers and musicians to encompass a wider repertoire than ever before, can the same person fully engage with Monteverdi, Rameau, Handel, Rossini, Verdi, Wagner, Berg and Adams? How much attention should be paid to historical style, or should this be subordinated to personal taste and priorities?
- This especially affects ornamentation, particularly in the *da capo* aria where improvisation was expected.
- The range of voices has changed with time, but crucially the *castrato* has been lost. How to cope with these roles remains a serious problem. Even where countertenors can attain the pitch, they seem to lack the necessary power. The female voice can encompass the notes, but rarely sounds like a (castrated) man; so, too, with the boy alto. A modern high male role such as Oberon in *A Midsummer Night's Dream* treats the voice differently to Vivaldi or Scarlatti. Britten writes for a modern voice with particular qualities rather than a *castrato manqué*. Especially with the older opera, what choice of singer has been made, why – and how – should it be 'listened to'? The audience needs to know why a woman has been chosen to sing *travesta* rather than a man with the part written down. Has the priority been the music or the drama?

Performance conditions

This includes several areas, all of which directly affect the presentation and experience of operas from different periods:

- The size of theatre crucially affects acoustics, audibility and visibility. No opera before the second quarter of the nineteenth century was written for a house the size of Covent Garden or the Met. Orchestras and the sound they produced were smaller and better attuned to the audibility of the solo voice. Singer and audience were also far closer so that the effect was more intimate and immediate. Part of the problem with hearing the words (and the debate over surtitles) is that singers now have to project more, in larger houses, and over larger orchestras, which makes articulation more difficult.

- This is made worse by the fact that until the mid nineteenth century lighting and sets meant that singers would have performed near or at the front of the stage so that again they would have been closer and more easily heard.

Each of these factors once again means that any opera in a modern production will be changed from what it 'originally' was.

Production[2]

Production processes and values directly affect the problems of 'authentic' performance. The basic question is what a modern production/performance is meant to be. This entails fundamentally different approaches:

- Recreation of the original. This may be authenticated through written records, illustrations, performers' recollections and designs. The results will always be of great historical interest, such as the productions at Drottningholm. They will make all kinds of discoveries about how an opera 'works' that can inform other styles of production. But there will always be the problem of their being something between a real event and an elaborate artifice, however fascinating.
- Modern equivalent of an original. This involves acknowledging modern taste and style but using these to the advantage of an older work. The realistic Met 1989 production of the *Ring* was intended to be what Wagner 'would have done if only he had had modern production methods available'. It was, in a sense, truer to the original than the original itself.
- Interpretations. These can vary widely, from setting the opera in a different place or time, to productions that are treated abstractly, focused on the symbolic elements or interactions that are (thought to be) at the heart of what the opera is about. Others may be realistic, but with the narrative moulded to reflect contemporary issues. In the English National Opera 1986 production of Rossini's *Mosè*, the Crossing of the Red Sea was staged with the Egyptians smashing through a giant newspaper covered with reports about the Israel–Palestinian confrontation.

Each of these categories is in part defined by contemporary taste. If operas from the whole history of the art form are to be performed, should everything be translated into contemporary terms, or should there be an attempt at least to find analogues for the original? What is the opera and for whom is the production?

The audience

The audience (as Fabio Biondi says on p. 91) plays a major part; but audience behaviour is culturally and historically determined. The decorum expected in Britain is quite different to Italy or other countries where it is assumed that the audience will express their feelings strongly and immediately. The darkness of the auditoriums has only been a regular feature since Wagner started to dim (but not extinguish) the house lights in the 1870s. Sitting in a large, lit space surrounded by clearly visible people on all sides must have made it difficult to exclude them from one's field of attention. When the Emperor accused Mozart of having written 'too many notes' in *Le nozze di Figaro*, what he probably meant was that the opera demanded too much attention: it was supposed to be an entertainment not something as obviously serious as a string quartet or church oratorio. Handel's operas are long, but it is unlikely that he would have expected – or perhaps even hoped – that his audience would attend to every note in the way a modern audience virtually has to, isolated in the dark. Does this mean that his operas should be cut? Or that they can now be enjoyed as Handel wanted but never expected? This applies to several other areas:

- It is a commonplace to divide opera-goers between 'canary fanciers' and 'serious lovers of opera as drama'. But some operas were written as vocal showcases, to allow a soloist to display his or her talents – sometimes to set two against one another in a theatrical rivalry that on occasion even reflected rivalries in real life. But with the modern shift towards dramatic truth can, or should, all *bel canto* operas be treated as drama? Does this risk jettisoning those that cannot be, and undermining the ones that can by denying their *raison d'être*. Does this risk pretending that they are, or ought to be, something that was never intended and judging them by proportionately wrong criteria?
- Beyond that, there is the social function of opera. *Opera seria* was an integral part of a very particular kind of world. Wearing casual clothing and general modern attendance habits shifts one of the conditions of the original work. The New York ground-breaking 1966 City Opera recording of Rameau's *Hippolyte et Aricie* casually adds at the end of the introduction in the accompanying booklet, that 'Following the precedent set by the composer in the 1757 revival . . . the prologue has been omitted in this recording' (Trowell, 1966). William Christie's recording of 1997 includes it, and it makes a huge difference: it embeds the opera – and the listener – in a very particular context, preparing the listener to engage with the aesthetic structures and demands of a very different time and place.

Many operas were not intended to entertain or interest in the way an audience now expects. Unless this is recognised – and made clear – however 'authentic' a performance may be, there will be a major discrepancy between the way in which the opera was written and how it works for a modern audience.

Opera and its performance is, of course, a creative process. All the above criteria, questions and problems can be faced, used and resolved provided that those involved in its creation are conscious of the decisions, shifts, changes and choices they have made, and why. Only this can result in a responsible realignment of the work and the audience's experience. At the same time this has to be made accessible to the audience, otherwise the result is mystification and indulgence. To ensure this, the objectives for which the choices have been made need to be clear in the production. Provided these conditions are met, opera, however old the repertoire, will remain a living artistic force, and the experience will be both 'authentic' and a reflection of an 'original', however complex the implication of both words may be.

Part II

The nineteenth century

Chapter 7

Romanticism and Romantic opera in Germany

The Romantic age grew out of the upheavals of the Industrial Revolution, the French Revolution and the subsequent Napoleonic Wars. As these spread across Europe, so there developed a modern sense of nationhood and popular freedom that was expressed according to each country's historic and political needs through their particular cultural traditions. However, a characteristic of Romanticism was its shared themes and the close relationship between all the arts, in particular music, poetry, painting and theatre.

Revolution and war

Eighteenth-century Sentimentality had begun to value the importance of emotional response, reflected in the German *Sturm und Drang* (Storm and stress). But a major change came from an increasing sense that the Enlightenment's belief in rationalism had failed. The rationalist project had sought to control nature, both within and without the individual, to create an ordered world. But by the last decades of the century it was clear that poverty, crime, disease, war – all the blights of mankind – were still its major condition. At the same time, whatever its merits, the project had depended upon centralist, aristocratic imposition. But as the century advanced so did the power of the bourgeoisie, who increasingly became the real driving force of the European economies. Despite this they were excluded from the machinery of state, able neither to advise upon nor influence the laws that regulated their role. This ultimately exploded first in the American and then the French Revolutions which had in common the struggle against unbalanced and inept financial management, taxation policy and legislation.

With the rise of Napoleon, the aspirations of the French Revolution were carried across Europe to countries where they were both welcomed and repudiated because they came as the gift of the conqueror. Despite the contradictions, Napoleon was perceived as a hero who more than anyone since antiquity appeared to 'bestride the world'. He seemed like a force of Nature and a model for all those who aspired, however waywardly, to change the condition of their lives. Famously, Beethoven had

Table 7.1 *Themes and passages in Romanticism*

Developments in science/technology increase advanced late eighteenth-century international trade/imperialism. Large-scale rivalry helps create the sense of consolidated, separate political units (rather than 'nations'). These are disrupted and enhanced by:

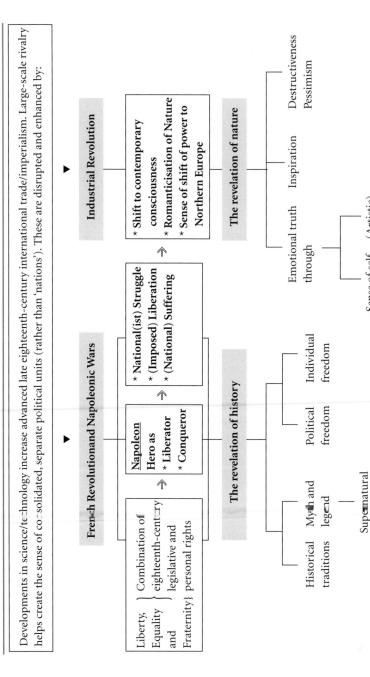

dedicated his Symphony no. 3 (the *Eroica*) to Napoleon the liberator before hearing that he had crowned himself Emperor and become 'like other men'.

History, art and myth

The popular struggle against French invasion helped create a new sense of national identity, history and traditions which now became a major theme in the arts. History, painting and opera turned from classical to national historical subjects. In France Delacroix and in Italy Hayez used historical subjects as expressions of nationalistic ideas rather than moral ideals. Myth, too, had became of increasing national interest ever since the publication of the *Poems of Ossian* by James Macpherson in 1760. As the Industrial Revolution rapidly promoted the north of Europe over the Mediterranean lands, so Britain, France and Germany all welcomed the discovery of mythologies, legends and poetry that made their culture as valid as that of the classical world.. This became of special significance in Germany as it strove to create a national identity (Table 7.1).

This eventually culminated in national unification or independence for several nations. In each case, the arts played a slightly different role. In Germany and Italy despite their disunity, cultural and musical traditions were firmly established and the accent was on national history, legend and myth. In suppressed nations such as Poland, Hungary and Czechoslovakia the rediscovery of national language and music was of prime importance. Russia was a special case: a single, if composite, state within which its own people and its culture were repressed. Their long struggle towards freedom was expressed through the reassertion of vernacular language and cultural traditions. France is only included because it was the inspiration, from 1789 onwards, for popular uprisings across Europe, and its use of the arts to rebuild its international standing after the defeat of 1815 (Table 7.2).

The Industrial Revolution and Nature

The Industrial Revolution was the engine of middle-class growth and the development of an increasingly militant urban working class. With industrialisation came the creation of a new kind of urban environment, one that redefined the relationship between man and nature. Huge demographic changes were effected by the magnet of available work and made possible by mechanised transport that could carry raw materials, finished goods and labour to wherever they were required. This rapid change affected the entire population, engendering a wholly new consciousness. Nature in particular was changed from being the major condition of life into something increasingly remote, so that it became an object of nostalgia, escape

Table 7.2 *Nationalist struggle and revolution*

	Countries with an established cultural sense; national aspiration is expressed through a new accent on myth and history			Countries where the struggle for independence is expressed, and conducted, through the rediscovery of national artistic traditions as well as history and myth			
(France)	Germany	Italy	(Russia)	Poland	Hungary	Czechoslovakia
1789						
1830	1830–2	1831		1830		
1848	1848	1848		1846	1848	
		1859		1863		
		1861 Unification				
1871	1871 Unification					
			1917	1918 Independence	1918 Independence	1918 Independence

			Major opera composers whose work expresses the national aspiration			
Meyerbeer?	Weber Marschner Wagner	Mercadante Verdi	Glinka Dargomïzhsky Borodin Musorgsky Rimsky-Korsakov	Moniuszko	Erkel	Dvořák Smetana Janáček

and idealism. But ironically, as artists and thinkers turned to look at Nature with a new sense of purpose, what they found was a reflection of the violent forces of the new industrial jungle: vicious cycles of slump and boom, the struggle to dominate markets, the battle between labour and employers. For Wordsworth in 1798 Nature had been 'The anchor of my purest thoughts, the nurse/The guide, the guardian of my heart, and soul/Of all my moral being (*Lines Composed a Few Miles Above Tintern Abbey*). By 1849 Tennyson was asking: 'Are God and Nature then at strife?' (*In Memoriam*, LV).

For Schlegel it was this very sense of contradiction that seemed to offer a truth that the neatness of the Enlightenment obscured:

> The whole of the ancient poetry and art is, as it were a *rhythmical nomos* [law] an harmonised promulgation of permanently established legislation of a world submitted to a beautiful order, and reflecting in itself the eternal images of things. Romantic poetry, on the other hand, is the expression of the secret attraction to a chaos which lies in the very bosom of the ordered universe, and is perpetually striving after new and marvellous births; the life-giving spirit of primal love broods here anew on the face of the waters. The former is simple, clear, and like to nature in the self-existent perfection of her separate works; the latter, notwithstanding its fragmentary appearance, approaches more to the secret of the universe.
> (Schlegel, 1809–11: 512)

Romanticism and pessimism

The late eighteenth century had anticipated this tension in its concept of the Sublime. Reading part of Edmund Burke's definition suggests the opening of Haydn's *Creation*:

> the passion caused by the great and sublime in *nature*, when those causes operate most powerfully, is Astonishment; and astonishment is that state of the soul, in which all its motions are suspended, with some degree of horror. In this case the mind is so entirely filled with its object, that it cannot entertain any other, nor by consequence reason on that object which employs it. Hence arises the great power of the sublime, that far from being produced by them, it anticipates our reasonings, and hurries us on by an irresistible force.
> (Burke, 2003: 517)

The Sublime did not exclude Reason, but it did relativise it. For the Romantics, man's natural responses were surer guides to the truth, and art's function was to enable and express this, however dreadful. German early Romanticism – *Sturm und Drang* – saw the beauty and terror of nature as an analogue for the realities within man. Whatever the suffering and loneliness, there was a strength to be drawn from knowing the truth of his condition. The over-riding tone of Romanticism became a pessimism as its artists faced a world of unknowable, uncontrollable forces, only

Table 7.3 *Opera: writers and painters of the Romantic period*

Author		Composer		Painter
Byron	*The Corsair*	Verdi	*Il corsaro*	
	Parisina	Donizetti		
	Mazeppa	Tchaikovsky		H. Vernet,
	Manfred	Tchaikovsky (Symphony)		John Martin
	Sardanapalus			Delacroix
	The Two Foscari	Verdi		Hayez,
	Heaven and Earth: A Mystery	Donizetti	*Il diluvio universale*	Delacroix
Dumas, père	*Charles VII*	Donizetti	*Gemma di Vergy*	
	Le Roi s'Amuse	Verdi	*Rigoletto*	
	Lucrèce Borgia	Donizetti		
Dumas, fils	*La Dame aux Camélias*	Verdi	*La traviata*	
Goethe	*Faust*	(Spohr), Berlioz, Gounod, Boito, Wagner (Overture)		Delacroix
Hugo	*Amy Robsart* (after Scott's *Kenilworth*)	Donizetti	*Elisabetta a castello di Kenilworth*	
	Hernani	Verdi		
	Ruy Blas	Mendelssohn (Overture)		
Scott	*Lady of the lake*	Rossini		
	Guy Mannering	Boieldieu	*La Dame Blanche*	
	The Bride of Lammermoor	Donizetti	*Lucia di Lammermoor*	
	Ivanhoe	Marschner	*Der Templer und die Jüdin*	
	Kenilworth	Auber	*Il castello di Kenilworth*	
		Donizetti	*Elisabetta al castello di Kenilworth*	
	The Fair Maid of Perth			
	Waverley	Bizet		
		Berlioz	(Overture)	
Schiller	*Die Räuber*	Verdi	I masnadieri	
	Kabale und Liebe	Verdi	*Luisa Miller*	
	Don Carlos	Verdi		Delacroix
	Wallenstein	Verdi	*La Forza del Destino*	
	Mary Stuart	Donizetti		
	Die Jungfrau von Orleans	Verdi, Tchaikovsky		
	Wilhelm Tell	Rossini		Ingres

Table 7.3 (*cont.*)

Author		Composer	Painter
Shakespeare	*Hamlet*	Thomas, Tchaikovsky (Fantasy overture)	Delacroix, Fuseli, Moreau
	King Lear	Berlioz (Overture)	
	Macbeth	Verdi	Fuseli, Martin, Moreau
	Measure for Measure	Wagner *Das Liebesverbot*	
	Much Ado about Nothing	Berlioz *Béatrice et Bénédict*	
	Othello	Rossini, Verdi	Delacroix
	Romeo and Juliet	Benda, Gounod, Tchaikovsky (Fantasy overture)	
	The Tempest	Halévy, Tchaikovsky (Overture)	Turner, Hayez

recognised through an emotional response. For Caspar David Friedrich 'If a picture leaves the feeling and responsive of the beholder cold and the heart untouched, however exemplary it might otherwise be . . . then it can lay no claim to the name of an authentic work of art.' (Friederich, 2003: 1025)

Romanticism: national and international

Romanticism therefore combined both national and international traits. Composers, dramatists, painters and poets learned from and followed one another. In particular opera, constantly searching for subjects and bases for libretti, turned to the leading writers and dramatists of the age. In addition, Shakespeare was universally adopted. His plays offered both the epitome of the individual tragic hero, above all in Hamlet, and also seemed to be the antidote to the straitjacket of French classicism (Table 7.3).

However, despite the international sharing of material, Romanticism was always tempered by national circumstances, including dramatic traditions which directly affected how these were expressed in opera (Table 7.4).

In addition, nineteenth-century opera is distinguished by the wholesale shift from a courtly to a commercial, middle-class audience. With this came an emphasis on the entertainment value of opera, increasingly focused on melody. Once again melody starts to draw attention to itself, potentially creating a tension with the dramatic

Table 7.4 *Development of national operatic traditions*

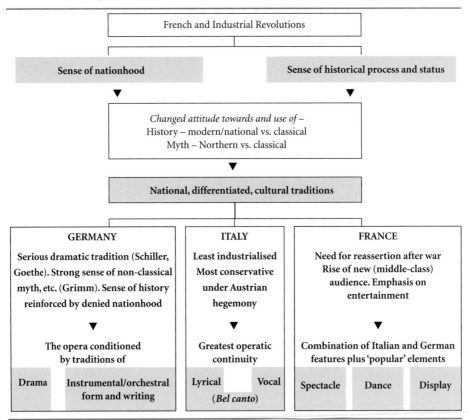

as a whole. There were two main responses to this. First, simply to create operas that were essentially frameworks for a sequence of melodic numbers. Second, where dramatic integrity was important, to find ways of drawing melodic numbers into larger units.

Germany

In Germany a number of specific elements affected the development of opera. The 1815 Congress of Vienna had specifically denied Germany nationhood despite the fact that it had suffered severely in the French Wars and played a major part in Napoleon's defeat. A unified Germany would have created opportunities for new international alliances which Austria and Great Britain especially feared. Germany felt this strongly. At the same time it had always been claimed that Germany was a barbaric state, the only part of western Europe that had never been 'civilised' by

Rome; that it had no real language – merely a hotch-potch of dialects; and according to Tacitus had no tradition of organised religion.

The interest in myth played a major role in helping reverse these ideas. The brothers Jacob and Wilhelm Grimm initially established modern German as a language, publishing the results of their studies in their *Germanic Grammar* and *German Dictionary*. But, in the course of their linguistic research, many of the working people whom they interviewed demonstrated their languages by telling stories. In these, the brothers heard echoes of ancient religious beliefs and myths: 'What all tales have in common are the remnants of some belief, reaching back to the most ancient times' (Grimm, 1966: 301). The 'Preface' to the later *Teutonic Mythology*, which became a major source for Wagner, concluded that 'Having observed that her Language, Laws and Antiquities were greatly undervalued, I was wishful to exalt my native land' (Grimm, 1966: LV). Out of this would come the kind of folk-oriented awareness that underlay the operas of Weber (*Der Freischütz*), Marschner (*Hans Heiling*) and Wagner (Table 7.5).

At the same time, Germany's major literary figures – Lessing, Goethe and Schiller – turned to history, stimulating a new kind of historical drama that was about the *processes* of history rather than being a sophisticated kind of fancy dress. Here, too, the emphasis was on the moral purpose of the German stage:

> Where the influence of civil laws ends that of the stage begins. Where venality and corruption blind and bias justice and judgement, and intimidation perverts its ends, the stage seizes the sword and scales and pronounces a terrible verdict on vice.   (Schiller, in DuKore, 1974: 441).

It is in this spirit that Beethoven, Weber and, later, Wagner, approached opera.

Beethoven and *Fidelio*

Fidelio stands between the operas of the late eighteenth century and the early Romanticism of Hoffmann (*Undine*) and Spohr (*Faust*). As a transitional work it has traditionally posed a number of problems, highlighted by Romain Rolland:

> he accepted what was given him; he began with the established conventions. But what we have to consider is not the point of departure but the point of arrival. These conventions that he so meekly and unwillingly endorses, this formal frock-coat in which his great chest suffocates during the first ten numbers – see him burst them and tear them in pieces with a single stroke.   (Rolland, 1980: 34)

The mixture of a farcical love triangle and a wife's self-sacrifice to save her husband from injustice seems, on the face of it, unsatisfactory. Yet Beethoven chose to express his loftiest ideals through this domestic subject and the popular *Singspiel* form.

Table 7.5 *Germany and Romanticism*

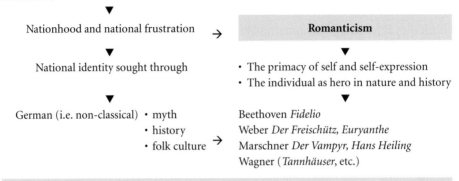

German identity and Romanticism

Germany after the Congress of Vienna, despite a major part in Napoleon's defeat, is denied nationhood

▼

Nationhood and national frustration → **Romanticism**

▼   ▼

National identity sought through
- The primacy of self and self-expression
- The individual as hero in nature and history

▼   ▼

German (i.e. non-classical)
- myth
- history
- folk culture →

Beethoven *Fidelio*
Weber *Der Freischütz, Euryanthe*
Marschner *Der Vampyr, Hans Heiling*
Wagner (*Tannhäuser*, etc.)

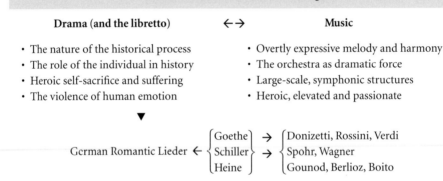

German Romanticism: drama and opera

Drama (and the libretto) ←→ **Music**

- The nature of the historical process
- The role of the individual in history
- Heroic self-sacrifice and suffering
- The violence of human emotion

- Overtly expressive melody and harmony
- The orchestra as dramatic force
- Large-scale, symphonic structures
- Heroic, elevated and passionate

▼

German Romantic Lieder ← { Goethe, Schiller, Heine } → { Donizetti, Rossini, Verdi; Spohr, Wagner; Gounod, Berlioz, Boito }

Singspiel literally means 'sing play' and was originally simply the German translation of *melodrama* 'music play', a synonym for 'opera'. By the mid eighteenth century it started to be applied to works that mixed vernacular speech with song and acquired a number of characteristics. Chief among these were an essentially popular appeal, as in *Die Entführung aus dem Serail* or *Die Zauberflöte*, without any necessary implication of triviality. The *Singspiel* was typified by:

- A world whose emotional range was recognisable, with empathetic characters whether the setting was realistic or exotic.
- A romantic love interest and associated love trial.
- (Often) a comic element.
- A clear, happy or at least moral, resolution.
- Music that was popular and above all tuneful.

All these elements are found in *Fidelio*; in fact, Michael Tusa suggests that:

> the 1805 version of the opera represents nothing less than [Beethoven's] attempt to conquer the operatic world with a work that would demonstrate an encyclopaedic competency in the . . . known operatic styles (comic and serious, lyrical and declamatory, Italian, French and German), forms (strophic, through-composed one-section forms, multi-sectional forms), and genres (songs, arias, recitative, melodrama, contemplative and active ensembles, finales and even a canon).   (Tusa, 2000: 207–8)

Beethoven, however, chose to take on this challenge because the libretto provided him with several elements that he required:

- A drama of heroic self-sacrifice in the name of liberty, justice and conjugal love.
- A story that was rooted in a recognisable world and real characters.
- A narrative in which the complications of the farcical love triangle were essential to the heroine's struggle to save her husband.

In addition, *Fidelio* reflected the vogue for the new 'Rescue Opera', a genre that for obvious reasons became increasingly popular immediately after the French Revolution (Solomon, 1998: 180; Warrack, 1976: 156–8).

   Beethoven's problem was how to integrate these elements in a way that would create an elevated moral experience. To do this he had to transcend the *Singspiel* form and the limitations of the narrative through a musical dynamic. Beethoven was supremely well placed to do this based on his development and mastery of the symphonic form, which would become the opera's true driving force. William Kinderman, writing about the *Eroica* symphony, composed just before *Fidelio*, says: 'What Beethoven explores in the *Eroica* are universal aspects of heroism, centring on the idea of a confrontation with adversity leading ultimately to a renewal of creative possibilities. Variants of this narrative sequence surface again and again in Beethoven's music up to his very last years' (Kinderman, 1995: 90).

Dramatic structures

Chapter 1 of this volume proposes that 'opera is a dramatic form whose primary language is music. A successful opera must work both musically and dramatically; to understand opera means understanding both elements and how they interact.' This implies that an opera text must be appropriate to the nature of 'the language of music' (see Chapter 15). The complex refinements of poetry are rarely appropriate, since they do not require, and often defy, musical setting. The detail of language in the spoken drama similarly means that it is rarely suited to musical setting. The play, however, offers not a literary but primarily a dramaturgical structure. The spoken drama, like opera, creates its effect and meaning more through the dramatic mechanism of plot than through the detail of the text. It is the dramatic structure that determines *how* the play, each of its acts and scenes, *works* – directing the audience and determining their response. In a stage play, attention does not move from 'literary' word to word, as in a novel or poem. The dramatic scene is constructed, like a piece of music, to lead the audience from a starting to a finishing point, often without using words at all (Table 7.6).

Good theatre writing, including the libretto, has nothing to do with literature: it is a dramatic action. In Stanislavski's terminology this is effected through:

- a 'Super-objective': the play's overall intention which is realised through the sequence of
- 'episodes' or 'units' that make up the stage action; in turn, each of these will have its own
- 'objective'; finally, the 'objectives' are realised through
- 'actions'.

These actions are events that create the meaning for an audience. In a play they can be physical, but are rarely words themselves: they are more often interactions between characters *using* words. In opera the major events are *musical* events. For example, in act I, scenes vii–ix of *Rinaldo* things happen, such as Almirena's magicking away: but this in itself does not affect the audience. They are affected by the *musical events*: Rinaldo's sequence of arias expressing his changing state of mind.[1]

The dramaturgy of the classical play was relatively simple: a single action leading to a necessary conclusion. Once that model was abandoned, dramaturgy (as in Shakespeare) became much more complex. In *Così* there is a dynamic but shifting

Table 7.6 *Dramatic units and objectives*

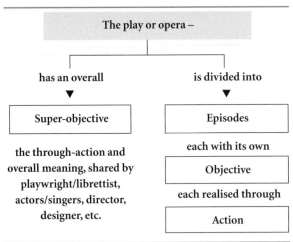

relationship between action, text and score. It is usually only the composer's main input (the music) that can be depended upon to indicate not the meaning itself, but where the meaning may lie (Table 7.7). Luca Zoppelli suggests a paradigm for this:

> In the . . . diagram the broken line joining author and objective represents the musical element, which crosses the frame superimposed upon the verbal act through which the characters communicate with one another.
>
> (Zoppelli, 1994: 17–18)

In other words the musical dynamic can confirm, enhance, or contradict the surface implications of any verbal passage.

Musical dramaturgy in *Fidelio*

In *Fidelio* the music serves several functions. First there is characterisation. Rocco's music is the most consistently in the popular *Singspiel* style, for example his aria 'Hat man nicht auch Gold beneiben' (If one has no gold whatever) (no. 4) and his part of the duet (no. 8) 'Jetzt, Alter, hat es Eile!' (Now, old man, we need to hurry!). Marzelline's music moves between the *Singspiel* writing of the opening duet (no. 1) and the sentimental sensitivity of 'Der arme Jaquino' (Poor Jaquino) (no. 2). Significantly, Leonora herself is first heard not in a solo but in the quartet 'Mir ist so wunderbar' (It is so wonderful to me). This extraordinary, quite unexpected piece, lifts the drama to a new level, the one at which the opera as a whole aims. It has no foundation in Bouilly's original libretto[2] and of all the numbers it is the one that remained untouched throughout the opera's development (Tusa, 2000: 207–8; *Grove*, vol. II, 1997: 185).

Beethoven was neither experienced not confident enough to handle his librettists in the way the mature Verdi could. However the changes to the dramatic structure in the 1806 and 1814 versions show him reworking the initial comedy/*Singspiel* so as to move as quickly and directly as possible towards the higher plane of the quartet. This involved reversing the original nos. 1 and 2 and removing the original no. 3 (Table 7.8).

In this way, the audience is led from the real but mundane world of the young couple's argument into Marzelline's assertion of emotional fidelity. Two passages of

Table 7.7 *Narrative and musical interaction*

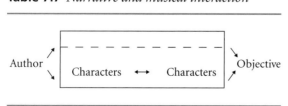

Table 7.8 Fidelio: *the revision of number order*

Léonore, ou L'Amour Conjugal (1798) (Bouilly/Gaveaux)	Fidelio (1805)	Léonore (1806)	Fidelio (1814)
Act I	**Act I**	**Act I Scene i**	**Act I Scene i**
Aria (Marzelline) ·········→ 1	································→ 1	⟍	→1
Duet (Marzelline, Jaquino) ······· → 2	································→ 2	⟋	→2
	3 Trio(Ein Mann is bald)		
	4 Quartet ···········	→3 ··································	→3
Aria (Rocco) ···················· → 5	························		→4

dialogue then create a hiatus before the major shift to the Quartet (no. 3). Within the narrative, it is the musical dynamic that establishes the opera's main objective. The quartet is a musical event that is pivotal to the whole drama – not as a narrative but as an ethical conception.

Once the real tone has been established, Beethoven can allow the music to indicate the layers of moral hierarchy. After Rocco's aria (no. 4) whose *Singspiel* attractiveness jars with the Quartet, the scene is consolidated in the Trio (no. 5). This precludes Jaquino who would reintroduce the farcical narrative at the expense of the real trajectory of the plot. The Trio was originally written to end act i (now act i, scene i) and its function is to draw together the two strands of the plot and these three characters as the basis for working out the narrative in acts ii and iii. It falls into two broad sections: A, where they determine to approach Pizarro, and B in which the characters reflect, again, on their hopes and fears but now in the context of the need for immediate action (Table 7.9).

It is essential to see the Trio in the context of the whole act. The most significant feature of *Fidelio* is Beethoven's control of the larger musical structure, parallel with his symphonic writing. This is evident in large-scale individual numbers, such as Florestan's 'Gott! welch' Dunkel hier!' (God! What darkness here!) (no. 11) at the opening of act ii. But act i, scene i as an entirety shows this in a more significant way, as Beethoven takes the fragmentary elements of the *Singspiel* and creates an over-arching musical shape whose dynamic drives the opera and its audience towards its emotional and ethical objective (Table 7.10).

The impact of this scene – and the rest of the opera – depends on the relationship between overall musical and dramaturgical structures. Within these, the words have a part to play, primarily carrying narrative information and providing the composer with the basis for the musical tone and structure which provide the narrative with its real dynamic.

Table 7.9 Fidelio*: act i, scene i, Trio (no. 4)*

A	In the first section each character has a separate verse of six lines in which Rocco encourages Fidelio, Fidelio replies affirmatively, and Marzelline encourages him. Each verse is set so that the words remain absolutely clear.

1–2	The Trio is based on a simple rising syncopated figure first heard at the very start in quavers
3–4	Rocco and Fidelio have the same opening melodic material, but
14–15	where Rocco is accompanied by jaunty rising quavers
(25)	Fidelio is more heroic, with pronounced chords in the woodwind and a strenuous decorated bar (bar 25) leading to high A♭ on her repeated 'hohe Leiden' (severe pain).
	By contrast, Marzelline's verse is set to a much simpler, complementary subject, with a decorative but standard run on her final words 'unnenbare Freuden' (boundless joy).

B	The second section is quite different, the verbal text is subservient to the musical structure as the characters sing across one another.

43–56	The first section opens with a figure of three rising crotchets, in fact a slower version of the quavers that began the trio. This is sung in canon by each character, followed by another short sequence for Rocco and Fidelio which leads
56–57	to a brief moment of consonance on the word 'Ja' (bars 56–57), and an *a cappella* statement followed by another quasi-canonic sequence in which each echoes the words 'glücklich sein' (to be lucky).
76	At the mention of the word 'Gouverneur' the music slows, casting a shadow over their hopes. But
76–119	it picks up speed immediately and in bars 76–119 all three reassert their aspirations.
120–203	The third section is an extended *crescendo* marked *Allegro molto* that only allows the word 'Tränen' (tears) to be properly – if disparately – heard: Fidelio: Er kostet bitt're Tränen It costs bitter tears Marzelline: O süsse, süsse Tränen. O sweet, sweet tears. Rocco: In süssen Freudentränen. In sweet joyous tears.

Weber and *Der Freischütz*

Where Beethoven's Romanticism is still tempered by Enlightenment aspirations, Weber embraced the gamut of romantic themes which he identified in his descriptions of the opera:

Table 7.10 Fidelio: *act 1, scene i, musical and dramatic dynamic*

ACT 1	Scene i	Scene ii	Scene iii	Scene iv					
	No. 1 Duet and dialogue	No. 2 Soliloquy and aria	Dialogue	Dialogue	No. 3 Quartet	Dialogue	No. 4 Aria	Dialogue	No. 5 Trio
Narrative action	Jaquino pursues the unwilling Marzelline	Marzelline hopes for true love with Fidelio	When will Fidelio arrive?	Fidelio seeks Rocco's trust – Rocco believes he seeks Marzelline's hand	All four characters express their fears and hopes	Plans for the wedding	Money is essential	Love is essential	Hopes and fears
	Roots the opera in a real world ▲			Dangerous complication tying Leonore's need for Rocco's trust to her involvement with Marzelline ▲					
Objective	The world of mundane love ▲		Anticipation ↑	Increasing sense of man's higher aspirations and potential					
Musical 'action'	*Singspiel* strophic writing confirms the social reality of the opera's world ▲				Strict canon form: an isolated and isolating moment of contemplation for characters and audience ▲		*Singspiel* strophic form – the world of scenes i and ii. The contrast with no. 4 shows the lower level (▲)		Concerted writing presents each character's attitude – but musically creates a symphonic driving dynamic for audience (▲)

- A sense of German cultural heritage from which the music, narrative, historical reference and themes derive.
- The wonder, power, terror and beauty of nature: 'The contemplation of a landscape is to me the performance of a piece of music. I feel the effect of the whole, without dwelling on the details which produce it' (Warrack, 1976: 96).
- Folk culture and the supernatural: 'There are in *Der Freischütz* two principal elements that can be recognised at first sight – hunting life and the rule of demonic powers' (Warrack, 1976: 221).

All the major tropes of Romanticism are here and, unlike *Fidelio*, are not simply part of the narrative, but give rise to the music itself:

> when composing the opera I had to look for suitable tone colours to characterize these two elements; these colours I tried to retain and use not only where the poet had indicated one or the other element but also where they could be made effective use of. The tone colour of the scoring for forest and hunting life was easy to find: the horns provided it. The difficulty lay only in finding for the horns new melodies that would be both simple and popular . . . I had to remind the hearer of these 'dark powers' by means of tone colour and melody as often as possible . . . I gave a great deal of thought to the question of what was the right principal colouring for this sinister element. Naturally it had to be dark, gloomy colour.   (Warrack, 1976: 221)

Like *Fidelio*, Hoffmann's *Undine* and Spohr's *Faust*, *Der Freischütz* is a *Singspiel*, in part chosen as a German operatic form, using the vernacular. But again, like *Fidelio*, this posed problems of balance between the sung and spoken elements and how best to create a dynamic that would carry the audience in terms of the opera's objective. Weber achieves this through his musical dramaturgy, essential to which are:

- Great melodic strength; where appropriate consciously reflecting, and occasionally using real, folk tunes (Warrack, 1976: 222).
- Evocative use of the orchestra and sensitive use of individual instruments to create character and atmosphere (Warrack, 1976: 227–9).
- Direct, often intense expression, especially in the treatment of the passages of emotional turmoil and the diabolical.

Der Freischütz launches its audience on a combination of melody and musical dramaturgy that supervenes the limitations of a libretto which, considered as 'literature', seems weak, platitudinous, or faintly comic. But, like Beethoven, Weber enables the opera to transcend its narrative parts to create an over-arching experience, in this case, the descent into darkness and ascent back to the light.

The Wolf's Glen scene, act ii, scene iv ('Finale') is structured as a single entity despite its combination of singing, speech, melodrama and theatrical effects. It is a strongly coherent unit in which the musical and dramatic dynamic work in unison to direct the audience. Weber paid particular attention to the musical and physical presentation of the opera and both the words and music have to be 'read' in the context of the detailed stage directions. The music is never mere illustration, but rather an analogue for the audience's emotional experience. The changes in tempo, key and dynamics; the switching between speech, recitative and *arioso*; the sudden changes in volume, create an experience for the audience that is the equivalent of the fiction on the stage. Table 7.11 shows how flexibily Weber employs this range of elements.

Weber stressed the integration of music, words and staging. He was one of the first composers to establish the modern rehearsal process (Warrack, 1976: 205–6). This began with the *Leseprobe* (reading rehearsal), so that the singers fully understood the text and the opera's dramatic structure. After the *Zimmerprobe* (chamber rehearsal) for individual singers and, where necessary, solo instrumentalists, came the *Sitzproben* (placing rehearsals) where the singers learned how to fit their roles into the production. Finally there was a full-scale *Generalprobe* (dress rehearsal) (Radice, 1998: 161–2). In addition to the musical preparation, Weber paid close attention to the lighting, costumes and scenery. He was especially concerned with the staging and scenic effects, in particular the Wolf's Glen scene.[3]

Weber is one of the first composers to make use of recurrent musical ideas attached to specific characters and themes, foreshadowing the Wagnerian *Leitmotiv* (leading motif). The overture consists of a series of ideas/motifs that are repeated in the course of the opera. This is not the same as the later *pot-pourri* overture, which is a simple *mélange* of the best tunes. Instead, it is a genuine introduction that establishes the tone and mood of what is to follow. Gluck had set the precedent for this, but here there is an extra dimension when the themes recur later and strike the audience in their dramatic context. Most notable is the second theme of the overture at bar 61. Growing out of an extended *crescendo* (bars 49–62) it explodes with a violence that is repeated at the casting of the seventh bullet (act II, scene IV, bar 373) accompanied scenically by a cataclysmic storm. Musically the motifs are both expressive and melodically attractive. But Weber's melodic gift once again raises problem of the potential for melody to disrupt the dramatic flow by creating a focus in its own right. This is especially the case when a complex drama consists of the separate numbers and spoken dialogue of the *Singspiel.*

Because of its melodic attraction, *Der Freischütz* is often patronised by critics such as Gerhart von Westerman: 'The peculiar charm of the music to *Der Freischütz* is its irresistible melodiousness which has made some minor numbers a part of German folk music' (Westerman, 1973: 141). In fact Weber uses his forms flexibly, creating something far more complex than a sequence of appealing, popular tunes. Only

Table 7.11 Der Freischütz: *act II, scene iv, 'The Wolf's Glen'*

1–39	*Sostenuto* incantation by tenors and basses, with bird screeching from sopranos and altos.
40	Bar's prolonged silence, before
41	a *forte* rush of the violins.
43–50	Caspar's whispered 'Samiel!', demi-semiquavers in the upper strings rising to *ff* as Caspar continues to call on Samiel.
51–104	*Agitato* 3/4 Caspar sings while Samiel speaks his replies. The music increasingly agitated until
105–109	4/4 Samiel grants Caspar's request and vanishes.
110–122	*Allegro* as the hearth begins to glow, with a ghostly rising figure of a quaver rest, quaver, minim and two crotchets.
123–133	Caspar again speaks, asking Samiel for help, as the strings play two slurred minims from *e* down to *b* below the stave.
134–153	The figure at 110 is repeated, Caspar continues his 'business' until
154–164	the brass sounds out as Max appears and begins his *recitative*, on an heroic high *G* sung *forte* over repeated demi-semiquaver strings and then
165	*andante*, sings *arioso* until
175	*recitative* (to bar 177) and then sings *a tempo* until bar 189 when another *recitative* starts marked, two bars later, *Vivace*.
196–198	Caspar thanks Samiel, speaking over the music. A long pause and then Caspar speaks to Max.
199–234	In bars 219–231 Max sees his mother's spirit; in 235–257 he sees that of Agathe. In between, Caspar mocks him – speaking. Max's line is divided between *recitative*, with constant changes in tempo markings. Finally
235–260	Caspar and Max address one another – but interrupted at bar 240 by two chords in the strings.
261–430	*Melodrama* and the casting of the bullets begins in which every resource of the orchestra – spoken voice, chorus and scenography – is employed to create this extraordinary scene.

four of the numbers are straightforwardly melodic, and in each case they suit the character and the dramatic moment:

- No.1, Kilian's celebratory 'Schau der Herr mich an als König'.
- No. 3, the waltz for the local people at the inn.

- No. 4, Caspar's 'Hier im ird'schen Jammertal (Here in the earthly vale of tears!), a drinking song headed *Lied* (*Song*) rather than 'aria'.
- No. 7, Aennchen's 'Kommt ein schlanker Bursch gegangen' (If a slim young chap comes along). Aennchen's character is derived from the *Singspiel/opera buffa* maid. Here she is integrated into the opera as Agathe's friend so that her straightforward style is appropriate to this secondary role as *confidante*.

The other numbers are lyrical but without any dominant melodic focus. Caspar's *Aria* 'Schweig! Schweig! Damit dich Niemand warnt' (Silence! Silence! So none shall warn you!) (no. 5) forms a deliberate contrast with his preceding *Lied* (no. 4), the toast to Bacchus designed to inveigle Max into his apparently good-natured power. This is a soliloquy in which he triumphs over Max's impending fall. It consists of an opening recitative followed by the aria proper, itself divided into two sections.

- The first 'Der Hölle Netz hat dich umgarnt (The toils of Hell ensnare you) opens with a strident theme suggesting diabolical strength (bars 11–15) but which is not repeated.
- The second, is a song of triumph 'Triumph,... die Rache gelingt!' (Triumph, revenge has succeeded!) (bar 63, where the key changes from F major to D). But again, although lyrical there is no dominant melody. Similarly the Trio (no. 2), and Duet (no. 6), both have clear melodic interest, but in neither case does this distract from the dramatic function.

In both Max's aria (no. 3) and Agathe's aria (no. 8) a series of melodic ideas is used, changing with the mood of the scene, and at various points reminiscing material from the overture; Table 7.11 shows how their fluid and fragmentary nature focuses on the dramatic function. Agathe's strongly melodious material in the aria (bars 17–60) is dramatically fractured by bars 35–40; similarly, the lyricism of bars 61–73 is left suspended as the music runs straight in the following *recitative* (Table 7.12).

Beethoven and Weber both strove to create dramatic unities out of the disparate elements of the *Singspiel*. Both succeeded in replacing the fragmented libretto, with its inherently weak dramaturgical drive, by a musical dynamic that controls the audience's experience. What both needed was a libretto whose dramaturgical structure actually promoted the composer's objectives. It is easy to look back at the history of operatic forms and read it as an evolution towards an admired goal – often Verdi or Wagner. However it is true that the future of opera was through-composed, with an increasing integration of all elements into the kind of whole represented by *Falstaff* or *Parsifal*, as Wagner understood: 'After all was done, the Impossible was bound to stay impossible for Weber too. Spite all his suggestions

Table 7.12 Der Freischütz: *act I (Max's aria, no. 3) and act II, scene ii (Agathe's aria, no. 8)*

Act I Max's aria (no. 3)		
1–31	*Walzer* – a folk-like, rustic dance in contrast to Max's soliloquy of despair	
32–66	Orchestral introduction	
67–84	Nein! Länger trag'ich nicht die Qualen No, I will no longer bear this torment	4/4 C *Allegro* Recitative.
85–125	Durch die Wälder, durch die Auen Through the woods, through the meadows	*Moderato* E♭: opens with a lilting, Italianate melody on the flutes and clarinets immediately taken up by Max as he sings of his lost joy.
126–141	Hat denn der Himmel mich verlassen? Have the heavens then forgotten me?	*Recitative*, with the sinister drum beats and *tremolando* strings (130–131, 133–134) from the overture (26–29).
142–169	Jetzt ist wohl ihr Fenster offen Now surely her window is open	3/4 G major, *Andante con moto*: a prayer-like apostrophe to Agathe.
170–257	Doch mich um garnen finstre Mächte Now the dark powers have hold on me	4/4 E♭ *Allegro con fuoco*: arioso-writing as Max increasingly despairs of God. There is no melody here, but – At bars 170–190 the relentless rising and falling motif refers back to bars 36–47 in the overture; – At bars 192–193 the sharp descending figure again refers to bars 61–64 in the overture and will occur again at the end of the Wolf's Glen scene.
Act II, scene ii: Agathe's aria (no. 8)		
1–16	Wie nahte mir der Schlummer, How could sleep draw near me,	4/4 B major *Andante, Recitativo*, but actually lyrical, *arioso* writing.
17–34	Leise, leise, fromme Weise Gently, gently, soft melody	2/4 *Adagio* Beautiful, lullaby-like melody for what is the first part of her aria as she prays, interrupted by
35–40	O wie hell die goldnen Sterne O how bright the golden stars	4/4 *Recitativo* proper as she has a premonition of gathering storm clouds in the distance.

(*cont.*)

Table 7.12 (*cont.*)

41–60	Zu dir wende ich die Hände To you I raise my hands	2/4 *Adagio* The second part of the aria, continues her prayer for protection from danger.
61–73	Alles pflegt schon längst der Ruh All have long since gone to rest	4/4 C major *Andante* Melodious writing as she ponders the beauty of nature – but leading directly into
74–80	Er scheint mich noch nicht zu sehn He does not yet seem to have seen me	*recitative* as she thinks she hears Max approach and then
81–106	Er ist's! Er ist's! It is he! It is he!	*agitato* as she believes him to be victorious in the shooting competition.
107–141	All' meine Pulse schlagen My pulse beats wildly	4/4 E major *Vivace con fuoco* She sings of her rapture using the melody from the overture (at bar 191).
141–154	Will sich morgen treu bewähren? Will it hold true in the morning?	A more recitative-like passage as she wonders whether Fortune will hold until tomorrow and pronounces her faith in Heaven, before
155–198	Himmel, nimm des Dankes Zähren Heavens take my grateful thanks	repeating the words to the melody used earlier (bar 107) to the theme from the overture (bar 191).

and instructions to the Poet, he could not procure a dramatic groundwork which he might entirely dissolve into his Melody; because he wished to call into being a genuine drama, and not merely a play filled out with lyric moments' (Wagner, 1994–5, II: 84).

Chapter 8

Opera in nineteenth-century Italy

The *primo ottocento* (Rossini, Bellini, Donizetti)

The challenge of integrated operatic form

As in Germany, Italian composers were faced with the problem of how to create a coherent musico-dramatic whole from disparate elements. While the Italians did not have the problem of the *Singspiel*'s alternating song and speech, it had always alternated between recitative and aria. This became exacerbated with the emphasis on virtuosic and melodic writing, which risked overwhelming the needs of the drama. It was against this background that opera of the *primo ottocento* (early nineteenth century) developed.

At the 1815 Congress of Vienna, the arch-reactionary Metternich had been told that Italy was Austria's affair (see Duggan, 2008: 74). The consequent repression meant that public political life and debate were virtually impossible. Where they did exist, in the movement towards the *Risorgimento*, they were radical and outside mainstream circles, secretive and often conducted in exile. This was reflected in the public arts, so that intellectual life had no public arena where the pressing issues of freedom and national unity could be addressed. In addition, Italy's lack of raw materials meant that industrialisation occurred late in the century, so that the independent bourgeoisie, who were so active in France, England and Germany, remained part of the Austrian-dominated world, reinforcing the role of the arts as entertainment and escape rather than becoming a force for change.

Dramatic aims

Given the censorship under which these operas were written (Kimbell, 1991: 405) it is hardly surprising that the kind of moral imperative that obtained in Germany – and which Mazzini was to demand (Strunk, 1998: 1035–194) – is rarely found in contemporary criticism, composers' or librettists' letters, let alone the operas themselves. Table 7.3 indicates the range of sources these composers shared with their French and German contemporaries. Common to these was a focus on personal, rather than political or historical issues, reinforced by the love theme. These operas present a vison of a world that is dominated by individual actions and passions. There is no sense of a political or historical process. As Mazzini complained:

> [Their heroes] are alone: this is the secret of their wretchedness and impotence . . . They have never realised the conception that Humanity [exists] in the multitude that have preceded, surround and will follow after them; never thought on their place between the past and future; on the continuity of labour that unites all the generations into one Whole . . . in our own day, we are beginning, though vaguely, to foresee this new social poetry, which will soothe the suffering soul by teaching it to rise towards God through Humanity.   (Kimbell, 1981: 12)

Instead, the dramaturgy, music and staging present a world where individuals and their society were caught, often helplessly, between the demands of the status quo and individual passions. Its most obvious expression lay in the role of the hero/leading singer, whose vocal artistry, at its best, became an analogue for their suffering.

Composers of this period are often accused of having no concern with dramatic let alone intellectual values. This is untrue (e.g. Kimble, 1998: 69–72), as Bellini's letter written during the rehearsals for *Il pirata* shows: 'I have in mind a new style and a music that can express completely the words and form a union of singing and drama, should I give it up because you don't want to [work] with me? In fact, you can co-operate with me, provided that you forget yourself and put yourself into the soul of the character that you represent' (Galatopoulos, 2002: 65).

These composers had to find a way of combining genuine drama, melody and vocal opportunity. Where in *Fidelio* or *Der Freischütz* individual numbers were subsumed into the musical development and dramatic dynamic, in Italy it was essential to maintain their separate appeal.

The physical nature of music

The opening of Stendhal's *Vie de Rossini* is about the history of music. Contrasting Italian and German music he says: 'The quality of music, which makes of it the most enthralling pleasure that the soul can know . . . lies in the powerful element of *physical* intoxication which it contains' (Stendhal, 1985: 15). The principle of Rossini's music is different to the symphonic development of a Beethoven symphony. He identified [his own] two essential elements: 'I do not doubt that "melody" and "rhythm" will predominate, the principal foundations of music' (Rognoni, 1968: 329). Rossini's music is therefore dominated by:

- melodies, melodic figures and motifs;
- a strong rhythmic pulse which sometimes forms melodic figures.

To these is added the repetition of melodies which creates its own larger-scale rhythm, together with the dynamic of the *crescendo*, with its physical excitement. All of this is demonstrated in the overture to the first of Rossini's complete successes, *L'Italiana in Algeri* (Rossini, 1981).

The 'Sinfonia' (Overture) is structured not through *development* but the *accretion* of repeated elements which Rossini uses in different ways:

- Melody itself is often made up of repeated figures. The oboe tune at bars 82–93 consists of a simple dotted rhythmic figure that is repeated three times followed by a series of descending triplets, the whole of which is then played again. At bar 110 another melodic figure appears, this time repeated fifteen times before bar 117.
- Whole units are repeated, both on a small scale (bars 19–24 repeated at 26–31; bars 82–93 repeated at bars 94–105); and, on a large scale, the whole *Allegro* section, (bars 40–138) is repeated (at bars 146–251).
- Rhythmic figures play a major part and are, in themselves, repetitive – for example bars 52–67 and 82–93.

In each case, however, the repetition transcends the simplicity of its rhythmic and melodic parts, creating something that is *physically* exciting. Within this, a crucial factor is the melodic attraction of each element (Table 8.1).

The same technique is used in the vocal writing, always tending towards a climax whose musical excitement becomes the dramatic experience of the scene.

Situazione and the functions of the libretto

The dramatic focus in this period is what Rossini refers to as *situazione* (situation). This is not a technical term but indicates how libretti were crafted, as Rossini explained: 'neither the subject not the characters displease me; the situations, without being especially original, are good, realistic and fit for music, which is the main thing... Aulo's exit, the following duet and the finale make an excellent situation' [Rognoni, 1968: 295–6]. In the early stages of preparing *Il pirata*, Bellini applied these, and other practical considerations, to the development of the libretto: 'Both Romani and I, and even Pollini, favour Arlincourt's La Straniera... Romani won't follow the comedy part in it but will more or less unite the best Romantic situations... All these may possibly be divided into four little acts, to give the impression of time and place. This is all very promising, but Romani thinks that it will be very difficult to do well without a good tenor for the part of Arturo' (Galatopoulos, 2002: 118).

Rossini and his contemporaries were all aware of dramatic structure and textual detail. However their ability to select and shape libretti depended on the time allowed

Table 8.1 L'Italiana in Algeri: *'Sinfonia'*

Andante		
Bar: 1–8	Figure[1]	Slow *pizzicato* with the audience suddenly surprised at bar 7 with a *ff* chord which is 'ignored' and followed by
9–15		*cantabile* solo on the oboe – and a second surprise at
16–18		two *sf* chords followed by
19–24	1	a repetitive figure in the strings rising from *p* (19) to *f* (22) and then *sforzando*, creating a false lull before
26–31		the theme is repeated by the oboe solo. Suddenly there is a bar's rest and then a change of tempo to
Allegro		
32–39		starting with an introduction on the woodwind using a figure of two semiquavers, quavers and crotchets that becomes
40–51	2	a sprightly motif in dotted quavers and semiquavers played by the woodwind and repeated with a *crescendo* at bar 50. This reaches
52–67	3	a *f* climax. A rapid rhythm is then set up in the flutes, second violins, cellos and basses, emphasised by timpani, as the first violins play and repeat a figure centred on a falling scale.
68–76	4	This is now enhanced by rising scales on the flutes and a repeated 'fanfare' figure in the wood and brass. Then
76–81	5	a sudden *piano* with a quiet rising and falling figure on solo cello and bass.
82–93	6	Over quietly 'beating' strings, the solo oboe plays a long melody which is answered (bar 90) by a complementary melody on the piccolo.
94–105	7	Both sections are repeated (bars 94–105)
106–117	8	An essentially rhythmic passage, wind and strings answering one another with a simple rising and falling motif, until
118–127	9	the whole orchestra starts to repeat what is really another series of rising and falling scales, emphasised (again) by the timpani. This is
128–138	10	enhanced by rhythmic chords played *ff* by the clarinets, oboes and brass. The 'fanfare' figure of bars 68–76 is then repeated and followed by
139–145	11	a bridge by the violins, played *p*, that trips into
146–251	12–20	a complete repeat of bars 40–138

by their hectic schedules and the authority that only came with recognition. Rossini's rather self-deprecating remark that he could set a laundry list to music is often quoted to show a diminished sense of dramatic interest. However, when Wagner insisted that he must have played a part in moulding the oath scene in the second act of *Guillaume Tell* (which Wagner greatly admired), he replied: 'That is true. That scene was actually profoundly changed, not without difficulty, following my indications' (Rognoni, 1968: 413). *Lucia di Lammermoor*, and 'the mad scene' in particular, shows the inventiveness and care with which (many of) the *primo ottocento* libretti were created. A comparison between the opera and its source, Scott's *The Bride of Lammermoor*, demonstrates how the focus of the opera was extracted from a long and detailed novel. It also shows what the main concern and dynamic were intended to be, and how the narrative was reconstructed to accommodate, and be expressed through, the conventions of the period (Table 8.2).

Once the episode had been decided upon, the librettist's task was to create a clear through-line as a series of dramatic moments (*situazione*) each built out of a sequence of vocal elements (arias, etc.).

Within this, the drama and characters are realised through the art of singing, with the music written in a way that allowed the singer to display a combination of virtuosity and expression in a variety of moods. This was what was understood by the (later) term *bel canto* (beautiful singing) (see 'Singing Rossini', in Senici, 2004), which Rossini defined as: 'made up of three elements: 1. The instrument – the voice . . . 2. Technique – that is to say the means of using it; 3. Style, the ingredients of which are taste and feeling' (Senici, 2004: 193).

The aria and the 'tripartite form'

The major building block of the musical structure was the aria, which could take several forms *cavatina, cantabile, cabaletta, stretta*. The meaning of these names changed in the course of the eighteenth and nineteenth centuries,[1] but the broad *primo ottocento* uses were:

- *Cavatina*: an introductory aria and/or one that required virtuosity. As a result 'cavatina' is often used indiscriminately to imply a solo, technically demanding aria.[2]
- *Cantabile*: literally 'singingly', a slow(er), flowing, usually *legato* aria which can either stand alone or be the first part of the tripartite unit.
- *Cabaletta*: a fast aria, often used as the counterpart to the *cantabile*, especially when part of the tripartite unit.
- *Stretta*: literally a 'tightening' of the action – coming at the end of scene or act and usually bringing together soloists and chorus.

Table 8.2 Lucia di Lammermoor: *act* III, *scene* ii *and* The Bride of Lammermoor: *Chapter* XXXIV

The Bride of Lammermoor (novel text in italics)	*Lucia di Lammermoor*
'*It is well known, that the weddings of ancient days were celebrated with a festive publicity rejected by the delicacy of modern times . . .*'	Chorus: Per te d'immenso giubileo (With great rejoicing)
Episode in which it is noticed that one of the ancestral portraits has been exchanged for that of a member of the hated rival family.	
As the dancing begins '*a cry was heard so shrill and piercing, as at once to arrest the dance and the music. All stood motionless; but when the yell was again repeated, Colonel Ashton snatched a torch from the sconce*'.	<u>Gran scena con cori</u> Raimondo rushing in to stop the celebration. Deh! Cessate quel contento (Oh! Stop this rejoicing!)
He then rushes out, leading Henry, Lady and Sir William Ashton to the bridal chamber '*Arrived at the door of the apartment, Colonel Ashton knocked and called, but received no answer except stifled groans . . . When he had succeeded in opening it, the body of the bridegroom was found lying on the threshold of the bridal chamber, and all around was flooded with blood.*'	Raimondo narrates how he heard a cry, went to Lucia's chamber, and what he found there Ah! Dalle stanze ove Lucia (Ah! From the rooms where Lucia)
They then search for Lucy and eventually discover '*. . . something white in the corner of the great old-fashioned chimney of the apartment. Here they found the unfortunate girl, seated, or rather couched like a hare upon its form – her head-gear dishevelled; her night-clothes torn and dabbled with blood – her eyes glazed, and her features convulsed into a wild paroxysm of insanity.*'	'*Lucia enters in a short white dress, her hair is dishevelled, and her face, covered with the pallor of death, makes her seem more like a spectre than a living creature. She has a stony stare, her convulsive movements and ill-omened smile show not only a terrified mind, but also sure signs that her life is near its end.*' ▼
As they carry her out she murmurs '*. . . with a sort of grinning exultation – 'So, you have ta'en up your bonny bridegroom?*'	▼ ▼

Table 8.2 (*cont.*)

The remainder of the scene is Cammarano's invention		
		Scene and aria Lucia enters
Recitative	Lucia: Il dolce suono (The sweet sound)	Lucia fantasies as she remembers her meeting with Edgardo at the fountain and the nuptials she wanted. The music is fragmented, with snatches of melody appearing and disappearing.
Cantabile	Lucia: Ardon gli incensi (The incense is burning)	She 'sees' her wedding. This is the *cantabile* section but initially it is the flute that 'sings' as Lucia continues in *arioso* over it. She starts to sing *cantabile* and then ends with a long cadenza[1].
Tempo di mezzo	Raimondo: S'avanza Enrico! – Enrico approaches!	
Cabaletta	1 Lucia: Spargi d'amaro pianto Spread with bitter tears 2 Lucia: Ah sì	1 This is a *coloratura* aria, but very slow for a *cabaletta*. 2 It becomes fast at the end on the words 'Ah sì' as the others join in to create a true *stretta*.
	Enrico: Si tragga altrov Lead her away	The scene ends quietly and darkly with a dialogue between Raimondo, Enrico and Normanno.

Note: Corghi (1981).

The two commonest forms of the aria were:

- Strophic-form aria, such as Desdemona's 'Willow Song' in act III of Rossini's *Otello*, or Nemorino's 'Una furtiva lagrima' in act II of *L'elisir d'amore*. These consist of several verses in each of which the melody is repeated. However, this apparently simple form can be used dramatically. In *Otello*, for example, the third verse of Desdemona's ballad is interrupted as she becomes aware that she has ominously sung the wrong words and the window is shaken by a sudden blast of wind before she continues 'Ascolta il fin de' dolorosi accenti' (Hear the end of these sad words).
- The two-part aria, consisting of contrasting sections, usually a slow *cantabile* followed by a fast *cabaletta*. Examples are Count Almaviva's 'Ecco ridente in cielo'

at the start of act I of *Il Barbiere di Siviglia* or Rosina's later 'Una voce poco fa'. Especially famous is Tancredi's act I, scene v 'Oh patria! Dolce, e ingrata patria!' with 'Di tanti palpiti' as the *cabaletta.*

As in the eighteenth century, conventions affected where arias were placed. The first act of an opera was considered as the *Introduzione* and usually consisted of separate numbers designed to set the mood and introduce the main characters. This could be varied to work on an audience's expectation, as in *Matilde di Shabran,* where the male lead does not make his appearance until the quartet, almost half an hour into the act.

The most significant formal use of the aria was as part of the kind of sequence shown in the second part of Table 8.2. This structured unit allowed the composer to make a *dramatic* unit out of a series of recitatives and melodies by treating the arias as 'movements' within a larger whole, each with its own dramatic and musical style and function. The libretto had, therefore, to configure the narrative into *situazione* that could be realised through a series of defined musical elements. The result was a formula common to all operas of the *primo ottocento* that was later referred to as the *solita forma* (the usual form) (see Senici, 2004: 97). This is not a technical expression, however, and is here called the tripartite form.[3]

The tripartite form or sequence uses the aria forms above, but with additional dramatic implications:

- The *cantabile*: contemplation of a predicament;
- The *tempo di mezzo:* a dramatic interruption with a noticeable change of mood and *tempo*;
- The *cabaletta*: a fast(er) section in which the character resolves to act. This can run into or become a *stretta.*

In addition there is almost always an introductory *recitative* which consolidates the predicament, and a *tempo d'attacco,* between the *recitative* and the *cantabile* (Balthazar, 2004: 49–68) (Table 8.3).

This formula was often applied quite mechanically, but it could be varied to great effect as in the *Lucia* 'mad scene'. Here Donizetti varied the musical patterns so as both to satisfy and challenge the audience's expectation. The introductory *recitativo* is unusually lyrical but made up of a series of melodic fragments; the *cantabile* ends with an unusually long cadenza[4] and the *cabaletta* is split between two sections, the first of which is unexpectedly slow with the normal tempo achieved only in the second part. Finally, instead of ending with the *stretta* as a moment of high musical drama, the scene simply fades away in the final dialogue.

Table 8.3 *The tripartite structure, with additions*

		Main sections	
A1		Orchestral introduction	Sets the tone and atmosphere of the scene
A2		*Recitativo*	Consolidation of the narrative position
A3		*Tempo d'attacco*	Stiffening of resolve
B	1	*Cantabile*	Contemplation of the predicament
C	2	*Tempo di mezzo*	An interruption (messenger, realisation of the need to act, etc.)
D	3	*Cabaletta* or *stretta* ('tightening')	The decision to act.

The tripartite form often includes a subsidiary character – a messenger, an attendant or *confidante* – as in the act I, scene iv *Scena e cavatina* from *Lucia di Lammermoor* (Donizetti, n.d.: 73–110) (Table 8.4).

The structure can also be used to develop a large-scale scene involving several characters and chorus, as in act I, scene iv of Bellini's *Norma*. This moves from recitative to the *cantabile* 'Casta diva', then through the *tempo di mezzo* to the final *cabaletta/stretta*. The *cabaletta* has an unexpectedly moderate first section as Norma reflects on her love for Pollione before she is drawn into the vehement *stretta*. Dramatically, it shows her opposition to the Britons' clamour for rebellion and, despite being Pollione's lover, having to join Oroveso and the chorus in the final section. The musical shape is itself exciting while developing the dangerous ambiguity of Norma's situation which lies at the heart of the opera (Table 8.5, p. 137).

The second act of Rossini's *Mosè in Egitto* shows how a longer, more complex scene could be created from a sequence of tripartite units. Act II, scene iii (no. 8) is a single-unit headed *Scene and quartet*. It consists of two linked tripartite units (bars 1–261 and 276–535) joined by a second *tempo di mezzo* (bars 262–275) (Table 8.6a, p. 138).

Within an overall shape that the audience would have recognised, Rossini creates tension and drama. Shifts in tempo and key signature reflect changes in mood, while the repeated rhythmic motif (marked * in Table 8.6b, p. 139), helps sustain the scene's musical unity.

Melody and its problems

Rossini had stressed the dual importance of rhythm and melody. But melody can easily disrupt dramatic flow. In the *Mosè in Egitto* example on p. 138, Elcia begins the

Table 8.4 Lucia di Lammermoor: *act i, scene iv*

	Figure			
A1	23	Orchestral introduction with prominent harp solo		Sets the tone and atmosphere of the scene.
A2	24	Recitative	Lucia and Alisa: Ancor non giunse He has not yet come	Alisa is frightened as they make their stealthy entrance.
A3		*Tempo d'attacco*	Recitative passage marked *crescendo e incalzando* (crescendo and increasing in tone and speed) for Lucia: Ah, tu lo sai Ah, you know	Lucia, increasingly breathlessly describes why the place is terrifying.
B	25	*Cantabile*	Lucia: Regnava nel silenzio Silence reigned	Lucia describes her vision of the girl murdered once by a Ravenwood.
C	28	*Tempo di mezzo*	Alisa and Lucia: Chiari, O Dio Clearly Oh God	Alisa begs Lucia to abandon the tryst.
D	29	*Cavatina*	Lucia: Quando, rapito in estasi When, rapt in ecstasy.	Lucia is overpowered by her burning love.

tune starting 'Mi manca la voce' at bar 267 which is then repeated by each character, using not only the same tune but the identical words. Finally they combine and sing it *ensemble*. Rossini could have given each character their own melody, or at least their own text. Instead, he ignores dramatic probability and simply repeats it allowing the audience to enjoy the tune *per se*. There is a kind of dramatic intensity as the musical dynamic urges the scene to its concluding *stretta*. Where Beethoven employs musical *development*, Rossini uses repetition and sheer melody. However melody *per se* can also inform the dramatic moment. The Finale of act ii of *Lucia di Lammermoor* is, again, a complex scene consisting of three numbers (8, 9 and 10) each with its own dynamic (Table 8.7a).

The detail shows Donizetti, and his librettist, using this traditional structure consonant with the demands of the drama (Table 8.7b).

The two focal points are the *cantabile* sextet and the *stretta*. The sextet is a moment frozen in time, not unlike 'Mi manca la voce' in *Mosè*, although here each character has their own text. The repetition creates a musical *crescendo* that parallels the scene's increasing dramatic tension.

Table 8.5 Norma: *act i, scene iv*

Scene iv: *Scena e cavatina*					
Recitative	E♭ 4/4	*Recitativo*	Norma, Oroveso, chorus	Sediziose voci Seditious voices	Norma addresses the Britons' call for rebellion.
Cantabile	F 2/8	*Andante sostenuto assai*	Norma, and then Oroveso, chorus	Casta diva Chaste goddess	Norma prays to the moon – while the others add a rhythmic undercurrent.
Tempo di mezzo	E♭ 4/4	*Allegro*	Orchestra	Approaching march	
		Allegro assai maestoso	Norma, Oroveso, chorus	Fino al rito The rites are ended	As the Romans approach, Norma and the others decide to act.
		Poco più lento	Norma	Ma punirlo il cor non sa But my heart cannot punish him	Norma reflects on her inner conflict.
Stretta/ cavatina	F 4/4	*Allegro*	Norma	Ah! Bello a me ritorna Ah! Bring back the beauty to me	She exclaims that she longs for her first love to return.
			Norma, Oroveso, chorus	Ma irato il Dio s'affretta But an angry god hastens	Chorus and Oroveso await revenge – Norma awaits a renewal of her love.

However the final *stretta* is another matter. Here the melody's short melodic lines and galloping rhythm seem inappropriately jaunty. It is supposed to be furious, anguished, violent, horrified – but is none of these. After the intensity of the sextet it is bathetic, a common problem. Within the tripartite form, where *cantabile* melodies are usually easily assimilated into the drama, this is rarer with the *cabaletta* and *stretta*, such as the second part of Tancredi's entry aria 'Di tanti palpiti' which scarcely sounds like a profoundly moved exile in agitated expectation. Composers

Table 8.6a Mosè in Egitto: *act II, scene iv, overall structure*

Scene	
1–43	Orchestral introduction
46–114	*Recitative* – including *arioso* passages
115–158	*Cantabile*
159–192	*Tempo di mezzo*
193–261	*Cavatina* – but in two sections, the second of which is *legato* and therefore seems to return to a *Cantabile* but is in fact followed by a
Quartet	
262–275	*Tempo di mezzo* – standing between the two main sections
276–325	*Cantabile*
326–366	*Tempo di mezzo*
367–535	*Stretta*

were conscious of this difficulty, as Pacini suggests: 'My *cabalette* did not spring, like limpid waters from a pure fount, but were very much the fruit of considerable thought and conscientious study of how to set the various poetic metres so that their melodies were not reminiscent of other musical ideas; something all too easy to do, especially in the first throes [of composition]' (Pacini, 1865: cap. XI).

Where this kind of writing is far more successful is in comedy where *brio* suits the situation, as Rossini recognised: 'I had a greater aptitude for the *opera buffa* I was happier dealing with comic rather than tragic subjects. But I hardly had a choice of libretti which were imposed on me by the impresarios' (Rognoni, 1968: 404). *L'Italiana in Algeri* provides an interesting example, particularly since Rossini had alterations made to a libretto which Luigi Mosca had set five years earlier. The most notable – perhaps notorious – of these were the 'new alliterative and onomatopoeic effects' (R. Osborne, 1993: 162) starting at fig. 66: Isabella, Elvira and Zulma's 'Nella testa ho un campanello/Che suonando fa din din' (In my head I have a bell/which sounds din din). But this is not Rossini happily setting nonsense. It is his understanding of how to construct the *finale* to an act whose narrative is potentially tragic but which has to allow the audience to enjoy the anticipation of comedic healing (Table 8.8).

Table 8.6b Mosè in Egitto: *act II, scene iv, detailed analysis*

Scene				
Orchestral introduction				
1–13		Andantino 4/4 E♭	* Repeated figure of two quavers, two demi-semi-quavers and a semiquaver.	Darkness and tentative entry of the characters.
14–23	91		* Repeated figure continues with solo clarinet melody.	
24–31			* Repeated figure continues with new solo flute melody.	
32–43	92		Resounding chords and a bridge passage end the Introduction.	
Recitative (but incorporating lyrical – *arioso* – sections)				
44–60	93		* Recitative over music from the Introduction.	Elcia: Dove mi guidi? Where are you leading me?
61–73	94		Recitative	Elcia: E in così mesta And in such a predicament
74–81	95		* Arioso over music from the Introduction.	Osiride: Se di maschil coraggio If with manly courage
82–87			Recitative	Elcia: Ah! Servir deggio Ah! I must obey
88–101	96		Recitative – but assertive and dramatic.	Osiride: Di Armenia la Regina The Queen of Armenia
102–114	97		* Arioso over music from the Introduction including the chords that ended fig. 92.	Osiride: Giorni felici Happy days
Cantabile				
115–134		Andante maestoso 2/4 G major	*Cantabile*: first melody – each singing complementary lines.	Elcia: Quale assalto What daring
135–158	99		Duet in parallel harmony: second melody.	Elcia: Rendi a me Restore to me Osiride: Tu di amor poter divino Thou divine power of love

(*cont.*)

Table 8.6b (*cont.*)

				Quartet	

Tempo di mezzo

159–185		Allegro 4/4 Eb	* *Arioso* over themes from the Introduction.	Elcia: Ah mira! Ah look!
186–189		Andante C major	Dramatic recitative.	Amaltea: Osiride!
190–192			Ensemble	Tutti: Al guardo mio non credo I do not believe my eyes

Cavatine (?)

193–237		Allegro	Amaltea, Aronne and Osiride again use the same melody in turn as they address one another.	Amaltea: Sperai che un folle ardore I hoped that a foolish passion
237–261	104		Elcia addresses Aronne but to a *legato* melody of her own.	Elcia: Non reo not guilty

Tempo di mezzo (?)

262–275	105		* Exclamations over music from the Introduction (as at bars 159–185).	

Cantabile

276–325		Andantino 3/4 Ab	A *cantabile* melody, sung four times. Elcia sings it through and then continues to repeat it each time with another character adding his or her voice.	Elcia: Mi manca la voce I lack the voice

Tempo di mezzo

326–342		Allegro 4/4 Eb	*Tempo di mezzo*	Amaltea: Costei dal suo lato Now remove from his side
343–366	109		*Tempo d'attacco* (?)	Elcia: Deh servi allo stato No, serve the state

Stretta

367–535		Vivace C major	*Stretta* for all four characters and chorus.	Fiera guerra mi sento I sense fierce war

Table 8.7a Lucia di Lammermoor: *act II Finale, overall analysis*

Number	Designation	Formal structure
8	Coro e cavatina	Introduction
9	Scena e quartetto	Recitative
	Sestetto e coro	Cantabile
10	Continuation and stretta of the Finale (Final ensemble)	Tempo di mezzo Stretta

As at the end of act I of *Il barbiere di Siviglia*, the *brio* of the *stretta*'s melody and rhythm are an analogue of the comedy. A dialectic is set up between the enjoyment of the *musical* situation and the potential tragedy of the narrative.

In this way the *primo ottocento* struggled with its material: not so much that between words and music or both and drama, but between drama and melody. In *Opera and the Nature of Music* Wagner writes:

> Driven by his prickling sense of Life, Rossini tore the pompous cereclothes from this corpse ... Beneath the jewelled and embroidered trappings he disclosed the true life-giver of even this majestic mummy: and that was – *Melody* ... he made the opera-public of the world a witness to the very definite truth, that people were merely wanting to hear 'delicious melodies where mistaken artists had earlier fancied to make Musical Expression do duty for the aim and contents of Drama'.   (Wagner, 1994–5, II: 41–3)

Verdi

Verdi's life and work overlapped with those of Rossini, Donizetti and Bellini, but continued into the Risorgimento and its aftermath. Like his older contemporaries, Verdi suffered from the Austrian censorship which required moving Victor Hugo's *Le Roi s'Amuse* from the historical court of Francis I to the fictitious world of the Duke of Mantua for *Rigoletto*; the court of Gustavus III of Sweden to the American world of Riccardo, Conte di Warwick for *Un ballo in maschera*, and a host of other such changes in almost all the libretti before 1861. But the temper of the period changed after 1849–50 with the, albeit failed, First War of Independence. In any case, Verdi was of a different cast. He was far more interested in musical and dramatic innovation, the integration of words and music to create a cohesive operatic drama, the nature of operatic form and the changing political world around him.

Table 8.7b Lucia di Lammermoor: *act II Finale, detailed analysis*

Introduction				
8	Coro e cavatina	Chorus: Per te d'immenso giubilo Great joy for you	The chorus opens the scene with their rejoicing.	
		Arturo: Per poco fra le tenebre For a little in the gloom	This is a brief aria 'carved out' of the scene (hence 'cavatina' – an 'excavation') interrupting the chorus and increasing the dramatic irony before.	
		Chorus: Repeat of their opening		

Recitative +				
9	Scena e quartetto	Arturo: Dov'è Lucia? Where is Lucia?	a melodious recitative, briefly interrupted.	
		Quartet: Oh dolce invito! Oh sweet invitation!	as all four main characters briefly sing together, contrasting their different positions.	
		Lucia: Me misera! – Wretched me	and then return to solo lines.	
		At this point Edgardo enters, Lucia faints – but recovers in time to take part in the sextet.		

Cantabile				

(9)	Sestetto e coro	Edgardo: Chi mi frena in tal momento?
		        Who restrains me in such a
		        moment?
		Enrico: Chi raffiena il mio furore!
		        Who restrains my fury?
			1 This begins with Edgardo and Enrico singing their own verses in duet. This is followed by	

		Lucia: Io sperai che a me la vita
		        I hoped that with my life
		Raimondo: Qual terribile momento!
		        What a dreadful moment!
			2 Lucia and Raimondo with their verses, while Enrico and Edgardo interject.	

			3 All characters plus the chorus sing *ensemble* to a *cantablile* version of the main melody	

Table 8.7b *(cont.)*

Tempo di mezzo +			
10	Continuation and stretta of the Finale	Arturo/Enrico: T'allontana, sciagurato Away with you, you wretch	All characters and chorus now enter the quarrel until.
		Edgardo: Maledetto sia l'istante Cursed be the moment	Edgardo breaks in with a short, *bravura* aria in which he repudiates Lucia. It is a crucial moment.
		Lucia: Ah	All turn on Edgardo and then
Stretta			
		Various: Esci, fuggi Go, flee	the final ensemble – *stretta*.

Verdi's career falls into three main phases. Significantly the second, 'mature' phase coincided with the most active years of struggle for national independence, in which he played his own part (e.g. C. Osborne, 1971: 123–5) (Table 8.9).

Verdi's late abandonment of set pieces and 'numbers', and the consequent integrated dramatic flow, his control of subject-matter, libretti and staging all broke the mould of traditional Italian opera and made new developments, such as the *Verismo* movement, possible. Although he was not a theoretician like Wagner, he understood and appreciated Wagner's achievement and his own practice effected as substantial a change in the way opera was thought about and created, as this interview shows: 'When our conversation turned to Wagner, Verdi remarked that this great genius had done opera an incalculable service, because he had had the courage to free himself from the tradition of the aria-opera. "I too have attempted to blend music and drama in my *Macbeth*"' (Conati, 1986: 109). Like Wagner, and unlike Bellini, Donizetti and Rossini, Verdi became intimately involved in every aspect of opera production (see Balthazar, 2004: 260). This began with the business details of the contract and went on to include choice of subject and librettist; casting, stage design and production; structure of the libretto – the detail of the actual text, ranging from comments on verses, requirements for verses with particular metres and, as he grew more confident, even providing verses of his own. Like Wagner, Verdi conceived of his work as whole.

Table 8.8 L'Italiana in Algeri: *act I Finale*

233–267 [66] [67]	*Andantino*	Introduction		Orchestral introduction: flute and oboe, then clarinet Trio.
			Pria di dividerci da voi Before I would be clear from you	
268–291 [68]			Oh ciel! Oh heavens	Pizzicato accompaniment as the voices fragment the melodic line as they recognise one another.
292–358 [69]		Cantabile	Confusi e stupidi incerti Confused and stupid uncertainty	Trio: flowing, legato melody but with a strong 'swaying' rhythm enhanced by Mustafa's strong rhythmic bass line.
359–412 [72]	*Allegro*	Tempo di mezzo	Va sossopra il mio cervello My head is topsy-turvey	*Tempo di mezzo* heightened by Isabella's *fioritura*.
413–446 [75]	*Allegro vivace*	*Stretta*	Nella testa ho un campanello There is a bell in my head	All together in a *stretta* that becomes increasingly confused.
447–613 [77]				'Nel testo . . .' a melody but which is a pure dynamic of entanglement and *stretta* (tightening) of the situation, at once final and comic in both its words and music.

The role of the librettist

For Verdi the librettist was not a playwright but someone who would dramatise extant material in a way appropriate for musical setting and, crucially, follow Verdi's own conception and instinct. As soon as his reputation allowed, he chose his own material: 'Last year I chose *Il corsaro* as a subject, but when it [i.e. Byron's poem] was put into Italian verse I found it cold and lacking scenic effect. I changed my mind, therefore, and decided, even if it meant doubling my expense, to have another

Table 8.9 *Development of Verdi's operas in their context*

Politics and contemporaries		Verdi		
		1813	Born	
1829	Rossini retires			
1835	Bellini dies			
		1839–46	The 'galley years'	*Oberto – Attila*
		1847–71	Maturity/'middle style'	
1848	Donizetti dies			*Macbeth – Luisa Miller*
1849–50	(Failed) 1st War of Independence	1847–49	Initial innovation	
1851–7	The Years of Waiting	1851–62	Consolidation of middle style	*Rigoletto – La Forza del Destino*
1859–60	2nd War of Independence			
1861	Italy declared independent kingdom			
1868	Rossini dies	1865–71	Increasing innovation within middle style	Revision of *Macbeth – Aida*
		1881–93	Radical change	1 Revision of *Simon Boccanegra* 2 *Otello, Falstaff*

libretto made: Schiller's *I masnadieri*' (C. Osborne, 1971: 38), and did everything but write his own libretti. From as early as *Ernani* comes one of the first statements of his conception of the relative roles of composer and librettist: 'My *Ernani* is progressing, and the librettist [Piave] is doing everything that I ask' (C. Osborne, 1971: 18).

Bellini, Donizetti and Rossini had considered librettists like Felice Romani, in the tradition of Metastasio, as poets with their own qualities who would write poetic texts following the conventions of the time. Verdi saw his librettists as instruments doing those tasks that he himself simply could not manage: 'Now the libretto [for *Aida*] must be considered, or, rather, the versification, because at this point only the verses are needed. Would Ghislanzoni be able and willing to do this job for me? It would not be original work: explain that clearly to him; it is only a matter of making verses' (C. Osborne, 1971: 150). In 1857 he wrote to Tito Ricordi showing how, from at least 1847, he had approached the first stages of a new opera:

> Ten years ago, I decided to compose *Macbeth*. I wrote the synopsis myself, and what's more I wrote out the entire libretto in prose, with its distribution into acts, scenes, vocal numbers, etc. Then I gave it to Piave to turn into verse. As I was not entirely happy with his versification, I asked Maffei, with Piave's permission, to rewrite some verses and re-cast the witches' chorus in the third act and the sleep-walking scene.   (C. Osborne, 1971: 114)

But once the structure was agreed upon, Verdi continued to make suggestions and demands: '[In *I Due Foscari*] I think that here you should insert a very short recitative, then a solo passage for the Doge and a big duet. This duet, coming at the end, should be quite short. Work yourself into the proper state of feeling and write some beautiful verses' (C. Osborne, 1971: 23). Such requests were always intended to improve the drama, either because of the dramatic development or because of its musical needs:

> [*La Battaglia di Legnano*] One final, tiny favour I ask of you. At the end of the second Act, I should like four verses for Arrigo and Rolando (together) before
>
> Infamati e maledetti [Dishonoured and accursed]
>
> I should like to give some significance to this passage before the finale, so I don't want at this point to repeat the words. I require these verses to be strong and full of energy. The idea I want to express is this: 'A time will come when your descendants will shrink in horror from bearing your name', etc. etc . . . then 'Dishonoured and accursed' etc.
>
> And tell me (don't be frightened to!): in the ensemble of the introduction I need to have another voice, a tenor. Could one include, for example, one of Arrigo's retinue? . . . He could help Arrigo when he is wounded. Let me know about this.
>   (C. Osborne, 1971: 59)

Wagner's ability to write his own libretto was a source of envy to Verdi and later Puccini, who regretted the time wasted waiting for his librettists to furnish material – or get it right to his specification. Part of the novelty of Boito's *Mefistofele* was that this was the first Italian opera with libretto and music by the same artist. But as Verdi grew in stature he felt more confident even in the literary area. The last scene of *Aida* particularly concerned him, above all the need to avoid the platitudes of a final farewell and death scene:

> Here, then, is the last scene, for which I need the following changes . . . At the end, I should like to avoid the usual death agonies, and not have words like 'I'm failing. I'm going before you. Wait for me. She is dead. I'm still alive', etc. etc. I

should like something sweet, other-worldly, a very short duct, a farewell to life. Aida should then fall calmly into the arms of Radames. Immediately, Amneris kneeling on the stone the vault, should sing a *Requiescant in pacem*, etc. I shall write the scene down to explain myself better.

[There then follows his versified version of the Final Scene, Verdi commenting] These are just mixed up words to be worked into beautiful verses by you. [And ending:]

Radames: Die? you, so innocent,
Die? You? (Eight beautiful seven-syllabled lines for singing)

(C. Osborne, 1971: 164–6)

Above and beyond these examples there is the magnificent correspondence between Verdi and Boito for the revision of *Simon Boccanegra* and then the creation of *Otello* and *Falstaff* (Weaver, 1994).

Casting

Casting was always a major concern, and might even affect the choice of subject:

As soon as possible I will let the Presidency know the subject of the opera, which will depend on the singers I will have. For example if I were to have an artist of the power of Ronconi, I would choose either *Re Lear* or *Il corsaro*, but since it will probably be best to rely on the prima donna, I could choose either *La fidanzata d'Abido* or something else where the prima donna is the protagonist.

(Weaver, 1977: 157)

Staging

Once an opera was complete Verdi became involved in every aspect of the production. The Romantic period saw a growing concern with historical detail on stage. This reached its apogee in the middle of the century with the productions of the Saxe-Meiningen company in Germany and Charles Kean in England. The latter were usually accompanied by essays on the historical provenance of Shakespeare's plays as a basis for the 'archaeological' approach to set design. It is in this spirit that Verdi writes to Tito Ricordi asking him to communicate important information to the French designer of *Macbeth*:

Please let Peronne know that the era in which *Macbeth* takes place is much later than Ossian and the Roman Empire.

Macbeth assassinated Duncan in 1040, and he himself was killed in 1057.

In 1039, England was ruled by Harold, called Harefoot and of Danish extraction. He was succeeded in the same year by Hardicanute, half-brother of Edward the Confessor.

Don't forget to tell Peronne this, because I believe he is making a mistake about the period.   (C. Osborne, 1971: 40–1)

There could be no greater contrast with the historic farrago of operas such as Mercadante's *Maria Stuarda, regina di Scozia*, where the historical is treated as no more than a suggestion for a romantic love tragedy.

Physically, staging with wings and backdrop remained as they had been in the seventeenth and eighteenth centuries. However as halls, palaces, prisons, etc. became a working part of the production, so anomalies such as entrances from the wings and thus apparently through walls, seemed intolerable. Sets with practical elements, such as doors and balconies, became increasingly important. Bellini's *La Sonnambula* (1831) demanded at least the roof on which Elvina has to somnambulate. In later productions this was extended to a plank perilously leading from the roof over a mill-stream: physical production was an inherent part of the dramatic effect of this climactic scene.

Verdi's operas for La Fenice in Venice were designed by the innovative Giuseppe Bertoja. Staging – scenery and lighting – became an inherent part of his thinking about the operas, and *Attila* shows the extent to which Verdi conceived his operas visually: 'The curtain must go up to reveal Aquileja in flames, with a chorus of people, and a chorus of Hun . . . ' (Radice, 1998: 226). The importance – as well as the novelty and cost – of this required the impresario Alessandro Lanari to write to the directors of the theatre: 'Maestro Verdi, who feels especially strongly, advises me that for several of the scenes he would like to fill the entire stage and, to use his own words, he says, "what I would like to be sublime is the second of scene six [second part of the Prologue], which is the beginning of the city of Venice. Let the sunrise be done well, since I want to express it with the music"' (Radice, 1998: 226). The scene requires both a practical balcony and the arrival of small boats, and there is a note added to Bertoja's design for the scene that refers to both the practical elements of the set and the lighting: 'As written in the opera by Maestro Verdi – All the buildings were [constructed] in separate pieces, and the background of the sky changed from the storm to the serene sunrise' (Radice, 1998: 226). Lighting is conceived as an essential part of the musical/visual score in the last scene of *Rigoletto*:

[the machinist] will have to accept my ideas and make the thunder and lightening occur precisely according to the music and not (as usually done) by chance. I would like the lightening bolts to transpire as a 'zigzag' on the upstage drop, etc. . . . etc. . . .

A human body! (*lightning flash*) My daughter! God! My daughter! Ah no! It's impossible! She's on her way to Verona! It was a vison! (*final lightning flash*).

(Radice, 1998: 231)

In some cases, aspects of the opera were only possible because of the new practical scenery. The quartet in act III of *Rigoletto* only works if the audience can see inside the tavern so that they can observe both the Duke and Maddalena while watching Gilda and Rigoletto's reactions outside. The music, with its separate lines for all four characters, is mirrored by the visual action: the combination is what makes the scene so dramatic, truthful – and ironic. The device is simple, but without it one of the most striking scenes in nineteenth-century opera would have been unthinkable. Significantly, this was the scene chosen for the cover of the first edition of the 1851 piano score. As with the text for *Aida*, Verdi went so far as to draw the way in which he wanted the stage set: 'You have some queries on the entrances and exits of the characters. Nothing is easier or simpler than this production, if the designer produces a set as I imagined it when I was writing the music . . . ' (C. Osborne, 1971: 250–2).

Musical form (*Macbeth*)

In his first operas Verdi used the same standard forms as Rossini, Bellini and Donizetti. This started to change in *Macbeth*. This is the first opera that clearly marks the beginning of his maturity, accompanied by growing insistence on complete control of his work. It is also the first opera that allowed him to engage with a drama worthy of his own musico-dramatic genius. 'Here is the scenario of *Macbet* [*sic*]. This tragedy is one of the greatest human creations! . . . If we cannot make something great from it, let's try at least to make something out of the ordinary' (Weaver, 1977: 168).

Verdi was clear that there were two vital moments in the opera:

> Tell them that the two most important numbers in the opera are the duet between Lady Macbeth and her husband, and the sleepwalking scene. If these two numbers fail, then the entire opera fails
> they must be acted and declaimed
> in a voice hollow and veiled:
> otherwise the effect will be
> lost. The orchestra muted.

(C. Osborne, 1971: 59–60)

Similarly, he insisted on the kinds of voices he needed, especially for Lady Macbeth: 'Tadolini has a beautiful and attractive figure, and I want Lady Macbeth to be ugly and evil. Tadolini sings to perfection, and I don't want Lady Macbeth to sing at all ... [her] voice should be hard, stifled and dark (C. Osborne, 1971: 59–60). Verdi required a singer for whom character depiction and drama were more important than, or the essential condition for, *bel canto* beauty *per se*.

The opening of act i, scene ii shows him exploiting the tripartite form in ways that deviate from an audience's expectations:

- The 'recitative' section becomes a *parlando* and evocative *arioso* (bars 26–51) interrupted by the repeated *tremolando* opening at bar 34.
- The *cantabile* is marked *Grandioso* and introduced by a misleadingly gentle orchestral section (bars 52–61). This is not a lyrical *cantabile* movement in any ordinary sense.
- The *cabaletta* is marked *allegro maestoso* and is unusually controlled and self-assuredly triumphant rather than merely urgent.

Similarly Verdi exploits the vocal line. For example, the powerful octave leap from G to high G at bars 39/40 which is followed by the repeated G and then a high C followed by the *fioritura* in bar 49. What should be the *cantabile* opens on a high F (bar 63) repeated at bar 67, combined with the insistent rhythm these turn standard forms into a powerful expression of Lady Macbeth's character (Table 8.10, p. 151).

The importance and problems of performing the *Gran scena e duetto* for Macbeth and his wife required innumerable rehearsals including a final session as the first-night audience waited. It shows how important it was to Verdi and how novel and difficult it was for both singers and audience at the time:

> Verdi asked us, as a favour for another piano rehearsal of that accursed duet ... The 151st took place, while the audience clamoured impatiently in the theatre.

> And that duet – to say that it aroused enthusiasm and fanaticism would be a great understatement. It was something unbelievable, new, unheard of.
>
> (Conati, 1986: 26–8)

The scene moves from Macbeth and Lady Macbeth's first meeting, through Duncan's arrival, into Macbeth's soliloquy, and the couple's duet following the murder (Table 8.11a, p. 153).

The duet radically consists of a series of short sections. Rather than the large blocks dictated by the traditional musical form, Verdi mercurially shifts his material to reflect the changing mood of two characters in desperate dialogue. A letter to the singers who would create the leading roles (Felice Varesi and Marianna Barbieri-Nini) shows where Verdi's priorities lay: 'I will never stop urging you to study the dramatic situation and the words; the music will come by itself. In a word, I would be happier if you serve the poet better than the composer' (Phillips-Matz, 1993: 199).

Table 8.10 Macbeth: *act* I *scene ii*

1–25	Orchestral introduction		Violent chords alternating with rising and falling *tremolando* in the strings, then *diminuendo* as Lady Macbeth enters.
26–28	*Recitative* (?)	Nel dì della vittoria In the day of victory	Lady Macbeth *parlando* as she reads the letter over a held chord in the strings.
29–33		Ambizioso spirto Ambitious spirit	Unaccompanied *arioso* as she launches into her hopes and fears for her husband.
34–38			Repetition of the opening *tremolando* strings and chords.
39–51		Pien di misfatti Full of misdeeds	Another outburst, with *tremolando* accompaniment and a florid ending on the word 'retrocede' (draws back).
52–61			The orchestra sets up a false expectation in its *piano* triplet introduction to the *cantabile*, interrupted by a bar's silence as
61–76	*Cantabile* – Grandioso	Vieni! T'affretta! accendere Come! hasten! arise	the key changes to E♭ major with an insistent syncopated rhythm in the strings, marked *grandioso*.
77–93			Repetition, but dominated by her call to the sprits 'Che tardi?' (Why tarry?). At bar 82 she almost seems to be wooing them, ending at bar 91 with another florid, but steely cadenza.
94–121	*Tempo di mezzo*	Al cader della sera il Re At nightfall the king	The key changes to A major as a servant enters. The music describes his hurried entry but also sustains the tension from the aria into the narrative section.
122		Duncano sarà qui? Duncan will be here?	As soon as he has left, Lady Macbeth cries out in wonder and exaltation, again, as at bars 29–33, unaccompanied and marked *Tutta forza* (With full force) at bar 127.

(*cont.*)

Table 8.10 (*cont.*)

130–135			As she ends *ff*, the orchestra breaks in with strongly accented chords, followed, again by a bar's silence.
136–166	*Cabaletta* – Allegro maestoso	Or tutti sorgete Now everything arise	The key shifts to E major marked *Allegro maestoso* for the *cabaletta*, ending (bars 161–165) in increasingly triumphant *fioritura*.
167–175			An orchestral bridge back into
176–225			repetition of 136–166 but with an added triumphant coda for Lady Macbeth herself.

He also shows how his whole thinking about opera was changing: 'this is a drama that has nothing in common with the others, and we all must make every effort to render it in the most original way possible. I also believe that it is high time to abandon the usual formulas and procedures, and I think that by doing so one could make much more of it, especially you, who have so many resources' (Phillips-Matz, 1993: 199–200). Throughout, the listener is constantly aware of the dislocation of the expected traditional forms of both the whole scene and its individual elements (Table 8.11b, p. 154).

Finally, an example of Verdi's handling of the finale. Rossini had despaired of the formulaic nature of the finale: 'And do you know what we called that [moment] in Italy at the time? The row of artichokes. I was perfectly aware of the silliness of the thing: it gave me the impression of a line of porters who had come to ask for a tip. It was a custom – a concession that one had to make to the public' (Servadio, 2003: 203). In act I of *Macbeth*, Verdi turns the Finale into a powerful musical and dramatic moment, isolating the solo characters in the great outcry for justice following the discovery of Duncan's murder (Table 8.12, p. 156).

Rigoletto: melody, subject and convention

Verdi was not unique in wanting to abandon the straitjacket of the musical and dramatic conventions of the *primo ottocento*:

> I have continued with the revolution begun in Il giuramento: forms varied – trivial Gabalette [*sic*] banned, *crescendo* exiled – Tessitura shortened – less repetition – Some novelty in the Cadenzas – Attention to the dramatic element: the Orchestration rich, without covering the Singing – Removed long solos in

Table 8.11a Macbeth: *act i, scene iii, nos. 5 and 6 prior to Macbeth and Lady Macbeth's duet*

No. 5 Scena e marcia	
1–23	Macbeth and Lady Macbeth greet one another and agree to the murder.
24–30	Distant sounds of Duncan's arrival.
31–35	They prepare to greet Duncan.
36-end	March as Duncan enters and exits to his rooms.

No. 6 Gran scena e duetto	
1–67	Macbeth's 'Mi si affaccia un pugnal?!' (Is this a dagger?!)
68–82	Macbeth goes to Duncan's chamber and Lady Macbeth's enters.
83–93	Lady Macbeth awaits Macbeth's return in a still, nocturnal passage, interrupted (bar 87) by a haunting figure on the cor anglais and bassoon. At bar 91 a cry from Macbeth increases the sense of lonely stillness.
94–316	The extraordinary *Gran duetto* that now follows can be divided into the traditional tripartite form. However, its fragmentation in response to the developing situation and the characters' rapidly changing reactions, completely transcends the traditional structure. The value in seeing how it may be divided is the demonstration of how radical it truly is:

Formal structure of the duet proper		
94–153	*Recitative*	Macbeth: Tutto è finito (All is done): *Recitative* section but with melodic fragments and *arioso* writing within it.
154–232	*Cantabile*	Macbeth: Allora questa voce (then that voice): *Cantabile* section, but with no vocal congruence. Rather, the effect is of the *cantabile* being continually broken.
233–271	*Tempo di mezzo*	Lady Macbeth: Il pugnal là riportate Take the dagger back
272	*Cabaletta*	Lady Macbeth: Vieni altrove! (Come away!)

concerted passages, which left the other parts frozen, spoiling the action . . . Others with greater genius and more imagination can complete this, and I shall be content with having instigated it.   (Mercadante, 1838)

The problem really lay in getting librettists to think beyond the conventional. For *Il trovatore* Verdi repeatedly asked for a libretto emancipated from anything that

Table 8.11b Macbeth: act I, scene iii, the duetto *proper* (bars 94–307)

94–97	Allegro		The shift to *allegro* and *tremolando* strings creates an expectation which enhances the dramatic effect of
98–99	Allegro Ab 6/8	Macbeth: Tutto è finito All is done	Macbeth's unaccompanied line, sung 'slowly with a stifled voice'.
100–104			A new urgency created by the sudden shift to 6/8 in quavers and then repeated semiquavers.
105–112		Macbeth: Fatal mia donna! Fatal lady!	Macbeth opens with a lyrical line echoed by Lady Macbeth. Both sing *sotto voce*: secretive and nervous.
113–120		Macbeth: Io (I)	The melody is lost. The musical and dialogue line fragments as the two nervously question one another.
120–126		Macbeth: O vista, oh vista orribile! O ghastly, ghastly sight!	Macbeth completely disrupts the flow with his exclamation, while Lady Macbeth attempts to calm him, singing a contrasting, even, musical line.
127–143		Macbeth: Nel sonno udii che oravano In sleep I heard them pray	Macbeth responds with a lovely melodic line. But instead of calm, it is his retreat into a memory/vision of the peace he has shattered. Now it is Lady Macbeth's turn to interrupt him with her impatient 'Folie!'
143–153		Lady Macbeth:. Folie! Folie! Che sperdono Folly, that will be dispersed	The line breaks down into dotted quavers and semiquavers – but the melody is carried by Lady Macbeth as she struggles to gain control.
154–172	Andantino Bb 3/8	Macbeth: Allora questa voce Then that voice	In a lyrical, sonorous declamation, accompanied almost entirely by wind and brass, Macbeth's inner voice condemns him.

Table 8.11b (*cont.*)

Bars	Tempo/Key	Text	Description
172–176		Lady Macbeth: Ma dimmi But tell me	Lady Macbeth understands the need to woo him back to sanity. She responds using the same musical line before launching into
176–187		Lady Macbeth: Sei van, O Macbetto You are proud, Macbeth	a lilting melodic line designed to calm him
187–195		Macbeth: Com'angeli d'ira Like angels of wrath	but Macbeth does not hear. Instead, he counters her melody with one of his own as he sees the angels of vengeance.
195–201		Lady Macbeth: Quell'animo trema His spirit quails	Lady Macbeth's line breaks down into quiet, urgent despair at her husband's frailty, while
201–210		Macbeth: Vendetta tuonarmi Thundering revenge	Macbeth abandons his melody and dwells on thoughts of Duncan's revenge.
210–232		Macbeth: Com'angeli d'ira Like angels of wrath	Macbeth returns to his previous melody, while Lady Macbeth continues to punctuate it with her quavers.
		In this part of the 'duet' the voices only behave in anything like the traditional way at bars 216–217 and 222–223. Verdi's duets are often referred to as 'disparate duets', and even this is almost two intertwined solos – yet producing a dramatic cogency and musical beauty at the same time.	
233–271	Allegro F 6/8	Lady Macbeth: Il pugnal là riportate Take back the dagger	This is the most normative section: following Macbeth's lyricism (*cantabile*) it is clearly the *tempo di mezzo* as Lady Macbeth returns the dagger.
272–307	Presto Ab 4/4	Lady Macbeth: Vieni altrove! Come away!	This is the only section that seems to conform to a traditional expectation. In a hurried *cabaletta* Lady Macbeth dominates as she carries the melody.
		The two voices genuinely complement one another although each has a quite different verbal and musical impulse. Unlike any traditional *cabaletta* this one ends *morendo* dying away into hurried silence as the two characters disappear to prepare for the murder's discovery.	

(*cont.*)

Table 8.12 Macbeth: *act 1, scene ii*, Scena e sestetto *Finale 1*

1–15	Allegro C 4/4	Macduff: Di destarlo per tempo / The time to awaken him	The key and rhythms create a new mood as Macduff enters and goes to wake Duncan.
16–29	Largo Eb	Banco: Oh, qual orrenda notte! / Oh, what a dreadful night!	All this changes as Banquo, left alone, is given a brief, lyrical aria of meditation on the previous night, full of foreboding and then drama at the *ff* bar 26. This is realised as
28–56	Allegro agitato	Macduff: Orrore! / Horror!	Macduff enters to report the murders. A strong rhythmic pulse impels the action forward until
57–59		Macbeths: Qual subito scompiglio! / What sudden disorder!	the Macbeths sing in unison (!) as
60–61		Banco: Oh noi perduti! / Oh we are lost!	Banquo enters, only to be
62–66		Soloists: Che fu? Parlate! / What is it? Speak!	interrupted by the anxious solo characters
67–72		Banco: È morto assassinato il Re Duncano / King Duncan is dead, assassinated	and then reveals Duncan's assassination in a high, solemn line accompanied only by a single note in the strings.

Bars	Tempo/Key	Text	Commentary
71–82	Adagio D♭	Tutti: Schiudi, inferno, la bocca ed inghiotti / Open, hell, your mouth and swallow	Immediately, over a drum roll, all sing in parallel, with portentous, thunderous tones.
83–109		Soloists: O gran Dio / O great God	There now follows an *a cappella* passage. All are stupefied (the score indicates *stupore universale* at bar 72). The soloists are echoed by the chorus, but with Banquo singing with the chorus until bar 92, setting him apart from the others.
			From bar 93 onwards portentous drum strokes punctuate.
		Macbeth: Da te lume, consiglio cerchiamo / We seek light and council from you	102–103: Ironically Banquo and Macbeth sing this line together, on their own.
110–133	Grandioso	Tutti: L'ira tua formidabile e pronta / Your anger awful and prompt	A throbbing rhythm starts over which soloists and chorus sing a driving melody that culminates in
134–153	Allegro	Tutti: Che stampasti sul primo uccisor / Who set a stamp on the first murderer	repetition of the final line, interrupted by
154–163			*a cappella* solo voices echoed by the chorus until
163–174		Tutti: In te fidiam / We have faith in thee	the final cry for divine justice.

would hinder the flow of the drama: 'the more Cammarano furnishes me with novelty, freedom of forms, the better I will do. Let him do whatever he likes: the bolder he is the more pleased I shall be' (Weaver, 1977: 183). He insisted:

> If in operas there were no more cavatinas, no more duets, no more trios, no more choruses, no more finales, and if the whole opera were one single piece, I would find that more reasonable and right. For this reason I tell you that it would be a good thing if, in the beginning of this opera, the chorus could be left out (every opera begins with a chorus); if Leonora's cavatina could be left out; and we begin right off with the Troubadour's song, and make one single act out of the first two acts; for these isolated pieces and the changes of scene ... make me feel that they are numbers from a concert rather than an opera. If you can do it, *do it.*
>
> (Phillips-Matz, 1993: 305)

In the event, Cammarano 'couldn't' and it was only Verdi's implacable desire to change the nature of operatic form that drove his librettists to innovate.

The 1850s, the unbearable 'Years of waiting' for liberation, saw a radical shift in Verdi's approach to subject-matter and musical forms. He turned to material that gave him unending problems with the censor – as he knew they would. Subjects became more political (*La battaglia di Legnano, Les Vêpres Siciliennes, Simon Boc-canegra, Un ballo in maschera*); or with more obvious social implications (*Luisa Miller*) and a radical shift in the notion of the hero:

> I want subjects that are new, great, beautiful, varied, strong ... and really strong, with new forms, etc. etc. and at the same time suitable for music ... for Venice I have written *La dame aux camélias* it is a contemporary subject. Another composer would perhaps not have done it because of the costumes, the period or a thousand other foolish scruples, but I did it with great pleasure. Everyone complained when I put a hunchback on the stage. Well, I wrote *Rigoletto* with great pleasure. The same with *Macbeth.*   (C. Osborne, 1971: 89)

Together with the prostitute and the crazed gypsy came the malign hunchback.

Like *Il trovatore*, *Rigoletto* contains a number of memorable melodies. But Verdi always uses these as a means to an end: 'Some want to be melodists like Bellini, some harmonists like Meyerbeer. I don't want to be one or the other ... Melody and harmony should only be tools for music-making in the hands of the artist' (C. Osborne, 1971: 196). Very few conform to the conventional models and when they do so it is for a dramatic reason. Melody is used to enhance the character's emotional state and the audience's seduction into the dramatic moment. There is, in addition, a constant sense of fragmentation as tempi shift in the longer scenes to reflect psychological change (Table 8.13).

The later operas continue to offer great melodic passages, such as King Philip II's *Introduzione e scena* 'Ella giammai m'amò' at the beginning of act IV of *Don Carlos*,

Table 8.13 Rigoletto: *the solo scenes and their musical and structural variety*

1 i	Duke: Questa o quella This one or that	Self-standing strophic *ballata* – a 'song' sung by the Duke in role.
I ii	Rigoletto: Pari siamo! We are alike!	Not an *aria* in any usual sense: closer to an *arioso* Shakespearean soliloquy, constantly changing tempo, and vocal line.
	Rigoletto: Ah! Deh non parla real misero Ah! Do not speak to hurt	For the first time the human face of the jester is revealed, in a beautiful and touching melody – that runs straight into his first duet with Gilda. The *scena* moves from *adagio*, through *allegro* (bar 16), *moderato* (31), *allegro* (42), *andante* (53), *allegro* (63) to *allegro vivo* as Gilda enters (70).
	Gilda: Gualtier Maldè . . . Caro nome Gualtier Maldè . . . Siveet name	Conventional *bel canto* but which establishes Gilda's innocence and naivety rather than being a technical display.
	Duke: È il sol dell'anima, la vita è amore It is the sun to my soul, light and love	In the middle of his attempted seduction, the Duke takes breath and sings a conventional – if attractive – love song: does he have real feelings?
II	Duke: Ella mi fu rapita! She has been stolen from me! Colei che prima potè in questo core She who first was able in this heart	A solo *scena* in four sections that seems to imply the standard tripartite form. But its extreme compression hardly conforms to the standard model as the Duke provides his own *tempo di mezzo* by repeating the opening line and then, in the final sections, instead of an impetuous *cabaletta*, sings a lilting meditation on Gilda that almost convinces us of the sincerity of his feelings.
	Ella mi fu rapita! She has been stolen from me! Parmi veder le lagrime I seem to see her tears	This *scena* again constantly changes tempo between *allegro agitato assai*, *allegro recitativo* (bar 23), *adagio* (36), *andante* (38), *allegro* (47), *adagio* (54) and then a change to 3/4 and G♭ (59) for the remainder.
	Rigoletto: Cortigani, vil razza dannata, Courtiers, vile damned race	This aria falls into four sections as Rigoletto moves from anger to begging for help. This first section is defined by its pounding rhythm.

(cont.)

Table 8.13 (*cont.*)

		Quella porta, assassini, m'aprite Assassins, open the door for me	The second section is a recitative explosion of futile anger and then
		Ebben piango ... Marullo Well then, I'll weep ... Marullo	beautiful melody with the orchestra quietly crying as he sings.
		Miei signori, perdono, pietate; My lords, pardon, pity;	Rigoletto finally begs, left almost with only the cello obligato to support him.
III		Duke: La donna è mobile Woman is fickle	Like his opening 'Questa o quella' this is a strophic 'song' that altogether shows the careless Duke's true nature.
		Rigoletto: Della vendetta alfin giunge l'istante! The moment of vengeance is here	This long scene is interrupted first by the dialogue with Sparafucile and then by the Duke's 'La donna è mobile'. But everything is designed to tighten the narrative and dramatic trap that Rigoletto has created for himself. Other than the Duke's song Verdi does not use melody at all, leaving it for the final duet, but here focussing everything on the tragic victim, Rigoletto, almost devoid of everything that the music of a Verdi opera is meant to provide.

or Carlo and Rodrigo's duet 'Dio, che nell'alma infondere amor' in act II, scene i. But from this period onwards Verdi makes free use of all the musical means at his disposal – melody, harmony, rhythm and traditional forms.

Final innovations (*Otello*)

By the time of the last two operas, *Otello* and *Falstaff*, Verdi felt able to write exactly as he wanted. No longer 'with one eye on the public and another one on art' (Weaver, 1994: xxi). Never one to lift the mask, he told a reporter: 'I write as I feel, the method does not concern me; if I think a certain style conveys my thought, I use it, even if it means composing in a new style. That is the way I have always composed' (Conati, 1986: 170). While to another who daringly asked 'Is it true there are no choruses in *Otello*?' he replied: 'There are choruses, duets, trios, a quartet, a finale ... are you satisfied?' (Conati, 1986: 178). This is just about true. Throughout these operas two, three or more characters sing together, but this barely constitutes 'duets', 'trios' or 'quartets' in the formal sense. When appropriate there are identifiable elements, such as Otello and Desdemona's duet 'Già nella notte' in act i, or Otello and Iago's duet 'Con questi fili' in act ii. But only because Verdi wanted to create a particular focus, and used conventional forms as a way of doing so.

The most obvious indication of the structural changes made in *Otello* is that there are no 'numbers'. Even in the late 'mature' operas such as *Don Carlos* and *Aida* the acts are divided between their musical sections which are either numbered or given headings such as *Scena e grande duetto*. Although dramatically *Don Carlos* is completely integrated, it is still built out of these discrete elements. By contrast, in *Otello* there are no such divisions. Each act is an indivisible entity, with the various actions and their music flowing seamlessly into and out of one another.

An impressive example is the ending (the term *Finale* is not used any longer) of act iii. This is an enormously complex sequence (which Verdi tried to clarify in his revision for Paris) in which several individual scenes often take place simultaneously. At the same time, unlike Wagner, Verdi maintained the true ensemble tradition. As a result, at several points it is the musical impulse that carries the drama forward, so that the characters' physical grouping on the stage rather than their individual words carries the narrative impact (Table 8.14, p. 162).

Structure, melody and orchestration

The distinguishing features of this passage are:

- the seamless flow as dramatic/musical episodes lead into and succeed one another;
- the subtlety and richness of the orchestration;
- the use of melodic motifs rather than distinct, let alone self-contained, tunes.

Through-composition

A comparison between the finales of *Macbeth* act i and *Otello* act iii reveals significantly different ways of thinking about operatic structure and composition. The *Macbeth* Finale consists of a sequence of separate, substantial blocks, each with its own musical logic. While there are distinct phases in the *Otello* Finale, these are all decided by their larger dramatic function. Unlike *Macbeth*'s series of elements, the *Otello* is a single long breath. However, one problem with such dense writing, in which so much happens musically and dramatically, is that the audience cannot follow every musical and verbal/dramatic line. This can make it seem as though the composer intended a purely musical effect. Verdi's comment on this passage is significant, not least in the light of the debate about the use of subtitles and surtitles:

> I too am a bit concerned about the printing of the third-act finale in the libretto, because I would really like the audience to be able to see and understand everything at a glance.

Table 8.14 *Otello: act III 'Finale'*

A 5	Allegro sostenuto 4/4 C	Chorus: Evviva! Alla riva Hurrah! To the shore	The people acclaim the Venetian embassy. Fanfares and the people's cries punctuate the final exchanges between Iago and Otello.
B 9			Iago leaves as the public scene takes over, leaving Otello alone to greet the ambassador. Complex fanfares sound and then

C		Chorus: Viva! Evviva! Viva il Leon
		    Hurrah! Hurrah! Long live
		        the lion
			a richly accompanied chorus welcomes the ambassadors – but this contrasts with the state in which the audience knows Otello has been left.

D		Lodovico: Il Doge ed il Senato The Doge and Senate	Ludovico greets Otello in a stately recitative, Otello responds in a suitably florid line; fanfares punctuate both.
E		Lodovico: Madonna, v'abbia il ciel My lady, may heaven	A descending figure at D 16 leads into a quieter, private scene as Lodovico greets Desdemona and Emilia comments (aside) on Desdemona's sadness.
E 12		Iago: Messere, son lieto Sir, I am delighted	Iago enters. His exchange with Ludovico is unaccompanied recitative save for the ominous woodwind.

F		Desdemona: Credo che in grazia tornerà
		    I think he will return to
		        grace
			Desdemona as so often, introduces a lyrical note with her sweet falling motif as she returns to the subject of Cassio: she is naive, good – and doomed.

G	Più mosso	Otello: Frenate dunque le labbrra loquaci Curb your babbling lips	The *più mosso* marking starts a new phase, as Otello turns on Desdemona to everyone's horror – above all Lodovico, who now
H		Lodovico: Quest'è dunque l'eroe? This, then, is the hero?	turns to Iago for an explanation.

Table 8.14 (*cont.*)

H 8		Otello: Eccolo Here he is	Cassio enters: Otello, aside, intends to study his reactions. Then a series of abrupt chords (bars 12–14) introduces a complex passage.
I		Otello: Messire! Gentlemen!	In stentorian tones, over *tremolando* strings, Otello announces his replacement by Cassio while
I5		Cassio: Infida sorte Treachesous fate	Cassio comments on fortune and
I 10		Iago: Inferno e morte! Hell and death	Iago angrily swears – emphasised by a sonorous chord.
I 14		Otello: Vedi? Non par che esulti See? He doesn't seem overjoyed	Otello, again over ominously *tremolando* strings, switches between public statement and vitriolic address to the weeping Desdemona until
J		Lodovico: Otello, per pietà Otello, for pity's sake	Lodovico, accompanied by solo wood winds, marked *con espressione*, begs him to stop.
J 4	Presto		Having announced his departure the next day Otello finally loses control: the tempo changes and a rush of downward strings followed by an upward sweep of strings and wind leads to
J 7		Otello: A terra! E piangi! To the ground! And weep!	a *ff* chord as he forces Desdemona to the ground singing high, almost strained unaccompanied notes followed by four pairs of bars in each of which a chord is played *decrescendo* by the full orchestra. Everything is set for an open confrontation between the various characters.

(*cont.*)

Table 8.14 (*cont.*)

J 18	Largo A♭	Desdemona: A terra!...si... To the ground...yes...	The strings now set up a faltering, rhythmic, descending figure played *pp* and *pizzicato*, while the woodwind create a disturbing progression from a single A to a second A/B resolving into a fourth, A/D, as Desdemona sinks, both physically and musically into the dust. She begins the passage *declamato* and then sings *cantabile* on the word 'piango' (I weep) as the chord progression is repeated. But her consistent vocal line turns this into a lyrical expression of her despair leading into
K	Più animato	Desdemona: E un dì sul mio sorriso And one day at my smile	a *tremolando* rising figure in the strings that sounds like the sun breaking through clouds as Desdemona remembers their first love, in a long melodic line, accompanied by quietly throbbing woodwind. This passage will reappear throughout the rest of the finale, before
K 6		Desdemona: Ed or l'angoscia And now the pain	the orchestra plays *stringendo* (contracting) as she contrasts the past with the present.
K 8		Desdemona: Quel sol sereno e vivido That sun serene and bright	The brighter sound returns in both the orchestra and vocal lines as she again recalls the past. Desdemona's pure, lyrical line, accompanied by a gently tripping *pizzicato* again portrays a character who remains pure and true: unable to comprehend what is happening to her or why.
L 5		Emilia, Cassio, Roderigo, Lodovico Chorus	All these sing *a cappella* apart from two *pizzicato* chords, pitying Desdemona as the female chorus interjects a plea for mercy.

Table 8.14 (*cont.*)

L 10	Desdemona: E un dì sul mio sorriso And one day at my smile	Desdemona's lovely phrase (K) now rises above the other characters in a long concerted passage in which:
L–Q		1 The female chorus is aghast at Desdemona's treatment; 2 The male chorus inveighs against Otello;
L 18–M 12		3 Iago persuades Otello to agree to Roderigo's murder.
N 1–4		Soloists and chorus continue as
N 5–O 10		4 Iago inveigles Roderigo into his plot.
O 10	Stringendo poco a poco – Tightening little by little	
O 12	Più mosso	The chorus, accompanied by pulsating brass, leads into a concerted outcry by all the characters, while
O 14	Iago: Corri al miraggio! Run after the mirage!	Iago mocks Roderigo's gullibility and admires his own duplicity; Roderigo resolves to follow Iago's advice.
O 19	Desdemona: Quel sol sereno e vivido That sun serene and bright	Desdemona's long line (K) sounds out alone and then continues with flowing string accompaniment as chorus and soloists resume, while Iago mocks and Roderigo resolves to act on his advice.
P	*Animando sempre poco a poco* Little by little more animated	This continues, but with a new, insistent triplet beat, driving all the characters forward to a point where something must happen.
P 7	Ritenuto	A version of Desdemona's lyrical line sounds out from the chorus and others, suggesting climax and finale, but

(cont.)

Table 8.14 (*cont.*)

Q	Allegro agitato C	Otello: Fuggite! Leave!	Otello completely loses control. All fall into confusion as he curses Desdemona and after the sudden eruption of a bar of brass semiquavers
R 7		Tutti: Orror! Horror!	recoil exclaiming in horror as the orchestra responds *tutta forza* describing their flight in descending semiquavers in the strings and rising figures in the woodwind.
R 13		Otello: Fuggirmi io sol non so! Only I cannot flee myself!	Over insistently rising quavers in the strings and with solo oboe and horn played *espressivo*, Otello states the real tragedy. Finally he can stand no more and faints.
T		Iago: Il mio velen lavora My poison works	Iago exults over the fallen Otello as the off-stage chorus continues to extol the heroic Otello.

Turn this page over and you will see what I would propose. If something better can be found . . . so much the better. Obviously, the page where there are the three columns should be complete in the middle of the libretto, with the stitching where there are the margins.

It is all right for Desdemona's solo to be printed at the bottom of the preceding page; in this way the audience will not be distracted, and would concentrate all its attention on her. Then, turning the page, they would find the whole hullabaloo of the ensemble laid out.   (Weaver, 1994: 103–5)

Orchestration

In this scene, the complexity of the vocal writing is enhanced by the role of the orchestra, which supports the singing while adding its own voice. Berlioz called the Italian opera orchestra a 'large guitar', by which he meant that its function rarely extended beyond accompanying the vocal line. This, of course, was never entirely fair. But compared with the growing sophistication of his own orchestral writing, it is broadly true. While Beethoven's orchestra in *Fidelio* accompanies and reinforces, it also plays its own role: commenting on the action, often adding its own voice as part of the narrative and the drama. This was rarely the case in Italy, and over the course of the century Italian music came to seem conservative and marginalised.

An important development over Verdi's career is his changing awareness of how the orchestra could be used. The list of instruments for *Macbeth* and *Falstaff* is the same, except for 'special effects' such as the guitar. What changes is his greater sense of colour, the independence of the orchestra's voice, and the more complex harmonic writing. Some direct comparisons illustrate this (Balthazar, 2004: 154–68):

- The atmospheric, but plain chords that open act I, scene ii of *Macbeth* and the complexity of the storm that begins *Otello*.
- The accompaniment, with its traditional (if apposite) use of woodwind, of 'Caro nome' (Dear name) in *Rigoletto* and the alert, commentatory voice of the orchestra in Iago's act II 'Credo'.
- The ballet music for the witches in *Macbeth*, and for the queen's entertainment in *Don Carlos*.

In each case the earlier writing is effective and apposite; in the later examples it is subtler, richer and more expressive.

Melody

Melody plays an important part in the *Macbeth* Finale, in particular consolidating the sequence in the imposing, broadly lilting last section 'L'ira tua formidabile e pronta' (Your anger awful and prompt). In *Rigoletto*, melody again plays a major part in characterising people and dramatic moments – as well as offering its traditional pleasures. This is not the case in *Otello*. There are fine, dramatically searching and attractive melodic themes (the act I duet, Iago's drinking song, the last section of Otello's act II duet with Iago, Desdemona's theme in the act III Finale, the Willow Song). But significantly only the fictionally 'sung' elements (the drinking and Willow songs) have self-contained melodies.

Inevitably Verdi was 'accused' by some critics of having become a Wagnerian. Eduard Hanslick offers a perceptive critique of how the music of the later operas works and how its style relates to the earlier operas:

> Verdi replied somewhat evasively to the suggestion that he had been influenced by Wagner: 'Song and melody should always remain a composer's prime concern.' In fact this is not the case in Falstaff, in the absolute sense of song and melody, as illustrated in the earlier Verdi operas . . . And yet the music of Falstaff possesses more the character of animated conversation and declamation than that of distinctive melody weaving its own beauty. That he knew how to blend this latter type of music perfectly with the flowing music of comedy, is proved by the second act of his Un ballo in maschera. (Conati, 1986: 245)

Grove, III (1997) notes that '*Otello* remains one of the most universally respected of Verdi's operas, often admired even by those who find almost all his earlier works unappealing' (*Grove*, 1997, III: 791). The implication is (probably) that even those who love Wagner are able to appreciate – even subscribe to – *Otello* (and *Falstaff*). Their through-composition and avoidance of 'numbers' with their focus on tunes seems to parallel Wagner's mature achievement. This may be, or seem to be, the case. Verdi was certainly aware of Wagner's music and had distinct, but carefully qualified praise, for several of the operas, in particular act II of *Tristan*, and understood the nature of his achievement: 'Verdi remarked that this great genius had done opera an incalculable service, because he had had the courage to free himself from the tradition of the aria-opera . . . Wagner surpasses every composer in his rich variety of instrumental colour, but in both form and style he went too far' (Conati, 1986: 245–6).

But more significant is Verdi's inherent development. This embraces not only technique but also a radical approach to, and understanding of, what opera, as a musico-dramatic form, was. By the late period, from *Don Carlos* onwards, Verdi was laying the foundations for a new kind of Italian opera that drew upon music and words, the voice and orchestra, set design and lighting and the singer as expressive vocalist and actor, to create an integrated expression of a single artistic vison.

Chapter 9

Grand opéra and the visual language of opera

Although '*Grand Opera*' is used as a general expression it is actually a technical term It refers to a specific kind of opera rooted in the French repertoire of the three decades following the Restoration. In particular it is associated with the serious operas of Auber, Halévy and Meyerbeer, significantly all written in collaboration with the playwright Eugène Scribe.

The interest in grand opera[1] lies in the works themselves, but also in their integration of words, music and physical presentation. While all operas are designed for stage production, grand operas were inseparable from the production practices and values that were built into their very fabric. This emphasis influenced Verdi and Wagner but beyond that changed the understanding of opera as a theatrical form and the audiences' expectation.

The role of the Opéra

Grand opera was in great part the product of socio-political trends. While the real beneficiaries of the Revolution had been the bourgeoisie, their place in the political world was initially resisted by the restored Bourbon monarchy. Both Louis XVIII and Charles X attempted to turn the clock back to the ethos of the *ancien régime*. This precipitated a series of violent confrontations between 1820 and 1848 as the monarchy, the middle classes and the newly developing radical (socialist) urban working classes, supported by intellectuals, students and idealists, jostled for political power. Throughout this turbulent period opera – and the Opéra itself – was used, supported, funded and attacked according to the needs of each successive administration (see Charlton, 2003: 26–7).

French international prestige had been destroyed by the Revolution and while Napoleon's Emperorship did something to raise the public image, this was undermined by the depredations of his warfare and his defeat at Waterloo. The task of the restored monarchy and successive governments was to rebuild the French state and economy, in part by reasserting its political and cultural identity. The opera, as the highest-profile art form, was required to play a significant role in this and became both a semi-official instrument of state and a barometer of changing public taste. As such, the opera's aesthetic was moulded as much by social as by artistic criteria. Grand Opera cannot be understood apart from these condition (see Hibberd, 2009). In addition, Grand Opera cannot be thought of outside the Opéra itself, whose funding, policy, directorship and artistic control directly reflected the disruption and changes in the state (Table 9.1).

The development of alternative forms: the Opéra-Comique

Through the eighteenth century new trends began to challenge the established repertoire. In particular, the performance of Pergolesi's *La serva padrona* in 1752 became a touchstone for those who found Italian opera more natural and melodious than the severe classical opera derived from Lully. The result was a shift towards a repertoire that was more overtly melodious, less rigid in its conventions and simply 'entertaining'.

The most obvious alternative was the development of the Opéra-Comique. In 1697 Louis XIV banished the Italian *commedia dell'arte* players (Comédie-Italienne) for their bawdy performances. Their repertoire, which mixed drama and song, was taken over by the popular Foire and Vaudeville theatres that had grown up in the great fairs at St-Germain and St-Laurent. This triggered a struggle with the recognised companies, but in 1714 they reached an accommodation, paying an annual fee to the Opéra under the generic title 'Opéra-Comique'. The name did not yet necessarily imply comedy, but opera that included dialogue. These comedic, melodious, light-hearted pieces appealed to, and helped develop, a middle-class, merchant audience. When the young Rameau arrived in Paris, he started by writing operas for the Foire theatres with his 1723 *L'Endriague* – a winged crocodile ultimately defeated by a knight in armour and Harlequin.

By the end of the eighteenth century the leading exponent of Opéra-Comique was Grétry. Two of his most popular works, *Zémire et Azor* (1771) and *Richard Coeur-de-Lion* (1704) were typical of the favourite subjects of opéra-comique. *Zémire et Azor* is a *féerie*, an oriental version of beauty and the beast, described as a 'comédie-ballet mêlée de chants et de danse'. *Richard Coeur-de-Lion* is a 'comédie mise en musique', based on romanticised history. Both include considerable spectacle. In act III of *Zémire*, the 'beast' Azor suddenly allows Zémire to see her distant family in a magic mirror, while act IV ends with the magical transformation of Azor's palace into one that is appropriate to his newly-restored human form. In act III of *Richard* there is a full-scale siege of the castle in which the king is captive.

Grétry's musical appeal was his combination of 'classical' numbers and attractive, simple melodies[2] such as Richard and Blondel's duet 'Une fièvre brûlante' (a burning fever) that they had supposedly composed together.[3] Grétry was wrongly accused

Table 9.1 *French constitutions and the Opéra, 1814–71*

	Regime change	Regime	The Opéra	
1789	French Revolution			
1790s			Run by the City of Paris	
1802			Taken over by Napoleon	
1807				Spontini: *La Vestale*
1809				Spontini: *Fernand Cortez*
1811			Funded by tax on other theatres	
Restoration				
1814	Restoration of the monarchy The White Terror	Louis XVIII (1814–24) Charles X (1824–30)	1815–30: subsidies of between 1,264,251 fr and 1,782,663 fr	
1819				Spontini: *Olimpie*
1820	Murder of the future heir			
1826				Rossini: *Le Siège de Corinthe**
1827			Run by the Comité de mise en scène	Rossini: *Moïse et Pharaon**
1828				Rossini/Scribe: *Le Comte Ory* **Auber/Scribe: *La Muette de Portici***
1829				Rossini/Jouy: *Guillaume Tell*
1830	July Ordinances July Revolution	'July Monarchy': Louis Philippe	Commission to examine running of theatres	

(cont.)

Table 9.1 (*cont.*)

	Regime change	Regime	The Opéra	
1831			Put on a fully commercial basis	**Meyerbeer/Scribe: *Robert le Diable***
1835				**Halévy/Scribe: *La Juive***
1836	Attempted coup			**Meyerbeer/Scribe: *Les Huguenots***
1838				Berlioz: *Benvenuto Cellini*
1840	Attempted coup			
1847				Verdi: *Jérusalem**
Second Republic				
1848	February Revolution	Louis Napoleon elected President		
1849				**Meyerbeer/Scribe: *Le Prophète***
Second Empire				
1852		Napoleon III: Hereditary Emperor		
1854			Overseen by the Imperial household	
1855				Verdi/Scribe: *Les Vêpres Siciliennes*
1861				Wagner: *Tannhäuser**
1864			Subsidy at government's discretion	
1865				Meyerbeer/Scribe: *L'Africaine* Verdi: *Macbeth**

(*cont.*)

Table 9.1 (*cont.*)

	Regime change	Regime	The Opéra	
1866			Directorship franchised	
1867				Verdi: *Don Carlos*
1870–1	Franco-Prussian War	Fall of Napoleon III	Run by the City of Paris	
Third Republic				
1871			Directorship franchised	

Note: *Operas especially revised for performance at the Opéra.

of having little technique. In fact, the complexity of the classical style was simply not appropriate to what he wanted to achieve. Even Berlioz could enthuse: 'It's delicious. The romance galvanizes the entire house. The whole thing has a fineness, a truthfulness, an inventiveness and good sense that are captivating' (Cairns, 1999, 2: 605). These operas make few demands on the listener, musically or intellectually. They are entertainment, designed for an unpretentious audience whose expectation was quality enjoyment after a day's work.

Opera in the Revolution and Restoration

Despite the Revolution, opera continued to be played in Paris, and under Napoleon's patronage it flourished as part of state policy, as one of his minsters declared: 'Through the union of art and talent, this unique spectacle provides a useful impetus to the fashion and luxury goods trade, attracts a throng of foreigners to Paris, and adds to the brilliance of this great city and – as befits it – to the genius and taste of the nation' (Barbier, 1995: 11). Finally, at the Restoration, the opera was given a special boost with the appointment of Rossini, the greatest name in European opera, as director of the Théâtre des Italiens. At the same time four of his operas were performed at the Opéra itself. Significantly, the third, *Le Comte Ory*, had a libretto by Scribe, while the last, *Guillaume Tell*, was on the grandest possible scale, in five acts and to a libretto derived from Schiller. Both set new standards of construction, length and grandeur.

Romantic demands

The scale of Rossini's last operas for Paris reflects a trend that was already manifest in French theatre. As in Germany, Romantic interest in history was accompanied by growing realism and physical detail in staging. In France this was pioneered by Victor Hugo:

> We are beginning to realize in our day that exactness in the matter of locality is one of the most essential elements of reality. The speaking or acting characters are not the only ones who leave a faithful impression of the facts upon the mind of the spectator. The place where this or that catastrophe occurred is an incorruptible and convincing witness to the catastrophe; and the absence of this species of silent character would render incomplete upon the stage the grandest scenes of history.   (Hugo, 1827: 689)

This became encoded in the script. *Hernani*, written three years after *Cromwell*, opens:

> Saragossa. A bedroom. Night. A lamp on a table. First scene. – Doña Josefa Duarte, *veiled, in black, with the body of her skirt sewn with jet, in the fashion of Isabella the Catholic;* Don Carlos.
>
>   Doña Josefa, *alone.* (*She draws the crimson curtains of the window and puts some papers in order. Someone knocks at a small concealed door on the right. She listens. There is a second knock.*)
>   – Can it be him already? (*Another knock*)
>   It's from the hidden flight
>   Of stairs. (*A fourth knock*)
>   Quickly. Open.
>   (*She opens the small covered door. Carlos enters, his cloak up to his nose and hat over his eyes.*)
>   Good day, good knight.
>   (*She brings him in. He removes his cloak and reveals a rich velvet and silk costume, in the Castillian fashion of 1519.*)   (Hugo, 1963: 51)

Everything is detailed with an eye to authenticity (the 'fashion of 1519') and the requirements of the action (the concealed door) that will make the drama all the more truthful because the stage has become a real space. The set, therefore, requires a series of practical doors, windows, curtains which become the condition of the action. Similarly, act IV of *Les Huguenots* requires a hidden door and a practical window without which the action cannot take place. Act III requires a church with a practical door and porch in which the audience can see Valentine hide and overhear the conspirators. However, rather than being an artistic expression of Romantic ideals, the new staging aroused purely visual and sensational expectations. The political and economic shifts of 1830 created the economic conditions for this to be adopted by the Opéra.

Finally, thanks to the innovations of Noverre and Angiolini (see Chapter 4) the Romantic ballet had become a truly dramatic medium. Full-length narrative ballets became a regular feature of the Opéra, some with libretti by Scribe (Charlton, 2003: 93–5). Continuing the tradition of ballet in the classical opera, this new dramatic version became a feature of the grand opera, such as the orgy in *Robert le diable* and the skating sequence in *Le prophète*.

Eugène Scribe and the *'pièce bien faite'*

It is hard to over-estimate Scribe's impact on nineteenth-century theatre and opera. One measure of this is the extent to which he was excoriated, here by Ibsen: 'God knows the public is anything but discriminating! The real reason is not difficult to find. When, year in, year out, one has grown accustomed, as our theatre-goers have, to Scribe and Co.'s sugar-candy dramas, well spiced with suitable quantities of various poetry substitutes' (Ibsen, 1970: 69).

At the heart of Scribe's dramaturgy was the notion of the *pièce bien faite* (the well-made play). This implied the careful, and clever, construction of a plot so as to maximise the audience's emotional engagement through a number of coincidences and accidents. These produced misunderstandings, often comic, sometimes tragic, depending on whether they could be sorted out or not. The result was a dramatic machine for creating tension and either brilliant resolution or tragic *dénouement*. In fact Scribe's only truly tragic plots were reserved for the opera: significantly, the tragic in a profound sense was not his *métier*.

In *Le Verre d'Eau* (The glass of water), the drama – and history itself – turns on the moment where the Duchess of Marlborough is manoeuvred into spilling a glass of water over Queen Anne: (*The Duchess, her hand trembling with anger, presents her with the glass of water which slips on the tray and spills onto the queen's dress*).

The build-up of tension is expertly handled, the characters, the increasingly heated atmosphere, the room and costumes all have every appearance of 'reality'. But this is not the 'reality' that Hugo wanted. It is escapist fancy dress.

Scribe's plots all use what seem to be 'real', everyday, 'normal', often trivial occur-rences, as the turning point for momentous events:

- In *Robert le Diable*, Robert is so moved by Alice's account of his mother's death that he cannot read her all-important letter. Had he done so, the rest of the opera could have been avoided.

- In *Les Huguenots*, because Raoul needs to prove himself as a new member of the assembly, it is he who spies on the encounter between Nevers and Valentine. His misunderstanding of what he sees leads to the St Bartholomew's Day Massacre.
- In *La Juive*, the moment for Eleazar to say who his daughter Rachel really is is constantly deferred by a series of engineered events, until he can only reveal it as she is thrown into the cauldron of boiling oil.

The result is a disparity between the momentous truths that *seem* to affect the audience and the dramaturgical devices that are the real experience. The result is history without history: political and social upheavals explained by trifling errors. These operas *imagined* history and presented it on the stage. But as a way of *understanding* it, plots based on personal foibles, coincidence and private passion are inadequate:

> I have not written to you about the opera's [*Les Huguenots*] subject because it is difficult to describe. The story is almost completely fictitious but the period and the ending are historical; that being the St. Bartholemew's Day Massacre. However, there are also some cheerful and lovely scenes in the first three acts.
>
> (Becker and Becker, 1993: 56)

In 1855 Verdi complained to the director of the Opéra about Scribe's behaviour in the run-up to *Les Vêpres Siciliennes*. This included 'altering the historic character of Procida into the conventional conspirator beloved of the Scribe system, and thrust[ing] the inevitable dagger into his hand' (C. Osborne, 1971: 96–8). Perhaps the most salient point is the phrase 'the Scribe system'.

Characteristics of stage presentation (Auber, *La Muette de Portici*)

Scribe enhanced the impression of importance by building a range of technical elements into his libretti. The major grand operas are studded with these, which are often the real climax more than the actual personal drama.

Spectacle and technical devices
- *Le Prophète*: the acclaimed sunrise as the troops prepare for battle at the end of act III, scene iii, and the violent explosion that ends the opera.
- *L'Africaine*: the storm and wreck, with the famous tilting stage/deck in act III.
- *Robert le Diable*: the spectral lighting effects for the return to life of the damned nuns in act III, scene ii.
- *Dinorah*: Dinorah's dance with her own shadow, created by an early moving spotlight.
- *La Muette de Portici*: the eruption and lava flow of Vesuvius at the end.

Ballet and divertissement

- *Robert le Diable*: the orgy-ballet of the dead nuns in act III, scene ii.
- *Le Prophète*: the skating ballet in act III, scene i, using the newly invented roller-skate.
- *L'Africaine*: the exotic ballet of priests, priestesses, warriors and jugglers that opens act IV.

Processions, ceremonies and crowd scenes

Particular use is made of large and impressive crowd scenes, processions and often religious ceremonial:

- *La Juive*: the entry of the Emperor in act I, and the final *auto-da-fé* and execution.
- *Le Prophète*: the coronation scene in act IV, scene ii.
- *Robert le Diable*: Bertram's descent into Hell and the sudden appearance of Palermo Cathedral for the wedding of Robert and Isabelle.
- *Les Huguenots*: the fight between Catholics and Huguenots in act III; the swearing of the oath in act IV and the final ball and massacre in act v.

The erotic and religious

A certain *frisson* is created in many of these operas by the use of either sensuality or threatened sexuality:

- *Robert le Diable*: the orgy-ballet of dead nuns who have been condemned for profaning their vows of chastity.
- *Les Huguenots*: the bathing scene.
- *La Muette de Portici*: the plight of the especially defenceless Fenella.
- *Robert le Diable:* the struggle between Bertram and Alice in act II.

Almost inevitably this raised the problem of how to stop the content being over-powered by the theatricality, as critics understood:

> Monsieur Halévy probably finds it regrettable that all those excellent things which abound in his score are locked in battle with scenic luxury . . . His style, learned, correct, grave in its harmonies, sober in its ornamentation, well crafted rather than inspired where melody is concerned, risks appearing somewhat severe and reserved in the midst of this orgy of scenery, costumes, horses and emperors. Had the visual sphere been less dazzling, the audience would have listened more attentively to the music.
>
> (Jordan, 1994: 64)

The first opera to include these elements was Auber's *La Muette de Portici*, and it immediately became clear that

A new genre was introduced [to the Opéra]. Until then, we clung on to pure tragedy, in its nobility and classical severity: Œdipe and La Vestale represented the model from which only fairy-tale operas were allowed to depart. With La Muette forms were varied: drama became available to issues [both] great and small, to sad and joyful emotions, it ventured into territory populated by gods and heroes; with Masaniello, the people invaded the domain reserved for pontiffs and kings, nymphs and princesses.   (Hibberd, 2009: 1)

La Muette combined expansive treatment of a political theme based on relatively modern history, played out by ordinary men and women. Its contemporaries must have seen it as a mirror of the turbulent world of French politics. But its success was equally to do with the production which followed the libretto's detailed requirements for:

- painted and architectural sets/scenery based on genuine topography;
- the blocking and movement of the singers;
- entrances, exits and behaviour of the crowds;
- lighting, including on-stage flares;
- climactic scenic effects.

This culminated in the final scene:

During this scene the cloud curtain has disappeared, uncovering Vesuvius in fury. [The volcano] throws up eddies of flame and smoke. The lava runs down to the bottom of the staircase. The music must be timed so that the chorus begins as soon as Fenella has disappeared into the lava.

After the final chorus, everyone moves about with the greatest fright. A man arrives at the top of the staircase. The roof of the terrace, with a sound like an explosion, collapses and overwhelms him and his three children – two holding his hand, one on his back. All see this scene of horror and form themselves into the following groups: Alphonse in the middle of the stage; Elvire, her head buried in his breast; the pages and ladies-in-waiting surround them, variously grouped.

The people fill the entire stage. Mothers carry their children; husbands support their wives. Some fall to the ground, others lean on the columns.

Those who enter by way of the terrace die on the steps. Finally, the terror in everyone's movements cannot be portrayed too strongly.

Subterranean noises continue . . . everything goes off at once. Almost at the moment when the curtain falls, from the flies, and reaching from Vesuvius to the staircase, comes a shower of stones of all sizes which are understood to be coming from the crater. You will need a lot of them.   (Radice, 1998: 188–9)

Grand opera thus drew upon a wide range of traditions taken from the opera itself, the ballet, the theatre and current cultural (mainly Romantic) concepts and ideas of history. But fundamental to the final 'mix' were two essentials:

- the commercial imperative that dominated the role, financing and work of the Opéra
- the growing demands by the bourgeois audience for entertainment that determined its subjects, ideas and aesthetic (Table 9.2).

Meyerbeer: words and music, spectacle and sense (*Les Huguenots*)

The potential excitement, and problem, was how to weld these elements into a unified work of art rather than a series of competing attractions. Meyerbeer was well aware of the challenge and he became famous for the detail of his scores (see Table 9.4b) and the incessant changes he made during rehearsals to ensure their effectiveness, as critics noted: 'every kind of change was made during rehearsals – libretto, orchestration, the music itself was subjected to perpetual tinkering. In the interest of perfection none was too humble for Meyerbeer to consult: he even approached the "chef de claque"' (Pendle, 1979: 437).

The operas' musical forms are essentially conservative. Meyerbeer strove to ensure that his principals were happy with the arias and other numbers, tailoring them to their individual talents. They were also designed to fulfil his audience's expectation of standard forms (*cavatine, romance, air, duo*, etc.). This is not in itself surprising. *Les Huguenots* was premiered in 1836, still well within the Italian *primo ottocento*. Yet, the focal moments did bring something new into opera. They expanded its language to include physical production, helping it become a theatrical form into which production was integrated as an essential part of the dramaturgy

- In *Le Prophète*, act IV, scene ii opens with the long coronation procession. As the crowd kneels only he and Fidès are left standing, so that they can see – and the audience can see them seeing – one another. As Jean's mother recognises him, his fall and the opera's tragedy become inevitable.
- In *Les Huguenots*, act IV, Raoul and Valentine's dangerous meeting in her room is interrupted by the entrance of her father and co-conspirators. Raoul hides but both are forced to hear the vituperation and the blessing of the daggers that precipitate the St Bartholomew's Day Massacre and their own deaths.
- In *L'Africaine*, act III, the slave Nélusko is steering Don Pedro's ship to disaster out of revenge. Vasco da Gama, despite being Don Pedro's rival, boards his ship to warn him of his danger. As the men challenge each other a storm erupts destroying the boat and all are enslaved and executed with the exception of Vasco da Gama

Table 9.2 *Antecedents and sources of grand opera*

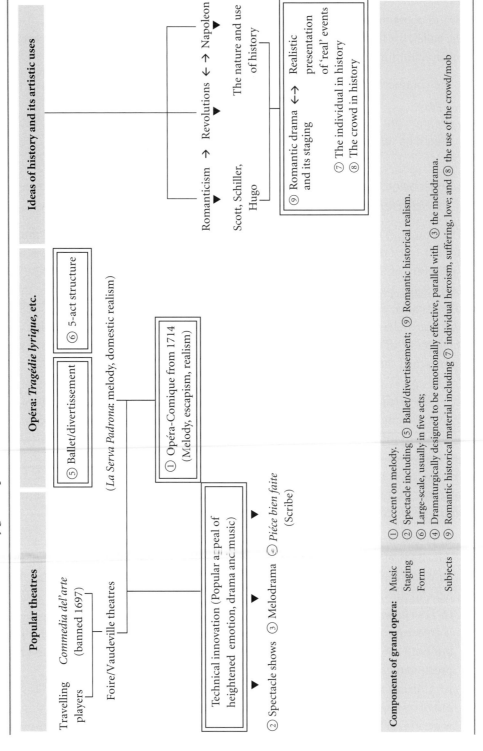

Popular theatres

Travelling players
Commedia del'arte (banned 1697)

Foire/Vaudeville theatres

Technical innovation (Popular appeal of heightened emotion, drama and music)

② Spectacle shows ③ Melodrama ④ *Piéce bien faite* (Scribe)

Opéra: *Tragédie lyrique*, etc.

⑤ Ballet/divertissement   ⑥ 5-act structure

(*La Serva Padrona*: melody, domestic realism)

① Opéra-Comique from 1714 (Melody, escapism, realism)

Ideas of history and its artistic uses

Romanticism → Revolutions ← → Napoleon
Scott, Schiller, Hugo

The nature and use of history

⑨ Romantic drama ←→ Realistic presentation of 'real' events and its staging
⑦ The individual in history
⑧ The crowd in history

Components of grand opera:
Music ① Accent on melody.
Staging ② Spectacle including ⑤ Ballet/divertissement; ⑨ Romantic historical realism.
Form ⑥ Large-scale, usually in five acts;
④ Dramaturgically designed to be emotionally effective, parallel with ③ the melodrama.
Subjects ⑨ Romantic historical material including ⑦ individual heroism, suffering, love; and ⑧ the use of the crowd/mob

who survives for his crucial adventures on the island 'in the Indian Ocean'. The storm, in which the boat's main deck famously tilted and rocked in the storm, is the dramaturgical fulcrum of the opera.

These scenes, for which the operas became famous, offered a new direction for opera:

> In pre-grand opera works scenic events are given pretty short shrift musically. The collapse of the statue of Baal in *Nabucco*, for instance, elicits from Verdi nothing more than a rapid descending scale . . . It is interesting to reflect how different Wagner's treatment of the final scene of *Götterdämmerung* would have been if he had composed his libretto straight away instead of waiting twenty years. The realisation of the musical potential of such important scenic moments is probably the key contribution of grand opera style.   (Charlton, 2003: 131–2, 133–4)

But such increasingly important and popular moments created difficulties as well. Verdi was concerned about the audibility of the words in the finale of act III of *Otello* (see Chapter 8), a danger that is constantly present in these momentous climaxes. The libretto for the 1970 Decca recording of *Les Huguenots* warns the listener that 'it is almost impossible, lacking the music stave, to keep pace with this final ensemble by means of the words alone. He must take the translator's word for it, therefore, as it is set down' (Cochrane, 1970: 36).

Scribe's dramaturgy is a mechanism designed to create and raise tension, enhanced by carefully placed lulls that heighten the audience's anxious anticipation of what will happen next. Table 9.3 suggests how *Les Huguenots* manipulates its audience through this steadily mounting tension articulated through a teasing series of peaks and troughs. Typically.

- The (potential) tension in nos. 2–4 of act I is lowered by the court and bathing scenes (7–10) of act II.
- Raoul's spurning of Valentine (12 B, C), which almost leads to violence, is followed by the relatively low-level confrontations at the opening of act III (13–14 C). Any residual tension is then dissipated by the Bohemian *divertissement* (15 and 16).
- Act V is one relentless *crescendo*, but a false lull is created by the *ballet* (25) at the beginning before the plot, like a tightly wound spring, is unleashed and the narrative/plot proceed to the final climax. The effectiveness of act V is compounded by the audience's understanding of what *must* now happen. There is no longer ironic expectation but resigned terror at the inevitable.[4]

The score of the fourth act opens with the description of

> An apartment in the Hôtel of the Comte de Nevers. Family portraits decorate the walls. At the back a large door, and a large Gothic crucifix. To the viewer's left a

Table 9.3 Les Huguenots: *narrative and plot mechanisms*

	Act I	
1	General rejoicing	
2	Introduction – and acceptance of – Raoul	
3/4	Marcel's 'interruption'	[Both treated with some good humour]
5	Raoul misunderstands Valentine's visit.	
6	General rejoicing	
	Act II	
7		
8	General pleasure of Marguerite's court (including the bathing scene)	
9		
10		
11	Marguerite's plan to unite Catholics and Huguenots	
12 A	The oath of union	
B	Raoul refuses Valentine's hand	
C	Anger and confusion	
	Act III	
13	Atmosphere of relaxation	
14 A	Huguenot soldiers are heard	
B	Catholic worshippers are heard	
C	The two comment on one another	
15	'Bohemian' *Divertissement*	
16		

Table 9.3 (*cont.*)

Act III		
17	The challenge is sent. A plot is to be hatched	
18	Marcel warns – and forgives – Valentine. He tries to warn Raoul	
19	The duel is about to begin – both sides are suspicious	
20	Partisans of each side appear and brawl. Marguerite stops the fight	
21	Saint-Bris learns that Valentine has betrayed the Catholics.	
	She is sent off to her loveless marriage	
Act IV		
22	Valentine laments her marriage	
	Raoul appears in Valentine's chamber	
Scene	The Catholics prepare the massacre	
23	The Blessing of the Daggers	
24	*Grand duo* of Valentine and Raoul – he leaves to warn the Huguenots	
Act V		
[i] 25	Ball in the (Huguenot) Hôtel de Nevers	
26	Raoul bursts in and warns them that the massacre has begun	
[ii] 27	Valentine comes to save Raoul – and converts	
A	Marcel blesses them	
B	Catholics break in	
C	*Vision* All three havea blissful vision. The Catholics pursue them	
[iii] 28	Marcel, Valentine and Raoul are killed together	

Table 9.4a Les Huguenots: *act iv, general analysis of no. 23, The Swearing of the Oath and Blessing of the Daggers*

No 23 *Conjuration et Bénédiction des poignards* – *The Swearing of the Oath and Blessing of the Daggers*		
638	Are the nobles willing to strike for the king and their faith?	
647	Who will now swear to join the sacred cause?	Main melody
657	Most agree; Valentine is terrified; Nevers refuses to join the conspiracy	
664	The leaders of the community and their followers enter. Nevers is arrested	Nevers rejects Saint-Bris, using the latter's melody
670	Saint-Bris tells the populace how to carry out the massacre	New melody
681	The monks enter and administer the oath	Chordal shifts rather than straightforward melody
690	Saint-Bris instructs them once again	
692	General cry for vengeance before all leave to await the signal for the massacre	697 Rhythmic 'furious' melody 710 The ensemble take up Saint-Bris' melody from 642
719 No. 24 Grand duo		

door that leads to Valentine's bedroom. To the right a large fireplace, and next to the fireplace the entrance into a closet, hidden by a tapestry. To the viewer's right, and at the front, a casement which gives onto the street.

Many of the musical markings are concerned as much with dramatic as purely musical effect. For example, the directions for the bells: these were real bells hung in the theatre flies (the first time this had been done). In order to create the impression of various distances they were muffled at various ponts. In act iv, towards the end of the Grand Duo, the note reads: 'It is very important that the Bells in F and C sound in the same octave as that written in the score, as the effect will be spoilt if these Bells were an octave too high.' In act v the instructions are more detailed. The act opens with the direction (p. 787) 'muffle the sound of the bells, by wrapping the clappers with a leather covering' adding 'as from afar'. At p. 794 'Cover the bells as in the entr'acte'. Then, 805, as Raoul enters to warn of the massacre 'Lift the covering'.

Table 9.4b shows how the long climax of act iv is 'orchestrated'. The music is vital, but only one function among others. After Valentine's despairing solo, Raoul later

Table 9.4b Les Huguenots: *act IV,* The Swearing of the Oath and Blessing of the Daggers

Page	Libretto	Stage and other directions in the score	Music: commentary
Scène			
635			Entry music followed by
636	Saint-Bris: Oui, l'ordre de la reine Yes, the queen's order		unaccompanied recitative.
No. 23 *Conjuration et Bénédiction des poignards* (Swearing of the Oath and Blessing of the Daggers)			
638		***Allegro moderato***	Dramatic rising figures in triplets.
639	Saint-Bris: Des troubles renaissants From reviving troubles		Stentorian recitative with chorus interjecting their agreement.
642	Saint-Bris: Eh bien! Du Dieu qui nous protège Well then, of God who protects us		Rapidly rising and falling sequences of triplets.
645	Nevers: Mais qui les condamné? But who condemns them?	(Struck with astonishment)	
646	Nevers: Nous! – Us!	(With horror)	
		Saint-Bris rises, all the others do the same; he looks at Nevers with distrust and addresses the following verses to him with clear intent	
647	Saint-Bris: Pour cette cause sainte For this holy cause	*Andantino* *Con portamento e ben marcato*	Melodic passage. Initially sung *ben marcato* with *staccato* accompaniment

(*cont.*)

Table 9.4b (*cont.*)

Page	Libretto	Stage and other directions in the score	Music: commentary
648	Saint-Bris: à mon Dieu, à mon roi! to my God, and my king	Very softly	now sung smoothly as Saint-Bris looks to heaven.
650	Ensemble		The melody takes over, accompanied by flowing rising and falling triplets with Valentine singing descant over the top.
653			The passage ends with Valentine's florid decoration and a light triplet motif in the wood wind
654	Saint-Bris: Le Roi peut-il compter sur vous? Can the king count on you?	***Allegro moderato***	returns to triplet figure as at 642.
657	Nevers: Frappons nos ennemis Strike our enemies	(With indignation)	Arioso/lyrical recitative.
658	Nevers: Il me commande en vain He commands me in vain	(With dignity)	
659	Nevers: Et parmi mes illustres aïeux And among my illustrious forebears	(With force)	Up-beat *pizzicato* string and dotted wind and brass accompaniment.
660	Nevers: Je compte de soldat, et pas un assassin! I count as a soldiers, but no murderer!	(With contempt)	
661	Nevers: Tiens! Tiens! La voilà Lo! Lo! Behold	(He breaks his sword)	
662	Valentine: Ah! D'aujourd'hui tout mon sang Ah! From today all my blood	(To Nevers with abandon)	

Table 9.4b (*cont.*)

Page	Libretto	Stage and other directions in the score	Music: commentary
663		At this moment the doors at the back open; armed *quarteniers* (heads of the city quarters), aldermen, leaders of the people, appear.	
664	Saint-Bris: Assurez-vous de lui Take care of him	(Addressing them, points to Nevers)	
665	Valentine: Puisse le ciel May heaven	(aside)	
666	Nevers: Ma cause est juste et sainte My cause is just and holy	(calmly)	Nevers adopts the words and music Saint-Bris used (650) to introduce the plot. This leads into an ensemble with the melody at its core.
669		(Nevers is led out)	
	Saint-Bris: Et vous qui répondez And you who answer	Récitatif	
670	Saint-Bris: Qu'en ce riche quartier la foule répandue. Let the crowd spill out into the rich quarter	*Allegro* (In a low voice, but clearly pronounced, to one of the leaders)	A syncopated motif, like a *moto perpetuo* begins, that brings a sense of inevitable, unstoppable power to the scene.
	Chorus: Tous, tous, frappons à la fois! All, all, let us strike together	(muffled voice)	Over this Saint-Bris sings a new melody. The chorus echo him as he turns from one leader to another.

(*cont.*)

Table 9.4b (*cont.*)

Page	Libretto	Stage and other directions in the score	Music: commentary
675	Saint-Bris: Écoutez, écoutez Listen, listen	*Un peu moins vite*	An alarm-like bar of sextuplets in the strings with dissonant chords from the woodwind that sound like the bells to which he now refers one after another.
676	Saint-Bris: Lorsque de St.-Germain When from St.-Germain	*Récitatif* (very seriously)	Saint-Bris sings the recitative over a single chord for 8 bars. The 'alarm' motif sounds again on pp. 677 and 678.
678	Saint-Bris: et lorsq'en fin And when finally	(Gravely)	The passage ends with unaccompanied recitative, as
679	Saint-Bris: le fer en main alors levez-vous with sword in hand, arise	*Allegro vivace* (vigorously)	the orchestra returns, but accompanying him only with punctuating chords
	Valentine: Mon Dieu! My God!	(aside with anguish)	followed by Valentine's lone voice, emphasised by string chord interjections.
680		The doors at the rear open, three monks carrying baskets containing white sashes advance slowly, followed by a group of novices	

Table 9.4b (*cont.*)

Page	Libretto	Stage and other directions in the score	Music: commentary
The entry of the monks			
681	[Saint-Bris sings with the third monk.]	*Poco andante*	The scoring for the brass and wind includes: trumpets in A♭ and E♮, five trombones (alto, tenor, bass) and ophicleide. Throughout there are instructions as to when and how the various brass instruments are to play, often with the 1st or 2nd bassoon.
	Monks/Saint-Bris: Gloire au grand Dieu vengeur Glory to the great God of vengeance		This striking passage is focused on ominous reiterated rising and falling chords. It starts with a bar-long C. Then a bar-long D is accompanied by the motif C, B C + E, D + F, E. When the voices enter, they repeat this confused, dramatic, clashing sound. Accompanying it is a syncopated figure in the basses and bassoons. The whole is repeated several times.
684		All those present draw their swords and daggers: the monks bless the arms	A series of bar-long brass chords as above.

(*cont.*)

Table 9.4b (*cont.*)

Page	Libretto	Stage and other directions in the score	Music: commentary
685	Monks/Saint-Bris: Glaives pieux saintes épées Pious blades, holy swords	(extending their hands) (in a monotone)	The basis of the blessing is, again, the same monotonous rising and falling figure, until
686	Monks/Saint-Bris: glaives pieux par nous soyez bénis pious blades be blessed by us		six *a cappella* bars.
687	All: Oui gloire au Dieu vengeur Yes glory to the vengeful God		The same rising and falling figure but now with strings, brass, wind and choir.
690	Saint-Bris: Que cette écharpe blanche et cette croix That this white sash and this cross	(showing to all the cross and the white sash that he wears)	Saint-Bris sings solo over violas and cellos divided into three voices.
691	Monks/Saint-Bris: Ni grâce, ni pitié Neither mercy nor pity		The rising and falling figure is repeated. But the wind now begins a series of rapid demi-semiquavers that increases the urgency.
692	All: Frappons, frappons, frappons! Strike, strike, strike!		A strong rhythmic passage (orchestra and voices) in which all cry out to strike the enemy as
696	Monks/Saint-Bris: Dieu! Dieu! ne les connaît pas! God! God! knows them not	sung in a half-voice	the four solo voices suddenly lower the temperature until

Table 9.4b (*cont.*)

Page	Libretto	Stage and other directions in the score	Music: commentary
697		***Allegro furioso*** 6/8 All rush furiously to the front of the stage, brandishing their swords and daggers	The brass blares out a furious fanfare, the trumpets instructed to play with the 'bells in the air'.
	All: Dieu le veut! Dieu l'ordonne God wishes it! God commands it		All sing *ff* in a strongly rhythmic figure until
700	All: et la palme immortelle and the immortal prize		a gentler passage, *p*, and then
	All: Dieu le veut, Dieu l'ordonne God wishes it, God commands it		the opening passage is repeated.
706	All: Dieu le veut God wishes it		The phrase is repeated, alternating with a series of rising scales in the orchestra creating an increasing sense of fury.
708	Saint-Bris: Silence, mes amis Silence, my friends		Solo voices of the monks and Saint-Bris interrupt, lowering the temperature again
709		The monks sign to those present to fall to their knees, and bless them moving slowly between the different groups	leading into a *rallentando* before
710	All: Pour cette cause For this cause		the melody first used by Saint-Bris at 647 returns and is taken up by the ensemble.

(*cont.*)

Table 9.4b (*cont.*)

Page	Libretto	Stage and other directions in the score	Music: commentary
714	All: À minuit! Till midnight!	(All retire slowly and mysteriously)	The voices fragment as the conspirators lower their voices ready to depart. Their 'departure' music is accompanied by a trivial flourish in the woodwind.
716	All: Dieu le veut! God wishes it	With fury	In extreme contrast, the chorus explode with a last outcry of vengeance before
	All: À minuit Until midnight	(The crowd passes out silently)	finally subsiding into silence as the orchestra plays a desultory, fragmented refrain version of Saint-Bris' melody
718		Raoul slowly raises the hanging, makes sure that everyone has left and runs towards the door; but he stops as he hears it being bolted from outside. He then turns to the door on the left and at that moment Valentine comes out of her room	over the prolonged *diminuendo*.

719 No. 24 Grand duo

enters by the door at the rear. He warns Valentine of the plot. Immediately Nevers and his colleagues are heard, but Raoul refuses to leave and stays to protect her. Valentine hides him in the closet. This is followed by the *Scène* in which Saint-Bris asks Valentine to leave – but, as a good Catholic, is allowed to remain. There follows No 23. *Conjuration et Bénédiction des Poignards* (Swearing of the Oath and Blessing of the Daggers). The main units of this complex scene are as in Table 9.4a.

In Table 9.4b the score page numbers are followed by the opening lines of the libretto, then the verbatim instruction in the score and finally a commentary on the music, etc. (Meyerbeer, 1980, ii: 627). It is significant that the scene has to be treated as a whole. The interest lies at least as much in the dramatic construction as its musical articulation.

Of all the climactic scenes in Meyerbeer, the Blessing of the daggers is the most satisfactory: it is also, like the rest of the opera, the most cogent. Berlioz 'found it superb in its beauty and refinement, and incomparably lucid and precise even in the most intricate passages ... The stretto on the Blessing of the Daggers was an overwhelming moment; it was some time before I could recover from it' (Berlioz, 1970: 396–7).

But there is always a haunting sense that the parts have not come together to create a genuine whole, that there is something missing. What these operas lack is the interest in character, a vision of the human condition, a genuine concern that is central to the grand operas of Verdi (*Otello* or *Don Carlos*), or the early mature operas of Wagner that were influenced by grand opera, as well as later operas whose grandiose conception was indebted to them. To a considerable extent the underlying fault lies with the librettists, Scribe and his imitators, whose qualities were not suited to the genuinely tragic. Despite this, early French grand opera redefined opera and the way it would develop. Looking ahead to the twentieth century, the sheer scale and ambition of much of the work of Strauss and Puccini, Britten and Tippett, Henze and Zimmermann is the result of opera being informed and extended by its production values.

Chapter 10

The Wagnerian revolution

Wagner changed opera in terms of its musical form and overall content, as well as how it was perceived – its aesthetic and social function. He was in a position to effect this because of his unique combination of musical, technical, dramatic and philosophical concerns which were expressed in

- opera;
- innovative involvement in all aspects of production and direction;
- theoretical writings.

He was, of course, influence by previous composers and thinkers, but what made him so influential was the force with which one person so successfully drew it all together. This turned Wagner into a kind of nineteenth-century hero, struggling to save and redirect art – as he portrayed himself, in figures such as Tannhäuser and Walther von Stolzing. The sheer range of interests in itself created a new ethos for evaluating a form that had become increasingly socialite, redefining it as a serious dramatic art, aimed at engaging the audience in moral, political and aesthetic ideas.

Wagner's theoretical writings and practice cover:

- The origins of art, especially the performing arts, as a social activity rooted in a particular group of people. This included the collective expression of group identity in myths and legends.
- The history and role of art, in particular opera, in Germany, together with special consideration of indigenous poetic forms, especially *Stabreim* (see p. 208) (Millington, 1992b: 264–8).
- The ideal function of art in modern society, proposed in his early writings as a revolutionary, socialist, force.
- How music and opera had developed, in particular the relationship between words and music.
- The nature of performance and the performer.

In addition, there are writings on religious, political and social issues, all contained in the eight volumes of his *Gesammelte Schriften* (Wagner, 1994–5).

For Wagner art, and in particular the stage, was an interventionist activity that should be grounded in significant ideas and seen as part of the larger socio-political sphere. The corollary was the need to reform current practice. His *The Art-work of the Future* (vol. 1) demanded that opera be

- recast as a genuinely musico-dramatic form – hence his term 'Music Drama';
- created (words, music, staging, direction) by a single mind (the 'poet' as in Greek ποιητής – *maker*);
- distinguished as a special activity, requiring a break with the socialite tradition (hence Bayreuth) (Table 10.1, p. 196).

Cultural and artistic purpose

Wagner died in 1883, twelve years after Germany finally achieved nationhood. His life was therefore framed by the struggle towards this, in the wake of the Napoleonic Wars and its denial by the Congress of Vienna in 1815. His growing concern was to make music and opera a real voice and national focus. This ultimately found expression in the dramatisation of Germanic myth and the creation of Bayreuth, which he saw as a national theatre. The idea of the stage as a public forum had been a theme since the end of the eighteenth century, as Schiller announced: 'The great of the world ought to be especially grateful to the stage, for it is here alone that they hear the truth. Not only man's mind, but also his intellectual culture, has been promoted by the higher drama. The lofty mind and the ardent patriot have often used the stage to spread enlightenment' (Schiller, in Dukore, 1974: 444). Wagner explained that he sought to realise this and found a substantial model in Greek theatre which showed how art could be derived from and made relevant to a community: 'Tragedy was therefore the entry of the Art-work of the Folk upon the public arena of political life; and we may take its appearance as an excellent touchstone for the difference in procedure between the Art *creating* of the Folk and the mere literary-historical *making* of the so-called cultural world' (Wagner, 1994–5, 1: 135).

This seemed an ideal of how art should function in the state, using commonly held myths to articulate fundamental concerns, in a presentation sponsored by the state as part of its religious and civil calendar. In addition, the Greeks had combined poetry, music, dance and painting (scenery), presented in a hallowed space whose seating was democratic – unlike the tiered and boxed theatres of modern Europe: 'Wheresoever *the Folk* made poetry . . . there did the Poetic purpose rise to life alone upon the shoulders of the arts of Dance and Tone, as the *head* of the full-fledged human being . . . Neither was the true *Folk-epic* by any means a mere recited poem . . . before these epic songs became the objects of . . . literary care, they had flourished mid the

Table 10.1 *Wagner's interests and influences*

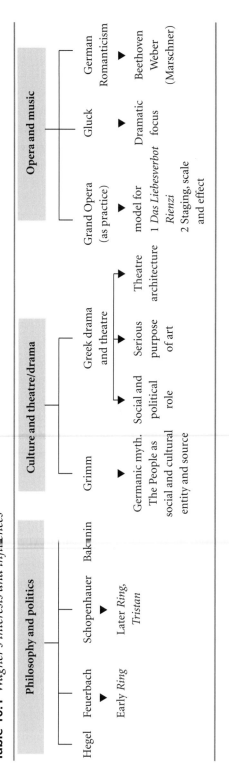

Philosophy and politics			Culture and theatre/drama				Opera and music		
Hegel	Feuerbach	Schopenhauer Bakunin	Grimm	Greek drama and theatre			Grand Opera (as practice)	Gluck	German Romanticism
	▶ Early *Ring*	▶ Later *Ring*, *Tristan*	▶ Germanic myth. The People as social and cultural entity and source	Social and political role	Serious purpose of art	Theatre architecture	▶ model for 1 *Das Liebesverbot* *Rienzi* 2 Staging, scale and effect	▶ Dramatic focus	▶ Beethoven Weber (Marschner)

Folk, eked out by voice and gesture, as a bodily enacted Art-work' (Wagner, 1994–5, I: 134–5) (Table 10.2, p. 198).

Convention and reform (*Der fliegende Holländer, Lohengrin*)

As a professional conductor between 1833 and 1839, Wagner became familiar with the standard repertoire, including Adam, Auber (*La Muette de Portici*), Beethoven, Bellini, Cherubini, Halévy, Rossini, Marschner (whom he especially appreciated as Weber's successor), Meyerbeer (*Robert le Diable*), Mozart (although *Don Giovanni* was 'distasteful to me, on account of the Italian text beneath it: it seemed to me such rubbish', Wagner, 1994–5, I: 3), Spohr, Spontini and, above all, Weber (*Preciosa, Der Freischütz, Oberon, Euryanthe*) (Millington, 1992b: 69–70). This experience is reflected in his own early and first mature operas (Table 10.3).

Immediately after fleeing Germany as a wanted political activist Wagner began what were probably his most important prose works. These followed the completion of *Lohengrin* and were written at the same time as the prose and verse versions of *The Ring* (between October 1848 and 1852):

1849   *Art and Revolution*
1850   *The Art-work of the Future*
1850   *Opera and Drama*
1851   *A Communication to my Friends*

In these, he worked out what he believed to be the origins and future of opera. His thesis was that Greek socially holistic theatre had fragmented as a result of the development of European religious, political and economic conditions. Capitalism had led to the commodification of the arts, mirroring the fragmentation of society and the substitution of purely material for spiritual values:

> the rulership of public taste in Art has passed over to the person who now pays the artist's wages . . . to the person who orders the artwork for his money, and insists on ever novel variations of his one beloved theme . . . and this ruler and this order giver is – *the Philistine* . . . the most heartless and the basest offspring of our Civilisation . . . it is the *artist* whose clear eye can spy out shapes that reveal themselves to a yearning which longs for the only truth – *the human being*.
>
> (Wagner, 1994–5, II: 374–5)

In his first operas Wagner had used generalised Romantic subjects: 'My path led me first to utter frivolity in my view of art; this coincides with my earliest practical contract with theatre as Musical-director . . . One strong desire then arose in me, and developed into an all-consuming passion: to force my way out from the paltry squalor of my situation' (Wagner, 1994–5, I: 297). He had then chosen an episode

Table 10.2 *Wagner's artistic models and objectives*

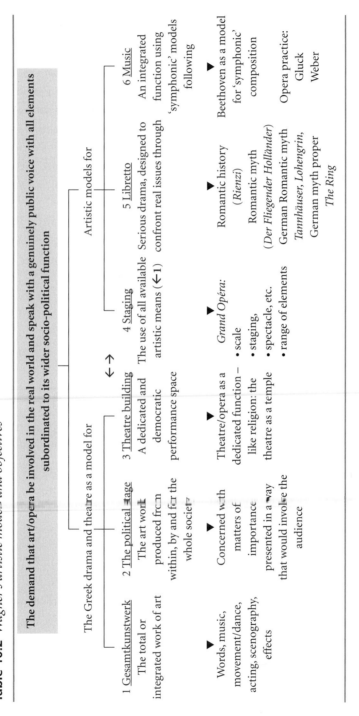

The demand that art/opera be involved in the real world and speak with a genuinely public voice with all elements subordinated to its wider socio-political function

Artistic models for

The Greek drama and theatre as a model for

1 Gesamtkunstwerk The total or integrated work of art	2 The political stage The art work produced from within, by and for the whole society	3 Theatre building A dedicated and democratic performance space	4 Staging The use of all available artistic means (←1)	5 Libretto Serious drama, designed to confront real issues through	6 Music An integrated function using 'symphonic' models following
Words, music, movement/dance, acting, scenography, effects	Concerned with matters of importance presented in a way that would involve the audience	Theatre/opera as a dedicated function – like religion: the theatre as a temple	*Grand Opéra:* • scale • staging • spectacle, etc. • range of elements	Romantic history (*Rienzi*) Romantic myth (*Der Fliegender Holländer*) German Romantic myth *Tannhäuser, Lohengrin,* German myth proper *The Ring*	Beethoven as a model for 'symphonic' composition Opera practice: Gluck Weber

Table 10.3 *Wagner's completed operas*

1833–40 'International' Romantic subjects	1843–50 Romantic 'Germanic' myth and history	1854–78 Mature works, German myth
1833 *Die Feen*		
1836 *Das Liebesverbot*		
1840 *Rienzi*		
	1843 *Der fliegende*	
	Holländer	
	1845 *Tannhäuser*	
	1850 *Lohengrin*	*Der Ring des Nibelungen*
		1854 *Das Rheingold*
		1856 *Die Walküre*
		1857 *Siegfried* i, ii
		1859 *Tristan und Isolde*
		1867 *Die Meistersinger*
		1869 *Siegfried* iii, iii
		1872 *Götterdämmerung*
		1882 *Parsifal*

of revolutionary 'history' in *Rienzi* – although based on Bulwer Lytton's romantic novel: 'From the misery of modern private-life . . . I was borne away by the picture of a great historico-political event [but] I still kept more or less to the purely musical, or rather: operatic standpoint' (Wagner, 1994–5, i: 298). Then, with *Der fliegende Holländer*, he turned for the first time to myth: 'The figure of the "Flying Dutchman" is a mythical creation of the Folk: a primal trait of human nature speaks out from it with heart-enthralling force . . . the longing after rest from amid the storms of life' (1994–5, i: 307). This combined Ulysses and the Wandering Jew with the 'longed for, the dream – of, the infinitely womanly Woman – let me out with it in one word: *the Woman of the Future*', a theme that would be repeated from Senta to Kundry. But more immediately significant was the realisation that: 'From here begins my career as *poet*, and my farewell to the mere concocter of opera-texts' (Wagner, 1994–5, i: 298). In *Der fliegende Holländer*, Wagner was able to cut through many of the conventions of Grand Opera. This was because he understood the tension set up by music at the service of inadequate, and inadequately handled, subject-matter. The more effective the *musical* drama, the clearer the vacuity became: 'The secret of Meyerbeer's operatic music is – *Effect* . . . we may translate "effect" by "a Working, without a cause"' (Wagner, 1994–5, ii: 96).

Wagner's own early works, typically followed the 'well-made play', with its sequence of engineered coincidences, confrontations and climactic moments.

However impressive these may seem, the real action remains theatrical, a series of planted/plotted traps for the main characters and the audience. Wagner learned to dispense with this, and put the purpose of the drama at the centre through straightforward action.[1] Where *Rienzi* consists of five sprawling acts, *Der fliegende Holländer* is dramatically tight, especially in its original one-act version. There is no dramatic waste, no deviation from the main theme as the opera brings together the Dutchman, searching for redemption, the haunted, idealising Senta, and her materialist father, Daland. Only the romantic, distraught lover Erik remains outside the core, although he is necessary as part of the dramatic action.

The notional structure still comprises a series of separate numbers, some of which look back to standard opera types:

- The middle part of the duet between Daland and the Dutchman (no. 3 at bar 222) with its swinging 6/8 'waltz' theme.
- The atmospheric, long-awaited wind blowing through the flutes and clarinets, but which leads into the jaunty Finale of act i (bar 470).
- Senta's ballad and the Spinning Chorus in act ii are both recognisably set pieces (Table 10.4).

Table 10.4 Der fliegende Holländer: *the dramatic action*

Act	No	Forms	Action
1	1	Introduction	Daland makes landfall and leaves for his nearby home.
	2	Arie	The Dutchman lands and narrates his history and fate.
	3	Scene, duet and chorus	Daland returns and accepts the Dutchman's offer All leave for Daland's home.
2	4	Scene, song and ballade	Senta sings her ballad — and invokes her vision of the 'portrait'. Erik is distraught at Senta's attitude.
	5	Duet	Senta explains her destiny to Erik.
	6	Aria, duet and terzetto	Daland and the Dutchman arrive. Senta and the Dutchman 'recognise' one another.
3	7	Scene and chorus	The two boats prepare to leave.
	8	Finale	Erik begs Senta to reconsider. Senta begs the Dutchman to stay, and then follows him 'faithful unto death'.

The first real hint of musical change is the Dutchman's opening monologue ('Arie') 'Die Frist is um' (The time is come). This uses a mixture of melody, motif and the extended arioso writing that Wagner ultimately substituted for both recitative and traditional melody-based Aria. The word Arie(a) is misleading: it is a monologue in three very different sections:

1 an opening recitative followed by the aria proper – or at least two sections with a strong melodic content,
2 bars 32–98 which repeat the storm melody from the overture, and
3 bars 127–260 which make repeated use of a 'prayer' melody.

The verse changes from unrhymed lines to a rhymed sequence for the aria, but mixing alternating rhymes (abab) and rhyming couplets. The real structure is dramatic: from weary narration, through despair, to hopeless defiance. In particular the repetition of melodic figures turns what might have remained self-standing melodies into something much closer to (reminiscent) motifs. The result is a profound character monologue (Wagner, 2000: 88–118) (Table 10.5).

Wagner has begun to loosen the musical elements. He is still featuring melody within a recognisable bi-part form, but he manipulates it as part of the dramatic flow rather than allowing it to determine the structure. The result is an effective compromise between recitative and melodic aria: an arioso but with one foot still in the older form. This kind of increasingly free writing was developed further in the course of *Lohengrin*, although the opera remained stylistically mixed. There are 'highlights': the Preludes to acts I and III, the wedding chorus in act III, and Lohengrin's arias 'In fernem Land' (In a distant land) and 'Mein liebe Schwan' (My dear swan). However both of these are written *around* melodic figures rather than being determined by them. But it is the handling of the *arioso* writing that is so significant, notably in the long dialogue between Ortrud and Telramund that opens act II:

> At the beginning of Telramund and Ortrud's dialogue the conventional musical structure is still visible: recitatives, only sporadically based on motives of expression or gesture, act as the foil to an aria for Telramund ('Durch dich musst' ich verlieren' – Through you I had to forfeit), which is constructed in regular eight-bar period . . .
>
> But the middle section of the scene (from 'Du wilde Seherin' – You cruel prophetess) anticipates the technique of the Ring. The vocal melody moves without a break from recitative to arioso and back again, without the stylistic distinctions between the two drawing any attention to themselves. The decisive factor is the rhythmic irregularity: two-bar groups alternate with phrases $1\frac{1}{2}$ or $2\frac{1}{2}$ bars long.
>
> (Dalhaus, 1979: 47–8)

Table 10.5 Der fliegende Holländer: *act 1, no. 2 Arie*

1	C *Sostenuto*	Orchestral introduction	Dark, ominous dialogue between horn, bassoon and bass tuba with deep murmuring in the low strings.	**1** (**'Recitative'**)
7	*Rezitativ* (etc.)	Die Frist ist um The time is up	This now alternates with unaccompanied recitative until	Narrative statement of the seven-year cycle and then
12	*Più mosso*	Ha! Stolzer Ozean! Ha! Haughty ocean!	the strings explode in a rapid upward figure.	the Dutchman turns on the sea, his enemy.
18	*Sostenuto*	Das Heil, das auf dem land ich suche The cure, which I seek on land	He returns to the opening unaccompanied *sostenuto* before the strings explode again. This alternation continues until the end of the section.	He alternates between rage at, and contemplation of, his fate.
32	E♭ *Allegro molto agitato*	Wie oft in Meeres tieftsten Schlund How oft in the sea's deep throat	The orchestra moves into the theme first heard in the Overture. (bar 97)	**2** The raging of the sea and storm, both in reality and in the Dutchman's mind as he narrates his search for release.
73		Doch ach! Des Meers barbar'scher Sohn Alas! The sea's barbaric son	The horn call is heard as the music relents: the motif of the Dutchman and his fate.	He tells how every man he has met and tried to buy over made the sign of the cross and dismissed him.
83		Wie oft in Meeres tieftsten Grund How often deep beneath the sea	The storm music resumes.	His musings again turn to anger.
98		Nirgends ein Grab Nowhere a grave	The vocal line is barely accompanied as the music virtually fades away.	Faced with this truth he states his eternal punishment as the storm dies away (115–116).

Table 10.5 (*cont.*)

127	*Maestoso*	*He raises his eyes to heaven* Dich frage ich, gepriesner Engel Gottes I ask thee, God's praised angel	Over a deep, growling *tremolando* accompaniment, the Dutchmen prays in a severe, but lyrical line.	**3** His prayer to God's angel for release – and then
161	*Un poco più agitato*	Vergeb'ne Hoffnung! Forlorn hope!	Stark chordal accompaniment and agitated rushing strings.	he abandons hope.
172			The bassoons growl towards a restatement of the prayer melody (bar 127).	
181	*Molto passionato*	Nur eine Hoffnung soll mir bleiben Only one hope remains for me	He resumes the prayer motif/melody and then explodes into	One last hope remains.
205		Tag des Gerichtes! Jungster Tag! Day of Judgement! Day of Doom	an expostulation rising to a high E and then falling an octave.	Finally he welcomes death and the Day of Judgement as
225		Wann alle Toten auferstehn When all the dead arise	After pronounced notes from the timpani he returns to the prayer melody, but now almost threatening.	his prayer melody becomes an ironic challenge,
260		Ihr Welten, endet euren Lauf! You worlds, your course will end!	A great upward surge of the strings leads to his final outburst and the last sounding of the Dutchman's horn motif.	as he understands that his own release is bound up with the destruction of the world.

Instead of using the regular phrasing imposed by traditional prosody, 'phrases are isolated by their irregular lengths' (Dalhaus, 1979: 49), breaking up the artificial symmetry, so that the setting can follow the words' natural sense and emphasis.

This can be seen in the contrast between the three sections which follow the orchestral introduction to act ii and initial recitative dialogue (Table 10.6a).

Telramund's monologue is like an aria proper in the way that lines and words are repeated to substantiate the musical shape; there is a clear break with the preceding

Table 10.6a Lohengrin: *act II, scene i*

1	Orchestral introduction		
72	Recitative dialogue	Telramund:	Erhebe dich
			Arise thou
101	Aria	Telramund:	Durch dich musst'ich verlieren
			Through you I had to forfeit
172	Recitative dialogue	Ortrud:	Was macht dich in so wilder Klage
			What are you doing with such wild noise
254	Arioso	Telramund:	Du wilde Seherin!– You cruel prophetess

dramatic dialogue and following it a highly articulated recitative It has no inherent musical interest although there are lyrical phrases:

> 176 Ortrud: Friedrecher Graf von Telramund
> Peace-loving Count of Telramund

> 189 Telramund: Von neuem grünen und herrschen in Brabant?
> Newly green and lordly in Brabant

> 240 Telramund: Je schwächer er
> So much the weaker he.   (Wagner, 1998: 34–7)

But these are the exceptions. This is followed by a change to a different style (Table 10.6b). Unlike the dramatically inflected vocal lines in the first part of the scene, Orturud's lines are relatively flat as she casts her mesmeric spell over Telramund. This is a potential problem: some thirty bars in a monotone make for dull music. So instead, the inflection, the musical interest *per se*, is moved into the orchestra. This has the additional benefit of giving the orchestra its own 'voice'. The result is musically interesting yet liberated from the grip of melody *per se* and the need to artificially distort the verbal patterns, as Dalhaus describes: 'The dialogue between Ortrud and Telramund is supported almost throughout by orchestral motives which, together and in conjunction with the vocal phrases, form the "melody" as Wagner understood the term' (Dalhaus, 1979: 47–8). What now followed, from the *Ring* onwards, was a series of redefinitions of all the elements of opera, creating a flexibility that allowed the elements to synthesis around a text and theme:

- Form: based on motivic cells that completely replaced the traditional sequence of independent numbers and recitative or spoken text with a through-composed 'symphonic' structure.
- Rhythm: this included traditional time but was essentially concerned with the dramatic pulse of the drama.

Table 10.6b Lohengrin: *act II, scene i, bars 254–288*

254	Telramund	*gripped by dread, in a soft, trembling voice*	Slow, muted descending chords (reminiscent of the 'Magic sleep' motif in the *Ring*.
256	Telramund	Du wilde Seherin, wie willst du doch Geheimnisvoll den Geist mir neu berücken! You cruel prophetess, how can you still wish To enchant my soul with magic!	A slow, oscillating lyrical line, as if the spell is being cast over him.
261	Ortrud	Die Schwelger streckten sich zur üpp'gen Ruh'; The revellers are laid to luxurious rest;	Ortrud replies in an almost hypnotic monotone, but the previous rise and fall of Telramund's line is sustained by the cor anglais.
265		Setz' dich zur Seite mir, die Stund' ist da, Sit by my side, the hour is here,	The clarinet continues to echo Telramund's line, while Ortrud sings, again in a monotone, then finally rising dramatically on the word 'da' (here).
267		Wo dir mein Seherauge When my prophetic eye for you	Ortrud's line becomes quietly intenser around the Db and then rising again (to F♯) on the first syllable of 'Seherin' (prophetic) until she finally
269		leuchten soll. will shine.	falls (to middle C) but followed by the 'spell-binding' chords first heard at bar 254.
272		*Friederich draws even closer to Ortrud and bends his ear attentively to her*	This ends in a *tremolando* over which the cor anglais and bass clarinet play a short, perhaps ominous, three-note figure.
273	Ortrud	Weißt du, wer dieser Held Do you know who this knight is	Ortrud sings two very similar phrases: while there is more variety than before, the near-repetition maintains the sense of 'spell' while the line's greater animation quietly challenges Telramund.
274	Ortrud	Den hier en Schwan gezogen an das Land? Brought here to this land by a swan?	The figure at bar 272 is repeated, unifying the passage as

(cont.)

Table 10.6b (*cont.*)

276	Telramund:
	Ortrud:
	Was gäbst du doch,
	  es zu erfahren,
	Wenn ich dir sag',
	Ist er gezwungen zu nennen,
	Wie sie Nam' und Art,
	All seine Macht
		Nein (No)
		
		What would you
		  give to learn it,
		If I told you,
		Were he made to tell it
		His name and race
		All his power
			the cor anglais and bass clarinet play a long variant on the ominous motif first heard in the Prelude (bars 18–20) and then in Act I as Lohengrin warns Elsa not to ask his name (bars 777–780).
			This extended phrase (277–279, 279–281, 281–283) grows, rising at each repetition, like a cry of quiet anguish, before eventually sinking into

284	zu Ende ist, Die mühvoll ihm ein Zauber leiht?	would end, His might given him by magic?	the chordal 'sleep/spell' music from bar 254 (and bar 269) which returns – Telramund is caught.

- Melody: the entire opera was an extended 'song' embodying the composer's overall theme.
- Text: based on (variants) of *Stabreim* creating a flexible, but always clear prosody.
- Harmony: increasingly released from key centres.
- Time: increasingly flexible and able to move with the detail of the libretto.

Form and motif (*Die Walküre*)

The word 'symphonic' is frequently applied to Wagner (see Abbate, 1989). However, this does not imply that the operas should be analysed in terms of the classical symphony. Essential to Beethoven's development of large-scale structures was his struggle to free symphonic writing from the dominance of melody. His note books show how he worked to reduce melody to cells that could be used as building blocks. Symphony no. 5 is perhaps the clearest example of music whose real interest lies in the dynamic evolution of large continuous structures from cells. While this was not directly applicable to opera, whose development relies on the drama/libretto, Wagner too used a series of musical cells associated with aspects of the characters, objects or themes. These ideas are what came to be called the *Leitmotifs* (leading motifs). However Wagner's own terms, *Grundthema* (ground theme), *Hauptmotiv* (chief motif) or *thematischen Motiv* (thematic motif) are all more useful and accurate, implying their primary roles in the compositional process (Millington,

1992b: 127). It is in this sense that the word 'symphonic' is not only apposite but crucial.

The idea of motifs that spanned works was not new. Berlioz had used them in the *Symphonie fantastique*, where a single idea, the *idée fixe*, recurs in all five movements, transformed as appropriate to each new context: a *reminiscence* as the 'beloved' is recalled. In Wagner's early mature operas motifs are used in this way and are essentially static. They occur at appropriate moments to recall an aspect of a character (the Dutchman's curse, Senta's 'vision') or a dramatic moment/idea (Lohengrin's warning about his name). At this level, the motifs bring their own interest to the scores but are not fundamentally compositional ideas. When Wagner looked back at *Lohengrin* through the experience of composing *The Ring*, he found 'a network of themes and how, in the direction I've chosen to go, [this] must constantly create new forms' (Deathridge, 2008: 39). This meant the need for 'symphonic' growth using the motivic cells rather than simply including them as reminiscences.

Debussy sneered at the motifs as 'calling cards', implying that the audience was meant to recognise each of them as they occurred. However, there are too many (over one hundred) for this, and much of the time they are used in varied forms. In some cases they are genuine reminiscences and are easily recognisable (and some are far more obvious than others, such as the Walküre or Sword motifs). But more generally they are what Wagner called *Gefühlswegweiser* (emotional pointers), indicating that they affect the listener in their own musical right. These form a multi-layered texture that, together with the libretto, are what Wagner called the *Versemelodie*.

Rhythm

In 'Poetry and tone in the drama of the future', Wagner talks about how the rhythm and meaning of the text give rise to 'Singing-tone' and then 'Musical Feeling' which produces Harmony (Wagner, 1994–5, II: 280). He understood 'rhythm' as the pulse of the drama itself, realised through the flow of the musical and verbal text. This, he hoped, meant that the fabric of the opera could 'only fall to the lot of the musician, in his turn, when he mounts from the depths, to the surface of Harmony; and on that surface will be celebrated the glorious marriage of Poetry's begetting Thought with Music's endless power of Birth' (Wagner, 1994–5, II: 280).

Melody

This 'glorious marriage' is what Wagner understood as melody: not simply tunes, but a complex onwards movement, developed from musical cells as the musical analogue of the drama: 'That wave-borne mirror-image is *melody*. In it the poet's Thought becomes an instinctively enthralling moment of Feeling: just as Music's emotional-power therein acquires the faculty of definite and convincing utterance, of manifesting itself as a sharp-cut human shape, a plastic Individuality. Melody is the redemption of the poet's endlessly conditioned thought into a deep-felt consciousness of emotion's highest freedom' (Wagner, 1994–5, II: 280–1).

Melody thus became the ultimate embodiment of the poet's intention and directly linked to the drama by the motifs. It was primarily seated in the orchestra so that the vocal line was left free to express the text in the most idiomatic way. There were exceptions, such as Siegmund's 'Winterstürme' (Spring Song) or Isolde's 'Liebestod' where the *voice* becomes the primary musical/melodic instruments. But these are comparatively rare, in the way that Shakespeare's soliloquies are the comparatively rare moments where meaning is almost entirely contained in the words as distinct from words accompanying, or being accompanied by, action.

Prosody and text, harmony and time

The sense of free, idiomatic flow, both verbally and musically, is in part enabled by the flexibility of the text. Wagner had sought a poetic style that could provide shape and ensure clear delivery of the words, but without the constraints of traditional versification. He found this in *Stabreim*, the verse form used in the Norse *Eddas* and early Germanic poems that provided the mythological part of the *Ring*:[2]

> In the *Stabreim* . . . poetic speech has an infinitely potent means of making a *mixed* sensation swiftly understandable.   (Wagner, 1994–5, II: 269)

Stabreim is unrhymed and structured through alliteration and natural stresses. It can consist of a series of long lines divided by a caesura (/) and with two stresses in each half:

> Pācience is a pōynt,/thāugh it displēse oft.   (Anderson, 1977: 31)

or an alternation of three- and two-stress freely alliterative lines:

> Hēill dāgr!/Hēilir dags synīr
> Heill nott oc nip! (D. Cooke, 1979: 75)

This combination of natural stress and metric freedom allowed Wagner to develop his flexible word setting. He now sought an equally flexible technique for handling keys. Modulation was not, of course, new. But effecting it as constantly as Wagner required began to call into question the whole *raison d'être* of the key system. This reached breaking point in the Prelude to *Tristan* whose music prefigures the opera's theme of the search for resolution. The Prelude appears to begin in C for bars 1–41, then changes to A for bars 42–71, and then reverts to C for bars 72–91. But, as so often, the C is misleading: it is really a kind of neutral within which Wagner uses accidentals to create a continuous ambiguity. The Prelude is structured as a tension between an harmonic progress towards the unstable, so-called 'Tristan chord,' and the long melody that eventually becomes the heart of the final 'Liebestod'. The audience is caught between these two kinds of music as Wagner constantly shifts ground so that the fixity of harmony and melody become illusory.

Finally, time itself was loosened. The Prelude to *Parsifal* moves through an almost bewildering sequence of time signatures: seven changes in the first seventy-eight bars. This, combined with three key changes, the very slow tempo and long-drawn chords, seems to undermine any sense of (definite) rhythm and even time itself, creating rhythmic ambiguity and a different kind of time, which is exactly what Wagner wanted.[3]

Formal moments

These innovations in text and prosody, role and kind of melody, melodic-symphonic development, harmonic freedom and rhythmic pulse, would challenge and change the direction not only of operatic writing but European music in general. Crucially, all of this grew out of the demands of the drama. The result was the abandonment of traditional operatic forms that would distort the dramatic flow or cover the actual words in arias, or duets. However where the *drama* required it Wagner used them to effect:

- The 'Summoning of the vassals' and the 'Revenge trio' in act II of *Götterdämmerung*, both of which are critical moments for the entire drama.
- The quintet in act III of *Die Meistersinger*, in which everything is drawn together in anticipation of resolution in the Song Contest.
- The duet in act II of *Tristan* where the intertwining of the lovers' lines is an analogue for the essence of the opera.
- The very different duet in act II of *Siegfried*, where two disparate individuals gradually draw together in musical as well as physical unity.
- Isolde's 'Liebestod' which becomes the song of her apotheosis through over-riding melody.

These ideas were first completely worked through in *The Ring*. Wotan's monologue in act II, scene ii of *Die Walküre* runs for 312 bars (677–989) and includes ten different motifs (Wagner, 2002: 898–93). It is not strictly a monologue, as Brünnhilde briefly interrupts it three times, but is typical of how Wagner uses the long monologue as retrospective narration. In the guise of informing Brünnhilde, Wotan tells the audience what has happened so far. But it is more than that: he endows the events with deeper meaning and, always crucial to Wagner's monologues, relives the events, so that they become part of the action and the character. This passage, as Wotan reveals the path the gods must take towards their destruction and the world's renewal, is often taken as a central moment in *The Ring*.[4] The first part, bars 683–689, allows Wotan to reveal things that are not allowed by suggesting that in speaking to Brünnhilde, one of his Wunschmädchen (Wish-Maidens, i.e. the Valkyries) he is speaking to his own Will (Table 10.7a).

Although Wagner has a reputation for (very) slow, (over-)extended music, his setting is in fact concise. It moves at a pace almost commensurate with speech and

Table 10.7a Die Walküre: *act ii, scene ii, the structure of Wotan's monologue*

693	Wotan: Was Keinem in Worten ich künde, / What in words I reveal to no one,	As he lost the passion of love he looked for power. There follows the narrative of the stealing of Alberich's ring and Erda's warning, leading to
	Da verlor ich den leichten Muth; / Then I lost all lightness of heart;	the begetting of the Valkyries and the gathering of dead heroes in Valhalla.
770	Brünnhilde's first interruption	The Valkyries have done this – what, then, does Wotan fear?
778	Wotan: Ein Anderes ist's: / There's something else:	Were Alberich to regain the ring all would be lost – Wotan is caught in this web.
	Nur Einer könnte was ich nicht darf, / One man alone could do what I myself may not,	Only one man can win back the ring, free of the laws that forbid Wotan himself from doing so.
871	Brünnhilde's second interruption	Why cannot Siegmund be that man?
874	Wotan: Wild durchschweift' ich mit ihm die Wälder; / I roamed the wildwood with him;	Because Fricka saw that Wotan urged him on – so he could not act of his own free will.
891	Brünnhilde's third interruption	Therefore the free hero cannot be Siegmund.
893–988	Wotan: Ich berhürte Alberichs Ring / I once held Alberich's ring,	Wotan is subject to Alberich's curse on the ring. Wotan now only wants the final end.

is articulated scrupulously following the words' natural inflection. In this it seems close to traditional recitative. But from bar 693, the singer is instructed to sing *streng im Zeitmaß* (in strict time): this is not recitative but *arioso* marrying natural speech rhythm and pace with musical interest, but without the falsification of melody. Parts are completely unaccompanied or only accompanied by long-held chords, while the vocal line itself can be relatively unvaried (the opening bars 693–695) or more articulate as Wotan recollects significant moments (bars 702–704). The motifs (see appendix 1) are played by the orchestra which becomes both accompaniment and commentary, so that the sung narrative and developing musical framework parallel one another (Table 10.7b).

Stage and theatre

Complex stage directions were an integral part of Wagner's scores; but unlike Parisian grand opera, where scenery and action were so often created for the sake of effect, here effect arose from dramatic need. This included scenic design, lighting, stage management and stage effects, as well as stage movement, the direction of the singers and the chorus. Although the scenography remained limited to late nineteenth-century Romantic realism, what was significant was Wagner's involvement in the detail of the mise-en-scène as a crucial part of the operas' meaning. His 1852 monograph, *On the Staging of 'Tannhäuser'*, showed how every aspect of production was integral to the opera's concept.

The 1845 design for act II, scene i of *Tannhäuser* included a floor plan showing the physical detail of the pilgrims' chorus. This prescribed how they were to move onto and around the stage to give time for the whole chorus to be on stage for the musical climax. But instead of the chorus simply entering, forming up, singing and then departing, the music was written to begin softly, as if from a distance, then gradually increase in volume as the pilgrims entered, and then fade as they left the stage, all as a continuum. To stage it otherwise would undermine the music and the effect it was designed to create (Carnegie, 2006: 38–9). The complex movement of the knights as they enter the Grail Hall in act I of *Parsifal* was indicated in a similar way (Radice, 1998: 275). In both cases, the stage action was 'orchestrated' as part of the entire 'text'.

The writing and composition of *The Ring* would have been impossible had Wagner not envisaged and understood the practicability of its vital scenic and production elements as part of the music-drama's language, the integration that Wagner meant by *Gesamtkunstwerk* (integrated or whole work of art). His ability to do this in itself had a major impact on the worlds of opera and theatre, as Henry Porges, who kept a record of the first rehearsals of *The Ring*, understood: 'This strange process was

Table 10.7b Die Walküre: *act ii, scene ii, bars 683–769 of Wotan's monologue*

Bar	Motif			(The motifs are named in **bold**)

677		*Very lightly*
		Was Keinem in
		  Worten ich künde
			What in words I
			  reveal to no one
				Sung over a dark low chord played by three and tenor bass trombones, a contrabass trombone and both cellos and basses.

679	20			As the first phrase ends, the first tenor's line rises, suggesting **Erda's motif**[1] [20] leading into the next line
680		unausgesprochen bleib'es denn	unspoken let it say	thereby creating another held, deep chord which ends as Wotan sings unaccompanied.
682		ewig	for ever	Another held deep chord and then

683		mit mir nur
		  rath' ich
			with myself I
			  commune
				Wotan sings unaccompanied again, followed by

684		red' ich zur dir.–	when I speak with you.–	another chord before his unaccompanied line ends, rising from low A to E and
686				a deep growl – low E two octaves below middle C on the contrabassoon played *pp* – brings this first section to an end.
688	32	A♭ *Still slower*		The **Dejection motif** [32a] is played on low strings and supported by the deep brass and wind. It sounds as though Wotan is descending into himself – and reliving the early history of the *Ring/world*.

693		*In strict time*
		  Als junger Liebe
			When youthful
			  love's
				The opening is accompanied by a low A♭ on the basses alone playing *pp*.

Table 10.7b (*cont.*)

Bar	Motif			(The motifs are named in **bold**)
697		Unwissend trugvoll	Unwittingly false	'Unwittingly' is at best questionable. The accompaniment marks the moment, as the cellos join the basses on a low E♭ in unison.
701	32	Loge der schweifend nun verschwand but vanished while roaming the world		Immediately after 'Loge' the tubas and contrabassoon take over from the low strings and the bar ends with the rising grace triplet of the **Dejection motif** [32a] in the cellos.
702		Von der Liebe doch Mocht' ich nicht lassen	Yet I did not like to give up love	Wotan's line rises more lyrically at 'Minne' ((romantic) love) while the low strings repeat the second part of the **Dejection motif** [32a] twice but rising with lyrical effect – again at 'Minne'.
705		Den Nacht gebar	born of the night	This abruptly ceases as Wotan reflects on Alberich, accompanied again by growling low brass and woodwind.
706	3	Alberich brach ihren Bund	Alberich severed its bonds	A semitone fall to a quaver in the wind and brass overlaps with Wotan singing the brief two-note **Woe motif** [3] at 'Alberich'.
707		Er flucht der Liebe	he laid a curse upon love	Low strings take over from the wind and brass, holding a chord until
708	5	des Rheines glänzendes Gold	the glittering gold of the Rhine	the wind and brass briefly re-enter with the **Rapture for the Gold motif** [5], also sung by Wotan
710	6			immediately followed by the **Ring motif** [6] played by the bassoons.

(*cont.*)

Table 10.7b (*cont.*)

Bar	Motif			(The motifs are named in **bold**)

715		**A**
		der Burg die Riesen
		    mir bauten
			the bulwark that
			    giants had built
			    for me
				The key brightens to A major as Wotan thinks back to the hope offered by the building of **Valhalla** [8] – whose motif sounds –

717	20			only to be interrupted by the **Erda motif** [20] as he remembers her warning and prediction.
719		Die Alles weiß	She who knows all	The music reduces to Wotan's line with its deep chordal accompaniment.

726	32	Da verlor ich den
		    leichten Muth
			Then I lost all
			    lightness of heart
				The **Dejection motif** [32a] is played with its initial grace triplets repeatedly rising through the orchestra creating a rich melodic continuum – but also suggesting Wotan's growing agitation.

733		Kunde empfing ich
		    von ihr
			Knowledge I gained
			    from her
				This subsides into a fragmentary repetition in the low strings as

734		von mir doch empfing sie ein Pfand from me though she gained a pledge		the descending quaver–semiquaver part of the **Dejection motif** [32a] becomes a sequence of crotchets and slowly turns into

739	26	gebar mich,
		    Brünnhilde, dich
			bore to me,
			    Brunnhilde, you.
				a motif associated with the **love of Siegmund and Sieglinde** [26] – but possibly suggesting love in generale – is repeated by the horns.

742		3/4 *A little more movement*		
742	30	Mit acht Schwestern	With eight sisters	The music starts to move more freely as hope appears to Wotan. The **Valkyrie motif** [30] sounds, albeit in a slow form.

Table 10.7b (*cont.*)

Bar	Motif			(The motifs are named in **bold**)
743	28	durch euch Walküren	through you Valkyries	A warning note is introduced on the timpani, perhaps a partial reminiscence of Hunding's motif horn which now runs through to bar 752, questioning Wotan's optimism.
750	30	Daß stark zum Streit	That our foe might find us	The **Walküre motif** [30] sounds in its recognisable form as Wotan becomes more animated, reflected in the orchestra until
754		Die Männer, denen	those men whose mettle	a more solemn note is sounded as Wotan describes the fallen heroes to be taken to Valhalla.
759	8	trügende Bande	blind obedience	Part of the **Valhalla motif** [83] is played by the cellos before
761	30/28	Die solltert zu Sturm	you'd spur them on	the **Walküre motif** [30].
770	8	Brünnhilde Deine Saal fülten wir	We filled your hall	The music metamorphoses into the **Valhalla motif** [8] proper as Brünnhilde naively responds to Wotan before he continues with the problems of recovering the ring.

Note: [1]The motifs noted in **bold** may be found in appendix 1 (p. 387).

apparent throughout the rehearsals of the first German stage festival, rehearsal which had such importance for the development of the new music-dramatic art' (Porges, 1983: 3).

The logical extension was the creation of an appropriate theatre (Festspielhaus). Bayreuth opened in 1876 with the first complete cycle of *The Ring*. The idea of a special theatre had occurred to Wagner as early as 1850 when he first thought about an opera on the Siegfried legends. Its basis was both practical and idealistic: 'I would have a theatre erected on the spot . . . and have the most suitable singers join me here, and arrange everything necessary for this one special occasion, so that I could be certain of an outstanding performance of the opera' (Carnegie, 2006: 70). Eventually this idea became the concept of a special space that would situate the audience in 'a new relation to the play . . . a relation quite distinct from that in which you had always been involved when visiting our theatres', and in which 'the mysterious entry of the music will next prepare you for the unveiling and distinct portrayal of scenic pictures that seem to rise from out an ideal world of dreams' (Wagner, 1994–5, v: 325). The specific features of the theatre were:

- '[T]he arrangement of our rows of seats [so that they] acquired the character obtaining in the antique Amphitheatre' allowing every member of the audience an equally good view. However
- the Greek theatre's 'actual form, with arms stretched out on either side could not be seriously thought of; for the object to be plainly set in sight was no longer the Chorus in the Orchestra . . . but the "scene" itself', so that a compromise was achieved between the Greek and modern illusionistic theatres 'bound by the laws of *perspective*' (Wagner, 1994–5, v: 324).
- The 'scene' was enhanced by the radical sinking of the orchestra so that 'the spectator would look right over it, immediately upon the stage' (Wagner, 1994–5, v: 333–4).
- Finally, Bayreuth stood apart from the ordinary world; it was reached with effort and always with a single purpose, emphasising the elevated role of art – the opera house/theatre as a temple rather than a place of mere entertainment.

Inheritance

The sheer range of Wagner's concerns would make it increasingly hard for composers to write an opera in the limited or even casual way that had been possible in the past. Even for those who thoroughly rejected Wagner's operatic writing, the need to recognise opera' in its social or political context became inescapable (Table 10.8).

Table 10.8 *Wagner's spheres of innovation and influence*

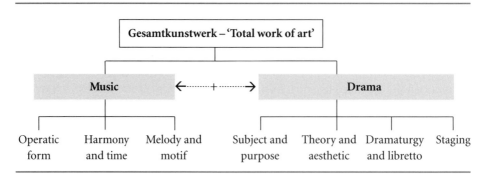

These ideas set the agenda for the arts in general and, more specifically, the future development of opera. They were able to do so for three reasons:

- their cogency – whether or not they were open to question;
- the impact of the work on fellow artists as well as the serious-minded public;
- the impressive fact that one man had managed to combine these arts so successfully, and demonstrated the validity of his theories in his own practice.

The last point is important – and offers a paradox. Wagner and his operas become the living embodiment of the integration that he saw as so important to art. At the same time that art, above all his music, was about fragmentation – of harmony, melody and time. His work stands at both a real and symbolic crux in European opera as it moved into the phase of the late nineteenth and early twentieth centuries. His work did not provide answers; instead, it brought to a pitch the questions of what and how art – in particular, opera – were meant to be in the modern world.

Chapter 11

Nationalists: vernacular language and music

Nationalist composers, principally in Bohemia, Hungary, Poland and Russia, were not isolated from mainstream European traditions. Their struggle was not, as is often naively proposed, to learn how to compose in countries where musical education was not available. In each of them there was a flourishing operatic and general musical life. But this was dependent on Western European models that represented the culture of alien dominant regimes from which the Nationalists struggled to emancipate themselves. In doing so, they contributed a series of major works to the international repertoire and, equally significantly, introduced or emphasised a number of elements that affected the future development of opera. These included:

- The use of vernacular elements drawn from the life of ordinary people, bourgeoisie and peasantry, especially in music, song and dance;
- In particular cases, the idea of deriving musical lines not just from the broad expression, but the precise shape and rhythm of language.

Nationalist composers are identified by their (musical) roots in folk material. But this is a simplistic and often misleading notion.[1] Despite this, however, it is clear that in part their drive was to create music from sources outside the languages of the international mainstream. This meant that they made a major contribution to the development of music itself, by providing one means of renewing music after the apparent impasse of late Romanticism.

Nationalism and folk culture

The gradual reaction against French-dominated, 'universal' Enlightenment ideas was a major theme of late eighteenth-century Romanticism. In Germany, the leading theoretical voice was Herder, whose *Fragmente über die neuere deutsche Literatur* (1766–7) and *Kritische Wälder* (1769) maintained that art was the expression of a people and could only be appreciated against its national or ethnic background. He invented the term *Volkslied* (folk song) and in 1778–9 published the ground-breaking *Stimmen der Völker in Liedern* (Voices of the peoples in song). In the post-Napoleonic world, the general move towards national identity led to a wide interest in folk traditions.

Nationalism was an important element in Germany and Italy, but in Poland, Hungary and the Czech lands the national culture was suppressed or, where not actually banned, social mobility and economic success depended on adopting the dominant culture.[2] In Russia, a combination of repressive censorship and the dominance of fashionable European culture meant that the development of a native voice was either ignored or seen as potentially dangerous.

Interest in folk art and music therefore had several roots:

- The articulation of a sense of nationality where the indigenous culture had been suppressed. This is typical of the Slav nations, above all Bohemia, Hungary and Poland, and later Finland.
- In Russia proper this was part, first, of the debate as to whether Russia's future lay in the European or Slav traditions; and, second, concern with the social, economic and political position of the peasantry which was associated with revolutionary activity.
- Romantic interest in folk art ran parallel with the general interest in Nature awoken by the Industrial Revolution.
- This foreshadowed a later concern that a musical heritage was being lost in the wake of urbanisation (Table 11.1, p. 220).

In general, the early collectors of national music looked to the rural peasantry. Their interest was part of the Romantic concern with Nature, and the rural population seemed to enshrine human activity uncontaminated by industrialisation and urbanisation. Their art was assumed to be both 'real' and ancient. But folk music is more complex, especially at the point where collectors began to gather it, using a range of sources, including the urban working class who, it was assumed, retained their rural traditions. This was not always the case. Much folk song collecting falsified material by making easy assumptions in a very complex field (Table 11.2, p. 221).

'Foreign origin' (no. 8) shows some of the dangers. Two of the most popular Bohemian 'national' dances, the *polka* and *beseda*, have Polish and French origins, respectively (Tyrrell, 1998: 216, 227). In Hungary the most popular form, the *Csárdás*, is the Austrian *Verbunkos* (*Werbung*) recruiting dance, translated into Hungary by gypsy musicians. As Richard Taruskin shows, the Finale of *A Life for the Tsar* – the famous *Slava* – 'is in a recognizable "period" style – that of the seventeenth- and eighteenth-century *kantï*, three- or four-part polyphonic songs that were the oldest of all "Westernised" Russian repertories (ironically, and perhaps unknown to Glinka, their ancestry was part Polish)' (Taruskin, 2000: 36). This suggests that it may always have been difficult to define 'genuine' folk music. Folk culture is identified at a particular historical moment and for a purpose which imposes the aims, attitudes

Table 11.1 *Examples of mid-nineteenth-century National(ist) folk music collecting and folk music-based composition*

		Folk song collections and arrangements	Compositions using folk material
Haydn	1792–1804	7 collections of British melodies (400)	
Beethoven	1814–25	6 collections of British melodies	
Glinka	1834 1834 1848		Symphony on two Russian themes Capriccio on Russian themes *Kamarinskya*
Brahms	1852–69 1854–73	Deutsche *Volkslieder*	Hungarian dances
Balakirev	1857–1905 1865–98	2 collections of Russian folk songs	Overtures on Spanish, Russian, and Czech themes
Tchaikovsky	1868–9	50 Russian folk songs	
Rimsky-Korsakov	1859 1875 1875 1875–6 1879	40 folk songs 100 Russian folk songs 15 Russian folk songs (choral)	Variations on a Russian theme 3 fughettas on Russian themes Overture on Russian themes Fantasia on Serbian themes Fantasia on two Russian themes
Dvořák	1877 1878–86 1878–87 1883	Two Irish songs Russian songs	Scottish dances Slavonic dances
Smetana	1854 1869 1872–94		*Slavnostni Symfonie* *Libuše's Judgement* *Ma Vlast*

and experience of the collector. An alternative way of thinking about folk music, is to consider *how* it was used This presents another set of variants, some of which, again, overlap with one another (Table 11.3).

Beyond this, there is the substantial question of whether being a 'Nationalist' composer requires being rooted in folk culture in the first place, as Schoenberg understood:

Table 11.2 *Range of sources and origins for folk song*

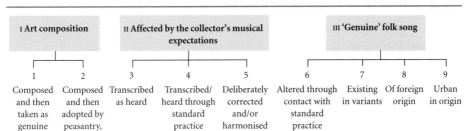

I Art composition		II Affected by the collector's musical expectations			III 'Genuine' folk song			
1	2	3	4	5	6	7	8	9
Composed and then taken as genuine	Composed and then adopted by peasantry, etc.	Transcribed as heard	Transcribed/ heard through standard practice	Deliberately corrected and/or harmonised	Altered through contact with standard practice	Existing in variants	Of foreign origin	Urban in origin

Table 11.3 *Potential uses of folk music*

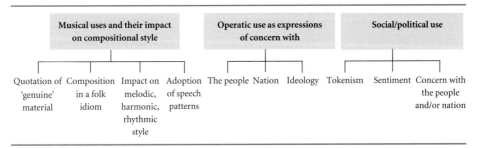

Musical uses and their impact on compositional style				Operatic use as expressions of concern with			Social/political use		
Quotation of 'genuine' material	Composition in a folk idiom	Impact on melodic, harmonic, rhythmic style	Adoption of speech patterns	The people	Nation	Ideology	Tokenism	Sentiment	Concern with the people and/or nation

> As a folk dance the *Thème Russe* [in Beethoven's *Razumovsky Quartet* no. 2] is certainly very pleasant. But that there now exists Russian music is due to the advent of some great composers ... the fact that Tchaikovsky's craftsmanship suggests the German school and, let us also add, the French and Italian contributions to the musical make-up of the world in his time – all this alters the national character of his music as little as it did that of Haydn, who was a pupil of the Italian.
>
> (Schoenberg, 1984: 162, 177)

Folk music or culture generally have to be understood according to how they were used. One distinction is between the merely picturesque or decorative and a profound identification with the people:

> Another durable and fertile tension attending Russian music concerns matters of interpretation and 'ownership.' Owing to the historical circumstances in which Russian artists have worked, the symbology of Russian art is exceptionally rich and multivoiced. In an autocratic or oligarchical society in which political, social, or spiritual matters could not be openly aired, such matters went underground into historiography and art. The art of no other country is so heavily fraught with subtexts.
>
> (Taruskin, 2000: xviii)

This affects the extent to which nationalist opera is merely decoratively folkloric or genuinely concerned with the questions it raises. Perhaps the most trenchant dramatic contribution made by nationalist opera was the introduction of the mass of ordinary people as real participants. Both in their chorus and individuals, Russian operas are notable for their social span; indeed for Musorgsky the mass of common people was the main character in *Boris Godunov* and *Khovanshchina.*

National struggle: Russia, Poland, Hungary and Bohemia

Table 11.4 indicates some aspects of the awakening of, and struggle towards, nation-hood in the nineteenth century. The background to this was:

- Poland: shared out between Russia, Austria and Prussia in the First and Second Partitions of 1772 and 1793. The Poles revolted against this in 1794 but were suppressed, leading to the Third Partition (1795) and the abdication of Stanislaus II. With this, the country ceased to exist. In 1807 it became a Grand Duchy, first under Napoleon and then in 1809 under Austria. In 1813 it came under Russian control and only regained independence in 1918.
- Hungary: divided in 1541 between Turkey, Austria and a free Southern Hungary. The Hungarian War of 1703–11 against Austria failed and the country finally lost its independence until the Dual Monarchy of 1867 and full independence in 1918.
- Bohemia: defeated by the Hapsburg/Austrians at the Battle of the White Mountain in 1620, ending Czech nationhood for almost three hundred years. This was cemented between 1720 and 1725 when the Emperor Charles III of Austria and VI of the Empire created a single crown for Austria, Hungary and Bohemia. In the nineteenth century a series of cultural rather than political events signalled the slow movement towards rebirth of the nation in 1918.

The situation in Russia was different: a series of uprisings, assassination attempts and civic unrest were all part of an attempt not to assert nationhood but to progress towards popular emancipation and a freer governance, only achieved (briefly) in 1917.

European art had dominated Russia from the reign of Peter the Great. But in the course of the century a small number of painters such as Ivan Nikitin and Mikhail Shibanov began to produce genre paintings that included scenes of peasant life. Emblematic of a growing change was the way Anton Losenko could turn from the neo-classicism of *Zeus and Thetis* to a depiction of Russian legendary figures in his *Vladimir and Rogneda.*

This shift was gradually reflected in opera which was originally dominated by Italian masters including Galuppi, Traetta, Paisiello and Cimarosa. As in Europe, it was comedy, with its greater sense of realism, that first broke the mould. Fomin's 1787 *The coachman at the horse stage-post,*[3] has a Russian libretto and, after its

Table 11.4 *Examples of National(ist) themes or subjects*

Category	Composer	Opera		Source
History	Glinka	*A Life for the Tsar*	Rescue of the founder of the Romanov dynasty	History
	Musorgsky	*Boris Godunov*	The suffering of Russia in the *smuta* (time of troubles)	Pushkin/history
		Khovanshchina	The suffering in the reign of Peter the Great	History
	Tchaikovsky	*The Oprichnik* *Mazeppa*	The rebellion in the reign of Peter the Great	Byron/history
	Smetana	*The Brandenburgers in Bohemia*	The 'German' occupation of Bohemia	History
		Dalibor	The struggle against aristocratic oppression	History
		Libuše	Founding of the Bohemian monarchy	History/legend
	Erkel	*Hunyadi László*	Internecine strife in mid-fifteenth-century Hungary	History
		Bánk Bán	National assertion in thirteenth-century Hungary	History
Myth/ legend	Glinka	*Russlan and Ludmilla*	Romantic folk tale	Pushkin
	Tchaikovsky	*The Queen of Spades*	Fantastic narrative	Pushkin
	Rimsky-Korsakov	*Snegurochka*	Symbolist nature folk tale	Ostrovsky
		Sadko	Quasi-folk tale	
		The Tale of Tsar Saltan	Quasi-folk tale	Pushkin
		The Golden Cockerel	Satirical quasi-folk tale	Pushkin
		The Invisible City of Kitezh	Symbolist, semi-historical folk tale	
	Rubinstein	*The Demon*	Romantic spiritual narrative	Lermontov

(*cont.*)

Table 11.4 (*cont.*)

Category	Composer	Opera		Source
Peasant and bourgeois worlds	Rimsky-Korsakov	*May Night* *Christmas Eve*	Quasi-folk tale Quasi-folk tale	Gogol Gogol
	Tchaikovsky	*Cherevichki*	Quasi-folk tale	Gogol
	Smetana	*The Bartered Bride* *The Two Widows* *The Kiss* *The Secret* *The Devil's Wall*		
	Moniuszko	*The Haunted Manor*		
	Erkel	*Dózsa György* *Brankovics György*		
	Dvořák	*The Cunning Peasant* *The Devil and Kate*		

Italianate overture, opens with Timofei's 'How ardent is a young man's heart' in which he alternates in the traditional manner with a polyphonic chorus based on the folk song 'My dear Matushka'. Khandoshkin's *Variations on 'Ah, on a bridge'* for violin and viola, written about 1780, is in the European style, but the theme is a Russian folk song. Teplov's 'O! that dread day', of about 1750, reflects Russian song although its melody is original. Dubiansky's 'The blue dove' is accompanied by the (folk) guitar and the binary melody is completely vernacular. It was also a great favourite of Pushkin.[4]

Pushkin

Pushkin's enormous achievement helped create the agenda for Russian art above and beyond literature. He showed that the Russian language, its folk tales and legends, historical and contemporary events, were all fit subjects for the serious writer – and composer. His writings established the literary forms for nineteenth-century Russia, and established the basis for some of the most important operas of the next hundred years (Table 11.5).[5]

This opening up of Russia to its own history and, above all, its people, reflected a major change in Russian sensibility caused by the Napoleonic invasion of 1812, which created a new sense of national identity. Much of the resistance had been

Table 11.5 *Major operas based on Pushkin, 1842–1922*

Composer	Opera title	Original title	Date	Form
Glinka	*Russlan and Ludmilla*[1]		1842	Narrative legend, poem
Dargomïzhsky	*Rusalka*		1856	Dramatic poem
	The Stone Guest		1872	'Little tragedy'
Musorgsky	*Boris Godunov*		1869	Verse tragedy
Tchaikovsky	*Eugene Onegin*		1879	Verse novel
	Mazeppa	*Poltava*	1884	Narrative historical poem
	The Queen of Spades		1890	Novella
Rimsky-Korsakov	*Mozart and Salieri*		1898	'Little tragedy'
	The Tale of Tsar Saltan		1900	Original folk tale, poem
	The Golden Cockerel		1909	Original folk tale, poem
Rachmaninov	*Aleko*	*The Gypsies*	1893	Narrative poem
	The Miserly Knight		1906	'Little tragedy'
Cui	*The Captive in the Caucasus*		1883	Narrative poem
	A Feast in Time of Plague		1911	'Little tragedy'
	The Captain's Daughter			Novella
Stravinsky	*Mavra*	*The Little House in Kolomna*	1922	Humorous narrative poem

Note: [1] Glinka had hoped to write *Ruslan* with Pushkin himself. In the event the Bayan's song at the beginning of act I was inserted as a eulogy for the poet.

conducted, as in Spain, by *guerrilla* forces. These were made up of, and often led by, members of the ignored peasant class, who proved themselves to be intelligent, patriotic and resourceful, as a member of the Semonovskii Guard observed:

> The 1812 war awoke the Russian people to life . . . All the instructions and efforts of the government would not have sufficed to expel the Gauls and the multitude of other tribes which had invaded Russia, if the Russian people had remained as passive as it was wont. But it was not owing to instructions from their authorities that, on the approach of the French, they withdrew into the forests and marshes, leaving their homes to burn.   (Hosking, 1998: 172)

The result was a growing commitment by a number of members of the officer class to bring about social change. In 1825 the attempt to present a petition to the new Tsar, Nicholas I, on his coronation day, 14 December, was met with gunfire, exile and execution. This was the context for Pushkin's poem of 1827:

> Away the bars, the shackling chain,
> Down with the prison and the captor.
> Freedom waits at the gate with rapture,
> Brothers shall hand you swords again.
>   (Pushkin, 1997: 46–7)

The Decembrist martyrs became the inspiration for the revolutionary aspirations that culminated in the 1905 and 1917 Revolutions.[6]

Glinka

It was against this background of aspiration and repression that Glinka wrote the first truly Russian opera. Far from being revolutionary, Glinka nonetheless became aware of the national identity of musical forms, as Stasov points out:

> He brought back from Italy, not what he had gone there for, but something entirely different – the idea of a national art, of a Russian music. As he attended the Italian theatres and concert halls, listened to Italian music and famous Italian singers, he . . . realised that the Italians are one kind of people and we Russians another . . . This . . . was the decisive moment in the history of Russian music. Then, for the first time, our music entered upon a genuine, full life of its own. Glinka thought that he was creating only a Russian opera, but he was mistaken. He was laying the foundations of Russian music, of a whole school of Russian music, of a whole new system.   (Stasov, 1968: 67)

The initial results were the *Overture on two Russian Themes* and *A Life for the Tsar*. These were followed by *Russlan and Ludmilla* (1837–42) and the orchestral *Kamarinskaya*, of which Tchaikovsky wrote: 'It's all in *Kamarinskaya*, just as the whole oak is in the acorn' (Brown, 1974: 1). In it, Glinka showed how it was possible to take genuine Russian folk material and use it to create an extended orchestral composition. He did this by varying the harmonic and rhythmic 'background' which allowed the melodies to be repeated without monotony. This was not, however, sufficient for an entire opera, and in *A Life for the Tsar* Glinka worked with vernacular material in a more expansive and creative way, as the critic Yanuary Neverov understood:

> Mr Glinka has . . . looked deeply into the character of our folk music, has observed all its characteristics, has studied and assimilated it – and then has given full rein to his own fantasy which has taken images which are purely Russian, native. Many who heard his opera noticed something familiar in it, tried to recall from which Russian song this or that motif was taken, and could not discover the original . . . in fact there is not one borrowed phrase, but they are all clear, comprehensible, familiar to us simply because they breathe a pure nationalism, because we hear in them native sounds.   (Brown, 1974: 112–13)

Musical elements

Vernacular material is used in a variety of ways:

- Genuine quotation of folk music used either extant or varied. (This is in fact relatively rare, most of what sounds like folk song is original and written in the folk idiom.)
- Music in various national styles used for symbolic, dramatic purposes.
- Folk music (melody, rhythm or harmony) as the inspiration for a new kind of musical language.

This series of options is more than formal. It means that Nationalist opera and the idea of *narodnost* – nationalism or national identity – depends upon and is defined not simply by its subject-matter and style but the ideological basis on which a number of decisions have been made.

The opening, chorus-based sections in *A Life for the Tsar*, *Eugene Onegin* and *Boris Godunov* show how varied the use, structure and meaning of Nationalist elements could be. Each of these operas has a quite different sense of nationality, which affects how the music is constructed and how national elements are used (Table 11.6, p. 228).

Two scenes for chorus

A Life for the Tsar is defined by its use of peasant material and characters. It is dramatically innovative in having a peasant as the hero of a serious, historical work. Its *narodnost*, however, has nothing to do with a progressive, liberal view of the condition of the peasantry. The opening of the first chorus (Glinka, 1965: 1) is based on the *protyazhnaya pesnya* (drawn out song), a traditional form in which a *zapevala* (intoner) alternates with a harmonised chorus. The men's stately theme is contrasted with the women's dance melody. But, once stated, the two are combined in a distinctly European fugue, only interrupted for emphasis at bars 282–287 as the tsar is named. As in *Kamarinskaya*, Glinka avoids the repetition becoming monotonous by alternating, overlapping and combining (traditional) elements to create an extended art-music that sounds completely vernacular (Table 11.7, p. 230).

In *Eugene Onegin* the peasant choruses are simpler, although their dramatic use is more complex. The passage falls into three sections (Table 11.8a, p. 231).

The first chorus is sung unaccompanied off-stage, and is in the same style as the first section of *A Life for the Tsar*, alternating responses between the *zapevala* (intoner) and the chorus. However, the use of the national style is not as straightforward as it seems. In the opening offstage 'Bolyat moyi skori nozhenki so pokhodushki' (My nimble feet ache after a long journey' the peasants complain after their labour. They then move into the second, deferential section where, despite their exhaustion, they

Table 11.6 *Examples of folk and folk-influenced elements in Glinka, Musorgsky and Tchaikovsky*

Category	Composer	Opera	Act/Scene	
Folk song	Glinka	*A Life for the Tsar*	act I (no. 3)	Susanin: Shto gadat' o svad'be? Why dream of weddings? In his *Memoirs* Glinka says he took this melody down from a coachman's song
	Musorgsky	*Boris Godunov*	Part I ii/ Prologue ii	Chorus: Uzh kak na nyebe solntsu krasnomu As the sun shines supreme in the heavens Words and melody from an old furtune-telling song
			Part I, scene ii/ act I, scene ii	Varlaam: Kak yedet yon, yedet yon, yon There he goes, goes, goes Wedding song 'The bells were ringing in Novgorod'
			act IV, scene ii	Varlaam and Missail Solntse, luna pomyerknuli The sun and moon have faded Epic song 'Of Volga and Mikula'
				Women: Ne sokol letit po podnyebesyu It's not a falcon flying across the sky Folk song: 'Did the hawk not soar aloft with the quail?'
	Tchaikovsky	*Eugene Onegin*	act I, scene i	Chorus: Uzh kak po mostu, mostochku On the bridge, the little bridge Traditional song
Folk style	Glinka	*A Life for the Tsar*	act III	Vanya: Kak mat ubili/U malogo ptenca When they killed the mother/Of the little bird
	Musorgsky	*Boris Godunov*	Part II ii act I ii	Varlaam: Song of Kazan Adaptation of a melody learnt from Rimsky-Korsakov
			act II (not in 1869)	Fyodor: Turu, turu, petushok Turu, turu little cockerel Folk verses with original tune

National styles			
Tchaikovsky	*Eugene Onegin*	act I, scene i	Chorus: Bolyat moyi skori nozhen'ki so pokhodushki My nimble feet ache after a long journey
Glinka	*A Life for the Tsar*	act II, no. 5 no. 6 no. 7	Chorus: Polacca Dance: Cracowiak Dance: Mazurka Each of these underlines the alien, Polish nature of the scene[1]
Musorgsky	*Boris Godunov*	act III, scene i	Marina: Kak tomitelno i vyalo O how slowly they pass Marina's aria is set in a (Polish) national (mazurka) style
Tchaikovsky	*Cherevichki*	act III, scene iii	Dances: Polonaise Russian dance
		act IV (Finale)	Musicians: Oy, ne veyte, vetri Do not blow, you winds Tchaikovsky characterises the imperial court earlier (III iii) by using the Polonaise, but uses Russian rhythms for the native dances and here for the final celebration
Speech rhythms	Dargomïzhsky	*The Stone Guest*	
	Musorgsky		
	Janáček	A stylistic preoccupation of both composers	

Note: [1] Glinka's use of a Polish style and dances in act II of *A Life for the Tsar* is especially interesting. In his *Memoirs* he noted that the basic musical concept of the opera was the opposition between Russian and Polish material. However, at the first performance 'a deep silence reigned' at the end of the act because the audience did not know whether it was appropriate – or even wise – to applaud the Poles.

Table 11.7 A life for the Tsar: *the opening chorus*

1	a	1–32	The first three of four repetitions of a tripartite sequence in which i the soloist (*zapevala* – intoner) sings a melody which	Solo:	V burju, vo grozu In storm, in gale
		33–65	ii the male chorus then repeat and extend, followed by		
		65–97	iii a refrain in the lower strings		
	b	97–103	The orchestra extends the melody into a bridge		
		103–132	and then introduce a new, dance melody		
	c	133–162	Fourth repetition of the initial tripartite sequence, but with the melody developed as a bridge into	Solo:	Mir v zemle syroj Peace in the damp earth
2		163–198	an extension of the dance melody followed by two repetitions of a double sequence of	Women:	Vesna svoe vzjala Spring has taken its course
		199–217	i the women singing their dance melody followed by		
		217–235	ii an orchestral refrain.		
3	a	236–256	Starting with the men, the two choruses combine both melodies.	Men:	Vyruchili my We have rescued
	b	257–275	Both sing a slowed-down version of the dance melody.	All:	Iz plenu, k nam domoj From captivity, back home to us
	c	276–281	Orchestral bridge.		
	d	282–287	Unison statement of the Tsar's name.	All:	Michail Fedorovich
	e	288–406	The melodies are combined in a fugue as the chorus ask who will now dare attack the nation.	All:	On u nas opjat' He is back with us
	f	407–408	Long, emphatic note repeating the question.	All:	Kto! Who?
	g	410–437	Using a version of the dance tune the chorus join in their promise to defend the fatherland	All:	My vse za nego stenoj We will all protect him like a wall
	h	438–462	ending in a series of chords.		
	i	462-end	Slow echoing of the two themes between strings and woodwind to end the section.		

Table 11.8a Eugene Onegin: *the main sections of peasants' entry and chorus, act I*

1	1–24	The peasants sing off stage. The words emphasise their weariness after harvesting
2	25–48	The peasants announce the completion of the harvest. Larina congratulates them and asks them to celebrate by singing a song. They thank her.
3	49-end	A peasant song follows

agree to entertain the mistress with their 'peasant song' (an original melody by Tchaikovsky), 'Uzh kak po mostu' (On a bridge). The two songs have quite different social and dramatic implications. That both seem 'Russian' or 'national' is only part of the equation (Table 11.8b, p. 232).

Musorgsky: words, music and truth

It was almost impossible in nineteenth-century Russia to avoid ideological strictures, whether the imperial imperative underlying *A Life for the Tsar* or more radical ideas. In a country with no political forum, extreme censorship and no access to debate, the arts inevitably became the place where ideas were expressed, albeit in covert ways. The hugely influential critic Belinsky had impressed on artists that: 'The poet receives his substance from the life of his nation, consequently, the merits, depth, scope and importance of that substance depend directly and immediately upon the historical importance of his nation's life and not upon the poet himself or his talent' (Belinsky, 1976: 15). In other words, art was primarily to be judged by its social and political truthfulness. Purely 'artistic' criteria were important but secondary. Perhaps the most obvious example was painting, above all the Itinerants,[7] whose aim was to paint Russia as it really was and then tour the paintings to the major Russian cities so that their citizens could see them and start to come to terms with the realities of their country (Table 11.9).

This was translated into music by Alexander Dargomïzhsky (1813–69) in his last, incomplete opera, *The Stone Guest*, based on Pushkin's play. His struggle to write music that directly grew out of the Russian language was as much moral as artistic: 'The majority of our musical amateurs and newspaper scribblers do not consider me inspired. Their routine viewpoint seeks flattery for the hearing of melody, towards which I do not drive. I have no intention of lowering the level of entertainment for them. I want the sound to express the word directly. I want truth' (Leyda and Bertensson, 1974: 105). The setting follows the text without the distortions of traditional operatic forms. It is an expanded recitative, but does not develop anything distinctively 'Russian'. By contrast, for Musorgsky this was part of his objective, an essential of the meaning of *Boris Godunov*. 'Musorgsky . . . was a very self-conscious stylistic innovator. His media, no less than Dargomïzhsky's

Table 11.8b Eugene Onegin: *The peasants' entry and chorus in act I*

			The singing of peasants is heard from off-stage, gradually coming nearer		
1	a	1	The responsive chorus is initially led, as is traditional, by the solo tenor *zapelava*.	*Zapelava*	Bolyat moyi skori nozhen'ki so pokhodushki My nimble feet ache after a long journey
	b	9	The *zapelava* role is then taken over by the basses (9) and tenors (16). From this point, the polyphony becomes more 'European' in its complexity.	Basses	Shchemit moyo retivoye syerddtse so zabotushki My zealous heart aches with care
	c	15	Running semiquavers in the orchestra now lend the complaint a new, sprightly character.		
2	a	25	*The peasants enter carrying a decorated sheaf*		
			2/4 The chorus defers to their mistress, telling her the harvest is in. The setting becomes distinctly European in its polyphony 3/2	Chorus:	Zdratvstvui, matushka-barinya Good fortune to you, your ladyship
	b	37	Larina welcomes them and suggests they celebrate with a song.	Larina:	Shto zhi, i prekrasno Is it, I thank you
	c	41	Despite their weariness they thank Larina for her request.	Chorus:	Potyeshim, barinyu Plcase allow us, mother
3		49	3/4 With the change in time they sing a strongly rhythmic, dancing melody in two phrases which they repeat through bars 49–64, followed by	Chorus:	Uzh kak po mostu, mostochku Oh on a bridge, a little bridge
		69	a bridge into a variant	Chorus:	Libo Sashu, libo Mashu Either Sasha, or Masha
		78	then a strong rhythmic bar (78) in the orchestra and		
		83	a final return to the original melody which is varied to create a rising harmonic climax; and then a	Chorus:	Ne bessud-ka, moidruzhochek drizhochek Do not grumble, my dearest
		92	final six bars of a lively *vayinu* (*la-la-la*)		

The chorus departs without notice

Table 11.9 *Passages towards Russian Nationalist art*

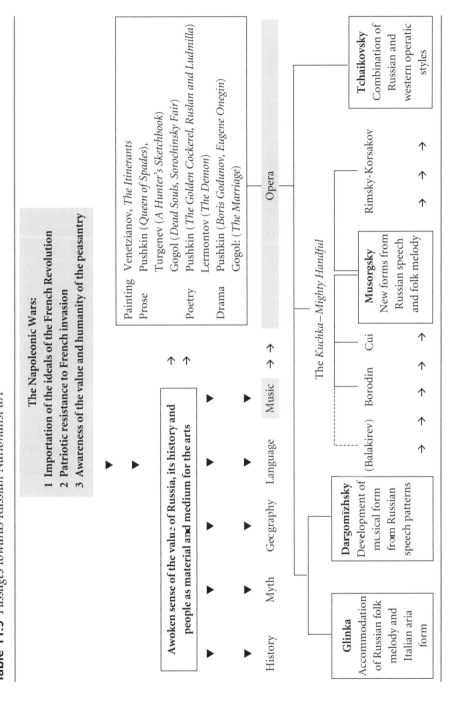

or Glinka's, were those of the European tradition; and yet he was more thoroughly and profoundly obsessed than any other member of his musical generation with *narodnost* [the national] and its full panoply of attendant historical and social issues' (Taruskin, 2000: 36).

In 1868, the year when he started work on *Boris Godunov*, Musorgsky asked:

> If one can assume a reproduction, through an artistic medium, of human *speech*, in all its most delicate and capricious shades, a natural reproduction, as natural as is required by the life and character of a man – would this be a deification of the human gift of speech? And if it is possible to tug at the heartstrings by the simplest of methods, merely by obeying an artistic instinct to catch the intonations of the human voice – why not look into the matter? – And if, at the same time, one could capture the thinking capacity as well, then wouldn't it be suitable to devote oneself to such an occupation?   (Leyda and Bertensson, 1947: 113)

The result, above all in the first (1869) version of *Boris Godunov*, was what Musorgsky had called an *opéra dialogué*. Far more than a conversational or *recitative* opera, this was to be an opera whose dramatic and musical form grew out of what he had called 'living prose in music, this is not a scorning of musician-poets toward common human speech, stripped of all heroic robes – this is reverence toward the language of humanity' (Leyda and Bertensson, 1947: 112).

Musorgsky's treatment of the peasants, in both the text and music, is quite distinct from either Glinka or Tchaikovsky. The opera has two protagonists: Boris himself and the people: 'I regard the people as a great personality, inspired by a single idea. This is my proposition. I have attempted to resolve it into an opera' (Leyda and Bertensson, 1947: 12). It presents the people suffering a series of catastrophes whose focus is the Tsar. Pushkin's play consists of twenty-four scenes that follow one another swiftly, like those in his Shakespearian model. In the opera these are reduced to seven in 1869 and nine in 1872, most of which are conflations of scenes in the play. By combining them, Musorgsky created a much stronger presence for his protagonists. The nobles are reduced to adjuncts to the main characters, while the Pretender becomes the motor that drives the narrative rather than the dramatic meaning. His role was greatly enlarged in the second version which was probably designed to increase the opera's acceptability by adding two more conventional scenes that included a major female role (Table 11.10).

The play opens with two nobles discussing Boris and his election. Musorgsky shifts the focus so that the opera starts with the people as they are forced to supplicate the Tsar, emphasising their coercion, brutal treatment, blind faith and self-manipulation. The opening (Musorgsky, 1975) is divided into six contrasting sections in which the crowd moves between their forced, formal supplication (C and E), dialogue with the police official (B and F) and argument among themselves (D) (Table 11.11a).

Table 11.10 Boris Godunov: *changing number of scenes and focus in original play and opera (1869 and 1872)*

	Play	Opera 1869	1872	
Total number of scenes	24	7	9	The 1869 St Basil scene is omitted in 1872, while the two scenes in Poland and the final scene in the Kromy forest are added.
People as dominant or major element	7	3	3	In the opera, the people's text is extended far beyond that in the play.
Grigory/Pretender	9	2	5	The pretender's scenes in Poland are a major addition, introduced largely to help 'normalise' the opera for the theatre's artistic committee.
Boris	5	4	3	In the opera, Boris is made far more central by reducing the number and inter-cutting of the play's scenes.
Nobles	3			Reduced to important but minor characters in the opera.

Table 11.11a Boris Godunov: *The main sections of act I, scene i/Prologue, part 1, bars 1–174*

A	1–25	Orchestral introduction and entry of the chorus and policeman.	
B	26–47	The officer abuses the crowd and demands that they beseech Boris.	'Dialogue' writing, following the contours of speech.
C	48–86	The people beseech the Tsar as required.	Strongly melodic in a 'folk' manner.
D	88–131	The crowd argue among themselves and with the officer.	'Dialogue' writing, following the contours of speech.
E	132–173	The people beseech Boris as ordered.	Strongly melodic in a 'folk' manner.
F	174	The people are told to attend to the Duma representative.	'Dialogue' writing, following the contours of speech.

Each section has its own kind of music, which is emphasised by the contrast between them. C and E, in which the people beg Boris to accept the crown, use a series of melodies that suggest both ecclesiastical and folk music, both appropriate to what they are required to do and their class. The sections where they are berated by the police official (B and F) combine recitative with strong motivic themes in the orchestra, suggesting their oppression; in the central passage (D), where they mock and argue among themselves, the music moves beyond recitative to reflect directly the intonation of the names, words and interjections. This is characteristic of the *opéra dialogué* style with which Musorgsky was concerned. A particular feature is the series of time signatures alternating 5/4 and 3/4 in the 'prayer' sections, and then 5/4 and 4/4 in the dialogue section (D: 88–131). These reflect the complex time signatures of Russian vernacular music and accommodate the natural word stress (Table 11.11b).

Musorgsky's approach is strikingly original. He creates a unified whole that is made up of dramatic, textual shifts that parallel Wagner's musical flexibility, structuring of monologue and dialogue. But Musorgsky's achievement is to make this both more flexible and a vehicle for realism. A comparison between Susanin's final aria, Tatyana's letter scene and any one of Boris's monologues shows how this close attention to the reality of a scene, character and precise language allowed Nationalism in radical hands to develop a new approach to what word setting in opera could achieve. But the most obvious demonstration of Musorgsky's radical departure is seen in the songs. A comparison between Glinka's 'Sleep my angel', Tchaikovsky's 'Evening prayer' and Musorgsky's 'Cradle song', from *Songs and Dances of Death*, shows how extreme music itself had become in Musorgsky's hands as he rejected everything but the sense, sound, rhythm and truth of the words.

The future of Nationalism?

As Schoenberg understood, the use of traditional, folk or folk-like material is, in a sense, incidental to the Nationalist composers' aims and effect. The important element is the use to which the material is put. The twin dangers of parochialism and musical limitation were identified, in an equally specific cultural context by Benjamin Britten: 'The English composers of today [1941] have consciously or unconsciously seen the danger-signals ahead. They are avoiding the pitfalls that some of their fathers and uncles have dug for them. It is only those who accept their loneliness and refuse all the refuges, whether of tribal nationalism or airtight intellectual systems, who will carry on the human heritage' (Kildea, 2000: 35). Smetana suggested a balanced view that recognised both the immediate historical importance of these works and their wider value:

> The programmes I suggest are to include masterpieces by heroes of every nation, but particular attention will be given to the works of Slavonic composers. And rightly so. Have works by Russian, Polish or Southern Slav composers even been heard in Prague? I hardly think so. Indeed, it is a rarity to meet one of our

Table 11.11b Boris Godunov: *analysis of act i, scene i/Prologue, part 1, bars 1–174*

A	1	**4/4 E major Andante** A slow dark introductory melody on the solo bassoon which then		
	10	turns into a faster (semiquaver), dotted version on flute with pizzicato accompaniment, which is then reduced to		
	14	a repetitive (semiquaver) figure in the violins which repeats throughout the scene (28, 32, 40, 111, 133, 157) and suggests oppression by the Officer, etc.		
	19	***Curtain*** Theme of bustle in the strings as the crowd appears, with (20) a new melody in the wind.		
B	26	**3/4 Moderato assai** An ominous chord on the trombones, and the oppressive motif in the strings.	Officer	Nu, Well?
	34	**C major** A single note repeated in the strings as the Officer sings.	Officer:	shto zh vi? What are you doing?
	40	Repressive motif as he urges the people to beg Boris to accept the crown.	Officer	Nu zhe! Da nu! Well then! Come on!
C	48	**A♭ major Meno mosso, quasi Andantino** The women start to pray for Boris using a formal melody that stretches over four bars in 3/4 and 5/4.	Chorus	Na kovo ti nas Why forsake us
	50	5/4	Chorus	pokidayesh, O and leave us, [O]
	51	3/4	Chorus	Otyets nash! father!
	54	5/4	Chorus	ostavlyesh [why] are you leaving
	55	3/4	Chorus	Kor/miletz! Provider!
	58	5/4	Chorus	tvoi siroti your orphans
	59	3/4	Chorus	bezzaschitniye defenceless
	67	5/4	Chorus	so goryomichi- with burn-

(*cont.*)

Table 11.11b (*cont.*)

	68	3/4		Chorus	-mi -ing [tears]
	76	The chorus beg – but using the repression motif		Chorus	Otyets nash! Our father!
	86	The chorus end their official prayer, and the strings subside into a repeated *f* on the violins. These semiquavers, echoing those accompanying the Officer at 34, now run until bar 129 when the chorus is forced, once again, to start beseeching the Tsar.			
D	88	**C major** 4/4}		Chorus (90)	Mityukha,
	96	3/4} The crowd argues among themselves.		Chorus (95)	Orala pushche vsekh She shouted worst
	98	4/4		Solo (98)	Nu vi, babi Now then, women
	110	3/4 Officer abuses them.		Officer (115)	Shto zh vi? What's going on?
	119	4/4		Officer (119)	Pro-uchu chu vas I'll teach you [what]
	121	3/4 They ask the officer not to beat them.		Officer (121)	. . . zhivo promptly
	126	4/4 and continue to complain about their treatment.		Chorus (126)	I vzdokhnut ne dast He won't let us breathe
	132	3/4 **A major** ***Con tutta forza*** They repeat their prayer to Boris from bar 48.			
F	174	4/4 The Officer demands silence for Shchelkalov.			

own people's names in our programmes . . . As a Czech I arrange Czech concerts. Surely we Czechs are allowed to have our own concerts. Or is the Czech public not fit for this? I think our reputation as a musical nation is sufficiently old and well known to justify this.   (Large, 1970: 129)

Apart from the innate quality of their operas, these composers highlighted the importance of national styles and speech for the wider development of musical language. This would offer a resource for renewal after the apparent exhaustion of harmonic and melodic potential in late Romanticism. Like Wagner, but in quite different ways and with different emphases, they also focused on opera as part of a larger intellectual enterprise that required an approach combining aesthetics and ideology.

Chapter 12

The role of the singer

The central 'attraction' of the operatic performance is the singer. But this is not a simple notion. The many ways in which the singer can be used define the operatic experience and, because of its centrality, has the potential to distort it. Consideration of the role and function of the singer entails four overlapping elements. In addition to the scope of the singer's functions as musician, interpreter and focus of public attention, there are the development of the range of voices used in opera (see appendix 2); the (social) history of the profession[1] and training and technical development (see Potter, 2000: Chapters 17 and 19). This chapter is concerned with the ways in which how the singer is handled and perceived affect the nature of opera.

The range of roles and attractions of the singer

Just as the singer can be asked to do different things, so audiences come to an opera with different expectations. Just as it is vital to know what any opera was designed to be, so it is essential to understand what the singer is meant to be doing in it. Without this, the opera and the singer are likely to be judged by wrong criteria. In Table 12.1, these roles are divided between those which belong to the singer *per se* and those which are part of an opera.

Despite the best efforts of modern directors, the *bel canto* operas of the *primo ottocento* are usually approached – or dismissed – as star vehicles and associated with illustrious names. In some sense, this is inevitable: opera is its living performance history. However there are dangers, as Bernard Williams points out:

> The historical conflicts between the dramatic and the performance aspects of opera have been concerned with the power of singers. They do not call in question the power of singing, which is at the heart of all opera . . . At a fine operatic performance, the audience is conscious of the singers' achievement and the presence of physical style and vitality; a feeling of performance and of the performers' artistry is more constantly at the front of the mind than it is with other dramatic arts.
> (Williams, 2006: 17)

Table 12.1 *The range of roles and attractions of the singer*

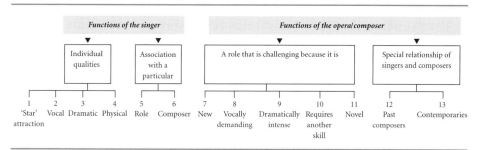

Functions of the singer

Star quality

The notion of the star performer is complex. Maria Callas is a good, if paradoxical, example. While admiration for her actual singing remains mixed, there was never any question of her dramatic ability. She was also a major force in the recovery of the *bel canto* repertoire after the Second World War (see Chapter 12 in this volume). All of this made good reason to attend her performances. However, in part because of her unhappy personal history, she also became an icon. She was someone whom it was important to have seen for her own sake, typical of the attitude towards the 'star'. This over-rode normal critical criteria, so that Callas's last recital performances were sought after despite the fact that everyone knew her singing was past its prime.

   Of course there may be excellent musical reasons for wanting to see or hear a singer who also happens to be a star, but star quality is itself a potent category that is irrelevant to any opera or its performance, as critics have always known: 'There have been better singers, there have been better musicians, there may have been better voices than Signor Mario. There has been no more favourite artist on the stage, in the memory of man or woman than he' (Potter, 2009: 57).

Vocal quality

Vocal quality and technical facility may be a draw, often irrespective of wider artistry. Although there have always been afficionados of the voice, this has been enhanced by recording that popularised singers and allowed them to reach beyond the confines of the opera house – or, in a sense, opera itself. Gigli was one of the first singers to achieve international popularity through the gramophone. The quality of his voice was never in doubt – although there were always critics of his vocal style, especially the Gigli 'sob' (Potter, 2009: 91). In particular there was no apparent ability to distinguish stylistically between Mozart, Verdi, Puccini or 'Neapolitan' songs. His acting, however, was consistently criticised. But despite this, he drew full houses, long after his vocal prime, as critics admitted: 'None of [these limitations] should blind us to the simple commitment of Gigli to share with his audience his understanding of what he knew better than anyone on earth at the time: the emotional and communicative power of the voice' (Potter, 2009: 92).

In the late twentieth century the power of recording, television and the media propelled Pavarotti to even greater heights of popularity, so that he became: 'the first tenor to transcend the aesthetic and musical world in which he matured as an artist... [his] voice has long ceased to be synonymous with the voice of music. It has become entertainment' (Kesting, in Potter, 2009: 186). This was in part due to the 'Three Tenors' phenomenon, as much part of the marketing industry as opera. The claim that it opened opera up to a wider audience was always in doubt because of its exclusive concentration on just one aspect of what opera is, as commentators show: 'If anything, the Three Tenors reinforced the tendency for the public to be offered a very limited musical diet, anthologised in the form of a "greatest hits" collection, with none of the vagaries of operatic plots or the contortion of recitative to contend with' (Potter, 2009: 178).

At the same time, sheer vocal quality is an essential component of opera, often demanded by composers such as Handel or Bellini. Joan Sutherland, not a natural actress, nevertheless was acclaimed as 'La Stupenda' on the basis of her flawless vocal technique in this repertoire: 'nobody living had heard before such a combination of vocal power and flexibility!' (Brook, 1995: 373). But even where the voice was rightly the centre of the event, critics have been aware of the imbalance between the musical and dramatic, as Charles Burney pointed out:

> Nicolini, Senesino, and Carestini gratified the eye as much by the dignity, grace and propriety of their action and deportment, as the ear by the judicious use of a few notes within the limits of a small compass of voice; but Farinelli, without the assistance of significant gestures or graceful attitudes, enchanted and astonished his hearers by the force, extent and mellifluous tones of the mere organ.
>
> (Burney, in Brook, 1995: 52)

Dramatic ability

A singer's dramatic ability may also be a major attraction. Tito Gobbi was admired as much for his acting as his singing. Audiences would choose to see him because of this combination of abilities over a finer 'pure' singer. In many ways he was an ideal opera performer, like Jean de Reszke whom Melba admired 'not only in his voice, which he used with an artistry which can only be called perfection – but in his appearance, his acting, his every movement' (Potter, 2009: 70). Equally, dramatic ability has sometimes compensated for relatively poor vocal quality. Wagner was inspired by Wilhelmine Schröder-Devrient despite the fact, as he says, that her 'effect by no means lay in any vocal virtuosity . . . for in this case that was scant and totally unsupported by any richness of the voice itself: the effect was simply due to the dramatic power of the rendering' (Wagner, 1994–5, v: 141).

Great actor-singers have always been acknowledged as a rarity and as an ideal for those who believe in opera as a dramatic form. When Stanislavski was invited to work with singers at the Bolshoi in 1919 'His teaching was based on the fusion of two masters, [the actor] Schepkin and Chaliapin. The System was the means, Chaliapin was the goal' (Benedetti, 1988: 234). Stanislavski was clear about the need for a balance:

> The opera singer has to deal with three arts simultaneously, i.e. vocal, musical and theatrical. Therein lie problems on the one hand and the supremacy of his creative work . . . All three arts the singer has at his disposal must be united as one, and directed to a common goal . . . The majority of singers only think about the 'sound', how to place and project a note towards the audience. They need sound for the sake of sound, a good note for the sake of a good note.
>
> In this regard the bulk of opera singers are still crude amateurs with little musical and theatrical education.   (Stanislavski, 2008: 330)

The question of what constitutes a full training for the opera singer has become increasingly important in the modern period when many theatre directors are deliberately brought into opera to emphasise its dramatic viability, as Richard Miller emphasises:

> One might ask why contemporary performance preparation should extend beyond the means available to artists of the past . . . today's performer must operate in an arena with even greater visual orientation than was the case in previous decades . . . A singer must be able to monitor his [or her] external behavior while performing, so that it conveys to an audience, through both voice and body, the desired artistic intention.   (Miller, 1996: 105)

Physical attraction

Opera has not usually been as susceptible to mere physical attraction as, perhaps, ballet or theatre (the 'matinée idol'). Singers are, however, sometimes praised for their looks. In the review of a solo *recording*, Danielle de Nise was described as 'an exotically magnetic stage presence' before the reviewer went on to ask 'how does she fare as an auricular rather than an ocular demonstration?' (Lawrence, 2008: 100). Maria Jeritza was described as having 'great physical allure and temperament, with a voice of individual timbre, if of no great power at any rate memorable. Memorable too was her acting' (Hope-Wallace, 1959: 142).

The danger of introducing this as a criterion was demonstrated when Deborah Voigt was withdrawn from *Ariadne auf Naxos* by 'the director, Christof Loy, [who] proclaimed her too heavy to wear a sleek black cocktail dress that he deemed integral to his concept. The dress has since become a symbol of skewed priorities among opera directors who value a singer's appearance over vocal artistry' (Tommasini, 2008).

Even the most superficial critics, such as Lady Granville, the British Ambassadress in Paris, have understood the limitations – let alone ethical undesirability – of this kind of attitude:

> Hideous, distorted, deformed, dwarfish Pisaroni. She has an immense head, a remarkably ugly face. When she smiles or sings her mouth is drawn up to one ear, with a look of a person convulsed in pain. She has two legs that stand out like sugar-tongs, one shorter than the other. Her stomach sticks out on one side of her body, and she has a hump on the other, not where stomachs or humps usually are, but sideways, like panniers.

> With all this, she had not sung ten minutes before a Paris audience was in ecstasies,... Every word is felt, every sound is an expression...I came home quite enchanted.   (Rosselli, 1995: 68)

The well-worn injunction to 'wait until the fat lady sings' emphasises the irrelevance of glamour in opera. Brecht wanted to cast 'unattractive' actors to play Romeo and Juliet, waiving conventional romantic platitudes and penetrating the true heart of the drama.

Association with a particular role or composer

Association with a role

There are singers who have been especially associated with a role. These are so-called 'legendary' performances, such as Christoff's Boris Godunov, Supervia's Carmen, Eva Turner's Turandot or Hotter's Wotan. This kind of mythologising has existed throughout opera history. But since the early twentieth century it has been per-petuated by audio and, even more, video recordings. These are always in danger of establishing stereotypes. They can interfere with casting, audience expectation and critical perception, making it difficult to come to a work afresh, as Brecht emphasised: 'the model is not set up in order to fix the style of performance; quite the contrary. The emphasis is on development: changes are to be provoked and to be made perceptible; sporadic and anarchic acts of creation are to be replaced by creative processes whose changes progress by steps or leaps' (Willett, 1977: 212).

Association with a composer

Similarly, a singer can be associated with a particular composer. In Wagner, for example, artists such as Melchior, Flagstad, Nilsson or Windgassen, again helped by recordings, have been taken as definitive. This is enhanced where there is some kind of claim to tradition: 'Melchior then returned to England for German lessons before going back to Munich to study the essential Wagner roles with the soprano who had once been Mahler's mistress and was a close friend of Cosima Wagner' (Potter, 2009: 156). These singers' undoubted quality means that there is a great deal that can be learned from them, by both artists and audiences. But again there is a danger of stereotyping works/roles so that innovation and experimentation cannot take place. In his 'Preface' to the first volume of EMI's *The Record of Singing*, Michael Scott argues that:

> when interpreting the music of the late eighteenth century and much of the nineteenth century, which still provides the bulk of most opera houses' repertory, it is as well to remember that the music was not composed for the theatres, singers, orchestra players and public of today. Our interpretations, however fine in their own way, can never be as stylish as those that were given by the composers' contemporaries. Changes in vocal method and technique, in the instruments of the orchestra, in the design of the theatres, and even, in a way, in the ears of the audience, have seen to that.
>
> (Scott, 1977: 4–5)

This again implies a 'correct' style and immutable composers' intentions which the recordings accurately reflect. The weight of evidence from composers' letters and reports of their conversation shows that this was rarely the case. Composers have often felt constrained by what the singers wanted or were expected to do. The notion of singers' special, even definitive relationship with a role or composer can only be evidence, useful example or critical criterion.

Functions of the opera/composer

New roles

Where a singer is well known, particular interest can be aroused when he or she has taken on an unexpected role. In 2005 Placido Domingo recorded *Tristan und Isolde*. He had performed rather more Wagner than is often thought, starting with *Lohengrin* in 1968, but *Tristan* aroused special interest, not least because of his age – and its implications for vocal stamina – balanced against his musical maturity worried reviewers:

> Of course, the 60-something tenor could never tackle this role on stage now, but it is not often one hears quite such a fantasy interpretation being realised on disc . . . the idea of him recording this masterpiece in full seemed a little far-fetched. The advantage of the recording studio is that his Tristan never seems to tire and he gives an ardent account, characterised by the almost baritonal warmth of his voice.
>
> (Allison, 2005: 73)

The recording was a great success and has become a 'recommended recording' (see March, 2008: 1536–7). But it creates a spurious sense of being a benchmark because it is irrelevant to the stage, however much it may illuminate aspects of the opera.

In a different move, in 2009 Domingo took on the baritone role of Simon Boccanegra. Because he has a major following, critics predicted that: 'Not many will care too much about the reception accorded the director . . . This was Domingo's show and his many fans will be eager to discover how he fared in his courageous move to baritone territory' (*Gramophone*, December 2009: 14). Again, the results may be illuminating in terms of what a mature and experienced artist can do with the role; but the danger is that it will become a stunt and a distraction from the opera itself.

Vocally demanding roles

Some roles are especially demanding, enabling virtuoso display, display as part of the character, or both. The Queen of the Night's virtuoso arias are expressions of her emotional state and steely nature as David Cairns says: 'The coloratura, which in her act 1 aria she turns on as it were to dazzle Tamino, is here shot from her by the force of an uncontrollable fury; the mask the Queen wore in act 1 is stripped from her and her Medusa gaze glares at us head on. This is music that demands to be sung with maximum vehemence, by a dramatic soprano with an extended top to the voice' (Cairns, 2006: 218).

Both singers and audiences can be attracted by virtuosity *per se*, but this will always distort opera as a holistic dramatic (or even musical) experience, as a contemporary wrote about Angelica Catalani:

> [Catalani's] excessive love of ornament proved a fatal stumbling-block, and ruined the beauty of this matchless voice. She cared for no simple air . . . She preferred the music of the most inferior composers, written expressly for her, to the most exquisite productions of the greatest masters . . . Her fantastical luxuriance and redundancy, her reckless daring, her defiance of the rules, disgusted connoisseurs as much as it astounded and charmed the multitude.   (Brook, 1995: 73)

With the development of more focused dramatic writing in the mid nineteenth century, roles such as Violetta, or Marguerite in *Faust*, make substantial *coloratura* demands as part of their characters. As a result, a composer such as Verdi, for whom the music was an equal partner with the drama, was strongly aware of the potential conflict:

> Tadolini, I believe, is to sing Lady Macbeth, and I am astonished that she should have undertaken the part. You know how highly I regard Tadolini, and she herself knows it, but for the sake of us all I feel I must say this to you: Tadolini's qualities

are far too fine for this rôle... Tadolini has a wonderful voice, clear, flexible, strong, while Lady Macbeth's voice should be hard, stifled and dark.

(Verdi, in C. Osborne, 1971: 39)

In the later twentieth century increasing vocal demands have been put on the singer that surpass the pyrotechnics of *opera seria* or *bel canto*. One tendency has been to write for an increasingly high *tessitura*. Act III, scene 5 of Zimmermann's *Die Soldaten* combines consistently high lines with complex ensemble. Thomas Adès' writing for Ariel in his *Tempest* is 'incredibly high and difficult to sing', and the singer who created the role has said that 'That first scene is very frightening, very punishing. It's always terrifying to come straight out and sing that high – a bit like asking an ice-skater to jump a triple axel straight after stepping on the ice' (*Gramophone*, August 2009: 15). One effect is to render the words themselves indistinguishable.

Dramatically demanding roles

This tendency is complicated by the increased theatrical demands made by modern composers and librettists who include complex directions in the score. In addition, the important move to treat opera of all periods as drama can lead directors to ask performers to sing while making physical demands that can add to the challenge of voice production. Even without this, it creates an expectation that was at most optional before the late nineteenth century. In both Verdi's and Wagner's operas there is a stream of detailed directions written into the scores, asking far more of the singer than generalised attitudes: 'From this point onwards, Wotan's expression and gestures grow in intensity, until they culminate in the most terrible outburst... gazing at length into her eyes, after which he strokes her hair in a gesture of spontaneous tenderness. As if emerging from deep thought, he finally begins in whispered tones' (Spencer and Millington, 2000: 148). *Verismo* operas, and their extension in Puccini, contain similarly detailed directions, parallel with those of the classic Naturalists such as Ibsen or Chekhov. Towards the end of act III of *La Bohème*, as Mimì lies dying, the score specifies the detailed scenario laid out in Table 12.2 (Puccini, n.d.: 395, 397, 398, 405).

In act II, scene ii of *The Knot Garden*, Tippett asks that 'This scene, though more naturalistic than Scene I, is played as by puppets, especially Faber' (Tippett, 1969: 16).

These demands are an essential part of the operas' vitality. However they may become an attraction in its own right, as Michael Kennedy describes:

> Klytämnestra is one of the juiciest roles Strauss created. It is short, but contraltos or mezzo-sopranos will ever be grateful to him for the chances it gives them to make audiences' flesh creep... quite apart from the music, which singing-actress

Table 12.2 *La Bohème: act III stage directions*

Fig.		Libretto words	*Directions*
25	Mimì	It was dark, and my blushing could not be seen	She remembers her meeting with Rodolfo on Christmas Eve
	Rodolfo		Mimì is seized by a suffocating spasm and lets her head fall back, exhausted
		Oh! God! Mimì	Terrified, he holds her up
26	Schaunard		returns at this moment; on Rodolfo's cry he runs to Mimì
		What's happening?	
	Mimì	Nothing... I'm fine.	She opens her eyes and smiles to reassure Rodolfo and Schaunard
30			A ray of sunlight falls through the window on Mimì's face; Rodolfo sees this and tries to shade her: Musetta points to her shawl. Rodolfo thanks her with a look, takes the shawl, gets up onto a chair and tries to spread it over the window

could resist the stage-direction's description of the queen on her entrance? – 'in the dazzling torchlight her wan and bloated face seems more pale against her scarlet robes. She is leaning both on her confidante and on an ivory stick, encrusted with jewels... The queen is completely covered in precious stones and charms. Her arms are covered in bracelets, her fingers with rings. Her eyelids are exceptionally large and it seems to cause her considerable effort to keep them open.'

(Kennedy, 1999: 156–7)

In each of these cases, attention is bound to be drawn to the singer as more than mere vocalist, and 'success' as singer and actor will be balanced and judged against one another. Directors, audiences – the whole apparatus of the opera – have to decide on their priorities.

Operas requiring additional skills

Papageno and Tamino are both asked to play instruments – which their creators were able to do. The soprano in *Les Contes d'Hoffmann* is required to sing three, very different, demanding roles, including Olympia with her mechanical actions. In a recent production of *The Turn of the Screw* by the Mariinsky Theatre, the boy singing Miles played the piano part himself. Meyerbeer understood the attraction value of this kind of demand. In *Dinorah* the heroine is required to dance with her own shadow at the crux of the action; in *Le Prophète* the chorus was taught to use newly invented roller-skates for the ice skating scene. While this can be dramatically valid, there is always the danger of such elements becoming a stunt.

Strauss was aware of the demands he was making, and the potential for sensationalism, when he wrote the 'Dance of the seven veils' for *Salome*. In this case, failure to realise the complete physicality of the main role would undermine the opera. The temptations, however, are manifold, as this reviewer appreciated:

> While not everyone's idea of a proper opera singer, there's no denying soprano Maria Ewing's artistry as a performer, which is why her portrayal of...[the] heroine in this 1992 staging is so riveting to watch. Her intensity, often misdirected in other portrayals, is focused on the teenage temptress she's playing, and she even performs a credibly sexy dance of the seven veils. Her then-husband, director Sir Peter Hall, makes sure that the audience sees his wife in the altogether at its conclusion (admittedly something not too many opera singers could pull off).
>
> (Filipski, 1992)

Well-known – or unknown – operas

Where an opera is unknown, or has been long ignored, there are obvious pressures to ensure that it succeeds. When revived, this may involve the central role, as with Callas and Sutherland in the *bel canto* repertoire, or the recovery of *opera seria* in general. This can create a tension between the responsibility to let an audience see the work itself (i.e. without interpretative intervention) and the desire to prove its viability as part of the modern repertoire. The singer can be easily caught between the two.

Ironically, where an opera is very well known (*Carmen, La Bohème, Aida*) there will, again be particular expectations of the main interpreters – as well as production – either to come up with something new or to meet the standards of previous productions and 'legendary' performers. This can, once again, produce a conflict between the work as it is known and loved, the desire to make it new, and mere novelty – any of which has implications for the performer. This is reflected in the next category.

Special relationship between singer and composer

Past composers

There are singers who have been instrumental in reviving 'lost' areas of the repertoire. This is usually where they offer a particular opportunity to the singer. Nonetheless, these are adventurous and artistically creative individuals who have added much to the repertoire.

Alfred Deller was neither primarily interested in opera nor a natural actor. However his recovery of the counter-tenor voice opened up new possibilities, inspiring contemporary composers such as Britten. It also involved a major reassessment of the *castrato* in the modern repertoire, raising both historical and musical questions:

> Opera seemed most likely to welcome the re-emergence of counter-tenor or alto voice, especially because the performance of very early opera had been handicapped without this voice, both as regards its musical effect and because of difference in stage 'presence' of a male rather than female singer. In addition, rôles were written for castrati which were and are well within the range of a large-voiced counter-tenor, with no need for transposition.   (Giles, 1993: 142)

Although not 'lost', the *bel canto* repertoire had become very restricted by the early twentieth century. With the appearance of singers to whom it offered particular opportunities, or those who saw a new dramatic potential in it, *bel canto* opera became part of the repertoire again. Many Rossini operas, for example, are only now being premiered in Britain. It is also easy to forget how recently Verdi has been taken seriously, as Francis Toye (writing in 1962) shows:

> Some five years ago I was lucky enough to hear several performances of Verdi operas at La Scala under Toscanini, and these performances brought with them a conviction that the importance attached to Verdi by conventional musical opinion in England was miserably inadequate...as a mere purveyor of tunes...Lip service might be paid to the merits of 'Otello' and 'Falstaff'; otherwise there was the same dreary repetition of the nonsense – for it is nonsense – about the 'guitar-like orchestra' in 'La Traviata' or 'Rigoletto'; 'Aida' was 'flashy' or 'empty'; 'Il Trovatore' 'just absurd'. Operas like 'La Forza del Destino' or 'Don Carlo' remained mere names, remembered, if at all, by some isolated numbers associated with famous singers.   (Toye, 1962: vii)

It was against this background that Callas's performances demonstrated the operas' combined dramatic and musical viability:

> By far her most interesting appearance of the 1950 season was that in Verdi's Il Trovatore...It is far from a polished performance, imprecise in ensemble and not musically complete, and yet not without interest, indeed it is remarkable as a portrayal of Leonora in which Maria Callas is newly discovering Verdi singing...Maria Callas performed the vocal part with all the finesse of *fioritura* and trills, thereby depicting the character. To take an example: there exist trills at the ends of phrases in 'D'amor sull'ali rosee' and 'Vanne, sospir dolente' just as in many other parts of the role.

> Yet their effect is lost when they are sung as if they were flute-like, merely decorative figures . . . Even Rosa Ponselle, or even an expressive singer like Claudia Muzio, do not dip the melodic line or the ornamental figures as deeply into the sound of *melancolia tinta* as Maria Callas. Putting it another way: Maria Callas has so much more to offer than notes spun out on a *fil di suono*. She does not make the part comfortable for her voice, but carries through every vocal formula and binds it into the larger shape.
>
> (Kesting, 1992: 296–7)

Cecilia Bartoli's artistry has allowed her to play an important role in bringing eighteenth-century operas to the public's attention – in many cases, works not heard since their original performances:

> Another composer for whom I have a passion is Vivaldi. I very much hope to revive his opera *La Griselda* with William Christie and Les Arts Florissants. Vivaldi is a very neglected composer, especially in Italy, which is unforgivable when one considers that he is such an important link in the Italian musical tradition. I don't see how any of us can presume to sing opera without knowing where it sprang from. And while the importance of Monteverdi, and to a lesser extent Cavalli, has been recognized, Vivaldi has yet to be fully appreciated.
>
> (Matheopolos, 1998: 249)

Contemporaries

Until the end of the eighteenth century most operas were written for specific singers and companies. In order to ensure success, the composer would want to please his singers, and be sure that the music suited their voices, range and technique to achieve the maximum effect. The result could lead to major changes in the course of composition or rehearsal, as Mozart wrote to his father:

> The Aria is excellent now – however, there's yet another change; Raaf is responsible for this one, but he is right; . . . He came to me yesterday, I trotted out his First Aria for him and he was very pleased, with it. – Well, now, the man is old, and in the aria 'fuor del mar ho un mare in seno,' etc., in the second Act, he is no longer able to show off his voice as he would like to; therefore, since he has no Aria in the third Act and cannot sing as much Cantabile as he would like to in his Aria in the first Act (because he has to concentrate on the expression of the words), he requested a pretty Aria after his last speech, 'O Creta Fortunata! ò me, felice!' to take the place of the quartetto.　　　(Spaethling, 2000: 214)

Britten similarly wrote for specific voices: 'I don't think I ever write an opera without knowing before I start who is going to sing the roles . . . I like to have their particular voices . . . in my mind when I write for them' (Kildea, 2000: 305). This was particularly so in his writing for Peter Pears who created all the central figures in his operas – but which created problems for other singers: 'Many of Pears' contemporaries and successors ... have taken on Britten roles and creatively extended the interpretative possibilities that were so rooted in the partnership between Britten and his tenor' (Potter, 2009: 134–5). Massenet was susceptible to both beauty and artistry – and, fortunately in his case, both inspired him positively, as he describes in a chapter significantly called 'A star':

> The master of the house hastened to greet them and I was presented to them almost at once.
>
> The younger was extraordinarily lovely ... What a fascinating voice! ... I was astounded, stupefied, subjugated. [Later when presented with a libretto by his publisher] I had scarcely run through a scene or two than I cried out in an outburst of deep conviction, 'I have the artiste for this part. I have the artiste. I heard her yesterday. She is Mlle. Sibyl Sanderson. She shall create Esclarmonde.
>
> (Massenet, 1970: 175, 177)

Some singers could advise both on the music being written for them and, because of their experience, more general aspects of an opera, as this passage from a biography of Halévy suggests:

> The part of Leopold had originally been offered to the tenor Nourrit who delicately pointed out that Leopold was a superficial character and that he, Nourrit, would much rather tackle the formidable part of Elazar. Halévy was taken aback. Tenors were supposed to be heart-throbs, not wizened old men. Elazar was definitely a mature bass. Nourrit turned on the charm and Halévy allowed himself to be persuaded. As he was working on Elazar's arias he discovered that a tenor voice was lending the part shades he had not visualised before. He was so taken with Nourrit's involvement that he did not flinch when the latter suggested a radical change in the score.
>
> Apart from being a beautiful and intelligent tenor, Nourrit was also a professor of singing at the Conservatoire, something of a poet, with a keen eye to dramatic development. He suggested that instead of bringing the curtain down on act IV with a finale, as was the convention, Halévy should end it with a solo for Elazar, to bring out the loving father side of his character. He offered to write the words himself. 'He wanted to choose the most sonorous syllables, those kindest to his voice', Halévy recalled. He negotiated the proposition with Scribe who graciously gave his consent. The result was *Rachel, quand du Seigneur la grâce tutélaire*, the aria that never falls to clutch at the heart strings wherever it is performed.
>
> (Jordan, 1994: 60–1)

Singers can adopt a quite different attitude, however, as with John Mark Ainsley during the composition of Henze's *Phaedra*:

In terms of Phaedra and Hippolytus we didn't communicate quite as much as one might expect, but that was more to do with how I like to work on new pieces. Quite often then I was invited to Marina, to his villa to talk about it, hear some things that he'd done, and see if I liked them, if I thought maybe he might change something. Now I always feel slightly uncomfortable and suspicious when a composer's quite that nice. And he is absolutely that nice. If I said I don't want to sing a high B on an 'e' vowel, he would have done his best not to write an 'e' vowel on a very high note. Personally I would much rather that any composer writes what's in their head and their heart and then deliver it and if there's something that is technically impossible for me as the protagonist then that's when the conversation I think is best had.   (Ainsley, 2007)

Any opera is susceptible to the careful balance between its music, dramaturgy and production. The role of the singer is crucial to all three and this has been redefined in each period. Unless that role is understood and attuned to the style and demands of the work, what the singer does can establish or distort the opera or the production. This is especially the case where technique and virtuosity are so identifiable and admired in their own right. For opera to be successful requires a sensitivity to the roles of the singer as vocalist, actor, interpreter and personality: a complexity that reflects that of opera itself.

Part III

The twentieth and twenty-first centuries

Chapter 13

The turn of the century and the crisis in opera

Naturalism and *Verismo*

Operatic Naturalism, most often associated with Italian *Verismo*, was the culmination of straightforward dramatic narrative and musical language: thereafter both started to fragment and develop more complex experiences. Until the later nineteenth century, the history of the arts presents a relatively clear development. From thereon, under a number of pressures, they began to fragment into a series of alternative, vying and often simultaneous movements. These 'isms' of the early twentieth century are most clearly seen in painting with several of them (highlighted in Table 13.1) paralleled in opera.

Naturalism is a philosophical movement that emerged in the mid nineteenth century as a response to growing industrialisation, urbanisation and the Darwinian scientific view of man. This responded to a view of the the human condition as completely determined by the material forces of the market and the social and physical environment this created. To Victor Hugo's emphasis on 'exactness in the matter of locality',[1] Zola now added specific period, saying that his *Rougon-Maquart* novels would have been impossible before 1889: 'I shall show this group at work, participating in an historical period . . . And thus the dramas of their individual lives recount the story of the Second Empire, from the ambuscade of the Coup d'Etat to the treachery of Sedan' (Zola, 'General Preface' to the *Rougon-Maquart* novels).

Although primarily a novelist, Zola was above all concerned with the relationship between the arts and social reality. He demanded the reform of theatre so that it could:

> put a man of flesh and bones on the stage, taken from reality, scientifically analysed, without one lie. I am waiting for them to rid us of fictitious characters, of conventional symbols of virtue and vice, which possess no value as human data. I am waiting for the surroundings to determine the characters, and for the characters to act according to the logic of facts, combined with the logic of their own temperament. I am waiting until there is no more sleight-of-hand of any kind, no more strokes of a magic wand, changing people and things in an instant. I am waiting for the time to come when they will tell us no more incredible stories, when they will no longer spoil the effect of real observation with romantic

Table 13.1 *The fragmentation of painting in the early twentieth century*

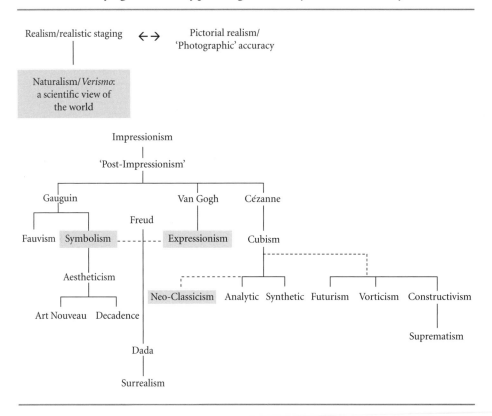

events ... I am waiting for a dramatic work, free from declamation, big words, and grand sentiments that has the high morality of truth, that will teach the terrible lesson that belongs to all honest inquiry.   (Zola, 1974: 711)

That inquiry was to be 'scientific' – an objective study of life that might give rise to a truthful ethic rather than a conventional judgemental imposition. Verga, Italy's most important naturalist, whose short story, *Cavalleria Rusticana* was the basis for Mascagni's libretto,[2] echoed this in the general preface to his projected five-novel sequence study of 'The fateful, endless and often wearisome and agitated path trod by humanity to achieve progress'. He intended this to run from the poor fishermen of *I malavoglia* to the highest echelons of society[3] so that: 'The person observing this spectacle has no right to judge it; he has already achieved much if he manages to draw himself outside the field of struggle for a moment to study it dispassionately, and to render the scene clearly, in its true colours, so as to give a representation of reality as it was, or as it should have been' (Verga, 1998: 'Preface'). When Zola turned to the problems of modern opera he predictably called for:

a more directly human drama, not taken from the mythologies of the North, but bursting upon us, poor human beings, in the reality of our misery and our joy. I'm not asking for operas in frockcoats or even blouses. No! I will be happy if instead of puppets, instead of abstractions drawn from legends, we are given living beings, gay with our gaiety, suffering with our suffering . . . It can be dressed in velvets, if one wants; but there must be people there, and coming from the whole work a cry of profound humanity.   (Zola, 1966–9: 832)

To create this, both theatre and opera needed all the resources of Realism, but as the external sign of Naturalism's underlying concern, the representation of the environment as the condition of human behaviour (Table 13.2).

Although Naturalism in opera is best known in its Italian version, *Verismo*, it was *Carmen* that made the breakthrough. Its subject was antipathetic to French operatic convention in its modernity, morality and class, as one of the administrators at the Opéra exclaimed: 'Isn't she killed by her lover? And these bandits, gypsies, and girls working in a cigarette factory! At the Opéra-Comique! The family theatre, the theatre for wedding parties' (Weisstein, 1964: 224). (One might be forgiven for thinking that the PR in 2011 for Mark-Anthony Turnage's *Anna Nicole* was positively designed to elicit such a reaction.) Bizet himself played a major role in structuring the libretto, well aware of the challenges he was creating, and making only three concessions to his audience's expectations: 'the duet between Micaëla and

Table 13.2 *Realism and Naturalism: priorities and implications*

Realism	Naturalism
The mere appearance of 'reality' in scenography, costume, speech used to dress otherwise sentimental, Romantic, or idealised drama	The use of realistic sets, costume, dialogue as the necessary condition of the world of the characters
▼	▼
Milieu as decoration	'Photographic' presentation and analysis
▼	▼
Performance as theatrical/operatic illusion[1]	Behaviour as truth conditioned by circumstances. (Special interest in working-class aspects of society)

Note: [1] 'The role of characters in Soviet novels and long poems, however, like that of the figures in mediaeval art, was to express the ideal of the Church. Some writers, those most adept at passing off lies as truth, took particular pains over the details of the clothes and furniture they described. They peopled their realistic stage sets with idealised, God-seeking characters' (Grossman, 2010: 93).

Don José in the first act, the entrance of the Torero in the second, and Micaëla's aria . . . these were the only pieces to attract attention and to be applauded, although indifferently . . . In the rest of the score, he tried only to impart the greatest possible degree of truth and passion to his work' (Weisstein, 1964: 224).

Carmen established the criteria for the Naturalistic opera that Zola had wanted, much of which challenged assumptions about opera as a refined and sophisticated art form. This new genre presented:

- modern life, usually of working people;
- a strong sense of genuine, local setting and behaviour;
- the use of vernacular music;
- an emphasis on sexuality more than romantic love;
- raw emotion and a tendency towards violence;
- direct musical and dramatic expression.

Carmen, however was not really followed up in France. Instead, it was Italy that needed Naturalism as a way of focussing on and expressing the realities of its working and middle classes in the post-Risorgimento world.

Mascagni (*Cavalleria rusticana*)

Mascagni's *Cavalleria Rusticana* is an example of *Verismo* at its purest. Its subject and dramatic treatment answer all these expectations, with the addition of dramatic compression. A characteristic skill of the *Verismo* composers was the ability to create a dramatic and musical unity out of a series of rapidly changing dramatic moments and emotions focused in powerful melody, as the conductor Edward Gardner says: '*Tosca* is, of course, filled with great arias; but in *Tosca* even more than Puccini's other operas, the listener doesn't get the impression of the drama pausing to allow the singers his or her moment' (Gardner, 2010: 8).

By the turn of the century Italian composers and theorists were much concerned by the challenge of German music in general, and Wagner's operas in particular. Both undermined Italian primacy, and presented new aesthetic demands, derived from the symphonic tradition:

> The idea of a unified musical conception was to become increasingly important to Verdi over the course of his career, arguably reaching its peak in *Otello*. Thus, by the turn of the twentieth century, a work perceived to be lacking in unity not only failed to meet the new demands of post-Wagnerian opera, but was also a retrograde step in terms of the Italian tradition itself.   (Wilson, 2009: 48)

Verismo paradoxically appeared to be both modern and regressive. The subject-matter and its dramatic treatment were precisely what Zola had demanded. But musically there were distinct, apparently retrograde, 'numbers', with identifiable, self-standing melodies. However, this duality was essential to its aims: the deployment of musical and dramaturgical forces designed to confront their audience with the realities of real life in the most animated way.

The duet between the distraught Santuzza and Alfio (Table 13.3) shows how this kaleidoscope of easily recognised and assimilated melodies is used to create an organic musico-dramatic structure. Much of the material is fragmentary and motivic, and is established in the 'Prelude' which is built out of themes that will be used throughout the opera. This is not a *pot-pourri*, however, but a tone poem, in which the peaceful atmosphere of Easter is destroyed by the anguish of the melody that later accompanies Santuzza's outpouring of frustrated love to Mamma Lucia. This is followed by Turiddu's *Siciliana*/serenade which interrupts the overture in an original stroke as the dramatic action 'invades' the overture.[4] Other motifs develop in the course of the opera itself. The theme first heard in Santuzza's 'Turiddu ov'è' (no. 3) becomes 'in effect a leitmotif... linked not so much to Santuzza as the deadly destiny she brings' (*Grove*, 1997: 781b). The introduced, ironic songs, Alfio's 'Il cavallo scalpita', Lola's *stornello* and the choruses, seem to relieve the tension, but in fact create an increasing emotional suspense as the audience waits for the drama to resume. The developing sequence of set pieces tightens the net around the characters as they move from crisis to crisis. The dramaturgical and melodic structures are the perfect analogue for the narrative's inner necessity and the audience's own experience.

Verismo proper was not a long-lived movement. Giordano, Leoncavallo, Mascagni and Puccini all turned to subjects that were beyond its original scope in period (*Andrea Chénier*, *Suor Angelica*), location (*Madama Butterfly*, *La Fanciulla del West*, *Iris*), or class (*Fedora*, *Tosca*). Part of the impetus came from publishers who believed the public wanted novelty and an alternative to the grim realities of *Mala vita*. But underlying its world view and its special use of realism, there lay an expressive directness, emotional and psychological truth that has continued to lend it great appeal and which has had a significant impact on subsequent composers however 'advanced' their musical idiom.

Puccini (*Tosca, Madama Butterfly*)

Towards the end of his life Puccini wrote: 'To turn to ourselves: I told you that I still want to make people weep: therein lies everything . . . We are not out to make original departures, nor do we rack our brains searching for something new. Love and grief were born with the world and we, our kind who have passed the half century, know well the impact of both' (Girardi, 2000: 329–30). What seems to be a very diminished response to the human condition in reality expresses a dominant twentieth-century view of man. It denies the grand traditional narratives and instead sees only the life and emotions of the individual, reinforced by Freud's emphasis on the reality of the private, inner world. There is a courageous frankness that traditional ethics

Table 13.3 *Cavalleria rusticana: analysis of the first part (formally identified elements highlighted in italic)*

1	Preludio e Siciliana	Turiddu:	O Lola cha'ai la, di latti la cammisa / O Lola, with your blouse as white as milk	Turiddu interrupts the 'overture' with his (off-stage) serenade to Lola.	Turiddu's 'interruption' is part of the opera's organic unity, so that the dramatic, but 'pure' music, is made part of the drama.
2	Coro introduzione	Chorus:	Gli aranci olezzano / The oranges' fragrance	The chorus cross the stage after the day's work.	
3	Scena e	Santuzza:	Dite, mamma Lucia / Tell me, Mamma Lucia	Santuzza reveals her plight to Lucia.	
	[Aria]	Santuzza:	Mamma Lucia, vi supplico / Mamma Lucia, I beg you	Santuzza begs Turiddu's mother for help.	This tiny aria (under one-and-a-half minutes, including an interruption) roots the tragedy and explains the opening Siciliana.
		Lucia:	Che dici? / What are you saying?		
	sortita di Alfio e coro	Alfio:	Il cavallo scalpita / The horse tramples	Alfio and the chorus praise the carter's life.	The tragedy is held in suspense by Alfio's robust entry.
				Alfio's 'song' lowers the emotional temperature – but the audience's suspicions are now aroused.	
4	Scena e	Lucia:	Beata voi, compar Alfio / You are blessed, neighbour Alfio	Lucia learns that Turiddu is still lurking in the village.	The narrative is resumed – and then made dramatic by Santuzza's aside to Lucia ('Tacete!' – Be silent!')
	preghiera	Coro: / Santuzza:	{Inneggiamo, il Signor / {Let us hymn the Lord	The villagers sing the Easter hymn. Santuzza – outside the church – becomes the emotional focus.	The focus now becomes the plight of the pregnant, betrayed and excommunicated Santuzza as the real focus of the tragedy

5	Romanza e scena	Santuzza:	Voi lo sapete, o mamma You know, o Mamma	Santuzza reveals her betrayal by Turiddu.	immediately confirmed by Santuzza's first long aria
6a	Scena	Turiddu:	Tu qui, Santuzza? You here, Santuzza	Santuzza warns Turiddu that Alfio will kill him but he merely accuses her of faithless jealousy.	The narrative resumes, with Santuzza established at the centre.
	[Duet]	Turiddu: Santuzza:	Bada, Santuzza Enough, Santuzza Battimi Beat me		A clear contrast between the two characters' very different passions in this brief duet – emphasised by the repetition – and
b	Stornello di Lola	Lola:	Fior di giaggiolo O gladioli flower	Lola taunts Santuzza with 'her' Turiddu	suddenly, ironically, interrupted by the *stornello*, itself
		Lola:	Turiddu, è passato Alfio? Turiddu, has Alfio passed?	broken off by the dialogue. Dramatic, melodic fragments are briefly asserted after Santuzza's 'e il Signor vede ogni cosa' and the ironic reprise of the hymn at Lola's 'E v'assista il Signore' before the reprise of her mocking melody.	
c	Duetto	Turiddu:	Ah, lo vedi Ah, can you see	Santuzza begs Turiddu to honour her – he refuses.	The drama is immediately reasserted but lead to Santuzza's controlled 'Turiddu, ascolta' as she begs rather than blames.
	[Duet]	Santuzza:	No, no, Turiddu	Santuzza begs Turiddu not to leave – he rejects her.	The melody is that of the Prelude whose ironic interruption by the *Siciliana* now bears dramatic fruit. Unlike the duet in 6a the two characters use the same melody: the tragic fate of each is bound up with the other, despite Turiddu's rough dismissal of Santuzza.

(cont.)

Table 13.3 (*cont.*)

d	Duetto	Santuzza: Oh il Signore vi manda / Oh the Lord sent you	Santuzza reveals Turiddu's infidelity to Alfio.	Alfio enters to a dark reprise of his opening song. The orchestra raises the pressure with an urgent version of the prayer beneath Santuzza's arioso 'Che mentre corrente'.
	[Aria]	Santuzza: Turiddu mi tolse / Turiddu robbed me Santuzza: Per la vergogna mia / By my shame	In the opening dignified melody – reminiscent of Verdi in its noble pathos and shape – Santuzza confesses her shame to Alfio – who responds with similar dignity although with violent words: both understand what is being projected. The melody has a controlled righteousness – and sorrow – that precipitates the tragedy. Once committed she becomes increasingly distraught in a second melody with throbbing accompaniment.	
	[Aria]	Alfio: Infami loro / Both infamous	Alfio commits to revenge. Santuzza despairs at what she has done.	Alfio's assertive melody expresses the violent direction of the narrative – while in a series of interjections Santuzza turns its strength against herself for betraying her lover.

and aesthetics have often preferred to avoid: 'They say that emotionalism is a sign of weakness, but I like to be weak! To the *strong*, so called, I leave the triumphs that fade; for us those that endure!' (Carner, 1974: 268). Puccini's appeal and effectiveness are not emotional exploitation or mere theatrical trickery, but a genuine vision of a truth. This has consistently been undercut by the suspicion aroused by his effectiveness and popularity, combined with his musical conservatism, as Alexandra Wilson proposes: 'the Puccini problem became a problem of progress and reaction, of modernity and tradition . . . Puccini's career was thus marked by popular success and critical doubt in the years since his death, these motifs have remained central to his musical and musicological reputation. The composer's popularity has only added to the problem' (Wilson, 2009: 6–7).

Opera is always prone to conservatism. This is partly due to its social function compounded by the growing proportion of historical material in the repertoire. As a result, opera is especially vulnerable to the friction between gradual and radical modernism. In the formative years between 1875 and 1914 there was an extraordinary overlap of musicians presenting one another and the public with an increasingly complex array of musical worlds. Schoenberg, Debussy, Stravinsky and, in a different way, Mahler, turned away from what they saw as the moribund tradition of late Romanticism, while others, such as Strauss, Rachmaninov and Sibelius were able to work within the harmonic and melodic tradition and achieved remarkable popularity (Table 13.4). This musical rift is directly paralleled in contemporary art as painting relinquished an aesthetic based on the easily recognisable, technical skill of reproducing the external world (appendix 4). Puccini's veristic inheritance meant that the world he created remained firmly recognisable in its subjects, characters and dramaturgy.[5] But this did not mean that it failed to address the modern condition. After seeing *La Fanciulla del West*, Berg reported that it was 'a score with an *original* sound throughout, splendid, every bar a surprise . . . No trace of *Kitsch* . . . I must say I enjoyed it very much . . . Am I wrong?' (Budden, 2002: 331).

Tosca, Puccini's fifth opera, demonstrates his musico-dramatic priorities. It departs from the original aims of *Verismo* in class and period, but it retains the desire to create a truthful world. The attention to detail dominates his correspondence, including demands for:

- genuine words and music for the religious ceremony at the end of act i;
- the correct topography for the panorama in act iii;
- real folk melody and words for the shepherd boy's music in act iii;
- accurate notation of the chimes of the Roman church bells in act iii (Carner, 1974: 123–44; Carner, 1992: 115; Budden, 2002: 188, 191, 193).

In turning the original play into a libretto, Puccini concentrated on isolating and expanding the significant moments and clarifying the characterisation. His librettists

Table 13.4 *Opera and contemporary music, 1874–1930: (see also appendix 5)*

	Non-operatic music	Other contemporary operas	Verismo	Puccini	Janáček	Strauss
1874			Bizet: *Carmen*			
1884				*Le Villi*		
1886		Verdi: *Otello*			*Šárka* (perf. 1925)	
1888						
1889	Mahler: 1st Symphony			*Edgar*		[*Don Juan*]
1890		Tchaikovsky: *The Queen of Spades*	Mascagni: *Cavalleria Rusticana*	*Crisantemi*		
1892		Massenet: *Werther*	Leoncavallo: *Pagliacci* Giordano: *Mala Vita*			
1893		Verdi: *Falstaff*		*Manon Lescaut*		
1894	Debussy: *L'Après-midi d'un Faune*		Massenet: *La Navarraise*		*The Beginning of a Romance*	*Guntram*
1895	Mahler: 2nd Symphony Rachmaninov: 1st Symphony					[*Till Eulenspiegel*]
1896	Mahler: 3rd Symphony (1891–1902)	Giordano: *Andrea Chénier*		*La Bohème*		
1898						

Year						
1899	Schoenberg: *Verklärte Nacht* Sibelius: 1st Symphony					
1900			Charpentier: *Louise*	*Tosca*		
1901	Mahler: 4th Symphony Rachmaninov: 2nd Piano Concerto					*Feuersnot*
1902	Sibelius: 2nd Symphony	Debussy: *Pelléas et Mélisande*				
1904	Mahler: 5th Symphony			*Madama Butterfly*	*Jenůfa*	
1905	Debussy: *La Mer*					*Salome*
1907					*Osud/Fate* (perf.1934/1958)	
1909	Schoenberg: *Five Orchestral Pieces*	Schoenberg: *Erwartung*				*Elektra*
1910	Stravinsky: *The Fire-Bird* Mahler: 8th Symphony			*La Fanciulla del West*		
1911	Strauss					*Der Rosenkavalier*

(cont.)

Table 13.4 (*cont.*)

	Non-operatic music	Other contemporary operas	Verismo	Puccini	Janáček	Strauss
1912	Schoenberg: *Pierrot Lunaire* Mahler: 9th Symphony					*Ariadne auf Naxos*
1913	Stravinsky: *The Rite of Spring*					
1917				*La Rondine*		
1918				*Il Trittico*		
1919						*Die Frau ohne Schatten*
1920					*Mr Brouček*	
1921					*Kát'a Kabanová*	
1924					*The Cunning Little Vixen*	*Intermezzo*
1925		Berg: *Wozzeck*			[*Šárka*]	
1926	Sibelius: *Tapiola*			*Turandot*	*The Makropoulos Case*	1933 *Arabella* 1938 *Daphne* 1942 *Capriccio*
1930					*From the House of the Dead*	

for *La Bohème, Tosca* and *Madama Butterfly* were Giacosa, the poet who supplied
the verses, and the dramatist Illica. After Giacosa's death, Illica felt free to state that:

> The form of a libretto is created by the music . . . It alone, Puccini, is the form . . . I
> shall therefore continue to give in every libretto importance only to the treatment
> of the characters, to the cut of the scenes and to the verisimilitude, in its natu-
> ralness, of the dialogue, of the passions and situations . . . The verse in a libretto
> is nothing but a prevalent custom, just as it is to call those who write a libretto
> 'poets'.   (Carner, 1992: 85–6)

The operas of Puccini and his contemporaries are a closely wrought combination
of highly charged melodic fragments/motifs, some of which are used to construct
larger numbers, that drive the listener through an almost uninterrupted musical
and dramatic *crescendo*. Act III of *Tosca* shows how this complex of fragments,
set forms and bold melody are welded into a whole. It has four main dramatic
stages, each subdivided between several musical elements, some of which are easily
identifiable arias and duets, all of which are very brief. The longest, Cavaradossi's
'E lucevan le stelle', has the advantage of being a self-contained scene, although it
runs for less than three minutes. Puccini's art, even more than Mascagni's, creates
this unremitting pace, moving the audience through fragments and sections. In his
response to Ricordi's criticism of the act III duet starting 'Amaro sol per te', Puccini
showed why it had to be so broken up: 'As for its being fragmentary, I wanted it
so. It cannot be a uniform and tranquil situation such as one connects with other
love duets. Tosca's thoughts continually return to the necessity of a well-acted fall
on Mario's part and natural bearing in face of the shooting party' (Carner, 1974:
138–9).

An overview of act III shows the range of action, incident and emotion Puccini
had to cover in just over half-an-hour (Table 13.5). This constant shifting between
a series of memorable but condensed dramatic and musical moments is in part
signalled by the frequent changes in key and time signatures. Within it there are
a number of identifiable formal arias and duets. But these are brief so as not to
hold up the action. This is the essence of Puccini's skill as composer and dramatist.
Essentially, he treats all melody as motif, always directly signalling character and
dramatic moment, even in something as extended as Lauretta's 'O mio babbino
caro' in *Gianni Schicchi*. Puccini was familiar with the Wagnerian *Letitmotiv* from at
least 1888[6] (the year of *Edgar*) and used reminiscence motifs as one way of creating
musical unity. In *Tosca* there are a number of these: the duet in act III uses ideas
associated with Tosca herself (Table 13.6b, at 14.1 and 14.10), Scarpia (at 15.6 and
17.1) and the attempted rape (at 17.7, 17.9 and 17.11). Puccini has been accused of
reprising the melody of 'E lucevan le stelle' in the closing moments simply because
it sounds dramatic. Although *Tosca* is historically based, with characters and an

Table 13.5 Tosca: *the overall structure of act III*

	Timings		
Prelude	4.40		The Prelude is designed to draw the audience, who have no stage action to follow, into the long wait for dawn. It consists of both purely atmospheric and melodic passages using incidental elements such as – the shepherd boy's song with its tension between triplets and the 4/4 time signature; – the shifting sound of the sheep bells; – the sequence of Matin bells, played at ten different 'distances'. This accompanies the scenic movement from deep night (with twinkling stars) through early dawn to the gaoler's entry – but still with his lamp, and Cavaradossi's entry accompanied by the troop of guards.
1 Cavaradossi	6.50	Aria	– Cavaradossi's conversation with the gaoler and the bribe of his ring; – From writing the letter to remembering his first meeting with Tosca in 'E lucevan le stelle'.
2 Tosca and Cavaradossi	10.00		this leads into the central section between Cavaradossi and Tosca which moves rapidly from – their ecstatic reunion, to
		Arioso	– Tosca's description of what passed between her and Scarpia in heightened *arioso* writing. The tension is then lowered as – Cavaradossi wonders at Tosca's fortitude in murdering Scarpia in the brief aria 'O dolci mani';
		Aria	– interrupted by Tosca's plan for their escape, following which
		Duet	– they join together in a duet but in sequence as Tosca's section responds to Cavaradossi's rather than uniting with it or using the same melodic material. – This is again interrupted as Tosca returns to their escape, leading to
		Duet	– the *a cappella* unison song of 'Triumph'.
3 The execution	5.00		Neither this nor the following section has a self-contained musical section (aria, duet). Instead, it is the dramatic trajectory that dominates: Cavaradossi is called to execution and then
		Ariso	– in the only solo proper, Tosca narrates – and creates for the audience – her impatience and tension as she waits for the execution. – This takes place followed by – Tosca ensuring that Cavaradossi plays his part and then – goes to raise him once the soldiers have left. – Finally she realises that he has, in fact, been shot dead.
4 Tosca's suicide	1.15		The final section brings the opera to its climax: – reinforcing the horror of Tosca's realisation, the guards and Scarpia's henchmen enter in pursuit of his murderer, and – Tosca escapes them by throwing herself from the parapet followed by – a reprise of the melody of 'E lucevan le stelle' – dramatically announcing the end of their life and love together.

event that presaged the Risorgimento,[7] Puccini typically avoids any celebration of heroism. For him Tosca and Cavaradossi's love in a cruel world is all in all. With Cavaradossi's execution and Tosca's death, that love is vanquished. The melody, as reminiscence, is the true judgement of the drama.

The duet falls into eight units (Table 13.6a). Throughout, the audience's attention and sympathy are balanced between the drama of the moment, the irony of the situation and empathy with the characters (Table 13.6b, p. 272).

This kind of musical structure also applies to self-contained arias, such Madama Butterfly's 'Un bel dì'. This frequently excerpted piece is a dramatic monologue, consisting of ten sections, formally held together with a *da capo* structure as the long opening melody finally returns, albeit with different words. The aria follows the heated dialogue between herself and Suzuki as to whether Pinkerton will return. It then starts abruptly, without any introduction, the transition marked by a shift into 3/4 time and G flat with the significant marking 'Andante molto calmo'.

Dramatically, it is a complex description of an emotional and psychological state which, as the opening direction asks, Butterfly actually lives through as she describes it. The ten sections are identified by three changes of time signature, using five melodic elements, one of which, the opening melody, recurs briefly at 15.1 and 15.11. But the strength of the melody and its consequent easy retention create a musical unity (Table 13.7, p. 275). Built out of a series of individual moments, 'Un bel dì' remains an 'aria'. The powerful opening melodic statement and its climactic repetition, the strongly lyrical vocal line even with its interruptions, combine to hold it together in a way that parallels the conventional aria.

The power of both these examples lies in the use of a series of impressive melodic fragments, and the rapid shifts in dramatic focus that are stylistic developments taken from *Verismo*. At the same time, there is a sense in which Puccini's sweeping lyricism can militate against *Verismo*'s essential concerns. The sheer beauty often creates a tension between the reality of the situation and its artistic filter. There is also the danger of distracting from the characters' suffering and falling into mere sentiment as the lyrical overbalances the event. In other composers' hands the lyrical can be more obviously controlled. This is especially true of Janáček: consistently lyrical, but with a firmly readjusted prioritisation of the musical and dramatic.

Table 13.6a Tosca: *act III, narrative sequence of the duet (figs. 14–29)*

15		16–18	19–21		22	23–28	29
Elation as Cavaradossi sees the pass	Suspicion as to how Tosca gained it	Tosca's narration of Scarpia's murder	Cavaradossi relents	The euphoria of his love	Instruction for the execution	Love duet	*A capella* paean to freedom

Table 13.6b Tosca: *act iii, duet sequence (figs. 14–29) (section 2 in Table 13.5)*

Fig	Bar			
14	1–10	*B,* 6/8	*Spoletta enters from the stairs, accompanied by the Sargeant and followed by Tosca; the Sargeant carries a lantern – Spoletta points to where Tosca will find Cavaradossi, then calls the jailer to come to him: he leaves with him and the Sargeant, but not before giving orders to the sentry on guard to watch the prisoner.*	
	1			*Tremolando* strings accompany one of the figures associated with Tosca, played in the woodwind.
	4			This accelerates and becomes
	7			a rapidly repeated figure
	10			climaxing and turning into a full statement of the 'Tosca' motif.
	11–14		*Tosca, who meanwhile has waited agitatedly, sees Cavaradossi weeping: she rushes to him, and unable to speak because of strong emotion, raises his head in both hands, showing him at the same time the safe-conduct: Cavaradossi, seeing Tosca, leaps to his feet in surprise, then reads the paper that Tosca has handed him.*	
15	1	C	Cavaradossi: Ah! Franchigia 　　　　Ah! Free pass	They sing with *tremolando* strings only accompanying.
	5	2/4	Tosca: Sei libero! 　　　You are free!	A huge upwards sweep of the strings but leading immediately into
	6	3/4	Cavaradossi: Scarpia! . . .	the Scarpia motif – and Cavaradossi's suspicions.
16	1	4/4	Tosca: Il tuo sangue 　　　Your blood	Tosca starts her narration with a nervous, pulsating accompaniment that resolves in
	4		Tosca: alla Madonna 　　　to the Madonna	the upward sweep of her (histrionic) appeal to the Madonna
	12		Tosca: il patibol le braccia leva! 　　　the gallows raises its arms!	and settles into her dramatic account of Scarpia's threats, while the orchestra supports her with a death march, culminating in

Table 13.6b (*cont.*)

Fig	Bar			
17	7 9		Tosca: pronto a ghermir! ready to seize its prey!	her imitation of Scarpia's triumphant cries with rising demi-semiquavers in the strings. Then
	11		Tosca: Si, alla sua brama Yes, to his lust	*tremolando* strings followed by a rapidly repeated figure derived from the moment when Tosca saw and seized the knife in act II. This is
18	1		Tosca: Là presso luccicava una lama I saw nearby a shining blade	repeated in full at the point when she narrates the moment.
	12/13			The music, and Tosca's line, rise to a climax as she recounts the murder, in an isolated, unaccompanied moment.
19	1		Cavaradossi: Tu! You	The music quietens as Cavaradossi understands what she did to gain the pass, and how wrong his first suspicions were.
	5	F, 3/4	*lovingly taking Tosca's hands between his own*	
			Cavaradossi: O dolci mani O sweet hands	This brief aria wavers between the personal and the public. It consists of five sections. The melody of his personal address to Tosca's hands is sung twice. Now
20	1		Cavaradossi: dunque in voi thus in you	the melody ceases as he is moved by her strength and what she has done in the name of both their loves
	4	2/4	Cavaradossi: Giustizia Justice	and justice itself.
21	1	2/4	Cavaradossi: Voi deste morte You brought death	Then a repetition of the music from act II and 18.1 describes the murder, before
	(4) 5	3/4	Cavaradossi: O dolci mani O sweet hands	returning to Tosca and reiterating his feelings of love – and finishes but with the aria suspended.

(*cont.*)

Table 13.6b (*cont.*)

Fig	Bar			
22	1	4/4	Tosca: Senti . . . l'ora è vicina Listen . . . the hour is near	Tosca prepares Cavaradossi for their departure. A new melody, accompanied by the muted strings and given a lighter feeling by the woodwind as she tells him about the fake execution.
	5		Tosca: Al colpo At the shot	The melody stops, creating a lull before the paean to freedom.
23	1	E, 2/4	Cavaradossi: Liberi! Free!	A lilting figure in the woodwind creates a moment of peace – perhaps suggesting the gentle movement of waves and the boat to freedom.
	9	C	Tosca: Senti effluvi di rose? Do you smell the scent of roses?	The downward part of the figure is taken up by the strings and accompanies Tosca's vision of freedom, leading into
24	2	G♭, 3/4	Cavaradossi: Amaro sol per te – Bitter only because of you –	the woodwind's rocking pulse which becomes a series of gentle chords against which Cavaradossi sings his melody, repeated at bar 10 and reaching a high B♭, when
25	1		Tosca: Amor, che seppe a te vita Love that could save your life	Tosca enters with a complementary melody but with the same accompaniment. Both extol a personal love – and then
	5	A		a key change as Tosca sings of the whole world changing –
	8		Tosca: . . . riguardare will be seen	but this is undermined by the decorative 'star dust' of the triangle and celeste.
26	1	G♭	Tosca: Finché congiunti alle celesti sfere Then joined to the celestial spheres	But Tosca takes her own dream seriously and then
	5		Tosca: A sol cadente In the setting sun	the main melody resumes and dies away on the flutes.

Table 13.6b (*cont.*)

Fig	Bar			
27		**D,** 4/4	Tosca: E non giungono No one is coming	Over the 'Tosca' motif Tosca instructs Cavaradossi how to behave at the execution.
	11	3/4	Cavaradossi: Parlami ancor Talk as before	Cavaradossi slips back into the 3/4, thinking of their love – not the present masquerade.
28			Tosca: Uniti ed esultanti United and exulting	He becomes more ardent as does Tosca in asserting love, art and freedom – over *tremolando* strings.
29		**E,** 4/4	Both: Trionfar Triumph	Singing unaccompanied – isolated and united – both exult in the victory of hope, passion and harmony and then
	13		Both: all'estasi d'amor to the ecstasy of love	the violins and the orchestra gently enter as they once again return to their personal love.
	18			The woodwind chords quietly wrap them in their love as the sound of a bell returns everything to reality.

Table 13.7 Madama Butterfly: *act ii, scene i, the structure of 'Un bel dì,'*

Fig	Bar	*(The scene becomes increasingly real to her and little by little she moves close to the shosi* [gods/idols] *at the rear)*		
12	1	**3/4 G♭** *Andante molto calmo*	Un bel dì, vedremo One fine day we shall see	Opening, long melodic line as Butterfly describes how the ship will be sighted;
	9	*Un poco mosso*	E poi la nave bianca entra And then the white ship enters	This is answered/completed by a complementary but quite different, more dramatic melodic line as she enters into the reality of her vision;

(*cont.*)

Table 13.7 (*cont.*)

Fig	Bar	(*The scene becomes increasingly real to her and little by little she moves close to the shosi* [gods/idols] *at the rear*)		
13	1	**2/4** *A tempo*	Mi metto/là I stay/there	Recitative-like setting creating a musical suspense parallel to her waiting. This then
	4	*animando un poco*	E . . . uscito dalla folla Then . . . out of the crowd	grows into a new *arioso* that creates her emotion as she 'sees' someone;
14	1	**4/8** **Sostendo molto**	Chi sarà? . . . che dirà? Who is it? . . . what will he say?	A short motif repeated on each of the four questions focuses the musical and dramatic tension;
	[4]5	*Lento*	[Chiamerà] Butterfly [He will call] Butterfly	A reminiscence motif of their love – already recapitulated earlier in the scene;
15	[11] 1	**3/4** *Andante come prima*	[per non mo-] rire [so as not to] die	The opening melody returns, *con forza* with the whole orchestra paralleling Butterfly's line as she allows her full emotion to burst out.
	9	*to Suzuki*	Tutto questo avverrà All this will happen	The line breaks into a complex of insistent triplets as she turns back to Suzuki and then
	11		Tienti la tua paura Bauish your fears	rises to a *fortissimo* as she rejects Suzuki's fears and
16	1	*Largamente*	[l'] aspetto I await it	reaffirms that she 'awaits' over an orchestral restatement of the opening theme.

Janáček

Puccini's ambivalent place in musical history is complemented by Janáček's. Like Puccini, Janáček's initial context was nineteenth-century opera with the addition of a strong nationalism. His operatic career almost directly parallels Puccini's (Table 13.4), but his music developed to sound more obviously twentieth-century. Typically, an important critic such as John Tyrrell has asked: 'Where does Janáček's Ká'ta belong? It owes little to Czech nineteenth-century models and belongs more . . . with works like *Pelléas et Mélisande* and *Boris Godunov* . . . Janáček's placing in fact presents an acute problem for his commentators' (Tyrrell, 1982: 6–7).

The conditions for Janáček's development were his relative musical isolation in provincial Brno; a strong sense of Czech nationality; and an over-riding concern with art as truth. The isolation, not unlike Haydn's, allowed him to develop away from the mainstream – in particular, German – influences. While he was aware of wider European trends, these never distracted him from his own vision:

> When I was twenty-five years of age, I already had Beethoven's Missa Solemnis at my fingertips. I conducted it in Brno on 2nd April 1879. It is no use denying it: Beethoven's works have never made me enthusiastic, never taken me out of myself. They have never transported me into the realm of ecstasy. I arrived at the bottom of them too soon. And quickly therefore, they have fallen to the bottom of my soul.   (Hollander, 1963: 78–9)

Janáček's first opera, *Šárka*, is one of the subjects in Smetana's *Ma vlast* and the same semi-historical narrative world of *Libuše*. But this generalised nationalist interest gave way to a concern with contemporary life and the Moravian world that he intimately knew. In what was probably his own programme note to *Jenůfa*, he claimed: 'it is the first work in this field which consciously attempts to be Moravian. – Prose was first used in opera by the French composer Alfred Bruneau in 1897 . . . Janáček . . . was the first to do this among the Czech composers, not at all after the example of the French, but on his own initiative, drawn to this direction by the principle of truth in recorded speech melody' (Tyrrell, 1992: 54–5).

Folk music

Janáček's strong individuality meant that vernacular musical traditions would be translated into something more radical than in either Dvořák or Smetana. He saw folk music as an expression of humanity rather than a local celebration of folk culture, a spiritual more than a nationalist experience: 'I lived among folk songs from childhood. Each folk song contains an entire man; his body, soul, his surroundings, everything, everything. He who grows up among folk songs, grows into a complete man' (Štědroň, 1955: 27). As with Bartók, Janáček transmuted folk music into a personal style. The fifth of the 1888 *Lachian Dances*, the 'Čeladenský', is a straightforward orchestral version of a folk dance melody, similar to Dvořák's *Slavonic Dances*. By 1904, in 'On that field of Hurašky', the fifteenth of the *Moravian Dances*, the folk root had been completely absorbed into a personal idiom. That the music has come from a folk source is not in doubt, but the radical shifts in rhythm and melodic line create a new kind of music. Finally, the second movement of the 1928 Second String Quartet is built on a sequence of dance rhythms revolving around a folk-derived melody. But the inter- and cross-cutting of rhythms and melodic lines creates a radically unstable music that has become a personal language.

Janáček's individual concept of music was explored in his theoretical writings as well as his compositions. These included his work as a critic and teacher, in particular his *Singing Teaching Manual* of 1899, and the 1911–12 *Complete Harmony Manual*. As with folk music, the emphasis in harmony is on how it can best be used as an expression of human values. As he says: 'we could enumerate the harmonic combinations which are agitating in effect, calming in effect, etc. This is the source from which our deepest musical feeling springs and which is capable of reaching the highest points and the most subtle nuances. This is the source of truth which must be apparent to all who possess a healthy sense of hearing whether they be laymen or artists' (Štědroň, 1955: 54).

This is compounded by the most trenchant of his musical concerns, *Nápěvky* – speech-motifs. By 1879 he had begun recording examples of speech inflections and rhythms. In 1903 he sat at the bedside of his favourite child, Olga, as she lay dying, and notated her last words:

> Melodic curves of speech? For me, music emanating from instruments, whether in the works of Beethoven or of any other composer, contains little truth. You see, with me it was always odd. When anyone speaks to me, I listen more to the tonal modulations in his voice than to what he is actually saying. From this, I know at once what he is like, what he feels, whether he is lying, whether he is agitated or whether he is merely making a conventional conversation. I can even feel, or rather hear, any hidden sorrow. Life is sound, the tonal modulations of the human speech. Every living creation is filled with the deepest truth. That, you see, has been one of the main needs of my life.   (Štědroň, 1955: 90)

Speech rhythms became the catalyst for his distinctive, fragmented style, focused on motifs as the cells from which the scores are built. The fusion of folk rhythm and melody, increasingly radical ideas about the function of harmony and belief in speech rhythms are the components of his style. Like Puccini, only a small number of his operas can be strictly categorised as Naturalistic: *Jenůfa*, *Kát'a Kabanová* and *From the House of the Dead*. Yet, again like Puccini, despite their exotic provenance the expressionist play adapted for *The Makropulos Case*, the symbolist *Cunning Little Vixen* and the fantasy/comedy of *The Excursions of Mr Brouček* – all belong to the same musical and emotional world, seeking human truth whatever the dramatic form.

Kát'a Kabanová

Janáček's love for Kamila Stösslová seems to have provided one impetus behind the female characters who are at the heart of so many of his operas. In 1919, during the negotiations for the performing rights to the Czech translation of Ostrovsky's *The Storm*, Janáček saw *Madama Butterfly*. This seems to have focused his mind on his new heroine and her relation to Kamila. He wrote that: 'I have just come from the theatre. They gave *Batrflay* [*sic*], one of the most beautiful and saddest of operas. I had you constantly before my eyes. *Batrflay* is also small, with black hair. You must never be as unhappy as her' (Tyrrell, 1992: 253–4).

Like Puccini, Janáček's over-riding concern is with emotional purpose, and he noted about the Ostrovsky that: '[The play] contains much that is touching, soft (in the Slav manner); what depth of feeling! If only I can find the right expression, just as deep!' (Tyrrell, 1992: 252). Similar, too, are his priorities in constructing the libretto: 'For musical reasons it was of course necessary to shorten much of the "talking". Also to concentrate the action on fewer characters' (Tyrrell, 1992: 255), 'and his own copy of the play shows how ruthlessly he cut the play to create new and greater focus' (Tyrrell, 1982: fig. 3).

Musically, however, the two composers stand divided by the fine line of early modernism. Where Puccini's scores are designed to hold a series of dramatic fragments together within a lyrical whole, in Janáček they are contained purely within the dramatic continuum. Although much of the writing is lyrical, extended lyricism, the grand sweep of melody and lyrical units, is rare. This melodic disintegration is in great part due to the speech melodies whose natural rhythms control the musical patterns and motifs. While all good word setting observes verbal flow and stress, in Janáček the music is wholly determined by them. They are the building blocks of the score out of which come the motifs attached to particular characters or aspects of the drama (Tyrrell, 1992: 21–8), precisely reflecting the character's words, moods and actions.

In Kát'a's first monologue in act II she starts to come to terms with her situation (Janáček, 1992: 162–6). The passage shifts ground rapidly as she moves between emotions: guilt at what she is about to do, terror as she hears her mother-in-law approach, relief as she realises she has not been discovered, resignation to her fate. Throughout, the motifs comment on the action in their own musical right, bind the monologue together as they are repeated and are manipulated to create a musical continuum – rather than a self-contained 'aria'. This is enhanced by the lack of key and time signatures. Instead Janáček constantly uses accidentals and configures his detailed rhythmic patterns through complex changes in note values as the music shifts with the character's developing mood (Table 13.8).

More than in Puccini, the unity and shape of the monologue is dominated by the dramatic, textual impetus. Puccini's larger paragraphs resolve themselves harmonically and melodically and ultimately refer back to an older aesthetic. In Janáček, this has given way to the textual dramatic imperative, resulting in a more overtly fragmented development held together by the drama and locating its aesthetic in the dramatic truth, regardless of what this may do to the lyrical line.

Naturalism is the last dramatic movement before the break-up of European cultural homogeneity and this, together with its very direct dramatic and musical

Table 13.8 Kát'a Kabanová: *act II, Kát'a's first monologue*

Fig	Bar			Motif	
6	9	**4/4 *Adagio***		a	The passage opens with the (repetition of a) theme associated with Kát'a herself, a line that rises delicately, is held for a moment and then drops. Here it has a fragile, hollow sound as the oboes double the violins and cellos. This is repeated *pp*
	12		Vida! This is it!	a	by a solo clarinet as Kát'a starts to resign herself.
	14			a	It recurs, but with *tremolando* strings as she
	17		*stares at the key*		
	18		Neštěstí! Tady je to neštěstí! Disaster! This is a disaster!		sings an unaccompanied but still lyrical line: in her anguish Kát'a remains a gentle, passive soul but
	21			b	the orchestra – low woodwind and strings – growls out the harsh implications of her situation in a foreboding motif of rising and falling semiquavers, before
7	1	*Più mosso*	*runs to the window*	a	an anguished *ff* restatement of the Kát'a theme as
	4		Zahodit klíč! Zahodit daleko do vody Throw the key! Throw it far into the water		she sings, over another *tremolando* accompaniment, but now rising to a series of anguished, high A flats followed by
	9	*Adagio*		b	a repeat of the foreboding motif followed by
	10	*Più mosso*		a	a series of repeats of the Kát'a theme *ff*. Then

Table 13.8 (*cont.*)

Fig	Bar			Motif	
	15		Abych ho nikdy nenašla! Where I could never find it!	a	for the first time her line is sung over the theme itself. But
	18			ai	the theme disintegrates into a repetition of its first two chords, leading to
8	1	*Adagio*		b	the foreboding motif as
	3	*Più mosso*	Pàlí mne jako žhavý uhel. It burns inside me like a living coal.	ai	the truncated Kát'a theme is played four times over another *tremolando* accompaniment.
	6	*[Adagio]*		b	The foreboding motif is extended downwards across two bars, and then
	8 9	*[Poco più mosso]*	Někdo přichází! Someone's coming! *She hides the key*		a chord is held *fp*, sustaining the mood, but with a trivial motif on the bassoons as the off-stage voice of Kabanicha is heard. Then, over Kabanicha's last word
9	1	*Andante*	Ne, ne! Nikdo. Tak mi srdce přestalo bít! No, no! No one. Oh my heart stopped then!	d	Kát'a's relief is heard in a flowing lyrical line that extends over the next four bars (1.1–4). The line consists of a series of paired semiquavers that gives the line a frail, hesitant feeling. The clarinets and strings accompany this with the same motif – something between weeping and the heart returning to a normal pulse.
	5		Ne,/nikdo. Jak jsem se polekala! No,/no one. What a fright I had!	d	The orchestra continues with the motif but with the second note becoming rising semiquavers which

(*cont.*)

Table 13.8 (*cont.*)

Fig	Bar			Motif	
	9			b	turn into the foreboding motif, breaking into her relief.
	10		A klič jsem schovala. And then I hid the key.		Her vocal line echoes the foreboding motif as
	11				the orchestra descends to
	12			a	a series of powerful *fp* chords over which the Kát'a theme returns, plaintively on the solo oboe
	14		Je vidět, osud tomu chce! I can see, that fate intended this!		returning to the opening of the monologue and her great struggle.

appeal, clear narrative and recognisable characters and situations, has meant that subsequent works have tended to be measured against it. 'Modern opera', like the other arts, has inevitably lacked the clarity of Naturalism, whose monolithic view of the world quickly gave way to a recognition of its contradictions. One narrative of the twentieth century is this growing rift between developing art and public conservatism, between the artist's aesthetic and moral vision and what the public wants to find in its art. No composer has been more caught up in those contradictions than Richard Strauss.

Modernism and Richard Strauss

The unyielding materialism of the Naturalists drove many artists to explore alternative versions of reality such as the artificial metaphysic of Symbolism or the inner world of Expressionism. Whatever their chosen path, when Nietzsche's Zarathustra wondered: 'Could it be possible! This old saint has not yet heard in his forest that *God is dead*!' (Nietzsche, 1971: 41), he pointed to a spiritual vacuum that horrified many. Violent changes in society in the run-up to the First World War further diminished the standing of both God and Man as his divine creation. It became the task of the artist to fill the vacuum. This demanded new kinds of technical and expressive language, and many artists turned away from the European mainstream. In some cases, radical alternatives were offered by traditions that made no use of European techniques, such as the Japanese print or the so-called 'primitive' arts. In the world of music Debussy called a halt when he looked back at Wagner and, as he put it, saw 'if we may express it in suitably grandiose terms . . . a fine sunset which might have been mistaken for the dawn' (Jarocinski, 1976: 100). Composers, too, looked for new languages, in non-Western types such as the Balinese gamelan, or the rhythms of jazz. At the same time, some looked to the European past, to baroque and classical models while, at its most extreme, Schoenberg gradually dispensed with traditional laws of composition and invented a new basis for music altogether.

The composer most obviously caught up in the throes of this change was Richard Strauss. He is important in part because, with Puccini, he is one of the last composers to find a permanent place in the international repertoire: *Der Rosenkavalier* is a staple opera, while *Salome, Elektra, Ariadne auf Naxos* and *Die Frau ohne Schatten* make regular if less frequent appearances. But Strauss' position is far more ambiguous, and, in its way, more crucial. While Puccini and Janáček stand complementarily on either side of the nineteenth/twentieth-century musical sound worlds, both were equally committed to Naturalism/*Verismo*. With his first operatic successes, *Salome* and *Elektra*, Strauss brought modernism into the public arena. The size and use of the orchestra, his reshaping of the vocal and lyric line, his harmonic exploration and his choice and treatment of subjects, were all challenging and aggressively progressive. In Strauss the musical world that Wagner had opened up is realised. In *The New Music* Schoenberg, who had attended the premiere of *Salome*, and to whom Mahler had given a copy of the vocal score, simply declared that: 'I was never *revolutionary. The only revolutionary* in our time was Strauss' (Schoenberg, 1984: 137).

But, at the brink of the modernist abyss, Strauss drew back, and two years later presented the public with *Der Rosenkavalier*. Hofmannsthal, who had provided the text for the radical *Elektra*, wrote to Strauss:

> If I rightly understood from the hints you threw out (which seemed to me remarkably promising), your intention is to write something quite new in style, yet which – for every new development in art acts like the swing of the pendulum – will resemble the older type of opera rather than *Die Meistersinger* or *Feuersnot*. Unless I am mistaken, you want to alternate set pieces with other passages which will approximate to the old-fashioned recitativo secco.
>
> (Hofmannsthal, 1927: 28–9)

Strauss is, therefore, an ambiguous musical and operatic personality. In *Salome* he brought the dramatic and psychological concerns of his time, together with the modernist developments that Wagner's music had indicated, into the opera house. In *Der Rosenkavalier* and its sequels, he selected aspects of his own and used them within an essentially conservative manner. The innovations, however, remained, including

- increasingly sophisticated and precise orchestration;
- tonal writing, but with a greatly expanded harmonic range;
- accommodating formal melodic units (arias, etc.) within the Wagnerian symphonic style;
- a conversational style that would be vital to subsequent opera.

Much of this had been developed in the tone poems with which Strauss had made his name.[8] But in his third opera, *Salome*, he created a sensation that signalled a fundamental shift in what opera could do. This was in part due to the choice of libretto, Oscar Wilde's *Salomé*. Written in French, this was part of the Decadent movement that took Baudelaire's *Les Fleurs du Mal* as their point of departure. Erotic, even transgressive love, has its own cultural tradition. In Puccini, the Finale of act I of *Madama Butterfly* combines Cio Cio San's romantic aspirations with Pinkerton's sexual urgency; in the second act of *Tosca*, Cavaradossi's torture becomes an aspect of Scarpia's sexual exploitation, ultimately leading to near-rape; in *Turandot* the torture-death of Liù, and Turandot's own blood lust, are combined in Calaf's unquestioning and irrational love for the princess. In both *Jenůfa* and *Kát'a Kabanová* the central characters are the subjects of illicit love leading to murder and suicide. But both *Salome* and *Elektra* explore sexuality more radically, in Salome's sadistic revenge and necrophilia, and Elektra's obsession with her own father. Strauss consciously chose these extreme subjects as vehicles for his extension of musical, operatic language.

The orchestra (*Salome*)

The final pages of *Tristan* require twenty-six staves and include divided flutes, oboes, clarinets, bassoons, horns, trumpets and cellos. The *Salome* orchestra needs thirty-four staves and includes heckelphone, contra bassoon, three additional timpani, a small tympanum, tam-tam, bass drum, side drum, tambourine, xylophone, castanets, glockenspiel, celeste and harmonium. In addition, the clarinets and horns are in three parts. This enormous force is employed with finesse, virtuosity and dramatic purpose. In Strauss' tone poems the orchestra reflects every detail of the narrative. In the earlier tone poems of composers such as Liszt and Smetana, the music certainly suggests the narrative, but it does so in relatively large blocks whose broad effects parallel elements of nature or action. In Strauss, this becomes highly detailed, reflecting every moment of the narrative. His achievement is to control this potential fragmentation and create a genuinely symphonic dimension. He now brought this into the opera.

The orchestra can be used illustratively. The initial stage direction requires that 'The moon shines very brightly' and the first three bars 'rise' with the both the curtain and the moon in two joined upward scales on the clarinet. A little later (fig. 2, bar 4), as Narraboth compares Salome's feet with those of 'little white doves', the flutes, oboes and bassoons play a fluttering dotted figure. Meanwhile, a series of long chords shimmer and spread like the moonlight itself. None of this merely decorates, it enriches the scene and becomes part of the larger musical fabric. Elsewhere, figures become motifs, such as the repeated four notes that accompany Salome's grasping lust, later triumphantly sounded (at fig. 316) as Jokanaan's head appears on the silver charger and she exclaims 'Wohl, Ich werde ihn jetzt küssen' (Well, I will kiss it now). There are also self-contained figures used to emphasise an actual moment, such as the rasping, insistent *sforzando* B flat played over the hollow rumble of the bass drum (fig. 304, bars 8–13) as Salome waits for the execution.

This integration of action, vocal and orchestral lines misled Fauré into calling *Salome* 'a symphonic poem with additional vocal parts' (Fauré, 1907), something that later critics have repeated. But this is to misunderstand Strauss' achievement. A major problem for the new music was how to create structures once traditional forms had been abandoned. This is why so many of Schoenberg's, Mahler's and early Stravinsky's scores either set words or use literary programmes. In his tone poems and operas Strauss similarly responded to the detail of the text while sustaining the musical whole.

Tonality

Strauss equally develops Wagner's destabilisation of harmony. The opening rising scale that 'creates' the moon consists of two joined scales played on the clarinet. However, the first is in *C* sharp major and the second is in G, almost at the other end of the spectrum. The passage is tonally recognisable and at the same time disquieting, as two usual, but normally incompatible elements, are joined. Typical of Strauss, it is innovative – but never beyond acceptable limits, as Richard Taruskin suggests: 'the opera's harmonic plan, one that owes nothing at all to the circle of fifths, but that, while maintaining the . . . [traditional] sound vocabulary of triadic functional harmony, connects the chords in a polymorphously perverse fashion' (Taruskin, 2010: 43).

In Strauss' highly personal modernism, the traditional bounds of harmony are broken, as they had been in the 'Prelude' to *Tristan*, but without moving into the atonality of middle-period Schoenberg.

The scene immediately prior to Jokanaan's execution exemplifies much of this. It begins with Salome's final demand for the Prophet's head as a reward for her dance.

Strauss' reflection of the detail of both character and action is extraordinary and he claimed that he lived with his libretti until he was completely familiar with them before even thinking about composition. This could lead critics to complain that: 'Every gesture of every character is mirrored in the music... [Although] the over-loading of detail is not as tedious as in other Strauss operas, and the whole is bound together with the greatest skill in a form comparable to that of the symphonic poem' (Kerman, 1956: 259). But as melody and traditional harmony became minimised as the century progressed, it was exactly this kind of structuring that would become essential to operatic composition (Table 13.9).

This is followed by a long, rapturous aria typical of Strauss. Its main feature is an apparently endless lyrical line, weaving like a piece of *art nouveau*: the kind of melodic writing which Hanslick had so criticised in Wagner. For the audience, it offers the paradox of seductively beautiful music fitted to a repulsive perversity. The tension between the two becomes a microcosm of the whole opera.

Lyricism and melody (*Der Rosenkavalier*)

The aria – the self-contained monologue with a strong, lyrical, usually melodic, base – becomes more apparent from *Der Rosenkavalier* onwards as Strauss manoeuvres into a less challenging style. In Wagner's later operas extended melodic passages are used sparingly, signalling moments of outstanding passion and rapture. There are a number of these in *The Ring* and, significantly, they are the sections most often highlighted. They are as varied as Siegmund's 'Spring Song', Siegfried and Brünnhilde's love duet at the end of *Siegfried*, Hagen's 'Summoning of the vassals', the 'Revenge trio' or Siegfried's funeral march. Each of these attracts attention to its sheer musicality in a way that Wotan's monologue in act ii of *Die Walküre*, an equally identifiable *dramatic* unit, avoids.[9] A comparison between Brünnhilde's final monologue in *Götterdämmerung* and Isolde's in *Tristan* shows the difference. Where Brünnhilde's is a dramatic continuum woven from a series of motifs, Isolde's is a lyrical outpouring based on the melody which runs through what is really an extended aria. It is this model that Strauss, a great melodist as his songs show, increasingly adopted.

After *Salome* Strauss' operas increasingly gravitated towards these large melodic episodes while also retaining more freely structured monologues. The result is a dichotomy between character/dramatic and purely musical interest. This is apparent in *Der Rosenkavalier*. The opera's central theme is the way human beings cope with the changes and revelations of time. In act i the Marschallin gradually faces her reality as an older woman in love with the teenage Octavian. In 'Die Zeit im Grunde, Quinquin' (Time, after all, Quinquin) she turns from earlier reminiscence to profound self-revelation. Nothing is allowed to distract from the character's inner

Table 13.9 Salome: *scene iv, figs. 297–315*

Fig	Bar		
297	11	4/4 *Langsam* Salome (*ferociously*) Gib mir den Kopf des Jo | kanaan Give me the head of Jo | kanaan	The woodwind play a single, shimmering, steely chord as Salome demands her reward 'ferociously' but *Langsam – Slowly* on a single insistently repeated E♭ before rising assertively to a high B♭ and then falling in a cascade of semiquavers to a low E♭ on the name 'Jokanaan'.
298	1	*Sehr schnell* *Herod sinks in despair back into his chair*	Despite the tempo marking, the orchestra explodes into a fury with rapid repeated figures on the timpani and rising scales in the wind and brass. These then break down into syncopated chords as Herod resigns himself.
	5		The orchestra subsides to *pp* leaving only two horns holding a note as
	8	Herod *Weakly* Man soll ihr geben, was sie verlangt! Let her be given what she asks!	Herod mutters the words that he does not wish to hear, before
299	1	Sie ist in Wahrheit She is in truth	a great, lush sigh from the orchestra as he despairs and then
	2	ihrer Mutter Kind! her mother's child!	no accompaniment, as he turns to hatred of, and casts the blame on, Herodias.
300		*Herod takes the death-ring from his finger and gives it to the first soldier, who takes it to the executioner*	As Herod frees himself of Salome, the clarinets whistle up a scale in sextuplets followed by whooping horns and a great trill. But the die is cast for both of them, and
301	3		everything descends into a nervous *tremolado* in the strings, trills in the low woodwind and agitated repeated notes by the trumpets and trombones.
	7	Wer hat meinen Ring gennomen? Who has taken my ring?	Then a sharp ascent and call from the first trumpet as Herod awakes to what he has done – but still trying to cast the blame elsewhere.

(cont.)

Table 13.9 (*cont.*)

Fig	Bar		
302	1	*The executioner goes down into the cistern*	Again the whooping horns – as Herod fails to rouse himself to halt the execution –
	2		and again the harsh descent, to *pp* as
	3	*Almost spoken* Ich hatte einen Ring an meiner rechten Hand I had a ring on my right hand	Herod half speaks, half sings in wonder at what has happened, while a clarinet wanders up and down, laughing at him.

303	2	*Softly*
		Oh! Gewiss wird Unheil über einen
		    kommen.
		Oh! I am sure misfortune will befall
		    someone.
			But the clarinet's line darkens as, *faux naïf*, he reflects that 'misfortune will befall someone' in a tightly rising line, before

	4	Herodias: Meine Tochter hat recht getan! My daughter has done well!	Herodias responds assertively, perhaps exultantly, but as might have been expected. The banality of her vocal line contrasts with
304	1	Herod: Ich bin sicher I am sure	Herod's internalised repetition of his 'certainty' at first on a repeated F but then rising and falling in a strange cadence that suggests a mixture of surprise and titillation at what may be to come.
	3		The low woodwind rumble ending in a *sf* chord and a long drum roll played with the wooden sticks, together with a *tremolando* on the basses, which continues
		Salome leans over the cistern	accompanied by a rasping *sf* B♭ played high on the basses. Strauss gives very detailed directions as to how this horrible sound is to be produced.

Table 13.9 (*cont.*)

Fig	Bar		
305	1	Salome: Es ist kein Laut zu vernehmen. There is no sound to be heard.	The naked *tremolando* and drum roll create suspense, isolating Salome in her voyeurism, and suggesting the darkness of the cistern. Her vocal line is almost a monotone, but with an intensity that is
	5	Warum schreit er nicht, der Mann? Why does he not cry out, the man?	released in the ejaculation on the words 'der Mann' – the object of her infatuation.
	6		The rasping *sf* becomes more insistent as it is taken up, one after another, by the first violins, the seconds and finally the violas.
	8	Ach! Wenn einer mich zu töten käme, Ah! If anyone tried to kill me,	Salome's line grows more excited, culminating in
306	1	ich würde es nicht dulden! I would not want to suffer!	a high *A* on the word 'dulden' (suffer).
	1/2	Schlag zu, schlag zu, Naaman, schlag zu Strike, strike, Naaman, strike	Immediately an insistent, barbaric dance rhythm begins, with the timpani instructed to play 'short and hard' notes, ending
	5		in a great chord and then an expectant silence created by *tremolando* violins and basses while the contra-bassoon plays a formless line suggesting, again, the depths of the cistern
	10	Nein, ich höre nichts. No, I hear nothing.	with which Salome joins, again in a quasi-monotone as the basses repeat their rasping B♭ and then a near-silence before
	15		a sudden crash made by the basses and cellos.

(*cont.*)

Table 13.9 (*cont.*)

Fig	Bar		
307	1	Ah! Es ist etwas zu Boden gefallen. Ah! Something fell to the ground.	Over *tremolando* basses and cellos Salome's recitative line becomes more rapid and varied, first on a repeated G♭ and then down to a repeated B.
	5		The timpani play a figure followed by the flutes in another of Strauss' rapidly rising scales, but this time introducing a long passage of mounting excitement, dominated by the woodwind. The whole section is harmonically diffuse, with scattered rising and falling figures thrown between each of the instrumental parts. Throughout this, Salome becomes increasingly agitated/excited and her vocal line grows fully expressive.
312	1	Hierher, ihr Soldaten, geht ihr in *die Cisterne* Come here, soldiers! Go down into the cistern	A *crescendo* as her frustration explodes: she orders the soldiers down into the cistern to do the job,
	5	[und holt mir den Kopf des] Mannes! [and bring me the head of the] man!	apparently climaxing on the word 'Mannes' (man) but in fact continuing
313	1	Tetrarch, Tetrarch	with hysterical repetition demanding that Herod order the soldiers and then culminating on
	4		the name 'Jochanaan' sung to an elongation of the motif she has used before – (see fig. 297, bar 11) – and falling in a swoon at the thought of everything she has by now associated with him and his execution. Then
	8	*A huge black arm, the arm of the executioner, reaches out from the cistern, with a silver charger holding the head of Jokanaan. Salome seizes it*	nothing but the bass drum until
	9		the orchestra explodes.

Table 13.9 (*cont.*)

Fig	Bar		
314	1		The trumpets play a version of the horn figure from fig. 306, bar 5 (at Salome's 'Naaman, schlag zu, sag ich dir' (Naaman, strike, I tell you)).
	4	Ah! Du wolltest mich nicht Ah! You did not want	Finally Salome launches into an ecstatic rapture as she greets the head with the Jokanaan name motif, while the orchestra sounds the motif associated with her power and lust, and then
315	1	Wohl, ich werde ihn jetzt küssen! Well, I will kiss it now!	climaxing on a high G and swooning by thirds down to E and C on the word 'küssen' (kiss) as she kisses the head at last.

journey, least of all melodic elements that might attract attention in their own right (Table 13.10).

By contrast, the famous ending of the opera, first trio and then duet, moves far away from this kind of writing. It is dominated by melody in its own right. In fact Strauss felt the musical need to extend the passage, and asked Hofmannsthal for more lines, who replied anxiously: 'Do my words for the last scene of all exactly fit the melody you have in mind. Send me a card to the Lido' (Hofmannsthal, 1927: 1).

Here, as in almost every opera from now on, the music itself creates resolution – for both the characters and the audience. The problem is not primarily that it is a relapse into melody and harmony *per se*, but whether the harmony and balm of melody are an adequate response to the opera's main theme – let alone the world in 1911.

Conversation

The contrast between melody-centred and freely constructed passages is taken further in passages of dialogue. Hofmannsthal was aware from the start that Strauss had wanted 'to alternate set pieces with other passages which will approximate to the old-fashioned recitativo secco' (Hofmannsthal, 1927: 28–9). The 'conversational' sections, of which there are many in this highly wrought comedy of manners, needed

Table 13.10 Der Rosenkavalier: *act 1*

Fig	Bar		
306	3	Die Zeit im Grunde, Quinquin Time, after all, Quinquin	The Marschallin begins by simply musing on the nature of time.
308	2	Sie ist um uns herum It is all about us	Her line takes on more definite, melancholy shape, rising softly to a high G♭ on the word 'uns' (us) and then falling – emphasised by a descending scale in the bassoon.
309	1		The trombones play a sudden *forte piano* chord with mutes as she realises how her appearance reflects the passing of time.
		im Spiegel da rieselt sie in the mirror it ripples, in meinen Schläfen fliesst sie around my temples it flows	The music loses any sense of key centre as she becomes caught in her personal sense of loss through time – including loss of her young lover and then
	9	Oh Quinquin!	comes to rest as she recollects herself and, knowing the truth of the situation, sighs the pet name of her lover.
310	5/6	Manchmal steh'ich auf mitten in der Nacht Sometimes I rise in the middle of the night	Conscious of what she is saying – and forecasting – Strauss enables the listener to join her as she 'hears' the clocks chiming in the night played by the celeste and harp. This is more than realism: it creates a shared, haunting moment for both audience and character

a new kind of musical writing that would give the very fragmentary text full prominence and at the same time sustain the musical flow without forcing it into a purely musical structure. A model was provided by similar passages in *Die Meistersinger*, such as the chaotic end of act II. Here Wagner used a kind of writing in which vocal fragments were allowed to become the musical norm. Instead of artificially forcing them into a larger melodic or even lyrical whole, he allowed the musical disintegration to reflect the social chaos. This fracturing is developed much further by Strauss, for example in the passage towards the end of act II where Octavian has challenged Ochs to a duel. This seems to deliberately reject musically structured writing with its increasingly irritating repetition of 'Die Fräulein' and final explosion at Octavian's indignant and naive 'die Fräulein mag Ihn nicht' (the young lady does not like you). The Police Commissar's act III 'Halt! Keiner rührt sich!' (Stop! No one is to move!)

is another example of a writing where the music becomes genuinely 'conversational', shaped purely by the text. In *Der Rosenkavalier, Arabella* and *Intermezzo* this works by contrast with the other, more lyrical elements of the score. But once the melodic has been dropped – in Berg or Britten – it becomes the basis for a new kind of music in its own right.

The paradox of Strauss is the apparent radicalism and innovation that had led Schoenberg and many others to regard him as a revolutionary, against the consciously conservative musical aesthetic that assured him popularity and a permanent place in the repertoire. But underlying this were more potent and fundamental questions about what opera was: the value and function of opera as an art form in society; the actual function of music, in particular lyrical music, in opera; and, finally, the relationship between dramaturgy, words, music and meaning. The exploration of these questions, raised from the very beginning of the art form, reiterated by the great 'reformers' Gluck, Mozart and Wagner, describes the course of opera in the modern world.

Chapter 14

First modernism: Symbolist and Expressionist opera

Debussy and Symbolism (*Pelléas et Mélisande*)

Pelléas et Mélisande and *Wozzeck* signal the true beginning of modernism in opera. *Pelléas* is revolutionary because of the kind of text Debussy needed to set, and the way in which he set it. A major preoccupation was how to get out of the impasse that Wagner had come to represent in music generally, and opera in particular, as Debussy himself wrote: 'Contemporary dramatic music, however, embraces everything from Wagnerian metaphysics to the trivialities of the Italians – not a particularly French orientation. Perhaps in the end we will see the light and achieve conciseness of expression and form (the fundamental qualities of French genius)' (Debussy, in Strunck, 1998: 1431–2). What he wanted was to 'purify our music! Let us try to relieve its congestion, to find a less cluttered kind of music' (1998: 1433). Just as painters and sculptors had turned to other, often 'primitive', traditions for new ways of looking at and representing the world, so Debussy turned to alternative forms of music encouraged by what he heard at the 1900 Paris Exposition Universelle:

> The tuned drums of the east were a new source of rhythmic subtlety and excitement. The persistent use of the pentatonic scale altered and, for the moment, freshened melodic utterances. In the long-drawn tremolos of the percussion instruments, with their peculiar tuning, were promptings for those successions of ninths that subsequently were to become fingerprints on Debussy's manuscripts. In the minor pulsations of the Gamelan, Debussy found an antidote for the great surges of the Wagnerian orchestra.   (Thompson, 1965: 92)

The result was not an imitation of the oriental, but an impulse to rethink how music might sound and be structured, and Debussy emphasised that:

> I have undertaken a task which was perhaps beyond my powers. Not having any precedent, I find myself obliged to invent new forms. Wagner could be of use to me, but I have no need to tell you how ridiculous it would be even to try him. I could use his system in the succession of scenes, but I should want to retain the lyrical line without letting it be absorbed by the orchestra.   (Orledge, 1982: 37)

All of this Debussy intended to apply to the opera, not simply in terms of music *per se*, but how it should work in a dramatic context. One result was the relentless search for a libretto that suited his musico-dramatic vision. Debussy's career is punctuated with more than sixty considered, projected, incomplete and finished stage works. As with Puccini, his search for material was determined by the kind of subject and the opportunity it offered for his kind of (dramatic) music. He had a number of requirements, all born of his early experience of setting words, mainly the cantatas stipulated for entry for the Prix de Rome, complaining:

> These great silly verses, which are only great in their length, bore me, and my music would be stifled by them. Then there's another thing: I don't think I shall ever be able to put music into a strict mould. I'm not speaking of musical form; it's a literary question. I shall always prefer a subject where, somehow, action is sacrificed to feeling. It seems to me that music thus becomes more human and real and one can then discover and refine upon a means of expression.
>
> (Lockspeiser, 1963: 25)

What he looked for was a particular integration of text, dramaturgy and subject with his particular understanding for how opera should work. He had made this clear in an interview given three years before he first encountered Maeterlinck's play:

> Debussy: I am not tempted to imitate what I admire in Wagner: I visualise a quite different dramatic form. In it, music begins at the point where the word becomes powerless as an expressive force: music is made for the inexpressible. I should like her to appear to emerge from the shadows and at times to return there, and she should always be discreet.
>
> Guiraud: What sort of poet could provide you with a suitable text?
>
> Debussy: One who, only hinting at things, will allow me to graft my dream upon his; who will not despotically impose on me the 'scene to be set' and will leave me free, here and there, to show more artistry than him and to complete his work. But he need not be afraid! I shall not imitate the follies of the lyric theatre where music insolently predominates and where poetry is relegated to second place.   (Orledge, 1982: 49)

This not only indicates what sort of text Debussy wanted as a composer, but the kind of dramatic world he wanted to create. He eventually found this in Maeterlinck's symbolist drama *Pelléas et Mélisande*, of which he wrote:

> The drama of *Pelléas*, which despite its dream-like atmosphere contains much more humanity than the so-called 'slice-of-life' plays, fitted in admirably with what I wanted to create. It has an evocative language whose sensibility can be extended in music and in the orchestral backcloth. I also tried to obey a law of beauty that seems to be singularly neglected when it comes to dramatic music: the

characters of this opera try to sing like real people, not in an arbitrary language made up from worn-out clichés. From therein stems the criticism concerning my so-called predilection for monotonous declamation where nothing ever seems melodic . . . First of all, that is untrue. Further, the feelings of a character cannot always be expressed melodically. Lastly, dramatic melody should be quite different from melody in general.   (Orledge, 1982: 51)

Symbolism

In Naturalism, direct narrative allowed the audience to watch events unfold as though in real locations. But for many artists the truth of the world lay somewhere other than in the material, day-to-day experience of life, in Yeats's 'artifice of eternity':

> Once out of nature I shall never take
> My bodily form from any natural thing,
> But such a form as Grecian goldsmiths make
> Of hammered gold and gold enamelling
> To keep a drowsy Emperor awake;
>   (Yeats, 1965: 217)

The problem was how to manifest this in something as physical as the theatre. Wagner had struggled with this. Moments such as the end of *Götterdämmerung*, the act II duet and act III 'Liebestod'/Verklärung in *Tristan* and the whole of *Parsifal* seemed to be straining beyond the mere physical images of some (albeit mythic) 'reality', to dramatise inner actions and truths. Wagner was right to be concerned about staging *Parsifal* at all, fearing that his own production would inevitably deny what the opera was intended to be, as Adolphe Appia understood: 'Through the medium of music [Wagner] conceived a dramatic action whose center of gravity lay inside the characters . . . He wished, moreover, to place this dramatic action on stage, to offer it to our eyes; but there he failed! . . . He did not conceive of a staging technique different from his contemporaries' (Carnegie, 2006: 175).

It was only in Appia's work some forty years later that a form of staging, based above all on lighting, could make the *inner* world manifest.

The sense that Wagner's work was an exploration of the interior life was one of the major impulses towards the Symbolist movement. In France it made a particularly strong impression. Mallarmé understood that, lost in Wagner's overpowering music, the spectator entered a longed-for world, albeit one that only existed within art, exclaiming:

> Yes, I *know*, we are merely empty forms of matter, but we are indeed sublime in having invented God and our soul. So sublime, my friend, that I want to gaze upon matter, fully conscious that it exists, and yet launching myself madly into

> Dream, despite its knowledge that Dream has no existence, extolling the Soul and all the divine impressions of that kind which have collected within us from the beginning of time and proclaiming, in the face of the Void which is truth, these glorious lies!
>   (Mallarmé, 1944: XIII)

Although Appia's techniques had been almost entirely developed in response to Wagner,[1] the results offered Symbolist playwrights a way of making their visions possible. Their most important exponent was Maurice Maeterlinck. His plays were intended to dramatise and reveal the inner meaning of a mysterious world, in which he described how:

> above the tumult may be heard the solemn, uninterrupted whispering of man and his destiny. It is [tragedy's] province to point out to us the uncertain, dolorous footsteps of the being, as he approaches, or wanders from, his truth, his beauty, or his God . . . The mysterious chant of the Infinite, the ominous silence of the soul and of God, the murmur of Eternity on the horizon, the destiny or fatality that we are all conscious of within us, though by what tokens none can tell.
>   (Maeterlinck, 1896: 726–7)

To achieve this, Maeterlinck developed a way of writing that exploited the inherent antithesis between the physical, including language, and actual meaning, insisting that: 'One may even affirm that a poem draws nearer to beauty and loftier truth in the measure that it eliminates words that merely explain the action, and substitute for them others that reveal, not so-called soul-state, but I know not what intangible and unceasing striving of the soul towards its own beauty and truth. And so much the nearer, also, does it draw to the true life' (Maeterlinck, 1896: 730).

Pelléas et Mélisande

All of this paralleled Debussy's desire for a poet who, he wrote, 'only hinting at things, will allow me to graft my dream upon his' and his sense that

> In the opera house they sing *too much*. One should *sing* only when it is worth-while and hold moving lyrical expression in reserve. There should be expressive variety, though. In places it is necessary to paint in cameo and to be content with greys . . . Nothing should impede the progress of the drama: all musical develop-ment called for by the words is a mistake. Besides, musical development that is even a little protracted cannot match the mobility of the text. I dream of poetic texts which will not condemn me to long, heavy acts, but which will provide me with changing scenes, varied in place and mood, where the characters do not argue but submit to life and destiny.   (Orledge, 1982: 49)

The paradox is that while Debussy wanted to get away from text and the literal, he needed a libretto where the language itself directly promoted the kind of world he wished to create. The text therefore became absolutely vital in both content and form. In *Pelléas et Mélisande* the inability to say anything real, anything useful, is apparent from the opening (scene ii of the play), as Golaud starts to question the young girl he spots by a pool in the forest – where he himself is lost:

> Golaud: Come, do not weep so. Where are you from?
> Mélisande: I have fled, fled, fled.
> Golaud: Yes, but where did you flee from?
> Mélisande: I am lost, lost! Oh! Oh! Lost here! I am not from here, I was not born there.
> Golaud: Where are you from? Where were you born?
> Mélisande: Oh, oh! Far from here, far, far.

The questions are real, so too are the answers – but they are disconnected and no sense emerges from them. The repetition of words only reinforces their inadequacy and, as Mélisande actually says, she neither wants to, nor *can*, answer Golaud.

The play offered Debussy a perfect text; one in which, as he had asked, 'the word becomes powerless as an expressive force: music is made for the inexpressible'. However, in order to achieve this Debussy realised that he needed to make radical changes not just to the sound of music and its structure, but to the whole way in which it worked with text. The first element to be addressed was the most fundamental: the role of singing in opera. He began by asserting that:

> Wagner tends to approximate to the speaking voice; or rather, he pretends to do so, while still treating the voices in a very 'vocal manner'. His kind of declamation is neither the Italian recitative, nor the operatic aria. He adds words to a symphonic continuum, while at the same time subordinating the symphony to the words. But not always enough. His works only partly embody the principles which he has laid down with regard to this essential subordination. He lacks the courage to apply them. He is too precise and meticulous, leaving no room for any unexpressed implication . . . And there is too much singing. There are only certain places where it is necessary to sing.   (Jarocinski, 1976: 98–9)

Perhaps the natural response to this was a reassessment of the entire musical structure and, therefore, the elements within it. Above all Debussy feared the falsification of the music-*drama* by purely musical demands:

> I should like to see the creation – I, myself, shall achieve it – of a kind of music free from themes and motives, or formed on a single continuous theme, which nothing interrupts and which never returns upon itself. Then there will be a logical, compact, deductive development. There will not be, between two restatements of the same characteristic theme, a hasty and superfluous 'filling in'! The development will no longer be that amplification of material, that professional

rhetoric which is the badge of excellent training, but it will be given a more universal and essential psychic conception. (Thompson, 1965: 103)

Above all, Debussy was concerned with the opera as a *dramatic* entity and experience, in which the music had to play its part. This required reassessment of the role of melody, the one element that historically had so often distorted the musical drama into a purely musical event. He replied to early critics:

> M. Gauthier-Villars reproaches my score because the melodic lines are never found in the vocal parts but always in the orchestra. I wished never to halt the action and to make it continue uninterrupted. I wanted to do away with parasitic musical phrases. On hearing opera, the spectator is accustomed to experiencing two distinct sorts of emotion: the musical emotion on the one hand, and the emotion of the characters on the other. Generally they are experienced successively, but I tried to ensure that both emotions were perfectly blended and simultaneous. (Orledge, 1982: 292–3)

In *Pelléas* Debussy broke with this tradition and completed the development of the sustained lyrical style that Wagner had initiated. He demanded of his audience:

> Before all, you will do well to eliminate from discussion whether there is, or is not, melody in 'Pelléas'. It must be decisively understood that melody – or song (Lied) – is one thing, and that lyrical expression is another. It is illogical to think that one can make a fixed melodic line hold the innumerable nuances through which a character passes. That is not only a mistake of taste, but a mistake of 'quality'. If in 'Pelléas' the symphonic development has, on the whole, small importance, it is to react against the pernicious neo-Wagnerian aesthetic which presumes to render, at the same time, the sentiment expressed by the character and the inner thoughts which impel its actions. (Grayson, 1986: 231)

Act ii, scene ii is the critical moment where Golaud first notices that Mélisande's ring is missing. But the scene begins as Golaud tries to understand Mélisande's malaise. It moves from Mélisande nursing Golaud who has had a hunting accident, through his attempt to sympathise with her to the confrontation over the ring. The scene demonstrates the flexibility and expressiveness of Debussy's writing whose overall lyricism mirrors the mysterious ebb and flow of Maeterlinck's drama (Table 14.1).

The key to *Pelléas*, and to Debussy's shift in the nature of opera, is his realisation of the Wagnerian aspiration to create a work in which all the elements genuinely combined to create a single dramatic whole, in particular by creating an equality between words and music as part of larger 'dramatic text', as he explained:

> Music has a rhythm whose secret force shapes the development. The rhythm of the soul, however, is quite different – more instinctive, more general, and

Table 14.1 Pelléas et Mélisande: *act ii, scene ii*

25	7	*un peu retenu*	Golaud	Mais on peut égayer tout cela But we can brighten all that	Golaud's recitative-like line rises hopefully, with sparse accompaniment, as he tries to comfort her.
26	1	*Plus lent*	Golaud	la joie, la joie joy, joy	He exclaims the word 'joie' with feeling – and regret
	3	*mutes lifted quickly*	Golaud	Mais dis-moi quelque chose But tell me something	and the orchestra flowers in a lyrical phrase as Golaud asks Mélisande simply to talk to him.
	9	6/4	Mélisande	Je l'ai vu pour la première fois I saw it for the first time	The solo flute plays a line of semiquavers, like a breath of fresh air blowing into the room before
27	1	4/4	Golaud	C'est donc cela Then that's what it is	Golaud thinks he understands. The orchestra subsides, accompanying Golaud's recit-like line.
	4				Triplets in the flutes echo those at 27.1 – although more ponderous, as Golaud now
	5	12/8	Golaud	Voyons tu n'es plus à l'âge Come, you are no longer of an age	changes role and gently begins to reprimand her for childish behaviour.
					The flowing triplets continue, suggesting a tenderness but the pizzicato in the cellos and basses, lends his voice authority
28	1		Golaud:	Tu vas voir le ciel tous les jours. You may see the sky every day.	and then, contradicting what he has said earlier about joy, attempts to woo her with the promise of seeing the sky every day, as he and the orchestra become overtly lyrical only to
	2		Golaud	Et puis l'année prochaine... And then the next year...	lapse into a barely accompanied, unfinished promise.

Table 14.1 (*cont.*)

	4	4/4	Golaud	Voyons, donne- moi ta main; Come, give me your hand;	He turns gently to her in a lyrical line with a stroking motion in the violins and violas.
	5				As he ceases, divided flutes play dainty triplets as the divided first violins rise and
29	1	12/8	Golaud	Oh! Ces petites mains Oh! These little hands	strings and wood wind gently rock – as though Golaud were attempting a lullaby, rising to an expressive high D before
	3		Golaud	Tiens, Wait,	this is dramatically interrupted by a single pizzicato on all the strings as Golaud realises
	4	4/4 *Animé*	Golaud	où est l'anneau...! where is the ring...!	that the ring is missing. He questions her in jagged triplets, accompanied by curt chords in the strings.
	5		Mélisande Golaud	L'anneau? The ring? Oui; Yes;	Her questioning rises nervously. He replies in a falling figure. There is no accompaniment until
	6/7		Mélisande	Je crois I think	a *pizzicato* interrupts her: she hesitates as she starts to find an excuse.
30	1	3/4	Golaud	Tombée? Fallen?	The strings rise slowly and threateningly, and then are repeated faster as Golaud turns on her.
	4	(4/4)	Mélisande	Non; elle est tombée No; it fell	Her reply is unaccompanied and then the strings play a rising figure similar to that which has just accompanied Golaud – but with sympathy.
	7		Golaud Mélisande	(Où est-) elle? Where is it? Vous savez... bien You know... well	A weeping figure in the high woodwind accompanies this exchange before

(*cont.*)

Table 14.1 (*cont.*)

	9		Mélisande	la grotte au bord de la mer? the grotto beside the sea?	a *pizzicato* pulse as she regains her composure and begins to make her excuses.
	10		Mélisande	Eh bien, c'est là Well then, it is there	The cellos and then violas play a meandering line that suggests the story she is weaving until
	13				it is taken up in the divided first violins and starts to sound more fragile as she sings increasingly breathlessly
	14	2/4			a feeling increased by two changes in tempo.
	15	3/4			
31	1	4/4	Mélisande	Il y en a de très beaux. There are some lovely ones.	She settles into her story, to a solid 4/4 and with the woodwind happily accompanying her, until
	3		Mélisande	puis la mer est entrée then the sea came in	the orchestra plays a descending line, suggesting both the fall of the ring and darkening the dialogue as
	5		Golaud	Es-tu sûre que ce soit là? Are you sure it is there?	Golaud sings, accompanied by *tremolando* basses which continue as Mélisande
	6		Mélisande	Oui, oui, tout à fait sûre Yes, yes, quite sure	replies – but again anxiously
	7	2/4	Mélisande	Je l'ai sentie glisser I felt it slip	accelerating as the marking changes to 2/4
	8	4/4	Golaud	Il faut aller la chercher You must go and find it	then back to a solid 4/4 as Golaud takes control, abandons the earlier gentleness and bears down upon her through to the end of the scene – with his ominous involvement of Pelléas.

> controlled by many events. From the incomparability of these two rhythms a perpetual conflict arises, for the two do not move at the same speed. Either the music stifles itself by chasing after a character, or the character has to sit on a note to allow the musician to catch up with him.   (Grayson, 1986: 277–8)

Debussy said that he believed he was 'working on things which will be understood only by the little children of the twentieth century' (Grayson, 1986: 35). But by 1913 *Pelléas* had received a hundred performances at the Opéra-Comique and had made a profound impression on other composers. As the Great War approached, Marguerite Long asked 'Did *Pelléas*, which had meant for us freedom and an escape from the Wagnerian fire, now foreshadow real drama? Would art survive the destruction to come?' (Nichols, 1992: 174). It would, although far more radical changes to art would be needed to cope with the new post-war world, above all in Germany where new music and new kinds of subjects would be required. These would be possible in opera in great part because of the way in which Debussy had completely broken the hold of 'melody – or song (Lied)' replacing it with 'lyrical expression'. In *Pelléas* the lyricism of the music is inextricably bound up with that of the text, both conditioned by the lyricism of the dramaturgy. The role of music is recreated: it is no longer even the most important element: it is a vital part of a larger whole.

Berg and Expressionism (*Wozzeck*)

Despite his innovations Debussy's music remained recognisably an extension, however radical, of late nineteenth-century harmony and lyricism. Enriched with chromatic scales and avoiding the restrictions of melody, it was new and modern, but listeners could understand where it came from even if they did not appreciate where it was going. By contrast *Wozzeck*, in many respects the dramatic continuation of what Debussy had achieved, was a far more radical departure. In 1904 Berg started lessons with Schoenberg, who by 1907 said he had 'renounced a tonal centre – a procedure incorrectly called "atonality"' (Schoenberg, 1984: 86). The period of Berg's formal studies with Schoenberg (1904–10), were the years of 'atonality' and Expressionism. This ended in 1922, a year after *Wozzeck*, with the formal beginning of the 'method of composing with twelve tones'.

The Expressionist period was marked by a freedom from tonal centres, but also by an extreme emotionality, as Schoenberg emphasised: 'I warn you of the danger lurking in the die-hard reaction against Romanticism. The old Romanticism is dead; long live the new' (Machlis, n.d.). For Schoenberg, the crucial features of his new music were never a denial of the emotionality of admired predecessors such as Brahms, Wagner or, more recently, Mahler. Responding later to complaints that he had abandoned the style of *Verklärte Nacht*, he insisted that: 'I have not discontinued composing in the same style and in the same way as at the very beginning. The difference is only that I do it better now than before: it is more concentrated, more mature' (Schoenberg, 1984: 30). This was achieved above all through an increased emphasis on formal organisation, with constant reference to classical models, and the paradigmatic relationship between harmony and melody, expounding his view that: 'Coherence in classic compositions is based – broadly speaking – on the unifying qualities of such structural factors as rhythms, motifs, phrases, and the constant reference to all melodic and harmonic features to the centre of gravitation – the tonic. Renouncement of the unifying power of the tonic still leaves all the other factors in operation' (Schoenberg, 1984: 87).

One of the key organising elements to which Schoenberg, Berg and Webern all turned was literary texts, which would provide music with form and direction. This made the search for, and sensitivity to, texts all the more urgent. On 8 May 1914, Berg attended a performance of Büchner's *Woyzeck*; as he left, a friend described him as: "deathly pale and perspiring profusely." "What do you say?" he gasped, beside himself. "But isn't it fantastic, incredible?" Then, already taking his leave, "Someone must set it to music"' (Jarman, 1989: 1). The play had made an enormous impression, both because of its subject and the way it was dramatised. Although written in a realistic, almost journalistic manner, several features made it revolutionary.

- Rather than a sequence of well-constructed acts, the play consists of twenty-five scenes that follow one another in a logical sequence but without any of the narrative apparatus of the 'well-made' play.[2]
- Woyzeck himself is unlike any traditional 'hero': a mentally subnormal soldier, desperately trying to earn enough money to support himself, his child and his prostitute mistress.
- Stylistically, the play alternates between ironic/satirical and realistic characterisation, accentuating the humanity of Woyzeck and Marie as victims of a society represented by the Captain, Doctor and Drum Major.

Even Schoenberg's initial reaction to Berg's choice was negative:

> I was greatly surprised when this soft-hearted, timid young man had the courage to engage in a venture which seemed to invite misfortune: to compose *Wozzeck*, a drama of such extraordinary tragedy that it seemed forbidding to music. And even more: it contained scenes of everyday life which were contrary to the concept of opera which still lived on stylized costumes and conventionalized characters.
> He succeeded: *Wozzeck* was one of the greatest successes in opera.
> (Schoenberg, 1984: 474)

Berg's attitude is quite clear from his statement that: 'The music was to be so formed that at each moment it would fulfil its duty of serving the action. Even more, the music should be prepared to furnish whatever the action needed for transformation into reality on the stage. The function of a composer is to solve the problems of an ideal stage director' (Jarman, 1989: 152).

Expressionism

Berg's commitment to the opera was, therefore, primarily dramatic: *Woyzeck* was a drama that he wanted to recreate because of the way it portrayed the world and the characters who inhabited it. He explained that his aim was: 'to compose good music; to develop musically the contents of Georg Büchner's immortal drama; to translate his poetic language into music' (Jarman, 1989: 152). But in the process of translation across almost a hundred years, the play entered the world of Expressionism. Zemlinsky had said that where Symbolism was the dream, Expressionism was the nightmare, and this can be seen in the contrast between two of Schoenberg's works. In the 1899 *Verklärte Nacht*, a man and woman walk through the night as she reveals that she is carrying another man's child. By the end, the man transfigures the child into his own as the final bars of Schoenberg's score cover them in starlight. By 1909 a very different vision of the world is presented. A woman wanders, stumbling, though a wood apparently looking for her lover, or her lover's body. The wood may be real or in her mind, the lover may be real, alive or dead. It is her *Erwartung* (Expectation) that dominates. The reality is the reality of, and in, her mind. In the fourth scene, on a 'Broad, moonlit road . . . The woman enters slowly, exhausted. A white stone balcony. Her dress is torn, her hair dishevelled. Bleeding scratches on her face and hands.' The monodrama ends

However, an important aspect of German Expressionism remained its relationship to Realism. Expressionism was perhaps most important in Germany, in particular after the end of the First World War, where it addressed the growing turmoil. Political and social contradictions were too vivid, omnipresent and dangerous to be avoided through idealisation or abstraction. In the work of leading painters such as Dix, Grosz and Beckmann, or the members of *Die Brücke* (Heckel, Kirchner, Schmidt-Rottluff), contemporary Germany is satirised, distorted, violated – but always recognisable.

Similarly Berg, in the 'Production and staging' section of his *Preparation and staging of 'Wozzeck'* insisted on realism, but explained that: 'the designer will be left sufficient scope for applying his own manner to his task. And this is so even if a realistic representation prevails throughout, as I think necessary, so that an immediate and unambiguous recognition and overall view of the place in which each scene is set is assured' (Perle, 1980: 205). He continues to ask for what he calls 'the greatest possible realism' throughout his commentary, adding important details related to the actual performance: 'Marie's murder, for example, occurs at the moment that Wozzeck – once only – 'plunges the knife into her throat' (bar 103). Everything that follows (bars 104–106) refers musically only to Marie and her death. Any further carnage must therefore be avoided!' (Perle, 1980: 206).

The problem of form

As a direct response to the inner world, Expressionism needed the freedom to be able to follow the dictates of the artist's feelings. Schoenberg writing as a painter, said that: 'One should paint what one feels inside and not go out and draw logs and stones which certainly in themselves are not significant and only in passing through the sensibilities of the subject can one get any form' (Smith, 1986: 50). But this raised acute problems of form. Part of the importance of *Wozzeck* is the way in which Berg addressed and resolved this. As Schoenberg and his followers developed, this became a major concern as they sought to extend music and not, as some contemporaries thought, destroy it. Schoenberg makes constant reference to how traditional forms can be used, and the Op. 25 *Piano Suite*, his first multi-movement twelve-tone composition, includes *Präludium, Gavotte, Intermezzo, Menuet* and *Gigue*. Once Berg had established the libretto, questions of musical form became paramount since, as he said 'Text and action alone could not guarantee . . . unity'. As a result: 'Once I had decided to write an opera that would last a whole evening I faced a new problem, at least as far as harmony was concerned: how, without the proven means of tonality and without being able to use the formal structures based on it, could I achieve the same sense of completeness, the same compelling unity?' (Jarman, 1989: 154).

The answer lay in two elements. The first, as in *Pelléas*, was a series of recurring harmonic and melodic figures, some of which are motifs (see Nichols and Langham Smith, 1989: 79–106), used primarily as structural devices.[3] These are associated with characters or aspects of character (12 The doctor, 13 The Drum Major posturing), objects (15 The earrings, 18 The knife), ideas (16 Marie's fear, 14 Seduction) and events or actions (5 Folk song, 6 Military march). These are usually linear (melodic) figures, but can also be rhythmic patterns and chords. They are used in various ways, played at different tempi, inverted, retrograde and so forth.

The second structuring feature is the design of each act as a series of formal, classical movements. These derive from a chart prepared with Berg's approval by one of his students, Fritz Mahler (Jarman, 1989: 42) (Table 14.2).

Several of the forms then have their own structure. For example the *Suite* (act 1, scene i) consists of: Prelude, Pavane, Cadenza for solo violin, Gigue, Cadenza for double bassoon, Gavotte, Air and Reprise. Analysis of the whole opera shows how the detailed construction of each movement, scene and act, together with the thematic/motivic interconnections, create Berg's 'sense of completeness' and

Table 14.2 Wozzeck: *the musical structure (Fritz Mahler)*

Act I	
Expositions: Wozzeck and his relationship to his environment	*Five character sketches*
1 Wozzeck and the Captain	1 Suite
2 Wozzeck and Andres	2 Rhapsody
3 Wozzeck and Marie	3 Military March and Cradle Song
4 Wozzeck and the Doctor	4 Passacaglia
5 Wozzeck and the Drum Major	5 Andante affettuoso (quasi-Rondo)

Act II	
Dramatic development	*Symphony in Five Movements*
1 Marie and her child, later Wozzeck	1 Sonata movement
2 The Captain and the Doctor, later Wozzeck	2 Fantasia and Fugue
3 Marie and Wozzeck	3 Largo
4 Garden of a tavern	4 Scherzo
5 Guard room in the barracks	5 Rondo con introduzione

Act III	
Catastrophe and epilogue	*Six Inventions*
1 Marie and her child	1 Invention on a Theme
2 Marie and Wozzeck	2 Invention on a Tone
3 A low bar	3 Invention on a Rhythm
4 Death of Wozzeck	4 Invention on a Key (D minor)
5 Orchestral interlude: invention on a key	
6 Children playing	6 Invention on a regular quaver movement (Perpetuum Mobile)

therefore 'compelling unity'. But this raises the seminal question of how this relates to an audience. Berg himself was quite clear:

> What I do consider my particular accomplishment is this. No one … from the moment the curtain parts until it closes for the last time, pays any attention to the various fugues, inventions, suites, sonata movements, variations, and passacaglias about which so much has been written. No one gives heed to anything but the vast social implications of the work which by far transcend the personal destiny of Wozzeck. This, I believe, is my achievement.   (Jarman, 1989: 153)

Table 14.3 Wozzeck: *act III, scene 2*

73	**3/2** *Forest path by a pool* (*It is dark*) *Marie enters right with Wozzeck*	Marie	Dort links / Over left	*The forceful music of the interlude between Scenes 1 and 2 rapidly falls away as the rising figure on the celeste suggests the moon rising, while the dark undertow of the basses starts to create the desolation of the scene, ending* / in a single quaver as Marie enters uncertainly, accompanied by the bassoon's meandering, elaborate figure. Her line is lyrical. But
74			geht's in Stadt. 's ist noch weit. Komm schneller! / lies the town. It's still far. Come quicker!	she is interrupted by an ominous interjection in the violins while the clarinets play triplets 'fleetingly' – emphasising her haste.
75		Wozzeck	Du sollst da bleiben, Marie. / You must stay, Marie.	The deep, ominous bass line continues as Wozzeck, otherwise unaccompanied, halts Marie in a steady, insistent phrase rising yearningly
		Wozzeck	Komm, setz' Dich. / Come, sit.	followed by a lyrical descending phrase – his love? – emphasised by the second violins.
76		Marie	Aber ich muß fort. / But I must go on.	The brief energy of Marie's rising phrase is parodied in the flutes and violas – but the energy falls away, still over the chord in the basses.
	They sit down	Wozzeck	Bist/weit gegangen, Marie / You have/wandered far, Marie	Ignoring her – and her music – Wozzeck's phrases are insistent, played 'zögernd aber poco. accel.' (lingering but with slight acceleration) accompanied by long steady phrases in the strings, before
78		Wozzeck	Füsse nicht mehr wund laufen. / [But your] feet will wander no more.	the demi-semiquaver figure in the bassoons falls to the words 'laufen' (wander). Throughout Wozzeck's passage, the text's irony is set off by the realistic colouring and commentary of the music. Now the clarinet plays independently, responding to the desolate mood of the place as

79		Wozzeck	's ist still hier! Und so dunkel. It's still here! And so dark.	Wozzeck changes from his brooding remarks to an awareness of the location. But this does not last:
80				He wakes to his purpose with a clearly harmonised, melodic and rhythmic phrase in the oboes, cor anglais and horns, pointed by high harmonic notes from the solo violin.
81		Wozzeck	Weißt noch, Marie, wie lang es jetzt ist, daß wir uns Do you, Marie, how long we have one another	Again Wozzeck sings in three clear, melodic, repeated phrases. Berg is particularly good at differentiating between Wozzeck's different states of mind: inner turmoil, purpose and straightforward awareness.
82		Wozzeck Marie	kennen? known? Zu Pfingsten drei Jahre At Whitsun, three years.	At this point, the music of the woodwind comes into focus, with the semiquavers in the clarinets creating a sense of pleading as Marie answers in a normal, conversational phrase. But
83		Wozzeck	Und was meinst, wie lang es noch dauern wird? And what do you think, how long we shall go on?	Wozzeck's sense of direct purpose remains. During his second phrase the high-pitched, insistent violin sounds become the relentless idea underlying his questions, while the pressing tuba creates a sense of inexorable purpose.
	[Marie] *jumps up*	Marie	Ich muß/fort I must/go	
84		Wozzeck	Fürchst dich, Marie? Are you frightened, Marie?	The powerful tuba line is sustained as Wozzeck moves to his real questions.
	laughing	Wozzeck	Und bist du doch fromm? And are you pious?	The tuba ceases but its line is taken over by the double bass, creating Wozzeck's own internal pressure which is now released in this rising phrase – as he laughs and

(*cont.*)

Table 14.3 (*cont.*)

Bar	Stage direction	Character	Text	Music
85		Wozzeck	Und/gut! Und treu! And good/And true!	continues to laugh, as the two musical phrases rise, first from D to middle C, and then from F♯ to a high *falsetto* F followed by
	he pulls her down onto the seat			an extraordinary series of *glissandi* in the strings, one section after another at the same time as demi-semi-quaver *glissandi* by the harp and celeste. This beautiful moment might be the point at which Wozzeck looks at Marie with love.
86	*he bends over her in deadly earnest, molto cantabile*	Wozzeck	Was! Du für süße Lippen hast, Marie! What! How sweet your lips are, Marie!	Wozzeck's line and the strings accompanying him become lyrical as he examines her.
88	*Kisses her*	Wozzeck	Den Himmel gäb' ich drum I would give the heavens	The woodwind, in sequence, enter and amplify this and the passage grows in intensity/ardour until
90		Wozzeck	wenn ich Dich noch oft so küssen/dürft if I could still sometimes kiss you	this phrase, when the woodwind ceases and he is left longing – and knowing that it is not to be.
91		Wozzeck	Aber ich darf nicht! But I may not!	A horn call arouses him from this reverie, repeated as he comes back to reality
92		Wozzeck	Was zitterst? Why shivering?	*Tremolando* flutes and then single notes on the harp create the cold – within and without.
93		Marie	Der nachtau fällt Night is falling	
	whispering to himself	Wozzeck	Wer kalt ist/den Who is cold/you	Wozzeck's line becomes subdued and inexpressive as he whispers to himself; the strings follow his line in broad strokes while a timp beats out a rhythm *pp*.

95		Marie	Was sagst du da?... What are you saying, there?...	Marie's line cuts across Wozzeck's leaving him
96		Wozzeck	Nix Nothing	unaccompanied to draw the section to a sombre conclusion.
	6/4 *A long silence* *The moon rises*			After a long silence the moon rises, sounded in the score by a long, slow ascent of the brass instruments entering in canon over a long chord in the strings which continues as the canon
98–99		Marie	Wie der/Mond rot aufgeht! How the moon rises red!	is echoed in Marie's slow, faltering ascending line.
100		Wozzeck	Wie ein blutig Eisen! Like a bloody knife!	This is followed by Wozzeck's much faster, assertive version of the same.
101	*he draws a knife* *she jumps up*	Marie	Was zitterst? Why shivering?	A steady pulse starts in the timpani. As Marie asks her question, the wind, strings and xylophone interject a short, nervous figure.
102		Marie Wozzeck	Was willst? What do you want? Ich nict, Marie Unk kein Not me, Marie. And no one	The orchestra is dominated by the pulse of the drum beat which continues as Wozzeck's line (*molto crescendo*) is sung in an hysterical, high *tessitura*.
103	*he seizes her and plunges the knife into her throat* [The exact point where he stabs her is marked ↓ in the score – see p. 291]	Wozzeck Marie	Andrer auch nicht! else either! Hilfe Help	Oboes, trumpets, horns and harp play a *ff* arc.

This emphasises the extent to which the dramatic and ethical experience was paramount for Berg, and this is constantly evident in the detail of the score:

> In *Wozzeck*, too, music makes new claims for sovereignty within opera. But Berg's method is directly contrary to that of the neo-classicists: utter submission to the text. The composition of *Wozzeck* outlines an exceedingly rich, multi-faceted curve of the inner plot: expressionistic in that it takes place entirely in an inner realm of the soul. It registers every dramatic impulse to the point of self-forgetfulness.
>
> (Adorno, 1991: 87)

The result is that, far more even than in Puccini or Strauss, any analysis has to follow the minutiae of the very dense and compact verbal and musical fabric (Table 14.3).

The extent of detailed continuity between libretto and music in both *Pelléas* and *Wozzeck*, supervening melody and any other individual, purely musical element, points to a significant shift in twentieth-century opera. Where Verdi or even Wagner composed in paragraphs or at least sentences, Berg writes word by word. The result is an extraordinary complex where words and music are inextricably bound together. Berg's success in achieving this meant that his operas would become an essential model for operatic composition from now on. As George Perle writes:

> Both [*Wozzeck* and *Lulu*] add new dimensions to the dramatic range of the operatic theatre and extend its relevance to life and to the world of ideas as radically and significantly as any work . . . of the past . . . They solve the perennial problem of operatic form in a new and unique way, integrating characteristic self-contained pieces that recall the classical 'number' opera within an overall cyclic and recapitulative design whose unity and scale are comparable only to the most impressive achievements in the literature.
>
> (Perle, 1980: xiv)

Chapter 15

The dramaturgy of opera: libretto – words and structures

Just as the essential elements of music were recast in the early years of the twentieth century so too were the basic components of dramaturgy. The emphasis that post-Wagnerian composers such as Debussy and Berg placed on the libretto, combined with the need to reflect an increasingly disrupted world, meant that basic assumptions about narrative and plot, as well as the relationship in the libretto between words and music, had to be rethought. Although dramatic structures had constantly shifted, the assumption of a straightforward sequence of events had never been challenged. This had led from a story, through the selection of events to form a plot designed to engage the audience's emotions and intellect (Table 15.1).

Both *Pelléas* and *Wozzeck*, in their different ways, started to interfere with this. In *Pelléas* there is a disparity between the events the audience sees and the rest of the narrative, so that the world of the opera and its characters are recognisable but always oblique. In *Wozzeck* the narrative is so fragmented that it only holds together within the main character and the audience's experience of and through

Table 15.1 *Narrative and plot*

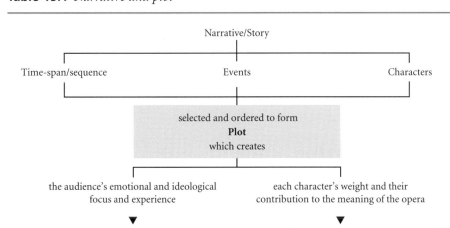

Both music and staging (original directions) become additional and major forces in determining each of these

him. A major feature of twentieth-century opera is the manipulation of this to create new, often provocative images of a world beyond realistic representation. All of this reinforces the libretto as a dramaturgical rather than a literary function, centred on plot. Dramaturgy is, therefore, what allows narrative, action, character – and ultimately music itself – to work; so that an understanding of it is not only vital for the complications of modern operas, but is a main key to the way in which all operas work as dramas.

Plot: the order of incidents

Chapter 1 began by quoting Aristotle on the relationship between narrative/action, plot and the other constituent parts of the drama. His starting point is that: 'In tragedy it is action that is imitated . . . The representation of the action is the plot of the tragedy; for the ordered arrangements of the incidents is what I mean by plot . . . Of [all the] elements the most important is plot, the ordering of incidents; for tragedy is a representation, not of men, but of action and life' (Aristotle, 1970: 39).

The first task is therefore to select incidents from the story and arrange them in a way that creates a particular sense and emphasis. For example, there could be operas called *Gilda, Maddalena, Monterone* or *Sparafucile*. Each of these is a character with their own lives and tragedies. In each case the broad events in *Rigoletto* would exist, but they would have to be ordered differently, with different weighting, with some left out altogether and others added, and each starting and ending in a different place, to ensure focus on the new main role. In this way the meaning of an opera – its reliable impact on an audience – depends at least as much on *how* the story is told as on the story itself. In fact there is, really, no *story itself*: the story will always be the story *as it is told*, and the telling is precisely the selection that turns narrative material into the mechanism of plot. Plot itself works through a number of devices, which together make up the dramaturgy: the way in which the librettist's and composer's intentions control the audience's reactions and understanding (Table 15.2).

Retrospective narration

The surviving Greek plays had a problem with narrative, because they took place in the last moments of the story. The *story* of Oedipus includes many elements that do not appear in the play. But even when released from the constraint of the unities, the librettist's first problem remained how to tell a story within the highly restricted time possible in the theatre – one major difference between the stage and the epic poem

Table 15.2 *Narrative, plot and dramaturgical devices*

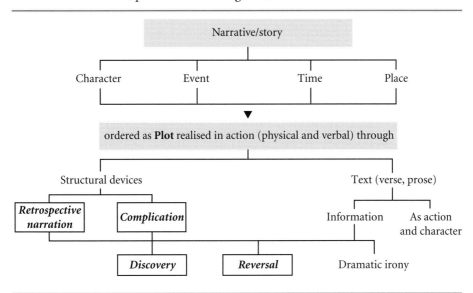

or novel. The problem is complicated by the fact that once the decision has been made which incidents are going to be shown, the information contained in those omitted will somehow have to be introduced. If this is not done, then the notorious complications of *Il trovatore* or *Simon Boccanegra* become inevitable.[1] This is usually done through *retrospective narration* in which, as naturally as possible, past events are introduced as part of the dialogue. In *Oedipus* the process of revelation is the process of the play itself. The audience becomes aware of what has happened about half-way through the play, which Oedipus, the incessant questioner, only understands too late to be able to stop. More typically, in Sophocles' *Antigone* the first episode is used to inform the audience of everything that has gone before.

The libretti of *The Ring* were written in reverse order as Wagner found the need to provide more and more information to make sense of (what was originally called) *Siegfrieds Tod*. Even so in *Die Walküre* there are three retrospective narrations:

- In act I, Hunding invites Siegmund 'der Frau hier gieb doch Kunde' (tell your tale to my wife), allowing him to narrate his part in the years between the end of *Das Rheingold* and his flight into Hunding's hut.
- Later, Sieglinde completes the story with her own history in 'Eine Waffe lass mich dir weisen' (Let me show you a sword).
- In act II, Brünnhilde asks Wotan 'Vater! Vater! Sage, was ist dir?' (Father! Father! What ails you?), allowing him to rehearse everything that has gone before in the long monologue 'Als junger Liebe Lust' (When youthful love's delights).

The opening of act I of *Siegfried* similarly fills in what has happened since the end of *Die Walküre*, while the later riddle scene rehearses the whole drama so far, as does the entire Prologue to *Götterdämmerung*. Wagner's skill as a dramatist is to make each of these sections more than just background narration or recapitulation. In each, the characters relive the events, as do the audience, creating an increasing sense of fatality.

A very different kind of opera, *Cavalleria Rusticana*, uses the same device. Santuzza's aria 'Voi lo sapete, o mamma' (You know, mamma), provides the background to the opera's tragic thrust, as she explains how Turiddu has treated both her and Lola. By contrast, Puccini rarely uses this device, preferring to let his characters create their tragedy as they go, conditioned not by fate but choices that are made in good faith as they become involved with a tuberculous embroiderer, an American naval cad, a painter caught up in subversive politics and so on. The audience watches choices being made and follows the consequences. As in *Così fan tutte* the world is what people make it – mistakes and all. In comedy, at least, they have the opportunity to learn from their mistakes and reach some accommodation, perhaps even start again.

The structuring of narrative into plot, and the devices it uses to inform the audience, are therefore the way in which dramaturgy creates the drama's *meaning*. While characters may *state/sing* their views of the world, it is the plot that tells the audience whose view counts. For all the power of the 'Credo' in act II of *Otello*, the opera does not belong to Iago's world of the 'cruel God'. Despite the anguish of the world, the audience is left with Otello's nobility and love. This is created by the decision to cut Lodovico's last lines in the play:

> To you, Lord Governor,
> Remains the censure of this hellish villain;
> The time, the place, the torture – O, enforce it!
> Myself will straight aboard; and to the state
> This heavy act with heavy heart relate.

Instead, there is Boito's version of Othello's last lines, not quite a translation but an extension that can carry the weight of conclusion. These are accompanied by the love motif, which leaves the audience not with hopeless reminiscence, or Lodovico's unfinished business, but the assertion, of, albeit tragic, love itself:

> Pria d'ucciderti... sposa... ti baciai.   Ere I killed you... wife... I kissed you.
> Or morendo... nell'ombra...   Now dying... in the shadow...
> in cui mi giacio   in which I lie
> un bacio... un bacio ancora...   A kiss... another kiss...
> Ah!... un altro bacio...   Ah!... another kiss...

Of course, it is not enough to focus on the words: in opera it is the function of dramaturgy to enable the music to achieve meaning. *The Ring* does not end with Brünnhilde's monologue. Wagner had great difficulty with the final words and at least four different versions exist, all of which try to sum up the 'meaning' of the cycle. He realised that no single character had the status to resolve the work and ultimately his answer to what *The Ring* meant was that: 'I have now come to realize again how much there is, owing to the whole nature of my poetic aim, that only becomes clear through the music' (D. Cooke, 1979: 2). This is not a fudge. The opera ends with the complex staging of the burning of the Hall, the flooding of the Rhine, the reclamation of the ring by the Rhine maidens, Hagen's drowning and the gathered men and women observing Valhalla catch fire. But the final statement is in the music: the motif, first heard in act i, scene iii of *Die Walküre*, where it accompanies Sieglinde's ecstatic lines as she realises she is carrying a child, sometimes called 'The redemption through love'. Even if an audience does not know what it 'is', the beatific glow of the last pages cannot but spread a sense of peace over the scene, however ironically modern directors may wish to use it.

Britten referred to Billy Budd as 'our Saviour, yet he is Billy, not Christ or Orion' (Morra, 2007: 109). But this is not how the novella concludes, with a song made by some 'tarry hand':

> Sentry, are you there?
> Just ease these darbies at the wrist,
> And roll me over fair!
> I am sleepy, and the oozy weeds about me twist.

E. M. Forster took up Britten and Eric Crozier's suggestion that: 'It seemed a natural development that the action on board ship should be "framed" by a prologue and epilogue of Vere as an elderly man looking back on the troubled days of his wartime command'.[2] This does more than 'unify' the opera. It allows it to conclude with Vere's reflection that: 'he has saved me, and blessed me and the love that passes understanding has come to me.' The opera is radically changed from the novella by the dramaturgical *structure* more than the actual words, which allows the audience to understand that Vere's final awareness is the meaning of the work as a whole.

For all its ambiguity – which is, after all, what the opera is about – *Così fan tutte* ends with all six characters joined in a resolute statement, set to forthright music that confirms their sincerity and unanimity:

Fortunato l'uom che prende	Happy is the man who takes
ogni causa pel buon verso,	everything for the best,
e tra i casi e le vicende	and through each event and the next
da ragion guidar si fa.	Allows himself to guided by reason.

In each case, librettist and composer have ensured that the arrangement of the incidents leads the audience *not* to the end of a story from which they need to draw their own conclusions, but a statement of intent. It is then left to the audience to test this against the evidence of the opera as a whole, as presented in its music, words and physical presentation.

Complication, discovery and reversal

The plot is therefore a way of manoeuvring the audience, and one major way of doing this is through the release of important information as the opera proceeds, deepening and complicating the characters and their situations. This can create dramatic irony, which affects the audience's view of the action and the characters. In *Otello*, Iago manufactures exactly this situation, so that he and the audience are complicit in knowing how each of the other characters is being manipulated. The result is an almost unbearable tension for the impotent audience. This sense of fatality can be introduced in other ways. In *Rigoletto*, Monterone's curse haunts Rigoletto and directs the audience's expectation. While curses were not literal for Verdi, the device makes the audience aware that this is a world in which there is no escaping the past, in this case Rigoletto's own behaviour. The same is true of the Marquis' curse at the end of act i of *La forza del destino*. In both operas, the curse is an analogue for how the world traps people.

   Fidelio is a curious case. Leonora does not actually reveal who she is until the last scene when she interposes between Pizarro and Florestan. This raises a number of questions. If the audience does not know who she is from the start, then how are they to understand her refusal of Jaquino, her dismay at Marcellina's advances and her insistence on helping Rocco with the unknown prisoner? In *Simon Boccanegra*, Amelia and Simon only discover that they are father and daughter at the end of act i – something that is equally a revelation to the audience. However once this has been revealed, Amelia keeps the secret from Gabriele until the end of act ii. The initial revelation produces relief and celebration, but then creates irony and tension. In *Il trovatore*, Azucena alone knows – if it is in fact true – that Manrico and the Count are brothers, a secret that she keeps until the very end of the opera. In *La Juive*, Eleazar similarly keeps Rachel's birth hidden until the last bars.

   The impact and hence ultimate meaning these devices create are different in each. In *Fidelio* it is part of a picture of a world of true love and self-sacrifice. What is moving is not the final revelation to the *audience* that she is who she is, but the moment of the revelation to Florestan which enshrines her love and sacrifice. By contrast, the ending of *Il trovatore* or *La Juive* run the danger of producing a mere *frisson*, a purely theatrical excitement. This can only be mitigated by the extent to which the audience has been enabled to empathise with the characters. Without this, the artificiality of the device threatens to undermine the whole drama: are such coincidences, secrets and machinations an adequate way of portraying the world? In the novel, Thomas Hardy constantly uses coincidence as an analogue for fate; but more often such things degenerate into merely thrilling effects. Gilbert understood this, and hence mixed-up babies (*HMS Pinafore*, *The Gondoliers*) and long-lost brothers (*Ruddigore*).

In *Rigoletto* there are three kinds of revelation, each demanding its own careful plotting. The first is straightforward, when the audience learns that Gilda is Rigoletto's daughter – which has been preceded in the first scene by ribald mention of her as the hunchback's mistress. This creates terrible irony and tension when the blindfolded Rigoletto assists in his own daughter's abduction, something that the audience alone realises. The second comes in act II as the courtiers tell the Duke what (they believe) has happened, until Rigoletto enters and reveals their true relationship. The effect is one of crushing pathos. The final revelation is when Rigoletto discovers that it is Gilda and not the Duke in the sack. In each case the audience is in a different position: they do not know initially that Gilda and Rigoletto are daughter and father; they do know whom Rigoletto is ignorantly abducting; they do know that they are father and daughter as they watch the Duke and courtiers. Do they know who is in the sack? If so, then it is the device of the curse that has raised their suspicion.

Underlying this are Aristotle's terms 'complication', 'reversal' and 'discovery' which together create 'feeling'[3] – the range of 'feelings' or reactions that are the aim of the work. He considers *Oedipus* to be perfect because the discovery (by Oedipus as to who he really is) brings about the reversal (from pride and nobility to horror and downfall) at the very moment which is the point of greatest emotion for the audience. 'Discovery' itself is most notably part of comic structuring, where coincidence is often used to remedy the situation. In *Le Nozze di Figaro*, the revelation that Marcellina and Bartolo are Figaro's parents clears the way to the marriage of the title; however the humbling of the count at the Countess's entry has a quite different impact. The first is a genuinely comic surprise and relief; the second is at best a bitter-sweet revelation of the truth. In each case it is plot, the arrangements of the incidents, the dramaturgy, that creates the overall meaning by creating the context within which the audience encounters characters, actions, words and music.

Words

Drama has often been taught as a form of literature. But the medium of the play is dramatic action, and while there are moments in the drama where words and their form – poetic or otherwise – are of the essence, these are rare. Most of the time words in plays, as in reality, accompany action. Shakespeare's blank verse is a working verse form, easily accommodated to the natural rhythms of the English language and easily variable as emotional and other pressures interfere with the regularity of speech. Similarly, the words/language of the libretto are not 'literature'. Many of the great librettists were playwrights and poets in their own right and often provided beautiful lines and verses. But it is also generally the case that the finest poetic work does not always suit musical setting: the words do not need it – there is no 'room' for the music, as Auden points out:

> Much as I admire Hofmannsthal's libretto for *Rosenkavalier*, it is, I think, too near real poetry. The Marschallin's monologue in act I, for instance, is so full of interesting detail that the voice line is hampered in trying to follow everything. The verses of *Ah non credea* in *La Sonnambula*, on the other hand, though of little interest to read, do exactly what they should, suggest to Bellini one of the most beautiful melodies ever written and then leave him completely free to write it. The verses which the librettist writes are not addressed to the public but are really a private letter to the composer.   (Weisstein, 1964: 359).

This does not deny the vital role of the libretto and its words. It is to emphasise that, as in the theatre, they play a particular part and can work in different ways: one element in the process of creating meaning.

It is in this light that verse forms need to be approached. In Italy in particular an elaborate system of versification had been developed that both suited and provided a stimulus for musical setting (see Balthazar, 2004: 69–87). But *Pelléas, Salome* and *Wozzeck* all have prose libretti. Musical setting had achieved a flexibility which meant that it neither needed the regularity of metrical verse nor wanted to be restricted by it. This did not mean that the verse libretto was abandoned, simply that it became an option. Puccini and Strauss continued to want verse libretti, Janáček had Ostrovsky's *The Storm* versified for *Ká'ta Kabanová*. But when modern and contemporary composers such as Stravinsky, Henze, Glass and Birtwistle use verse libretti, this is a deliberate choice, usually where they see opera as a hieratic art that requires the formality of verse as part of a larger aesthetic.

Points of division

The *Camerata* created opera for a serious purpose, and even when this was almost lost the major composers continued to create works that were important reflections of their societies. Wagner insisted on this as the essential purpose, through his own practice and, perhaps more lastingly, his theoretical writings. While composers may have rejected the views themselves, they accepted the concept of opera as an art form with a social, political and ethical role as Tippett wrote: 'For the purpose of

The Midsummer Marriage I had accepted and reenforced Wagner's thesis, but it is no guarantee that for the purposes of a new opera I shall not turn it upside down' (Tippett, 1974: 66).

At the same time, however, a major change took place. Naturalism was the last culturally homogeneous artistic movement. Thereafter, as in every other aspect of the arts, vying possibilities, styles, forms and ideas became the general condition. This is evident in Strauss' oeuvre. Table 15.3 is a tentative typology of his operas. The range of genres and subjects is very wide – perhaps wider than any artist might be expected seriously to encompass. In addition, only four of the operas fit easily into their categories: the romantic *Guntram*, (proto)expressionist *Salome* and *Elektra*, symbolist *Die Frau ohne Schatten* and naturalist *Intermezzo*.

This is made more complex by ironic subtitles such as 'Song poem', 'Merry mythology' and 'Bucolic tragedy'. The 'period realism' of *Der Rosenkavalier*, *Ariadne auf Naxos* and *Die Schweigsame Frau* is further qualified by their musical irony, while *Capriccio*'s aesthetic metaphor over-rides its apparent (period) realism. *Arabella* has a modern setting, but is caught between the romantic Arabella/Mandrika elements and the more obvious Naturalism of the other characters. *Die ägyptische Helene*, *Daphne* and *Die Liebe der Danae* all have classical narratives, but their irony is far removed from Fauré's *Pénélope* or Stravinsky's *Oedipus Rex*. This is typical of a period where new forms were being created and old ones left to be played with. The operas are distinguishable not by Strauss' music, but by his librettists, creating a tension between a consistent musical language and a variety of dramatic styles.

In the future, no composer would be able to apply a single style to such a range of dramatic types as choice of libretto became not so much a matter of personal preference as commitment, as Schoenberg foresaw:

> The future of the opera depends on the future of the drama, and both have new ways forced on them by the fact of the cinema, which can offer all the theatre offers except speech... The future of the drama, can therefore rest only with speech. The coming drama will be a *verbal* drama... and if the drama is to be a verbal drama, then the opera will have to be an opera of *musical ideas*... How will it look? One cannot say – one can only do!   (Schoenberg, 1984: 336–7)

This implies that, more than ever before, operas in the twentieth and twenty-first centuries have to be approached as dramatic types within which musical form/style is a crucial, but only one, element. This is because the multiplicity of visions of the world is directly paralleled in the different dramatic forms designed to express them so that there is a continuum between world view and narrative/subject-matter. While some kind of narrative is basic to most operas, its manipulation creates very different kinds of experience. The initial stage in this was the departure from

Table 15.3 *The range of Strauss' operatic types*

Symbolism	Pre-Expressionism	Period Realism	Naturalism	Classicism	Romanticism
Die Frau ohne Schatten Opera	*Salome* Music drama	*Der Rosenkavalier* Comedy for music	*Intermezzo* Bourgeois comedy	*Die ägyptische Helena* Opera	*Guntram*
	Elektra Tragedy	*Ariadne auf Naxos* Opera	*Arabella* Lyrical comedy	*Daphne* Bucolic tragedy	*Feuersnot* Song poem
		Die schweigsame Frau Comic opera		*Die Liebe der Danae* Merry mythology	
		Friedenstag Opera			
		Capriccio Conversation piece for music			

traditional notions of the narrative as a simple, linear reflection of the way events occurred in 'reality' (Table 15.4).

Each of these narrative types required the right balance between a comprehensible sequence and an equally comprehensible disruption as part of the creation of dramatic meaning. The focus had to be the real intention of the work rather than its narrative surface. The result was a reconsideration of the function of the music, the dramaturgical structure and operatic form as a whole. Furthermore, change in the twentieth century became increasingly radical, occurred with far greater rapidity and followed several different lines simultaneously. Together, these imply a number of different ways in which modern opera can be categorised (Table 15.5).

Table 15.4 *The fragmentation of narrative as expressions of dramatic meaning*

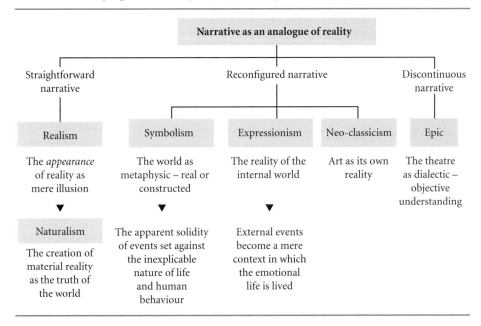

Table 15.5 *Alternatives for categorising twentieth-century opera*

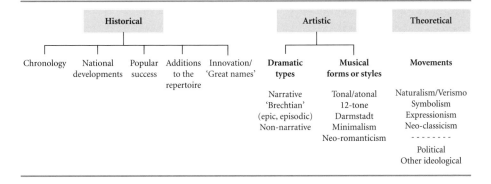

As a result any approach must provide analytical access without creating false coherences or distinctions. In the first half of the period this is less difficult to deal with. It is sufficiently distant to be more easily assessed, and composers mainly belonged to, or were identifiable with, broad movements. After the Second World War this ceased to be the case, creating a range of alternative approaches. But whatever the opera, composer, or style, it is the overall dramatic purpose and function that will determine the aesthetic structure within which it is to be understood:

> when I decided to write an opera [*Wozzeck*], my only intention, as related to the technique of composition, was to give the theatre what belongs to the theatre. The music was to be so formed that at each moment it would fulfill its duty of serving the action. Even more, the music should be prepared to furnish whatever the action needed for transformation into reality on the stage. The function of a composer is to solve the problems of an ideal stage director.
>
> (Jarman, 1989: 152)

Chapter 16

Narrative opera: realistic and non-realistic

The emphasis on disparate dramatic forms and kinds of music meant that composers would now be faced with a variety of choices in every aspect of their work. Even composers using historical conventions, as Stravinsky did in *The Rake's Progress*, or writing in a relatively conservative idiom, as Britten did, were conscious of how they were positioning themselves. What neither could do was take the tradition/al for granted. The stylistic range of operas surrounding four of the operas in this chapter shows how broad the dramatic and musical choices could be (see appendix 4 for a more complete chronology and cultural context) (Table 16.1).

The central concern was the way in which music – linear form, tonality, vocal and orchestral writing – would be used to reinforce, comment upon, or contradict

Table 16.1 *Five operas and their contemporaries*

1925	Berg: *Wozzeck*	Wolf-Ferrari Holst Ravel	*Gli amanti sposi* *At the Boar's Head* *L'enfant et les sortilèges*
1926		Puccini Szymanowski	*Turandot* *King Roger*
1943		Orff	*Die Kluge*
1945	Britten: *Peter Grimes*		
1946	Britten: *The Rape of Lucretia*	Prokofiev Menotti Weill	*Betrothal in a Monastery* *The Medium* *Street Scene*
1951	Stravinsky: *The Rake's Progress*	Britten Menotti	*Billy Budd* *Amahl and the Night Visitors*
1966	Henze: *Die Bassariden*	Britten Barber Dessau	*The Burning Fiery Furnace* *Antony and Cleopatra* *Puntila*

dramatic structure. In one sense, this was nothing new: it is the subject of the Calzabigi/Gluck 'Preface' to *Alceste*. What is different in the twentieth century is the range and radical nature of the alternatives, compounded by the demand that artists respond more or less directly to the wider context and the question of the role and responsibility of opera in society (Table 16.2, p. 326).

Precisely because of the growing stress on ideological content, composers were forced to ask Aribert Reimann's 'important question... whether the particular subject-matter needs music – not some sort of incidental music, simply to underline atmospheric and dramatic situations, but autonomous music which independently develops its own structure' (Reimann, 1989).

Realistic narratives

Britten: the composer in society

Britten had to make important choices because he so consciously saw himself as establishing an English operatic tradition while at the same time developing a musical language that would accommodate his audience. This meant coming to terms with specific social and cultural conditions, as well as broader considerations of the purpose of opera and the challenge of contemporary music, dramaturgy and production. While he was well aware of English operas of the past three hundred years, he also knew that none of these had established a discernible tradition. The exception that proved the rule had been Purcell who becomes an explicit model for Britten, who explained in the 'Introduction' to *Peter Grimes* that his aim was to 'try and restore to the musical setting of the English language a brilliance, freedom and vitality that have been curiously rare since... Purcell' (Kildea, 2000: 50).

Table 16.2 *The complex of factors determining operatic form and style*

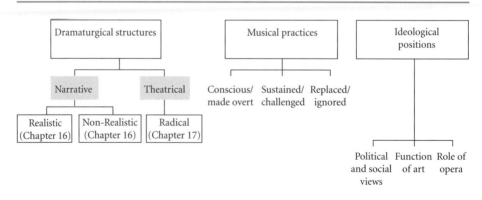

Britten consistently aimed to write music that should be comprehensible and useful: 'I believe that the artist must be consciously a human being. He is part of society and he should not lock himself up in an ivory tower . . . I would rather have my music used than write masterpieces which were not used' (Kildea, 2000: 311).

This directly affected his view of tonality and melody as well as dramatic structures. He believed that: 'The craze for originality, one result of the nineteenth century cult of personality, has driven many artists into using a language to which very few hold the key, and that is a pity' (Kildea, 2000: 215).

His concept of *Gebrauchtmusik* (useful music) often led to writing for specific groups. Three of his operas were composed for children, while the three Church Parables, as he says, were intended to 'suit the buildings and the occasions down in Suffolk' (Kildea, 2000: 294). One reason for establishing the English Opera Group was to enable opera to produce new work, experiment and reach communities that would otherwise never see live opera. (See Britten's evidence to the Arts Council, in Kildea, 2000: 86–101). Writing for smaller, more economical or community-based venues encouraged experimentation with musical and production styles: 'I think also that when you go to the theatre you don't want – at least I don't want – to see just a little touch of people's everyday lives. I want to see something heightened; I want to see something stylized. And that is why I believe the operatic form, like the poetic drama, is so much more illuminating than, for instance, just a straight drawing room comedy. I like the idea of the stylistic vision of people's lives' (Kildea, 2000: 308).

Although the narrative sequence in Britten's operas is straightforward, they also use production devices that extend beyond realism, reflecting this interest in stylisation, influenced by his experience of oriental theatre and contemporary theatricality:

- The Church Parables use sparse, largely symbolic scenery and costumes, enabling them to be performed in almost any space, but as a result invoking an active, imaginative response from the audience.
- *Curlew River* drew upon Japanese theatre for its theme, staging and the casting of a tenor in the role of the Madwoman.
- In both *Billy Budd* and *The Rape of Lucretia* the action is framed by a chorus (or choric figure in Captain Vere) not so much to distance the action as direct the audience's attention and understanding of the action.
- In *Death in Venice* the key characters of Tadzio and his family friends are danced rather than sung.

However, this experimentation does not break with traditional narrative sequence, tonality, or melodic lines. It is this that has helped ensure the operas' accessibility and popularity, allowing Britten to expand the language of opera from *within* the tradition.

The aim for accessibility led to a clarity about the relationship between musical tradition and innovation, as Britten explains:

> [musical] language is a means to an end – a means of saying what one wants to say, and should be as simple & direct as one can make it . . . Of course, however simple the language, it is no use pretending that appreciation will necessarily follow. New ideas have a way of seeming bewildering & shocking. Again – new ideas often need startling new developments in language to express them. But it must be this, not the other way round – the new ideas must lead to the new language, otherwise artificiality & self-consciousness occurs.
>
> (Kildea, 2000: 238)

But the most easily identifiable aspect of Britten's operatic writing is his acute response to language. This was not constrained by a mere literalism, and his rationale for an artificial style is significant:

> In the past hundred years, English writing for the voice has been dominated by strict subservience to logical speech-rhythms, despite the fact that accentuation according to sense often contradicts the accentuation demanded by emotional content. Good recitative should transform the natural intonations and rhythms of everyday speech into memorable musical phrases (as with Purcell), but in more stylized music, the composer should not deliberately avoid unnatural stresses if the prosody of the poem and the emotional situation demand them.
>
> (Kildea, 2000: 50)

This inevitably involved the (vexed) question of language – both for new English operas and the performance of foreign-language works. Britten was quite clear about this:

> I believe passionately in the intelligibility of the words . . . Because I do not speak Italian, it was not until I heard Mozart and Verdi operas sung in English that I realized to the full their fabulous subtlety, wit and dramatic aptitude. I always encourage my works to be sung, abroad, in the vernacular . . . Of course, something is lost, but not a great deal when you substitute the gibberish which can result from singers using languages they do not understand and cannot pronounce.
>
> (Kildeas, 2000: 208)

Jane Brandon (Walker, 2009: 78–83) has shown how much several of Verdi's operas, in particular *Rigoletto*, *La Traviata* and *Otello*, influenced Britten's dramatic structures and their relationship with musical forms, quoting Britten's statement that: 'I am especially interested in the general architectural and formal problems of opera, and decided to reject the Wagnerian theory of "permanent melody" for the classical practice of separate numbers that crystallize and hold the emotion of a dramatic situation at chosen moments' (Kildea, 2000: 50). This is emphasised by the way he began work on a new opera; Eric Crozier, his librettist for *Albert Herring*, describes how:

> we blocked out the action in three acts, and the probable contents of each scene. Britten went carefully through these lists with me, to establish what musical forms he would like to use at each point – plain or accompanied *Recitative, Arioso, Aria, Duet, Trio* or *Ensemble*. (Herbert, 1979: 29)...it was the prolonged consideration of the formal units and relationships among them that finally gave rise to the melodies and harmonies that would express them most vividly.
>
> (Walker, 2009: 75)

Peter Grimes

Committed Anglicanism spanned Britten's career, from the early *Hymn to the Virgin* to *The War Requiem*. Pacifism was a subject from the early *Pacifist March* to *Owen Wingrave*. Together with aspects of his personal life, these combined to produce the theme of the outsider and the tension between the individual and society that runs through almost all the operas and which he explained in his 'Introduction' to *Peter Grimes*: 'So many of the great things of the world have come from the outsider, the lone dog, and that lone dog, or outsider, isn't always attractive. That is what I try to portray in *Peter Grimes*' (Kildea, 2000: 305). Although *Peter Grimes* appears to be a perfectly natural narrative sequence, it is in fact mined from separate poems in Crabbe's *The Borough* where Grimes and Ellen exist in their own separate poems and have no connection. Beyond being rough fishermen who kill their apprentice/s, there is little relationship between the Peter Grimes of the poem and that of the opera. Crabbe's picture of a man driven to late penitence is replaced by a study of what Britten identified as 'the reaction of the people to Grimes, . . . to someone who is a gifted eccentric – a person who doesn't fit . . . I am interested in the people who don't think the same' (Kildea, 2006: 304–5).

Grimes's attraction lies in his vital ambiguity, which dominates the structure and music of all his scenes, in particular the central arias:

- ɪ ii: 'Now the great Bear and Pleiades'
- ɪɪ ii: the *scena* 'Go there!/In dreams I've built myself some kindlier home'
- ɪɪɪ ii: 'Steady. There you are. Nearly home.'

In each of them, Grimes moves between a range of contrasting, sometimes contradictory moods, enhancing and commenting on them – while always insisting on his essential humanity. Britten's sensitivity to words is empathetic without his ever being: 'afraid of a high-handed treatment of words, which may need prolongation far beyond their common speech-length, or a speed of delivery that would be impossible in conversation' (Kildea, 2000: 50). In fact it is this that emphasises the artistic truth rather than a mere realism.

The most complex of these is 'Go there!/In dreams I've built myself some kindlier home', which is divided between four main sections (Table 16.3a).

Britten's response to each section, subsection and individual words is detailed and fluid. But at two points (Bi and Ci) he arrests the flow with defining key signatures. Both are moments of transition for the audience and Grimes himself as he transcends his outer self through his dream of a life with Ellen (Table 16.3b).

In Britten's operas there is a quiet but resolute realignment of opera and its musical language in a way that makes it modern without threatening the traditional expectation of what an opera – and its pleasures – should be. His innovative artistry is propelled not by dogma, but a desire to make his art new, alive and relevant: 'to me [opera is the most fascinating of all musical forms]. I think it is the combination

Table 16.3a Peter Grimes: *structure of act II, scene ii, 'Go there/In dreams I've built myself some kindlier home'*

A	i	55		Go there!	Grimes's violent entry and treatment of the boy.
	ii	56		Here's the jersey	Reminiscence of Ellen's love.
	iii	56		I'll tear the collar off your neck!	Return to the opening violence.
B	i	57	D	Look! Now is your chance!	The sudden vison of the sea and its promise.
	ii	58		They listen to money –	A dream of what he could do with the money he earns.
	iii	59		Coat off! Jersey on!	Return to the reality of the siutuation.
C	i	60	A	In dreams I've built myself some kindlier home	A reverie as he returns to his inner world and love of Ellen.
	ii	63		But dreaming builds what dream can disown	Realisation that this is vision and not reality.
	iii	64		Sometimes I see that boy here in this hut	A haunting vison of what happened to his last apprentice.
D ▼		65		There's an odd procession here	The intrusion of the mob brings him back to reality again.

Table 16.3b Peter Grimes: *act* II, *scene* ii, *'Go there/In dreams I've built myself some kindlier home'*

		The 'Passacaglia' is profoundly ambivalent. It begins almost playfully and moves through refined, sympathetic figures to a violent climax. This parallels the ambiguity of Grimes's character, as this passage shows.		
55		*Allegro*	The 'Passacaglia' reaches its climax, dominated by the brass, as the curtain rises on Grimes's hut and as the woodwind play a rapidly rising and falling sequence of semiquavers marked *fff*, ending with deep, accented notes for the bassoon, cellos, basses and percussion as	
	1		Go There! Go there! Go there!	Grimes enters 'in a towering rage' with the boy and sings starting on a high G *ad libitum* that extends into a long descending cadence ending on his last phrase – violent and unanswerable.
	4	*quasi tempo della Passacaglia*		Woodwind and brass reintroduce the calmer chordal music of the 'Passacaglia'; but this is broken by a sharp rap on the side drum before
	6		Here's your sea boots! *He throws the sea boots at the boy*	Grimes orders the boy to dress, singing *con violenza*, with several notes accentuated in a grimly stark line, sung over held wind chords.
	7			The tension between the two characters is suggested by the agitated figure in the wood wind from the 'Passacaglia' accompanied by a sympathetic figure in the lower strings.
	9		There's your oilskin	Grimes sings *con forza* over a chord in the lower strings. This time his line steadily rises as he prepares to go to sea.
56	1		The music changes character, returning for a moment to the more tranquil section of the 'Passacaglia': an echoing passed between the violins and flutes. It suggests the other side of Grimes' personality as he leaves the brutality of his dealings with the boy and enters his own mental/visionary world, associated with his feelings for Ellen.	

(*cont.*)

Table 16.3b (*cont.*)

	3		Here's the jersey that she knitted With the anchor that she patterned.	Lyrical, *arioso* writing with the words 'here's' and 'she' lingered over.
	6	*Molto accelerando*	*He throws the clothes off the boy – they fall on the floor around him*	A complete change of mood as the woodwind's sudden rising scale blows like a piercing wind, introducing
	7		I'll tear the collar off your/neck!	a jagged, stressed line, sung unaccompanied and *con violenza*. This leads into
57	1		the biting string/woodwind figure of the 'Passacaglia'. *The boy is crying silently and Peter shakes him.*	
	5		Steady! Don't take fright, boy! Stop!	But this dies away to *ppp* as Grimes becomes conscious of what is happening – perhaps remembering his last apprentice – pulling up short with the *glissando* on the word 'Stop!'
	7		The luminous, echoing sounds of the brass, again from the 'Passacaglia', as *Peter goes to the cliff door, opens it and looks out* The final brass chord leads to a *tremolando* chord, *ppp* in the strings.	
	12		Look! Now is your chance!	Grimes is rapt at the sight of the sea world. An essentially monotonous line becomes a lyrical expression of his vision.
58	1	6/8 D *Vivace*	Time and key signatures mark this off as a brief, self-contained aria. The orchestra plays an animated, flowing figure dominated by the woodwind as	
	3		They listen to money	Grimes dreams of marrying Ellen.
59		4/4 (C) *Andante*	*He turns to see the boy still sitting on the rope coil, tears off his coat and throws the jersey at him*	
	1		The chords of the 'Passacaglia' return, but interrupted by drum beats. Following Grimes' aria about his future with Ellen they become the insistent sound of his vison of a new world.	

Table 16.3b (*cont.*)

	2		Coat off! / Jersey on! My boy . . . We're going to sea!	Each phrase (across five bars) is sung on a single note, but rising by a 3rd and then falling to F♯. As so often in Britten, this creates a closed cadence that gives a sense of completeness – although
	6	*con fuoco*	*Peter gives the boy a shove which knocks him over. He lies sobbing miserably.*	the strings explode into a *ff tremolando* rising and falling figure enhanced by the woodwind. But this may be Grimes's' energy now – not his anger.
	12	*rallentando*		Eventually this subsides into a gently rocking figure in the violins.
			The libretto is now in regular rhyming triplets, marking the inner core of the aria.	
60	1	3/4 *Lento tranquillo*	In dreams I've built myself some kindlier home,	The whole feeling changes. The strings create a warm accompaniment to the lyrical, almost rapturous vocal line as Grimes again enters his visionary world.
61	1	*A Adagio*	And she will soon forget her schoolhouse Ways.	This is enhanced by the change of tempo and key as he goes on to invite Ellen to join him. The repeated triplets in the woodwind have a lullaby feel, as the cradle – or the sea – rocks Grimes in his reverie.
	9		store/Of wisdom than we'd close behind our door	As he becomes more enrapt in his vision Grimes's phrases grow richer and more ornamented
	13		the rich man would be poor.	
62	1		I've seen in stars the life that we might share:	
	3	4/4		As the tempo changes his entire line becomes even more delicate.

(*cont.*)

Table 16.3b (*cont.*)

	9		a woman's care!	These words are repeated and again the musical cadence reaches a point of rest.
63	1	[C] Più mosso	But dreaming builds what dreaming can disown.	A sullen chord – followed by trampling *pizzicati* breaks the mood as Grimes begins to return to the real world (Hobson's drum will be heard after fourteen bars at Fig. 64).

of the human being in his or her daily life and music which can point up the events of people's lives and their emotions in the most marvelous way' (Kildea, 2000: 308). His modernism is always comprehensible, a combination of human truth and conscious artistry: the ability to create, and show the creativity, at the same time, each enhancing the force and truth of the other.

Henze: opera as dialectic (*The Bassarids*)

Where Britten's ideology was essentially cultural, Henze's was framed by an acute political consciousness. His social and political position was conditioned by his experience of the Nazi regime and subsequent revulsion at what Germany had perpetrated: 'Ever since I have felt ashamed of our country and of my fellow Germans and our people' (Henze, 1988: 53).

This sense of alienation grew with his increasingly left-wing political views. But these were complicated by his intense opposition to any kind of dictatorship, political, intellectual or ideological: 'For as long as I can remember, I too have been accustomed to regard free music, the music of freedom, as something mysterious, hostile to authority' (Henze, 1982: 123).

As a result he found himself antipathetic to the influential Darmstadt school under René Leibowitz. While Leibowitz himself was an important influence on him, the monopolisation and dictatorship of taste by the group, with Webern's music as its absolute yardstick, became intolerable: 'I found this entire development regrettable. In those days, everything that did not fit into this scheme was rejected; the whole thing was run according to rules and principles, without a trace of humour or humanity' (Henze, 1982: 43).

Similarly, as he moved towards the political left, he always sought alternatives. In 1957 he started to work with Visconti: 'a communist, with a clear Stanislavskian conception of theatre and music drama. In his work I detected a relationship between art and politics fundamentally different from Brecht's' (Henze, 1982: 55). Although he started reading Brecht and was even able to attend his rehearsals, he would not accept either of them as a delimiting authority.

A Marxist dialectic, which led him to see clearly the contradictions within bourgeois culture, increasingly became the basis for his analysis of the role of music. The essential contradiction for him was that music had developed, and was made possible by, patrons and the commercial enterprise of publishers, agents and concert management. This meant that music was embedded in the very socio-political world he stood against. The result was a series of tensions and contradictions: 'to maintain that one can write music today that is not fractured, that does not reflect the state of devastation to which people are subjected, means writing music with blinkers, to put it mildly. On the other hand I welcome any attempt to further the development of music despite everything, because it must go on' (Henze, 1982: 170).

The answer lay in 'the decision that in my work I will embody all the difficulties and all the problems of contemporary bourgeois music, and that I will, however, try to transform these into something usable, into something that the masses can understand' (Henze, 1982: 180).

Henze's rejection by the German *avant-garde* was therefore not the result of his political stance, but because of what he identified as his: 'desire to write music that was emotionally engaging as distinct from music that was abstract, not to be connected with everyday life... The existing audience of music-lovers, music consumers, was to be ignored. Their demand for plain music was to be dismissed as improper' (Henze, 1982: 40). Although this seemed to lead to a complex and difficult style, Britten, who admired Henze, described him as having: 'swung right away from the strict serial techniques because he has *felt* a need of stronger communication' (Kildea, 2000: 212). Henze himself seems to confirm this: 'My music has an emotional dimension that is unfashionable, an emotional untimeliness... I operate with old structures... My own music is traditional in that it operates on a horizontal plane, with the vertical plane related to it both dramaturgically and harmonically... The traditional principle whereby the dissonance has to be resolved remains valid in my writing (Henze, 1998: 56). Typically, his use of dissonance was never a matter of style but of meaning: 'With my dissonances I stress the distance between the modern world and Mozartian reality. Dissonance is not an empirical fact of life but an expression of pain' (Henze 1998: 56).

While Henze's music is more aggressively 'modern' that Britten's, both *The Bassarids* and *Peter Grimes* share important structural elements, most obviously their use of narrative and traditional forms. *The Bassarids* was Henze's second collaboration with Auden and Kallman who, he says: 'were keen that... I should learn to overcome my political and aesthetic aversions to Wagner's music... and I willingly agreed... to attend a Wagner opera without walking out after only ten minutes'

(Henze, 1998: 206). However this only helped confirm the extent to which neither the form nor the musical style would be Wagnerian. Despite the fact that it is *Durchkomponiert* (through-composed), Henze says that he wanted the libretto to be 'designed to make it a symphony in four movements' (Henze, 1996: 609). In part this reflected his broader musical thinking: 'I write operas because they are a musical form like quartets and symphonies... When I choose a plot for an opera, I don't think about what it will be like as a "show", but of certain musical ideas I want to express in a visual form.' (Henze, 1996: 608). As a result he describes the opera as formally divided between the *Satzen* (movements) of a symphony:

> [The first movement/act is in] Sonata form in which the two opponents of the drama (Dionysus and Pentheus) will be counterposed by different themes, and the clash of their two worlds is exposed in the exposition of the sonata form: both on the stage and in the score. [The second movement/act, is] the scherzo: a suite of Dionysian dances which ends very dramatically with the moment when Pentheus is going to be hypnotized by Dionysus and is going to face his doom. [The third movement/act,] the hypnotization movement, the central movement of the whole piece, is an Adagio and fugue... Into the Adagio the Intermezzo is interpolated as an alien element... The fugue has a very large coda, the hunt on Mount Citheron, and [the] last [fourth movement/act] is a huge passacaglia.
>
> (Henze, 1974: 830)

The Bassarids is potentially problematic because of the music's tonal and orchestral complexity, compounded by the dialectical relationship between action/text and music. In part this is mitigated by the use of traditional forms. Although Henze preferred the designation *Musiktragödie* to Auden's 'opera seria', the practical consequence of this was, as in *Peter Grimes*, a series of identifiable elements that help create focal points – aria, duet, ensemble, chorus – within the action (Table 16.4).

In performance this use of traditional forms helps the audience follow the interplay between accompaniment and text/action, clarifying what would otherwise be a series of contradictions or confrontations. For Henze this was essential to his larger purpose as a composer and political thinker, insisting that. 'Art has to go right among the people. Art has to mobilize its combative spirit and go into the attack [in order to] play its vital role in the shaping of a new and better society' (Henze, 1982: 276–7).

Stravinsky: opera as tradition (*The Rake's Progress*)

In quite different ways both Britten and Henze saw their art as a social force, which is why it is interesting to look at them together and out of chronological sequence with Stravinsky. In both, however different their styles, realistic narrative was wedded to traditional operatic forms. In *The Rake's Progress*, Stravinsky ostentatiously used traditional forms in a very different way, in one respect precisely to avoid social

Table 16.4 The Bassarids: *examples of traditional forms*

Movement/ Act	Aria	Duet/ensemble
1	Hauptmann: Wir, Pentheus, König von Theben We, Pentheus, King of Thebes	
	Pentheus: Zu frei war das Gesetz Too lax was the law	
2	Pentheus: Treue Beroe!/Dionysos! Dionysos! Faithful Beroe!/Dionysus! Dionysus!	
	Agave: Auf dem alten Waldweg On a forest footpath	
	Stranger: Ich fand ein Kind I found a child asleep	
3 i		Pentheus, Stranger: Du hattest recht./Sag mir: wann sind diese... You were right./Tell me: when are these...
3 ii		Dionysus, Pentheus: Wie sie. Schau. Blut verrät sich. Herself. Look. Blood will tell.
4	Agave: An deiner Bahrs At your bier-side	
	Dionysus: Ja, ich bin er Yes, I am he	

or political engagement. This was based in Neo-classicism, whose rejection of late Romantic and Expressionist emotionality suited Stravinsky's own temperament. In 1921 he insisted that 'Even in the early days, in the Fire Bird, I was concerned with a purely *musical* construction' (Ross, 2008: 108) and later formalised this: 'I consider music by its very nature powerless to *express* anything: a feeling, an attitude, a psychological state, a natural phenomenon, etc.' (Ross, 2008: 108) and described his *Octet* as 'a musical object. This object has a form and that form is influenced by the musical matter with which it is composed. The differences of matter determine the difference of form' (J. Cross, 2003: 29).

This would seem to contradict the essence of opera or any kind of stage work, concerned as they are with drama, human interaction and (usually emotional) conflict. Despite this, Stravinsky consistently wrote for the stage, and in 1947 decided to base an opera on Hogarth's *The Rake's Progress*. Initially the opera was to be a *Singspiel*, and he told Auden that: 'I will compose *not* a Musical Drama, but just an Opera with definitely separated numbers connected by spoken (not sung) words of the text' (Griffiths, 1982: 10). Although this aspect was dropped, he continued to insist that: 'The story is told, enacted, contained almost entirely in song – as distinguished from so-called speech-song, and Wagnerian continuous melody' (Griffiths, 1982: 2). Instead, it was to use earlier, 'classical' conventions to avoid the emotionality or expressiveness that he eschewed – and believed that music could not achieve (Table 16.5).

Although there are arias embedded in *Peter Grimes* and *The Bassarids*, in *The Rake's Progress* these are made an overt feature. The opera was described as a *Favola in tre atti*, echoing Monteverdi's *Orfeo: favola in musica*. As Stravinsky said, this did not imply an intention to 'reform' opera 'in the line of a Gluck, a Wagner or a Berg' (Griffiths, 1982: 2). Instead, he was counterpoising the dramatic force of an emotional narrative with music at its most obviously artificial.

Ultimately, this was bound to fail. Unless very deliberate steps are taken, music becomes the emotional impact. The fatal game of cards in the graveyard and the Bedlam scenes in act III are both dramatic and moving. The fact that each is divided

Table 16.5 The Rake's Progress: *numbers sequence of act I, scene i*

Prelude	
Duet and Trio	Anne: The woods are green
Recitative	Trulove: Anne my dear
Recitative and Aria	Rakewell: Here I stand
	Rakewell: Since it is not by merit/We rise or fall
Recitative	Shadow: Tom Rakewell
Recitative and Quartet	Shadow: Fair lady, gracious gentlemen,
	Rakewell: I wished but once
Recitative	Shadow: I'll call the coachman, Sir
Duettino	Anne: Farewell, for now

between *recitativo, aria, arioso*, etc. and use elements of 'classical' style, is no bar to the high dramatic context. Stravinsky's mastery of the forms enables them to work *for* and not *against* their effect.

In scene iii, the finale of act I, Anne's recitative and *cabaletta* 'My father calls/I go, I go to him' is an example of the way Stravinsky plays with received forms, in this case overlapping an eighteenth-century structure with a nineteenth-century one. The scene consists of a series of solo numbers that can be seen either as an eighteenth-century recitative/da *capo* sequence (A, B) or a nineteenth-century tripartite scene (X) (Table 16.6).

Within this brilliant technical manipulation of two musical traditions, the overriding effect is Anne's growing intensity and resolution. As in Handel, the *da capo* structure enhances the drama as Anne moves from realising the need to act ('I go to him'), through moral resolution ('O should I see/My love') to the repetition of the first section whose force and increasing decorative emphasis becomes the action. Using the classical form does not impede the depiction of character or the narrative flow but expresses it. The neo-classical style itself overlays the narrative not with a sense of indifference or disengagement, but with the irony of the work as an opera about operatic convention and means.

Adams: opera in plain English (*Nixon in China*)

John Adams (b. 1947) is one of the American composers associated with Minimalism, along with Steve Reich and Philip Glass. They, however, are more consistently rooted

Table 16.6 The Rake's Progress: *formal structure of act I, scene iii*

Designation	Libretto	Eighteenth-century *da capo* aria ▼		▼ Nineteenth-century tripartite structure	
[Orchestral introduction]			A		
Recitative	No word from Tom.	Formal recitative			
Aria	Quietly, night, O find him	Aria		X	*Primo tempo*
Recitative	My father! Can I desert him	Formal recitative	B		*Tempo di mezzo*
(Ritornello) Cabaletta	I go, I go to him	*Da capo* aria I go, I go to him O should I see I go, I go to him	Bi Bii Biii		*Cabaletta*

in the style than Adams who has developed away from it since writing *Nixon in China*, which gives it a particular place in his own development and that of contemporary opera generally. Like Neo-classicism, Minimalism was a reaction against specific musical trends. As with Henze, the Minimalists rebelled against the tyranny of serialism. Adams objected that: 'the works of Webern gained pride of place in composition and analysis seminars... [whose] methodological arcana and hyper-compressed expressive world, fit the prerequisites of college analysis courses to a tee' (J. Adams, 2008: 33). In creative terms they felt that serialism was over-cerebral, limited and potentially arid, leading him to say that: 'atonality... rather than being the Promised Land so confidently predicted by Schoenberg, Boulez and Babbitt, proved to be nothing of the kind. After a heady first planting, the terrain these composers discovered was unable to reproduce its initial harvest' (J. Adams, 2008: 106–7).

Adams describes Minimalism as 'Building large, expansive structure by the repetition of smaller elements' (J. Adams, 2008: 93). But it was more than a structural method. Stravinsky's Neo-classicism had questioned whether music was anything other than itself. His music had remained complex and highly wrought. By contrast, as Reich explains, Minimalism was in part designed to expose the elements from which music is made: 'What I am interested in is a compositional process and a sounding music that are one and the same thing... The use of hidden structural devices in music has never appealed to me' (Reich, 1998: 1385). As a result Adams became clear that his version of Minimalism' 'did not deconstruct or obliterate the fundamental elements of musical discourse such as regular pulsation, tonal harmony, or motivic repetition... To me it felt like the pleasure principle had been invited back into the listening experience' (J. Adams, 2008: 90). The danger was that Minimalism would replace one orthodoxy with another. This explains why Adams' development, while based in Minimalism and its aims, has moved away from its initial purity to become part of a number of musical elements: 'Minimalist procedures pointed to a way. I felt that the classics of the style were groundbreakers for sure, but I also recognised that Minimalism as a governing aesthetic could and would rapidly exhaust itself... As enchanted as I was by this marvellous new music, I missed the shock of the unexpected, the possibility of a sudden revolution in mood or coloration' (Adams, 2008: 93–4).

Adams wanted to use Minimalism in a way that was both expressive and dramatic, with ideas that were melodically interesting and appropriate to significant issues, believing, as he says, that: 'Something tremendously powerful was lost when composers moved away from tonal harmony and regular pulses... Among other things the audience was lost... [Whitman] has nobility, he was a social radical, and he wrote plain English' (May, 2006: 113). For each of his three large-scale operas – *Nixon in China*, *The Death of Klinghoffer* and *Dr Atomic* – Adams has chosen major, controversial subjects based on his own experience, as he shows: 'Nixon had been thoroughly disgraced by Watergate, and the American love for a good rehabilitation story had yet to be extended to him. Nixon, nevertheless, was undaunted, and he had written books attempting to establish himself as a wise elder statesman . . . The more I thought about it, the better I liked the idea of putting Richard Nixon to music' (J. Adams, 2008: 135).

The formal, 'operatic' dimension was inherent from the beginning, as his librettist Alice Goodman describes: 'We discussed the atmosphere of each scene and worked out where the various arias and choruses would go' (Goodman, 2000).

The essentially traditional dramaturgy and musical forms, together with an easily accepted tonality, have helped make *Nixon* such a success. However the score is deceptive: the constant, easily felt rhythms and *ostinati* give the impression of simplicity. But this is the 'art that hides art'. Nixon's 'News' aria at the start of act I shifts irregularly between 3/2 and 2/2 which creates the intensity and excitement of a rhythmic pulse while avoiding mere repetition. Rhythm and motivic repetition dominate the score, but are used in different ways. In the orchestral passages they produce a sense of expectation, such as the opening of act I with its sense of early-morning mist and mystery, the dramatic landing of Air Force One, and the sunlit start of act II.

Vocally, the musical repetition emphasises the 'operatic' dimension, turning the text into a series of musical patterns. The arias are carefully placed through the opera, with a major opportunity for each of the main characters:

Nixon	I.i	News
	I.iii	Mr Premier, distinguished guests
Mao	I.ii	We no longer need/Confucius
Chou	I.iii	Ladies and gentlemen/Comrades and friends
Pat	II.i	This is prophetic
Chiang	II.ii	I am the wife of Mao Tse-tung

Adams uses identifiable traditional forms to establish significant musical and dramatic moments:

- Pat and Nixon's duet at the start of *I*.iii begins as dialogue:

Nixon	You must be worn out
Pat	No I washed/And rested

and then seamlessly develops into the duet proper 'At least/This great Hall of the People stands';

- Nixon's 'News' aria stands out while, at the same time a purely musical effect is created by the voices that cut across it.
- The ensemble writing is especially effective, such as the end of *I*.iii, 'Cheers'.

- Choral passages are a major feature of the first two acts, from the opening 'Soldiers of heaven hold the sky'/'The people are the heroes now', through 'Look down at the earth' [interrupted by Pat's 'This little elephant in glass'] to 'It seems strange' towards the end of II.ii.

The success of *Nixon in China* is in part due to the way Adams was able to adapt his style and techniques to create a work that confirms the sense of traditional opera while moulding it to a contemporary musical style and subject:

> I had the good fortune to understand one important thing . . . that a good opera composer needs to be flexible and must learn to make his musical language capable of the slightest shift of mood or psychology on the parts of his characters. Modernism, with its obsession [with] form, purity and rigor in musical rhetoric, had proven to be a debilitating artistic ground for effective music drama. My natural suspicion of orthodoxy and stylistic rigidity had given me a leg up when it came to writing for the stage.   (Adams, 2008: 144)

Turnage: opera as 'spikes of feeling' (*The Silver Tassie*)

Mark-Anthony Turnage (b. 1960), is an iconoclastic composer. His melodic and harmonic writing is recognisably derived from traditional practice which, however, he refracts and distorts, introducing a range of non-'classical' styles. In general he writes in unconventional forms but, despite an initial nervousness of opera has increasingly become one of its major exponents in Britain. Contemporary British operas have used realistic narrative in a variety of ways: the aggressive naturalism of Turnage's *Greek* (1988); Dove's social comedy *Flight* (1998) and his fantastical *Pinocchio* (2007); Adès's Shakespearean *The Tempest* (2004) and his episodic naturalism in *Powder her Face* (1995). In each case the composer and his librettist faced the challenge of creating an opera that is new, would express their artistic aims and sustain enough of the tradition to enable the audience to understand what is happening and what each of the components – music, words, production – is doing, in a world where neither composer nor audience can take anything for granted.

In *The Silver Tassie* (1999) Turnage had the opportunity – and challenge – of writing on a full operatic scale. Initially: 'I had a real antipathy to [opera] from my childhood . . . I just found it irritating . . . I had no interest in it until I decided to do *Greek*, and I needed to be persuaded by Hans Werner Henze to write that' (Clements, 2000: 13–14). Turnage's political commitment is clear, but unlike Henze or Adams is expressed less obviously. In *Greek* it is the celebration of a counter-culture whose intensity and violence underlie the original play and the score's violence: 'I cannot describe my loathing for Thatcher's Conservatism . . . Glasses clink in the City, as the FT Index rises . . . But unemployment rises too. State benefits shrink, smack and aids spreads through the council estates . . . But the economy is doing well . . . And Thatcher wins the election . . . There will be more riots in England soon' (Turnage, 1990). In *The Silver Tassie* the politics lie in the interplay of a naturalistic depiction of working-class Irish society with a profound sympathy and visionary despair at the First World War as an analogue for modern Ireland: 'Every line [of the play] is within the Irish tradition . . . It was during one of the cease-fires and I was very aware of Irish politics. I think, living now, to ignore the Irishness of it is almost obscene' (Turnage, 2001: 15).

Turnage, like Adams, consciously addressed the nature of opera as a musical, dramatic form, explaining that: 'good concert composers go into opera and think that they can just produce the same music they would compose for the concert hall, but it just doesn't work, you have to be aware that you are writing a piece of theatre' (Clements, 2000: 15–16). This is evident in the way he writes about the play's operatic potential, describing it as: 'quite symphonic. It's not sonata form, but there is a first movement that's a sort of exposition of all the ideas . . . The second act, for me, was the slow movement. The third . . . is a sort of *scherzo*, although it is more than that because there is a slower ending. The last act is all dance movement, like a finale' (Turnage, 2001: 10).

Parallel with the musical aspect was the importance of the language, in particular what Turnage calls the 'incredible expressionistic writing' and chanting of the second act (Turnage, 2001: 10). He asked his librettist to: 'produce a text that remains utterly faithful to the spirit of O'Casey's original . . . and rewriting a substantial portion of O'Casey's lines to make them operatically apposite' (Clements, 2000: 74). Unlike *Peter Grimes*, the play/libretto was not shaped to include obviously 'operatic' elements. But once the composition started Turnage says he began to think: 'very carefully about what would be recitative and aria and what would be speech. It was very structured in that way' (Clements, 2000: 17). Once again, his understanding of the difference between operatic and other kinds of composition, was crucial: 'In *Three Screaming Popes* I was manipulating melodic lines and note cells. *Greek* had been slightly different because it was a theatre piece, and I was trying to make the characters believable and also to give them a distinctiveness' (Clements, 2000: 26). All of this came together in his concern with musical characterisation: 'I wanted the vocal lines to have their own character. Sometimes there's a real weakness in new operas where one character sings a line that is almost exactly the same as the one somebody else sings next. I wanted each character's lines to have little quirks of their own' (Clements, 2000: 17–18).

Turnage, again like Adams, had to consider how to use tonality, melody and, in this case, quotation, especially important because of the number of 'songs' and musical references in the play. There are themes that run through the work and melodies 'but as he points out they're usually disguised. There are harmonies and melodies, and interludes which act as transitions' (Turnage, 2001: 12). The result is a complex musical structure which is potentially problematic for the audience, something of which Turnage is well aware: 'I'm not being elitist, but I've got a much more sophisticated audience – it's a fact – so what? Why should you be ashamed of that? That's what I want to do. I do like simple things, it's not that I don't like simple things, but they must have a purpose' (Clements, 2000: 40–1).

The last scene (4) of act 3 is a duet between Harry and Susie which shows Turnage's combination of lyricism, unsettled rhythm and tonality. It uses orchestral motifs, melody, constantly changing time-signatures and precise directions for both the action and vocal style (Table 16.7).

In the notes he kept while writing *Greek*, Turnage insisted that: 'I do not want to write mathematician's music. Nor do I want to write glossy, luscious, gooey music. I'm looking for something sensuous, for the great spike of feeling you get in [the play] Greek, but also for a hard polemical edge' (Turnage, 1990).

Non-realistic narratives

In each of these operas the narrative and its plotting create credible worlds inhabited by characters whom an audience can recognise and whose dilemmas they can follow, even where this is an ironic eighteenth-century London or mythical Greece. However for other composers the truth of the world lies in something beyond an (apparent) materialism: archetypal relationships (Tippett), surrealist nightmare (Dusapin) or the relentless undertow of history (Sallinen). Especially in English-speaking cultures, there is a strong resistance, with the possible exception of Beckett, to metaphysical drama. As a result these operas are considered to be 'difficult' above and beyond their musical styles.

Tippett: a world of archetypes (*The Midsummer Marriage*)

Unlike Britten, Tippett wrote extensively about society, art and culture in general. He not only explained his own processes, but identified some of the major problems faced by the composer in society, of opera as a vehicle for contemporary, often complex ideas, and the function of music in the operatic drama. All of this was framed by his belief in the spiritual dimension of the human being, in which both individual and collective problems – and their resolution – lie.

Tippett insisted on the public role of the artist and what he saw as his 'great responsibility; to try to transfigure the everyday by a touch of the everlasting, born as that has always been, and will be again, from our desire' (Tippett, 1974: 18). For Tippett, the artist is caught between his or her own vision and the state of the public,

Table 16.7 The Silver Tassie: *act 3, scene 4*

33	1	3/4			Series of seven 'tonal' chords.
	2		*To Harry, making as if to move the chair*	Susie: It's your	
	3			bed time Twenty	The accent is on the sharpness of the 'Twenty Eight' – the descending semiquavers and low D – that Susie uses rather than Harry's name.
	4	4/4		Eight	
	5	2/4			
	6	3/4	Harry's first section is in alternating 3/4 and 2/4 as he turns a series of overtly lyrical sentiments and vocal phrases against themselves, ending		
	15/16		*Colla voce*	Harry: more than the shrivelled thing that I am	This is sung rather than *parlando* but abandons irony for stated bitterness and
	16/17/18	2/4	*Interrupting Harry's soliloquy*	Susie: Don't be foolish Twenty Eight	the repeated sharpness of the number.
34	2	3/4	*Sweet and delicate*		
			Susie's interruption is lyrical but accompanied by an ambiguous figure in the woodwind. This is a jerky triplet that eventually settles down into three rising notes (two semiquavers and a quaver or three semiquavers). Susie's attempt to comfort Harry is an uncomfortable platitude.		
35	5	3/4	*with intense bitterness*	Harry: I'll say to the pine	
			The woodwind figure continues, as Harry takes Susie's metaphor of the trees and flowers and, again, inverts it.		
	11/12	3/4		Harry: pine. I'll catch/butterflies	Beneath the woodwind's triplets the bass voices begin to assert themselves.

(cont.)

Table 16.7 (*cont.*)

36		4/4	*Suddenly turning nasty*	Harry: I'll twist and mangle them	In unambiguous 4/4, the triplets disappear as the full orchestra, emphasised by timpani, accompany his open cry of bitterness.
37		2/4	*Lighter*		
		2	Marked 'lighter' – not in tone but much more animated. The opening shifts constantly between 2/4, 5/8, 2/4, 3/4 and 3/8 creating a strong but uneven rhythmic sense as Harry loses himself in his vision of revenge and cries out against God.		

asking: 'Why won't the big public ever come any way to meet artistic integrity when it takes extreme forms of expression? . . . Surely the matter is that the very big public masses together in a kind of dead passion of mediocrity, and . . . is deeply offended by any living passion of the unusual, the rare, the rich, the exuberant, the heroic, and the aristocratic in art' (Tippett, 1974: 98). The core of the ethical/aesthetic task is intimately bound up with 'Beauty [which] is another absolute' (Tippett, 1974: 18) and a matter of wholeness:

> The endless dualisms, of spirit-matter, imagination-fact, even down to that of class, have led to a position psychologically where modern man is already born into division, and his capacity for balanced life seriously weakened . . . A lot of modern art attempts to find expression for the anguish of these divisions, but in the long run this state is fatal to art . . . The only concept we can place over against the fact of divided man is the idea of the whole man.   (Tippett, 1974: 23)

This was the basis of his opera *The Midsummer Marriage*, which he called: 'the kind of opera which might present division and wholeness' (Tippett, 1974: 51).

Tippett knew that dramatising this vision would result in an 'admittedly risky opera' (White, 1979: 48) in the way that *Ulysses* was risky, antagonising readers who, expecting a 'Victorian' novel and, as he says: 'Not finding what [they] expected of art, that is, not finding motive and choice and theme and sense, project [their] resentment first upon the book, then upon the author. But suppose the virtue of the art is precisely in the absence of these things?' (Tippett, 1974: 38–9). Crucial to his success was the libretto. When he had asked Eliot to provide words for *A Child of Our Time*, Eliot had advised that: 'while I don't think that a really poetic gift is necessary, I do feel that the author of an operatic libretto should have some theatrical gift' (White, 1979: 46). Later, from his experience as a playwright, Eliot again emphasised the physical and dramaturgical at the expense of the verbal and literary: 'during the period of gestation the composer is advised to eschew the advice of dramatists and seek the advice of stage producers' (Tippett, 1974: 65). This was especially important in *The Midsummer Marriage*, which mixes together contemporary characters and those from another dimension of time and place and in which the stage action has to manifest 'The transition between the world of the marvellous and the world of everyday' (Tippett, 1974: 61).

The model for this was *Die Zauberflöte*: 'The most enchanting expression of a general state where theological man is balanced against natural man is in Mozart's *Magic Flute*. From *this* point of view such masterpieces as *Fidelio* and *The Ring* appear to decline from the height reached' (Tippett, 1974: 23–4). This was essential to three levels of transaction and development – theatrical, dramatic and spiritual – involving:

- The use of the magical and theatrical marvels as an analogue for a spiritual journey.
- Symbolically contrasted characters: Pamina/Tamino – Jenifer/Mark; Papageno/Papagena – Bella/Jack; Sarastro/Queen of the Night – King Fisher/Sosostris.
- Operatic convention as an analogue for the spiritual dimension. Tippett recognised that: 'it is only in the course of my plot that my characters become aware of their real selves. I took a *prim'uomo* and a *prima donna* whose illusions were, so to speak, spiritual; to match against a *second'uomo* and a soubrette whose illusions were social' (Tippett, 1974: 54).

Writing about *The Mask of Time*, Tippett quite simply states: 'The text for *Mask of Time* is compounded of metaphors . . . These are swallowed up within the music, so the libretto should *not* be read as "literature"' (Tippett, 1983: 5). Instead, there is a consistent use of metaphor in which he says: 'The music and the action and the setting [can create] the requisite image or symbol which constitutes the experience in the form we can apprehend it. It cannot be analysed or paraphrased' (Tippett, 1974: 64). The problem lies in the temptation for an audience to make literal sense of action, words or characters that only exist as part of a larger transformatory, 'magical', experience. *The Knot Garden*, for example, takes place within two symbolic structures. The first is the knot garden of the title, an image for the complexities faced by and between the characters. The second is *The Tempest*, a play about the possibility of learning, in which the teacher/director – Prospero in the play, the psychiatrist Mangus in the opera – himself becomes equally involved. Like *The Midsummer Marriage*, the audiences's perplexity comes neither from the symbolic nature of the action nor the music, but because the apparently realistic locations, actions and characters exist *within* a metaphor. A partial 'suspension of disbelief' is needed to understand that what is being enacted is not a distortion of reality, but the point of entry into another level of reality altogether.

Tippett's music has a formal clarity combined with harmonic and rhythmic complexity. Ian Kemp writes that: 'After hearing the second movement of his Quartet no. 1 Tippett decided that he would discard the Sibelian approach to the sonata-allegro in that movement and return to the Beethovenian model' (Kemp, 1987: 88). The music is essentially tonal, however adventurous – and always sensuous: 'The artistic use of the tonal system is based on the fact that music whose tonal centres are rising in the scale of fifths produces an effect of ascent (struggle, illumination), while tonal centres descending the scale of fifths produces an effect of descent (resignation, despair)' (Kemp, 1987: 90). This equivalence between ascent and illumination, descent and resignation, became central to the narrative of *The Midsummer Marriage*.

Tippett anchors the opera by using a series of clearly identifiable standard forms which help the audience enter the world of the opera and its meaning. Many of the set pieces are overtly 'operatic', often expansively florid, such as Mark's large-scale *scena* in I.i. This grows more intense and ecstatic as it proceeds – ending in the anti-climax of Jenifer's entry without her wedding dress (Table 16.8).

Other set pieces are:

- King Fisher's I.vi 'So you, so you – are Mark's fine brood of friends'.
- Bella's II.iii 'Oh my face/They say a woman's glory is her hair'.
- Sosostris' climactic III.v aria 'Who hopes to conjure with the world of dreams'.
- The duets, such as Jack and Bella's II.i 'If there's a little house to rent', reflecting Papageno and Papagena's 'Welche Freude wird das sein'.

In particular, there are the large-scale choruses, such as:

- I.viii 'Let Mark and Jenifer'
- II.ii 'In the summer season'
- III.i 'O-hay! O-hay!'
- III.viii 'Carnal love'
- And the final scene, scene ix 'Was it a vision?'

Tippett's musico-dramatisation of complex ideas was only possible because of his ability to use theatre and theatrical devices as part of the artistic event and its meaning. The opera's success depends as much upon the strength of the vision's theatrical translation as the vitality of the score. In this, he confirmed Schoenberg's prediction that 'The future of the opera depends on the future the drama' (Schoenberg, 1984:

Table 16.8 The Midsummer Marriage: *act i, scene iii*

24	1	3/4 A *allegro molto*	Chorus: O Mark, who are they?	Sudden, busy semiquavers in the strings as the chorus come out of hiding and question Mark about the Elders.
24a	1		I don't know who they really are	The semiquavers continue as Mark begins, but then quickly die away as
25	1	*tranquillamente*	I've come here on summer nights	their pulse continues in the clarinets – but instead of the original busy motor this becomes a gently rippling sound, emphasising Mark's serious tone as he sings steady repeated notes over long chords in the strings.
	13	*a tempo*	I call them the Ancients,	The music becomes more animated – as he 'warms to his theme' – with semiquaver figures rising and falling.
26	1	*Un poco meno allegro*	They'll come back, so let them be	A brief recitative passage as Mark – who takes the Ancients in his stride – turns to his marriage.
	7	8/8	To give the/ring to Jenifer Here in this magic	
	9	4/4	wood And on midsummer-	The woodwind introduce a playful, joyful sense as Mark rises
	10	2/4	day	
	11	4/4	If no new dance,	
	14	*poco più largamente*	for For what can match the splendour	to his expansive statement about himself on this day in a broad lyrical figure.
27	1	2/4 G *allegretto non troppo*	Ah, the summer morning dances	The remainder of the *scena* is consciously 'operatic': strongly lyrical with extended florid passages rising in an ecstasy until
30	3	*allegro*	But – but – your dress? Upon our wedding day?	Jenifer enters and the rhapsody is abruptly cut short.

336), which has become increasingly true as composers search for a relevant contemporary voice on the stage. The challenge has been to find, from among the many theatrical forms available, something that both suits the composer's intention and is suited to his or her musical style.

Sallinen (*The King Goes Forth to France*)

Aulis Sallinen (b. 1935) is one of the composers who have developed a strong national school in Finland after Sibelius. In particular, he and Joonas Kokkonen have created an operatic repertoire which reflects both Finnish traditions and wider historical concerns. Sallinen's first two operas, *The Horseman* (*Ratsumies*, 1975) and *The Red Line* (*Punainen Viiva*, 1978) are essentially realistic. In both, there is a strong sense of Finnish history and the struggle of ordinary people. Their dramatic and musical language is recognisably descended from Puccini or Janáček, expressed through traditional tonality and melody. In *The Red Line* especially there is a pronounced political context. Both Riika and Topi have extended arias in act I, scene i that combine their sense of personal and class suffering:

> Riika Voi tätä elämää! Kurjuota!/Muistan kun ennen nuorena
> Woe is this life, Woe is this misery/I remember the old days
> Topi   Taas sinä kerrot minulle paratiisista, jonka kapotit kuna minulle tulit.
> You always talk of that paradise you lost when you married me.

Both are forceful, emotional expressions of their plight, rising in lyrical, securely tonal lines that directly affect the audience. Similarly, later in scene 2 Riika repents her harsh words to Topi in an introspective aria that balances regret against despair:

> Pahasti tein – kun sanoin Topia tolloski
> It was wicked of me to call Topi a simpleton.

In his third opera, *The King Goes Forth to France* (*Kuningas lähtee Ranskaan*) Sallinen retained the tonal, lyrical style of the earlier works but used them quite differently. Again the theme is the cruelty and suffering of man, but realised here through a non-realistic, only partially satirical, reworking of history. It is an allegory of power and suffering in his own world, as its subtitle, 'A chronicle for the music theatre of the coming Ice Age', suggests. Sallinen had deliberately looked for a dramatic form that would challenge him and help him move in a new direction: 'I wanted to call it quits and enter a wholly different world. When one starts at zero, the work remains vivid and interesting' (Hako, 2006: 10). However what emerged was not so much a different musical style as a different use of that style, with different emphasises, although as Sallinen says, based in the need to: 'arouse strong collective emotions, especially at the end. Collective passion is the only salvation left to mankind. When one individual's selfishness is elevated into national selfishness, the only result is certain destruction' (Arni, 1987). This is evident in the brooding 'Prelude' to act III and the dramatic final chorus 'Pariisin! Nyt Parisiin!' (We go forth to Paris at last!)

Sallinen uses a variety of styles to characterise and indicate different functions. The Nice Caroline, for example, is given strongly lyrical music, making her the sympathetic voice of humanity and sincerity. By contrast, the Prime Minister's music is a rather flat patter, reflecting the Italian *buffo* tradition, although without any real humour. The style effects a distance between what he says and its implications. By contrast, the King's dark, often sadistic statements, are treated without any irony or ambiguity. It is this flexibility in the *use* of his musical style that gives the opera its particular effectiveness.

Scene 3 of act I introduces the four female characters: the Nice Caroline, the Anne Who Strips, the Anne Who Steals and the Caroline with the Thick Mane[1] (Table 16.9, p. 352).

Sallinen's music creates a rapidly changing series of characters, attitudes and subjects, from satire, through caustic conversation, sympathetic but distanced portrayal of a deranged mind, to expressions of profound sympathy and understanding. Music and intrinsic meaning are drawn together, to create his vision: 'The terrible way human beings behave in this world is such that they no longer deserve the gift of music, but then perhaps it is right, after all, to break the silence' (Weitzman, 1987).

Dusapin (*Perelà, l'uomo di fumo*

Pascal Dusapin (b. 1955) is a prolific if highly unorthodox composer. He writes in many forms, almost all of his own devising, and in so doing he challenges traditional structures and concepts of musical form. This is especially true of his stage works. Where Sallinen's first two, realistic, operas belong to the first section of this chapter and his third in this, non-realistic section, so Pascal Dusapin's first three operas belong with the 'radical' operas of Chapter 17. In *Romeo et Juliette* (1989), *Medeamaterial* (1992) and *To be Sung* (1993) (perhaps also the 1991 *La Melancholia*, significantly designated 'Operatorio'), Dusapin was concerned with challenging the nature of opera itself, consistently opposing musical and literary priorities, as he says:

> in the first three [operas] . . . that project was initially a musical one, a theoretical, even a conceptual project. In a sense, there was an authoritarian prerequisite, an attempt to 'demonstrate' something. Each time, I had a precise desire for a musical object, and based, what's more, on a text that occupies a very special place in literature. Then I threw myself into an operatic project that would be somewhat 'militant'.   (Dusapin, 2004: 37)

Table 16.9 The King Goes Forth to France: *act 1, scene 4*

860			The scene opens with a jaunty/satirical melody in the woodwind.
862	Nice Caroline	Kuulin väärin, näin unta I must've heard wrong	Nice Caroline sings, accompanied by the continued woodwind melody until
890	Anne Who Steals	Ajatella Just imagine	the two Annes begin to discuss the preparation for war: the melody ceases and the woodwind interject small figures over an increasingly dark bass line.
900/1	Caroline with the Thick Mane	saa, luopua ketunmetsästyksestä he must give up all this fox-hunting	After her first phrase, Caroline with the Thick Mane's line becomes overtly lyrical as she evinces her humane sentiment but
900/6			the flow is abruptly interrupted by the piano and vibraphone as if alerting the audience to a problem.
900/7		se on julmaa it's a cruel sport	The music slows down and the tapping side drum distances the audience from the emotion as she starts to slip
910/4		Kuulitteko Did you hear	into her fantasy about her wedding
920	Anne Who Steals	Oletko sinä hereillä? What are you talking about?	broken into by a chord on the piano, marimba and vibraphone – and Anne Who Steal's interjection.
930	*Larghetto* Caroline with the Thick Mane	Tiedän I know	The score takes the audience deeper into Caroline with the Thick Mane's fantasy with sympathy until
940/4	Anne Who Strips	Oletkop sinä olemassa? What on earth are you on about?	she is again interrupted, this time by the other Anne.

Table 16.9 (*cont.*)

900/9	Caroline with the Thick Mane	Minun häitäni, tietysti! For my wedding, obviously!	Caroline, aroused to a sense of 'reality' by the sniping rounds on the Annes – in sung-speech: half-real half still within her fantasy world.
960	*Like a sermon*	To olette kuin keskiaikaisia naisia Your noses are long	The music acquires a grandeur – while Caroline sings on a single C – accompanied by wedding/celebratory bells as she reasserts herself – but within the fiction of the wedding.
970/8			A chord in the strings marks the end of the 'sermon' and then
980			a simple, lyrical downward figure returns
980/3	Caroline with the Thick Mane	Hän tahtoo He wants me	Caroline to her fantasy – a simple line, almost unaccompanied except for the vibraphone, leaving her alone in her dream.
980/8			A metallic sound again reasserts the distance between Caroline and how she is to be perceived.
990/9			The brass sound fanfares – as for the wedding.
1010/14	Nice Caroline	Ei olla Carolinelle pahoja, tytöt. The poor thing. We should pity poor Caroline	The orchestra plays a broad lyrical melody as Nice Caroline – the true voice of humanity and pity throughout the opera – first asks for pity on Caroline with the Thick Mane and then
1040/1		Se on silkkaa julmutta, julmutta joka asuu meissä The nature of man is cruelty, pure and simple	the opera's crucial lines.

In *Romeo et Juliette* the libretto by the poet Olivier Cadiot assumes familiarity with Shakespeare's play – but used obliquely as a foil: 'The action is divided into two parts: before the Revolution and after the Revolution . . . Romeo et Juliet is the story of a project: how to sing together with a single voice, how to come together, how to become a true [opera] duo. Text and music, speech and song, Romeo & Juliet' (Gindt, 1990: 8). The opera is really an elusive discourse between text and music which coexist rather than cohere. Much of the time the libretto is subsumed by the music or through the characters' combined speaking and singing, while the text itself uses French, English and at certain points 'nonsense' or syllabic sound-words, paraphrases of moments in the original play and lines quoted or part-quoted from it. All of these elements combine, for example, in the quartet that opens the second part of the opera, section 6 ('Après') in which each voice sings its own text creating a musical structure, accompanied by stage action, but which remains largely impenetrable beyond its purely musical effect:

mate genayuwa	mate	genayuwa	red rock
he he ye	mate	he heye	red
mate	mate genayuwa	mate mate	red
awe genayuwa	he he	he'heye	red
awe yuhwatiga	heye	it's	red
it's right here	it's right here	it's	red
it's right here	it's right	it's	red
ki kokeki kekei	here	right here	red
c'est là oui c'est là	ici, ici	the land	he he'ye
heye heye	the land	the land we're given	he he'ye
c'est là	the land	the land	oh
the land	it's right here	it's here	oh
o	Kikokikokikokike	frog	red
o April night	chantons	bee	red

There is a narrative: but it is the audience's own passage between the score, action and libretto. *Romeo et Juliette*'s post-modernist language isolates and 'quotes' traditional elements, reassembling them into a statement/experience of dislocation, precisely because Dusapin believes there is no coherence to be found in or from the past.

However in 1993 Dusapin became fascinated by the Italian Futurist novel *Il codice di Perelà* by Aldo Palazzeschi. As a result, he says that 'a lot of things were transformed, in my relationship to opera, maybe even my own culture. *Perelà* had an effect on me like a transfusion from the world of music towards an almost mystical literary world, and the other way around' (Dusapin, 2004: 37). One crucial change was in his attitude towards narrative: 'After the first three operas, I knew why I wanted a story, even though for me that desire had never been a prerequisite to writing an opera' (Dusapin, 2004: 38).

The opera is divided into ten 'Chapters', reflecting its origin in the novel. These form a sequence from Perelà's 'birth'/arrival through a series of increasingly political confrontations to his eventual fading away. The result is consecutive and 'realistic' but with a central character who is made of the subtitle's ['man of] smoke'. The action is sequential and credible but unreal at the same time. More radically than in *The Midsummer Marriage*, the audience is confronted with actions, characters and events that are perfectly comprehensible in themselves, and 'logical' within the work's surreal ethos. The characters, including Perelà, are well developed both dramatically and musically, often through extended solo passages/arias, such as the Marchesa Oliva di Bellonda's 'Vi ricordate di me' (Do you remember me?), or Perelà's 'L'amore! Quante volte io sentii salire fino a me questa parola' (Love! How many times have I heard that word come up to me), both in Chapter 5. There are several impressive scenes of dramatic conflict heightened by the use of the chorus, such as Chapter 6 scene i, when Alloro's daughter describes her father's death and the chorus begin to turn against Perelà. Within this, however, the text is treated in different ways, sometimes set quite clearly but at others used for the sake of musical texture.

The essentially dramatic, expressive score uses the full resources of the large orchestra, which Dusapin describes as 'a highly "psychologised" protagonist. It is never indifferent, and is driven by exclusively dramatic functions. What is new for me is the use from time to time of illustrative techniques' (Dusapin, 2004: 41). Dusapin's style is, in general, instinctive and unbound by dogma. In *Perelà* the writing is always moulded by and to the action, which he contrasts with : 'Boulez [who] used to explain . . . musical ideas like form, motive, etc. For my part, I have no musicological opinion on such ideas. When I am composing I have no preconceived plan, although I still know where I am going' (Downey, 2007: 1). In fact, some scenes are entirely orchestral, atmospheric accompaniments to action that is either mimed or a projected text. Chapter 7, for example, consists of a single sung line followed by a long stage direction describing Perelà's flight, accompanied by a solo flute over the quiet but long-drawn sounding of the gong.

While much of the vocal writing allows the character's words to be heard quite clearly (The Valet and Chamberlain at the start of Chapter 1, scene 3; or Perelà's 'Che cosa accade' (What is happening?) at the beginning of Chapter 7, scene 2), at other points it pushes the voices to an extreme, especially the high voices, such as Alloro's daughter in Chapter 6, or the hysterical falsetto of the Archbishop in Chapter 4, scene 2. As in *Romeo et Juliette*, but less extreme and more varied, the opera unsettles the audience through the variety of aesthetic experiences. The result is a process of constant engagement and disengagement – or engagements at several different levels. Together, this ensures that the disjunction of realities – on stage and between stage and auditorium – becomes the over-riding experience of this version of a reality. More extreme than either Tippett's exploration of a psychology or Sallinen's historical allegory, *Perelà* makes 'real' an essential unreality.

Chapter 17

Radical narratives

In the first years of the twentieth century dramatists began looking for alternatives to the 'hermetic' drama, whether Naturalistic, Realistic, or Symbolist. Each of these was designed to draw the audience into an empathetic relationship with situations and characters so that they saw them and their dilemmas as inevitable and unchangeable. As Brecht wrote: 'We would not wish to create the illusion of reality... Were one to create such an illusion that is all it would remain, and the audience would only see and consider it as such. Were the reality of life simply imitated then there would be nothing more to see or feel than in life itself. Which is not enough' (Brecht, 1948: 38). What was needed was a dramaturgy that allowed the audience to understand that in every case a choice had been made and that there were alternatives. Brecht's aesthetic and dramaturgy were derived from Marxist dialectics and worked at two inter-locking levels:

- The audience had to be enabled to read each action and decision as part of a man-made situation that was neither natural nor inevitable.
- Each aspect of the action and its staging had to be made part of this process by declaring its own mechanism.

For Brecht this was part of a larger, Marxist, politic. But this kind of staging and dramatic theory produced a range of other applications. It allowed composers to separate out the different elements of which an opera was made so that coherence took place in the audience's consciousness. This shift is a hallmark of much late twentieth- and twenty-first-century opera (Table 17.1).

Dialectical organisation of text and score

Brecht and Weill: narrative and montage (*Aufstieg und Fall der Stadt Mahagonny*)

Brecht formulated his ideas most clearly in the 'Notes' to *Aufstieg und Fall der Stadt Mahagonny*, where he demonstrated the differences between what he called

Table 17.1 *Variants and uses of non-narrative dramaturgy*

	i Dialectical organisation of text and score			ii Meaning as part of the totality of performance		
	Brecht/Weill	Nono	Zimmermann	Glass	Stockhausen	Birtwistle
Dramaturgy	Dialectical using montage of scenes	Episodic	Simultaneous action/scenes	Parallel actions: the separation of text, action and narrative	Interplay of independent elements	Layers of cultural reference and action
Narrative	Direct but interrupted: 'episodic'	Achronological montage of 'moments'	Direct but distanced by the simultaneity	Achronological Dependent on action – not text	Complex but direct journey	Overlays of 1 response to each action 2 Series of mythologies
Text	Direct	Collage of texts related to each historical part	Direct	Outside the stage action: 1 sung Sanskrit 2 'synopsis' independent of action	1 direct 2 esoteric 3 Purely musical (act II)	Overlay of texts 1 direct 2 invented or dismembered language
Score	Direct relation to text except for the interpolated songs	Dramatic but not directly related to the text	Polystylistic Largely direct relation to text	'Minimalist' setting of the Sanskrit	Self-contained world of sound	Expressive but oblique complex of electronic and acoustic

Aristotelian 'Dramatic theatre' and his own 'Epic theatre' (Brecht, 1978: ii, 37). The text is designed to be read horizontally and vertically (Table 17.2).

This dramaturgy resulted in:

- a strong, clear narrative, rather than a plot designed to create empathy, which was then
- broken into episodes by devices that forced the audience to stand back from the action.

This *Verfremdungseffekt* (Distancing or alienation effect) was neither undramatic nor unemotional. Instead the audience was drawn into scenes but then forced to stand outside the action and their own reaction. Typical devices are songs injected into or between scenes, breaking up the narrative flow; texts or images projected onto the stage; or an actor alternating between character and a citizen addressing the audience in his own person.

Crucial to this was demystification of the theatrical act itself so that the audience did not lose their sense of reality. The staging declared its means of (theatrical) production by exposing its elements, unlike traditional theatre that typically 'worked its magic' behind a closed curtain. The opening directions of *Mahagonny* show some of this:

> Instead of the normal curtain, a small white half-curtain ('Gardine'), no higher than $2\frac{1}{2}$ metres from the stage floor, is hung from a wire so that it can be drawn

Table 17.2 *Brecht's contrast of the 'Dramatic' and 'Epic' theatres*

Dramatic Theatre	Epic Theatre
Plot: implicates the spectator in the stage action wears down his capacity for action provides him with sensations	*Narrative*: turns the spectator into an observer but arouses his capacity for action forces him to take decisions
Experience: The spectator is involved in something	*Picture of the world*: he is made to face something
Suggestion: instinctive feelings are preserved the spectator is in the thick of it, shares the experience the human being is taken for granted he is unalterable eyes on the finish one scene makes another	*Argument*: brought to the point of recognition the spectator stands outside, studies the human being is the subject of the inquiry he is alterable and able to alter eyes on the course each scene for itself
Growth linear development...	Montage in curves...
Man is a fixed point	*Man is a process*

to the left or right. All the scene texts [Szenenüberschriften] are projected onto this half-curtain.

As the music begins the Arrest Warrants for Leokadja Begbick, Dreieinigkeitmoses and Fatty, the 'confidential clerk' [Prokuristen] are projected. The charges read: For procuring, and fraudulent bankruptcy. A note: ALL THREE ARE FUGITIVES. Also photos of the wanted.

At fig.1, bar 8 the stage directions introduce the scene proper:

Over these projections, in red letters the caption for the first scene 'FOUNDING OF THE CITY OF MAHAGONNY'

At fig. 3, bar 3 the scenery is created by simple projection:

Half-curtain off. On the backdrop Projection No.1 representing a desolate region. A large,...lorry drives on. The carburetor backfires...the motor dies...the lorry stops.

This is followed by dialogue over music and then at fig. 11 Widow Begbick sings first recitative and then breaks into *arioso* at fig. 13, bar 7 ('Sie soll sein wie eine Netz', It will be like a net), ending with the words, repeated by Fatty and Moses

Aber dieses ganze Mahagonny ist nur, weil alles so schlecht, weil keine Ruhe herrschaft und keine Eintracht, und weil es nichts gibt, woran man sich halten kann.

But Mahagonny only goes on because when everything is so rotten, and there is no rule of peace and no harmony, how can there be any stopping it.

Immediately

The half-curtain closes quickly and the caption for Scene 2 is projected: 'IN THE NEXT WEEKS A CITY AROSE, AND THE FIRST SHARKS SETTLED IN.'

Jenny and six girls come on in front of the closed half-curtain with a large trunk. They sit on the trunk and sing the Alabama Song.

Scene 2 consists of the 'Alabama Song'. There is no dialogue and therefore no narrative connection with the preceding (or following) scenes. In addition, its popular style is quite different from the music of scenes 1 and 3. By breaking the narrative sequence the audience has to stand back and consider what they have just seen rather than allowing themselves to be simply absorbed by a story. Similarly with the seven girls in this self-contained unit, the audience has to work out the scene's meaning rather than relying passively on the flow of events.

Ultimately, Brecht was dissatisfied with *Mahagonny*. There were two problems, both concerned with the intention behind the dramaturgy. The first was that, unlike the music in his plays, the musical continuity here reduced the distancing effect of the song passages. Second, the songs were dangerously attractive in their own right, and became a distraction from their primary, dramaturgical function. For Brecht, *Mahagonny* remained an 'opera' whose 'content is pleasure' (Brecht, 1978: II, 36). The attraction was such that the audience's experience and awareness remained *in* and *of* the opera, rather than enabling them to extricate themselves to achieve an objective consciousness. Nonetheless he had shown a completely new way of constructing opera as awareness rather than sensory experience. This now became central to one line of development in modern opera.

Nono: dislocation and montage (*Al gran sole carico d'amore*)

Luigi Nono (1924–90) was a long-standing member of the Communist Party, and saw his works as an extension of his radical views of society. In his 'Scenic action in two periods' (the word 'opera' was not allowed), he took Brecht's dramaturgy much further in order to put dialectics at the heart of the experience. His earlier opera *Intolleranza 1960* has a straightforward narrative, although the libretto is a montage of texts by writers including Brecht, Sartre, Paul Éluard and Mayakovsky. In *Al gran sole carico d'amore* Nono dispensed with conventional narrative; instead there is a montage of texts assembled around two events: the Paris 1871 Commune in Part One and the 1905 Russian Revolution in Part Two. Both had failed and therefore demanded that lessons be learned for the future. The libretto consists again of texts taken from several sources, some contemporary or later reflections, while others come from parallel events. In Part One, for example, these include

- the contemporary trial defence and other writings of Louise Michel;
- Marx's *The Civil War in France*;
- Brecht's dramatisation, *The Days of the Commune*;
- voices from other periods and struggles, such as Russian Revolutionary songs and the writings of Che Guevara and Tania Bunke in South America.

Even where the text is emphasised the setting is never straightforward: the audience has to work to become fully aware of it. For example, the second part of the opening 'Come preludio', has the title 'Struggle: yesterday – today' which is the theme of the work and the key to how it is organised (Table 17.3). The text is from Marx's *The Civil War in France*, but it is sung and spoken in the original German, with the voices overlapping so that the audience can neither listen passively nor respond emotionally to it. In scene iii the 'discussion' between Thiers and Favre is interspersed and overlaid with quotations from Lenin sung by a solo soprano, the large choir and the 'People of Paris'. This montage of texts, personae, sounds and music demands that the audience ask what the relationship is between them. At the same time the

Table 17.3 Al gran sole carico d'amore: *part one, scenes i–vii*

Scene	Directions/titles in the score — Title	Content/Action	Text sources	Cast and instruments
Come preludio	*Beauty is not incompatible with revolution*	Invocation in the names of beauty, revolution and humanity	Che Guevara, Louise Michel	Soprano solo, large chorus, percussion, tape
	Struggle: yesterday – tomorrow	Invocation of the heroes and martyrs of the Paris Commune	Marx: *The Civil War in France*	Orchestra, tape and women's voices
	First Time 'We shall return a crowd without number'			
i	*Resolution of the Communards I*	Revolt against a law that denies people their rights and the demands for those rights	Brecht: *Days of the Commune*	Chorus and orchestra
	Questions of Tania the guerrilla fighter		Tania Bunke	Soprano solo
	Resolution of the Communards II		Brecht: *Days of the Commune*	Chorus and orchestra
ii	*Questions of Tania the guerrilla fighter*	In a world of rich nature why can people not find a way to work the land and live?	Tania Bunke, Che Guevara	Soprano solo, tape
	For Tania fallen in the struggle			Chorus
	Reflections I			Orchestra with tape
iii	*Thoughts of Lenin on the Commune*	Sentiments of political and military opposition to the Communards and the reaction of the proletariat	Lenin, Brecht, Revolutionary song	
	Reflections II			Orchestra
iv	*'Les Mains de Jeanne-Marie'*	Baudelaire's outcry at the slaughter of ordinary men and women	Baudelaire	Large choir, orchestra Soprano solo, large choir, orchestra

v	*Paris rises*			Orchestra, tape
	Resolution of the Communards III	The Communards' demands	Brecht: *Days of the Commune*	Soprano solo, large choir, small choir, orchestra
	'The Commune lives'	The political nature and achievement of the Commune	Marx: *The Civil War in France*	Woman's voice, orchestra
	Resolution of the Communards	Call to action by the Communards	Brecht: *Days of the Commune*	Soprano solo, large choir, small choir, orchestra
vi	*Self-defence of Louise Michel*	The teacher Louise Michel declares she has nothing to defend herself for!	Louise Michel	Soprano, large choir, orchestra tape
		The Russian revolutionary song urges comrades to march	Revolutionary song 'We are no longer the Paris Commune'	Soprano solo, small choir, orchestra, tape; Communards: choir basses
	Episode at Montmartre	Louise Michel's admission of participation / Threats by the Communards / Louise Michel admits her participation	Louise Michel / Brecht: *Days of the Commune* / Louise Michel	Soprano solo, small choir, orchestra, tape / Soprano solo, tenor solo, small choir, large choir, orchestra, tape / Soprano solo, small choir, large choir, tape
	Self-defence of Louise Michel	Her desire to burn down Versailles	Louise Michel	Soprano solo, tape
	Reflections III	Reflections III		Orchestra
vii	*Massacre of the Communards*	Bismarck, Thiers, etc. vow to crush the Commune	Brecht: *Days of the Commune*	Soloists, percussion, tape

score adds its own interest and weight. For example in part i, scene ii, the *Questions of Tania the guerrilla fighter*, the soprano solo is accompanied by tape and a chorus of tenors. The effect is intense and lyrical while the sparse accompaniment gives the words an unusual clarity despite the wide-ranging vocal line and high *tessitura*. But it does not obviously reflect the words' sense or emotion. The words and the music in effect run parallel with one another.

More important than the individual roles or voices is the chorus. Nono explains that in his 'work the choruses will also play a greater role than the soloists. That is both a theatrical and a social ideal . . . Musical means of expression are utilised in order to encompass the expression of individual and collective utterance in one person' (Nono, 1999a: 22). The choral writing is varied and can be both arresting and dramatic. Scene iv, 'The hands of Jeanne-Marie', is set in a recognisably 'choral' style with an orchestral accompaniment that is full of pain. In scene v the chorus sings a sequence that begins with a strident choral setting, followed by muted, confused whispering that rises to a climax and then a more clearly defined chorus of the Communards. The result is dramatic but again the impact of the music and the text are separated so that there can be no easy emotional response.

Throughout the score there are no stage directions. It is for the performers to understand the work and how to use it in the creation of an active experience for the audience. The work is to be *used* rather than simply performed. The narrative becomes the audience's own journey to the point of understanding: not of the historical events, but of their own place in the historical process. Nono enables this by invoking significant historical events and then putting critical distance between them and the 'operatic' means used to create them: 'My works always take their bearings from a human stimulus: an event, an experience, a text of our life touches my instinct and my conscience, and demands of me that as a musician and as a human being I should bear witness' (Nono, 1999b: 10). The result is the manifestation of the 'bellezza' (beauty) declared at the very beginning which is demonstrated to be not 'reñida con la revolución' (incompatible with revolution). Through this special musico dramaturgical process 'beauty' is made compatible not so much with revolution *per se* as with the revolutionary impulse, consciousness and need.

Zimmermann: simultaneous staging and quotation (*Die Soldaten*)

Bernd Alois Zimmermann (1918–70) explains that he chose Lenz's play not because of the

> issues of the class struggle, social factors, a critique of the 'military condi-
> tion . . . [but] the way that Lenz's characters . . . were caught in a web of con-
> straints that led them inexorably, though they were more innocent than guilty,

to rape, murder, suicide and, in the end, to total annihilation. It is not so much destiny . . . [as] the combination of class, circumstances and disposition that determines human existence, and from which there is no escape.

(Zimmermann, 1996)

Here there is no historical dialectic offering the possibility of changing the way people behave. Instead there is only a constant, universal predicaments; so that, as Zimmermann intended, the opera should 'not tell a "story", it represents a situation. Better still, it proposes an account of a situation which, from its place in the future, threatens the past . . . in that we are all constantly confronted by the rotating temporal sphere where past, present and future blend together' (Zimmermann, 1996). This difference between 'chronological time and time as experience' (Schmidt, 1991: 36), is what Zimmermann calls 'Kugelgestalt der Zeit' (sphericality/sphericity of time) and is a central theme of the opera. The dramaturgy, staging and music had to maintain Lenz's narrative but, at crucial points, make the audience stand back to understand that they are watching something more than an isolated, fictitious event.

To create this sense of simultaneity of action and time, the opera was originally written to be performed simultaneously on twelve separate stages arranged around the centrally seated audience, each with its own projection screen and orchestra. When this proved impracticable, Zimmermann reduced it to a single stage but with a series of levels and areas within them, and three orchestras, one in the pit augmented by a large percussion section, another on stage and a Jazz combo. What remained was the simultaneous presentation of several of the scenes that either combine different locations or have multiple scenes going in within a single location. In ii.i, for example:

> The coffee house: galleries left, in the background and right. Two steps on the left and right lead to the gallery in the background. Below this are the bar, two doors and two more, one each to the left and right.

Zimmermann designates six tables, at each of which a separate activity takes place and which overlap one another. However in the next scene, ii.ii, there are two separate locations with three separate actions played at the same time following Marie's seduction by Desportes:

> (Gradually the stage darkens and assumes an unreal character: in the background left 'off-stage' [but visible] the lovers Marie and Desportes; in the foreground right Wesener's old mother, knitting and praying; in the background right, raised up, Stolzius's house in Armentières.) Stolzius seated at a table with a lamp, reading a letter, very depressed, his mother by his side . . . (The three groups are like separate islands, all visible at the same time.)

These scenes could have been shown sequentially. But although the *narrative* would have been the same, the audience's experience would be completely different. The simultaneity enables the audience to experience events from different times and places in their own single time. For Zimmermann: 'we live in harmony with a huge diversity of culture from the most varied periods . . . on many different levels of time and experience, most of which are neither connected with one another nor do they appear to derive from one another . . . we are capable of constantly experiencing this huge diversity together with all the changes that occur as a result' (Griffiths, 1996). Importantly, the score itself works in the same way through Zimmermann's polystylism or pluralism which he bases on his view that: 'Bach's chorales and jazz sit next to the rudiments of "number" operas and "music theatre" – each one combined, as it were, in a pan-acoustic form of musical performance' (Zimmermann, 1996). The complexity of the music, however, means that it is easier to appreciate a general sense of period than recognise specific quotations. For example in the act ii, 'Intermezzo', the sudden sound of the organ (letter **b**) suggests an older, ecclesiastical/moral world, but the treatment of the plain-chant and its brevity mean that the theme itself gets lost. Similarly, the jazz band creates a general sense of achronology and atmosphere/ethos.

At the same time these quotations and references are essential to Zimmermann's own musical thinking, helping him create structures and maintain the intellectual, philosophical thread through the score. This is reinforced, as in *Wozzeck*, by giving each scene a formal, non-operatic, designation. Act i, for example is broken into: Introduzione; scene i (Strofe); scene ii (Ciacona 1); Tratto 1; scene iii (Ricercari 1); scene iv (Toccata 1); scene v (Nocturno 1), etc. Little of this is discernible in performance because of the score's density and the elusiveness of the forms themselves. Their real purpose is to enable Zimmermann to control his material as the expression of a meaning that lies outside the emotional narrative. This does not mean that the music is cerebral or unemotional. The opening, for example, is explosively aggressive, while in many of the domestic scenes there is delicacy and sensitivity, such as the dialogue between the distraught Stolzius and his mother in i.ii. It can also be very beautiful in a stylised, self-consciously 'operatic' way, as in iii.v in the initial dialogue between Marie and Charlotte.

Die Soldaten projects its meaning beyond the basic narrative through the special way Zimmermann organises its scenes and music:

- physical dislocation of narrative in the simultaneous staging;
- juxtaposition, perhaps confrontation, between polystylistic musics;
- 'operatic' stylisation;
- the (often) aggressive modernism of the composer's own period as well as;
- sometimes highly sympathetic accompaniment of the action.

All of this, including the extraordinary forces and production demands, is necessary for realising the vision of a composer confronting the cyclical nature of time, history and the human condition – perhaps the German experience in particular. The 'difficulty' of Zimmermann's opera – its uncompromising score, the simultaneous action – can be easily exaggerated. What these ensure is that what might have been merely a personal tragedy becomes instead an objective vision of a world whose essential motor is its repeated, unthinking corruption of itself.

The totality of performance as meaning

The second set of works redefine opera from 'A dramatic form whose primary language is music' to one whose 'primary language' becomes the complete production. In all opera the meaning and impact lie in integrated performance, but in traditional works it is relatively simple to see how the narrative encapsulates the meaning and how other elements relate to it. In these works it is far more difficult, and central to this is radical change in the role of narrative (Table 17.4).

Glass: layers in parallel (*Satyagraha*)

Like Adams, Philip Glass (b. 1937) is a Minimalist but in a far more trenchant and profound way. In his hands, Minimalism has a spiritual purpose that informs all his work and particularly the operas. Nono's dislocation of narrative, events and text, prompts the audience to a dialectical awareness of history. In Glass's trilogy *Einstein on the Beach* (1975), *Satyagraha* (1980) and *Akhnaten* (1984) the disjunction is, if anything, more absolute, but to quite different ends. In these operas

Table 17.4 *The changing function of narrative*

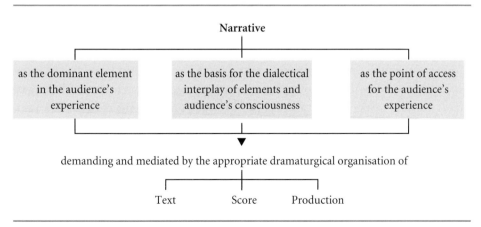

the libretto, score, narrative and stage action operate in parallel, with no direct connection between them. The result leads the audience not into a dialectic, but a contemplative, spiritual experience of what he calls 'the history of "great spirits"' (Glass, 1999: 213). For him, these are 'three operas about social change through non-violence . . . [and in] *Satyagraha* . . . I was thinking about a religious revolutionary. Again with *Akhnaten* and with his impact on the social order – in terms of the society as a whole or the individual in society' (Glass, 1999: 325).

Perhaps the most obvious feature is Glass's musical style: 'I want to say right away that this is a misnomer. It is *not* "minimal" music . . . This technique is capable of supporting music of richness and variety.' (Glass, 1999: 50). Instead, he describes his technique as 'music with repetitive structures' (Glass, 1999: 99). Like Adams, this was in part a reaction against the post-Webern *avant-garde*: 'As a young man, this was not the kind of music that was attractive to me. So I had to find a different language to work in, and I took a very extreme position. I reduced all the music that I knew to something that was based on the simplest materials . . . It was in kind of opposition to this very evolved technique' (Glass, 1999: 206). It was also important that 'everything I write is playable and listenable. I don't write ideological music or theoretical music' (Glass, 1999: 25). This has two implications for how *Satyagraha* works:

- it creates a continuum that helps hold the different levels togther;
- if creates its own spiritual dimension that directly reflects what the operas are about.

As a result, this accessibility, with its emotional appeal, went hand-in hand with Glass's philosophical concern: 'Music is one of the few places, perhaps one of the only places, where we find the meeting of our intellectual life and our emotional life. The possibility of forming a perfect match can take place there. We can use our brains in one way and at the same time respond' (Glass, 1999: 198). Glass emphasises the theatrical essence of opera: 'Before I start writing I get an idea of what the stage presentation is going to be like' (Glass, 1999: 274), while at the same time this does not imply simple assumptions about what opera is or how it works: 'I don't really take opera composers as my models . . . I like to listen to the same works that everyone listens to . . . But it never occurred to me to write like any of them . . . These works occupy a world of their own, one that enriches us all. I am a devotee of museums, but I don't want to live in one' (Glass, 1999: 7).

Glass sees the significant shift lying not so much in the opera as the audience and its exposure to a range of media experiences: 'We're all twentieth-century people and in various ways have learned to look or visualize that way, whether we know it or not' (Glass, 1999: 141). This is significant because, important though it has always been, the visual has rarely been at the core of the operatic experience. At crucial moments – the end of *Götterdämmerung*, the quartet in *Rigoletto*, the unveiling of the chair in *Le nozze di Figaro* – the stage picture has been vital, but most of the time the meaning is created directly through the words and music. In film, however, there is a completely different balance of words, music and action/image. One of the things that opera can do much more effectively than film, however, is use all of these elements but keep them separate: 'Early on in my work for theatre, I was encouraged to leave what I call "space" between the image and the music . . . which is required so that members of the audience have the necessary perspective or distance to create their own individual meanings.' (Glass, 1999: 141). However, unlike Brecht's or Nono's interrupted or discontinuous structures, Glass's are continuous but parallel or overlaid (Table 17.5):

> You know I gave a problem once in architectural school where I said, why don't we take this plan, let's say it's a Frank Lloyd Wright plan, and why don't we take this other plan which is a Le Corbusier plan. And I laid one right on top of the other – same kind of site plans – and said, build it . . . Have you ever thought that there is a possibility in music of doing overlays like that?   (Glass, 1999: 313–14)

In *Satyagraha* the narrative, the stage action, the text and the music are overlaid in just this way (Table 17.5), so that the coherence, and thus the meaning, resides entirely with the audience, but not, as in Brecht, as a point of consciousness, but rather a point of spiritual immersion: 'I liked the idea of *further* separating the vocal text from the action. In this way, without an understandable text to contend with, the listener could let the words go altogether. The weight of "meaning" would then be thrown onto the music, the designs and the stage action' (*Grove*, 1997: 190a). Given this disparateness, the work becomes dominated musically, in part because the Sanskrit text lies outside the audience's immediate scope. The score is made up of repeated orchestral figures and vocal lines, and it is this continuity which sustains the experience: an unwavering lyricism that embodies the idea of 'Satyagraha – truth-firmness' itself. The closing lines, as Gandhi sings Krishna's words:

> I come into being/age after age/and take a visible shape/and move man with men/for the protection of good, thrusting evil back: and setting virtue/on her seat again

are set as a repeated eight-note scale that rises over gently rippling *ostinati* interspersed with small repeated figures played over them in the woodwind. The effect is mesmerising, fixing the audience's attention on an intensely *musical* statement as an analogue for Gandhi's spiritual vision. This relationship between music and meaning is vital for Glass who believes that: 'The only way that music can be profoundly successful, is if the musical language is part of the *argument* of the piece' (Glass, 1999: 268). The music at this point enshrines the meaning, not of 'Gandhi'

Table 17.5 Satyagraha: *the parallel levels of activity in act 1 – Tolstoy; scene 1 –* The Kuria Field of Justice

Synopsis	Setting	Staging	Libretto/text
A great battle is impending between two royal families, the Kuruvas and the Pandavas.	Dawn breaking (sky with clouds). Mythological Battlefield/South African Plain.	Far upstage is a dawn sky backdrop in front of which is a truncated pyramid twelve feet high, where Tolstoy is seated at his desk with all its papers, knicknacks, etc.	
At a signal from the aged king, the trumpeter blew his conch, loosening the tempest in the waiting armies assembled on the sacred plain. From both sides, warriors and chieftains blew their battle shells announcing their readiness to fight with a din resounding between heaven and earth.		From far upstage to the pit, the floor is covered with golden grass varying in height from knee-high to trampled.	
And seeing the battle set, weapons unsheathing, bows drawn forth – Prince Arjuna spoke to Lord Krishna, wishing to look more closely at these men drawn up spoiling for the fight with whom he must do battle in the enterprise of war.		Two armies are situated stage right and stage left with an open area separating them. Centre stage right and left (at the heads of the armies) are Arjuna and Duryodhana in their chariots. Krishna stands downstage in the open area separating the armies.	
		The armies are backlit, appearing in silhouette, and as the scene progresses, lights come up on the armies to reveal them as Indians and Europeans respectively, also revealing their weapons as everyday objects.	
		Indian army, stage right, is wearing whites and light grays. European army, stage left, is wearing blacks, grays, beiges, off-whites. Krishna, Arjuna and Duryodhana are in resplendent, full colour. Gandhi in Satyagraha dress.	

Gandhi appears upstage centre and begins walking downstage between the two armies. After covering one-third of the distance, he starts solo.	**Gandhi** yo-tsyu-ma-na I see them here assembled
Joined in duet by Arjuna.	**Gandhi, Arjuna** kar-pun-yu My very being is oppressed
Joined in trio by Krishna.	**Gandhi, Arjuna, Krishna** u-thu chat But if you/will not
Followed by short chorus section, two armies singing.	**Gandhi, Arjuna, Krishna, chorus** tum th-tha kri-pu-ya-vish-tum To him thus in compassion plunged
Ending with Gandhi, in solo, downstage.	**Gandhi** khu-duk-kha hold pleasure and pain

as biography, but as myth: 'I never worked with the real Gandhi and I took poetic license or artistic liberty to do that . . . The Satyagraha movement and Gandhi himself have been kept alive by politicians, particularly Martin Luther King, Jr., but also by artists . . . I idealised the existing myth' (Glass, 1999: 326).

Satyagraha is a theatrically complex work that makes peculiar demands: the ability to suspend the usual expectations of the relationship between text, action and score. Instead there is a parallel series of artistic events, two of which, the *Bhagavad Gita*, and Gandhi's life, the audience has to know if they are fully to experience the staging and, above all, the score. As in Nono, the work requires a different kind of commitment by the audience as the true meeting point of all its elements.

Stockhausen (*Donnerstag* aus *Licht*)

Glass's Buddhism underlies his commitment to Gandhi and the idea of Satyagraha (Glass, 1999: 316). For Stockhausen, the main drive is his belief in the visionary role of the artist: 'I think there have always been different kinds of artists: those who were mainly mirrors of their time, and then a very few who had a visionary power . . . those who were able to announce the next stage in the development of mankind' (Stockhausen, 2000: 31–2). The visionary is based on inspiration which Stockhausen sees as a metaphysical fact of life: 'The essential aspect of my music is always religious and spiritual . . . mysticism is something that cannot be expressed with words, that is: music! The purest musicality is also the purest mysticism in the modern sense. Mysticism is a very incisive capacity to see right through things' (Kurtz, 1988: 199).

This idiosyncratic metaphysic of music does, however, also reflect a more traditional view. Stockhausen writes that: 'Music is a miniature of the harmony of the whole universe, for the harmony of the universe is life itself, and man, being a miniature of the universe, shows harmonious and inharmonious chords in his pulsation, in the beat of his heart, in his vibration, rhythm and tone' (Kurtz, 1988: 190). This is the essential subject of his seven-part opera *Licht*, begun in 1977 with *Donnerstag* (Thursday), which shows the development of musician/man as a key point of creation.

The dramatic form is in part influenced by Stockhausen's understanding of ritual and non-sequential aspects of oriental theatre, what he calls the 'lyric': 'the approach I now call lyric [which] in our western tradition is very rare, given the predominance of sequential and developmental conventions. Not so in the oriental traditions of Japan for instance . . . What counts there is the here and now; they do not always feel compelled to base their composition on contrast with what has gone before, or where a moment may be leading' (Stockhausen, 2000: 59).

Most importantly this applies to character, which Stockhausen does not see as a unified entity. Instead he writes about it as a way of looking at a series of disparate moments in time/life which seem to make a single sense because they happen to/within the same physical being: 'there is a general tendency in literature as well to think one should be able to follow the developments of characters in a drama or a novel, is something very old fashioned ... So character development, continuity of character, no longer seems to be important any more: what really matters is the way he appears, the manner of playing' (Stockhausen, 2000: 56).

The challenge in *Donnerstag* was to create an opera that traced the development of the man–musician without suggesting a simple homogeneous growth. Underlying each section of the opera there is therefore greater complexity than the broad biographical narrative suggests (Table 17.6).

The complexity arises because within this narrative there is a series of relationships and struggles between three cosmic forces, each of whom also has a series of manifestations:

- The principal characters are:
  - Archangel Michael as 'creator angel of the universe';
  - Lucifer, for whom Man is an unworthy object of creation;
  - Eve, the mother of human birth/rebirth as musical being.
- All three transform into other characters within the opera, so in 'Childhood':
  - Eve is/becomes Michael's mother;
  - Lucifer is/becomes his father;
  - Michael is/becomes the child.
- At different stages each character is played by three different kinds of performer:
  - a singer;
  - a dancer;
  - an instrument/alist (Michael – trumpet; Eve – basset-horn; Lucifer – trombone).

This means that any scene has to be understood on several actual (rather than analogous) levels. In the 'Examination' sequence, for example, Michael both sings and 'plays' episodes from his own life and in section v of Examination I, the text is both whispered and sung in a consciously 'singerly' style, while the examiner's (Lucifer's) continuous commentary is in recitative. The second act, 'Michael's Journey Round the Earth', has no verbal text at all and consists of an extended trumpet 'concerto'. The stage is dominated by a giant globe, out of which Michael appears to play his trumpet in partnership or confrontation with the orchestra and the two mocking swallow-clowns/basset-horn and clarinet.

In *Satyagraha*, the complexity is in part mitigated by the score's accessibility; this is not the case here where, in addition to disrupted action and narrative, the music

Table 17.6 Donnerstag: *narrative structure*

Act	Title	Section title	Broad action
Thursday Greeting			Played in the foyer
Act 1	Michael's Youth	Childhood	Michael is educated in music by his mother and worldly things by his father
			Michael's mother goes mad and is taken away
			Michael's father abandons him and goes to war
		Moon-Eve	Michael learns that both parents are dead
			He learns sensuous beauty from Moon-Eve
		Examination	Michael excels in music before the admission panel – playing his life
Act II	Michael's Journey Round the Earth		Michael travels the globe and experiences the variety of human life
			He (and Moon-Eve) struggle with mocking swallow-clowns
Act III	Michael's Return Home	Festival	Eve welcomes Michael home
			He struggles with Lucifer
		Vision	Michael is the human embodiment of the immortal/God
Thursday's/Michael's Farewell			Played outside the theatre

is itself enormously challenging. The score ranges from direct accompaniment of the action, such as 'Michael's battle with the dragon' in section 30 of iii.i, to being completely self-contained, although often with a luminous beauty, as in section 4 of iii.i, Michael's 'Thank you'. The opera alternates between Stockhausen's personal, mystic vision, concrete if oblique stage action and music that is concerned with its own unity and structure rather than dramatic function. At times it seems as though Stockhausen is most interested in a kind of metaphysic of performance that carries its own meaning, rather than an opera – however diffuse – as a concrete event:

> I now compose the spaces in which I imagine my music being performed . . . The invisible choirs in *Donnerstag* aus *Licht* are much more important than the visible choirs. There are sixteen channels of polyphony sung in the invisible choirs, and in the First Act they are heard very far away as an undefinable acoustic horizon, while later in the Third Act the same choral music approaches and is heard close-up, very close from a circle of loud-speakers surrounding the public. When that happens, what you see on stage seems almost like a miniature projection of what you hear, which is invisible. (Stockhausen, 2000: 146)

The audience is confronted here with an extraordinary range of ambiguously inter-related but separate elements, presented by singers, mimes, dancers and character-instrumentalists. The result is an inverted version of Wagner's *Gesamtkunstwerk*: not a totality but an accretion. The dramaturgy creates a series of congruencies that redescribe opera as an artwork where meaning itself has become just one aspect of a larger muscio-dramatic event.

Birtwistle: artifice as reality (*The Mask of Orpheus*)

Harrison Birtwistle (b. 1934) has been a major force in contemporary opera since his first opera, *Punch and Judy*, in 1968. His works include instrumental pieces as well as operas, all of which have a strong underlying intellectual approach to art and its reality. In *The Mask of Orpheus* there is a dislocation of elements similar to *Donnerstag*, but used in a more obviously coherent way. A tension is set up between the opera's dominant idea and the deliberately separated elements that embody it. Peter Zinovieff calls his introduction to the libretto 'The children's story', implying that it is a straightforward version of something more complex. In it, he recounts the myth of Orpheus and Euridice but using several variant sources and with particular emphasis on the story of Aristaeus. This serves two purposes. First, it acquaints the audience/listener with the full range of the story, which goes far beyond Monteverdi or Gluck's versions. Second, for the listener who knows the narrative, it shows that the opera is concerned with the multiple ways in which the story has been used. This is, in fact the real subject: the opera is not a dramatisation of the story, instead it is *about* the nature of story and myth, as a construct over time and through cultures.

Essential to this is the idea of time and sequence. The title of Birtwistle's *The Triumph of Time* is taken from an engraving by Brueghel which he describes: 'in the foreground, the overall image of a procession: a freeze frame, only a sample of an event in motion; parts of the procession must already have gone by, others are surely to come; a procession made up of a [necessarily] linked chain of material objects which have no necessary connexion with each other' (Hall, 1984: 82). In other words, the image implies a sequence that is a fiction constructed by the artist and/or viewer. Those in the procession, most of whom cannot be seen, have individual experiences which are not truly defined or described by the procession – which they in turn cannot know: the apparent 'reality' is composed by the artist alone. The myth/story of Orpheus is similarly not a 'real' or even a single story, but the result of an historical process of accretion. The opera is designed to explore the multi-faceted nature of perception and 'reality', and is therefore made up of events that are repeated and, Birtwistle says: 'accompanied by some distortion such as the event being seen from another character's viewpoint. For example the death of Euridice is seen at least five times from different situations and each time represents a new judgement' (Hall, 1984: 121).

Fracture is therefore essential to Birtwistle's work: 'If I sketch a passage . . . that consists, say, of seven phases or ideas in which one leads smoothly to and logically to the next, I break these up when I come to compose the work and reorder the events. The logical sequence is still there, but it has been fractured, disturbed, messed up' (Hall, 1998: ix). The result is the paradox of a dramaturgy that is a whole while showing the fragments – which may conflict with one another – of which it is made. The philosophical and artistic point is that there may be a coherence that does not create a false homogeneity. Piero della Francesca's *The Flagellation of Christ* is a painting famous for its mixture of precise geometry, violent subject-matter and sense of acute stillness. For Birtwistle:

> The lyricism, mystery and formalism it contains are qualities I've always wanted to emulate. The actual flagellation is taking place in the background on the left of the picture. There's a symmetry which is not a symmetry. In the foreground on the right are the figures of three men standing as if lost in their own worlds. But they're not puppets, they're genuinely human, and as far as information is concerned, they constitute the most important element in the picture. In fact the flagellation is not what the painting is about at all. The essence of the painting lies beyond its subject. It's about something else.   (Hall, 1984: 148)

The painting has pulled together disparate subjects to create an artistic whole which is about something other than any one of them. Apparent reality is a mere construct, an evasion of the fractured nature of experience and therefore: 'In *The Mask of Orpheus*... I invented a substructure which is not analogous with the text. There's a musical level and a dramatic level and they don't start coming together until the last act. But this was part of the formal compositional design and is completely artificial' (Hall, 1984: 145).

Wozzeck and *Die Soldaten* both use baroque forms to help stabilise the scenes and their music. By contrast, in *The Mask of Orpheus* formality creates a sense of ceremony and art. This allows fractured reality and its enactment to become metaphoric, each element reflecting on the other and back upon itself: 'In writing the piece I wanted to invent a formalism that does not rely on tradition... I wanted to create a formal world which was utterly new (Hall, 1984: 145).

The fractured, over-layered dramaturgy is a metaphor for the opera's theme. This is effected scenically, as well as in the text and action (see Table 17.7). In act ɪ there is the image of the 'Passing clouds', and in act ɪɪɪ 'The tides'. Both are images of repetition that also contain change. None of this is merely 'illustrative', but adds its own resonance to the refraction that lies at the heart of the opera's experience. Most impressively, act ɪɪ is dominated visually by the image of a seventeen-arch aqueduct, running across the stage from left to right, each arch given its own title: 1 = Countryside; 2 = Crowd; 3 = Evening; 4 = Contrast; 5 = Dying; 6 = Wings; 7 = Colour, etc. In addition, 'Water containing movement flows towards the future' across the arches from right to left, while a river flows through the seventh arch from the rear of the stage, 'from the past toward the present'. The first nine arches are those of 'going forward', ten to fourteen are those 'of the return' and the last three are the 'Arches of awareness'. Finally there are mountains 'of the living' at the back left of the stage and those 'of the dead' back right.

The score responds to the constantly shifting focus in text and action, ranging from the atmospheric opening electronic murmuring of Summer and Aristaeus' bees, to the incipient violence of 'Third terrible death' in ɪɪɪ.iii. ɪ.i's 'First act of love/First duet of love' demonstrates the complexity, musical coherence and sheer beauty of much of the work. The final lines of the preceding 'First Poem of Reminiscence', 'I remember my singing... I am Orpheus' overlap with it while the texts proper are spoken and sung simultaneously, with the sung and orchestral parts weaving a slow, delicate, hypnotic line. The overlay of styles and vocal types mirrors the complexity of the libretto so that there are three distinct vocal 'elements' rather than traditionally vocal 'parts': the spoken text, Orpheus' repeated cry of 'Euridice' and the sensuous beauty of the melodic line initially centred on Euridice herself. The experience is intense and engaging, fragmented and disparate but at the same time creating a complete aesthetic experience.

Like *Donnerstag* the opera uses detailed scenography and physical action; instrumental, electronic and sung music; sung text, *Sprechgesang*, speech and made-up

Table 17.7 *The Mask of Orpheus*: i, i

1st DUET OF LOVE
Duet of Hope
5   ^{0}s&p ^{E}s&p   A

SINGERS: ORPHEUS (SINGER AND PUPPET), EURIDICE (SINGER AND PUPPET) in variou
pairings on and off stage

*This song is a conclusion to the 1st Act of Love. It is interrupted and frozen by the 1st Passing Cloud
of Abandon, and leads into the 1st Ceremony (The wedding) by the Troupe of Ceremony entering and
shouting 'answer'. Extensions of the words are used as fixed patterned echoes three times during each
of the three ceremonies. The duet and extensions are by one Orpheus/Euridice pair on-stage and one
pair off-stage. The latter always sing syllables from the words 'Orpheus' and 'Euridice'. Which pair
sing is indicated below. The words show the change in Euridice's attitude to Orpheus' love for her.
At first she asks for hands and not love. Later she regrets not having accepted Orpheus completely.
Finally she understands the meaning of Orpheus' love.*

ORPHEUS (Singer)	EURIDICE (Singer)	
	1	
	Euridice reaches out her hand	**1st ACT OF LOVE**
Touch follows	Hands, Orpheus,	Act of Tenderness
These vows through fingers given.	Givehands:heartslater	4 ^{E}s M
(Crowns kiss rings in		
summertime)		
I remember, Euridice, this summer	Kisses, vows: all later.	
Willing across jewelled hands.	Give hands, Orpheus.	
Euridice	Orpheus.	**1st PASSING CLOUD**
		OF ABANDON
	Freeze of song as mime	The Story of Dionysus
	action crosses stage.	T. of P.C.
	2	6 M
Love follows	Words, Orpheus,	
Words through fingers taken,	Tell words: songs later.	
(Sounds touch lips in		
summertime).		
I remember, Euridice, this summer:	Hands, Orpheus,	*Troupe of Ceremony*
Forcing across jewelled hands	Give hands: hearts much later.	*slowly enter and adopt*
Silent willing love.		*formalised positions. Sun*
		sets. Ceremony starts
Euridice	Orpheus.	*during verse 2.*
Euridice		

language; events that are enacted by singers, dancers, puppets and masks. The main characters are each represented by three different kinds of performer, for example Orpheus is seen as:

The Man	singer	1st high baritone
The Hero	mime	Actor
The Myth	puppet	2nd high baritone

But, unlike *Donnerstag*, these are not alternative embodiments, but reflections of Orpheus as the process of myth. The result is not an illustration of the legend or its aesthetic articulation, but a refraction of experience that supervenes analysis, however careful (see Hall, 1984: 135–42). As Jonathan Cross writes: 'Any attempt to provide a synopsis of the plot of *The Mask of Orpheus* will be incomplete and, in a sense, doomed to failure in that it will impose a linear structure on a work which . . . is concerned with eschewing such a singular kind of narrative' (J. Cross, 1997: 14). *The Mask of Orpheus* takes the complete apparatus of opera to the limit. Its density and rich multiplicity are analogues for the way the composer understands 'reality'. As such it is both analysis and statement, complexity and irreducible fact. It is the world become art as its own truth. Opera has been constantly beset by the conflicting demands of words and music. Ironically, here it is precisely that opposition that allows it to become a vision of the world as the continuum of separate, repeated and contradictory realities.

Chapter 18

Directors and the direction of opera

> The most important thing is: I believe that you are *not* one of the producers who look at a work only in order to see how to make it into *something different*. Such a wrong could never be greater than if done to me, since while composing I had all the scenic effects in mind, seeing them in the utmost precision.
>
> (Schoenberg, in Stein, 1964: 139)

A performance of *The Mask of Orpheus* is unthinkable without a director.[1] It needs a single artistic/organising mind to focus its technical and scenographic components. Effectively it is written assuming the director. The rise of the director has changed the way opera is conceived.

From the early nineteenth century parallel developments took place in music, ballet and theatre as a result of growing artistic and technical complexity. The increased size of orchestras and length of scores required the conductor to hold the players and the work together. Once in place this led to the conductor as interpreter – adding, as it were, his own voice to that of the composer. In theatre and opera this had been the responsibility first of the playwright, librettist or composer and then the Stage Manager who understood the technical resources and staging tradition. Until late in the nineteenth century everyone knew what an opera 'looked like'. Increasing technical resources simply added to the realism of the stage picture: interpretation did not arise. There was almost no currency to the idea of older works having to be performed other than in the current production style.[2] However, as David Pountney says, increased technical resources meant that: 'This was the era ... in which production-books first became common ... the scale and intricacy of the stagings that became a fashionable and necessary ingredient of grand opera occasioned the practical demands that would lead to the invention of the director' (Pountney, in Charlton, 2003: 132).

Although Wagner's scenography remained far behind the other aspects of his visionary work he made extraordinary scenographic demands, in particular in *The Ring*. Added to this, what was to be produced was not just an opera, but a vision – so that production became an integral part of the work. Therefore, as Henry Porges recorded during the first rehearsal of *The Ring*, he directed the operas himself, to ensure that 'every movement, every expression, every intonation played its part in a living breathing organism' (Porges, 1983: 3).

At the same time, stage Naturalism demanded a new kind of truthfulness in staging and acting. The vital response was that of Stanislavski, who developed strategies for creating this with both actors and singers. After describing the implications of the brief orchestral opening of *La Bohème*, he goes on to say: 'The music presents you your inner state, the shades of your emotions, thus the inner rhythm of your life. But a driving rhythm is not necessarily expressed in energetic external gestures. A person can be full of drive and inwardly excited while remaining completely motionless' (Stanislavski with Rumyantsev, 1998: 214). This kind of detailed, inner reading of the score only made sense if it were adopted by the entire cast, so that the idea of ensemble became paramount: 'The core of our [Opera] Studio will consist of good singers of what we may call average talent, but who love their work; cultivated singers and actors who are welded together into an ensemble' (Stanislavski, 1998: 2). This itself increased the need for the director, as Stanislavski had realised: 'As I am quite sure that the only salvation for future opera is in ensemble opera, I agree that the role of the producer is becoming more important. Indeed, the producer is a creative artist' (Stanislavski in Graubard, 1986: 55). However, this also meant that, unlike the Stage Manager, the director no longer simply told his performers where to enter, stand and exit, but how to act – interact and realise their characters, the world of the play or opera and its meaning.

Until the late nineteenth century new works had made up almost all of the repertoire. After 1900 this changed, as the public's taste increasingly lagged behind musical developments. Not only were older works continually revived, but gradually managements and scholars looked back to parts of the repertoire that had been simply dismissed – such as Handel and Monteverdi. But if they were to live on the stage they needed to have a modern life. It was possible to undertake archaeological reconstruction which would be fascinating, but primarily as a basis for informing modern performance. The responsibility for this translation lay with the director. It once more emphasised the interpretative voice and, beyond that, the potential to become the voice of his or her time. The opera now became the material for the director's work. This posed two possibilities. The first was some kind of 'traditional' staging with all the questions discussed in Chapter 6. The other was far more challenging: to make the opera new while being true to it – however the 'it' might be construed.

Determining a production 'concept', however 'traditional', entails a series of questions implicit in the history of any opera, however recent:

- How was the opera originally conceived within its artistic and social context?
- Why has it now been chosen, and for whom?
- How are these two elements to inform the production?

Understanding the original work depends on how much is known in the first place. Not only is this variable from period to period but, as Peter Sellars has said: 'No one will ever know how much of this Wagner was aware of or not. His texts are saying both more and less than he intended . . . We look at them with our contemporary eyes and read a lot more into them than their creators perhaps intended to be showing, in terms of sexual subjects, in terms of political awareness and so on' (Sellars, in *Directors in Opera*, 2006/7, 2: 42). This means that the idea of the 'originator' is 'much more negotiable than those who think that there is a single thing called an intention which careful scholarship will elucidate' (Jonathan Miller, in *Directors in Opera*, 2006/7, 2: 16). At the same time all operas do have a point of origin which provides some indication at least of what the opera was and, within limits, was intended to be. No responsible director can ignore this as part of his working material (Table 18.1).

As taste, artistic conventions, audience expectations, political, social and financial circumstances change, so any opera will be seen differently and need to be adapted. This may range from the kind of generalised 'traditional' presentation to which arena productions aspire, through the refinement of Zeffirelli's realism, to the challenge of Deborah Warner whose 'interest is always to take things to the extreme' Warner in *Directors in Opera*, 2006/7, 2: 70). After its initial production, an opera takes on

Table 18.1 *The choices essential to the opera as meaning in original performance*

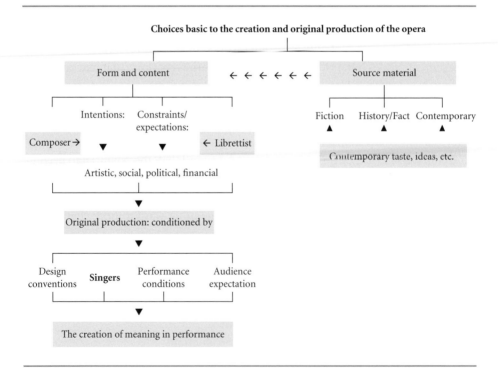

a life of its own. Even with minimal change, as with the D'Oyly Carte's productions of the Savoy Operas, the audience continues to change around them.

The audience therefore poses some of the major questions that management and director have to consider. Any house's policy is essentially determined by its understanding of its audience and how it wants to approach them. Without in any way denying the intrinsic merits of *La Bohème*, its constant, often 'traditional' repetition is a function of audiences with a very limited view of the operatic repertoire. This inevitably constrains the director and starts to eat into the real life of the standard repertoire itself. The decision to do an opera – commission a new work, revive a standard, or perform something rare or perhaps forgotten – will largely depend upon finance and how the house sees its function. All of this becomes a source of information for the director. It does not mean that the production has to conform to the audience's expectations, but it does mean that if the production is to succeed it must take the audience into consideration. If not, the result will be incomprehension. This means that 'The choices essential to the opera as meaning in original performance' of Table 18.1 are replaced by the criteria in Table 18.2.

At one extreme there are directors, such as David Alden, for whom a production is an expression of their own concerns: 'I can't really direct something until I feel that what I have to say personally I can say through the piece. I think that is what an artist is supposed to do . . . My productions are very much about my inner emotional life' (Alden in *Directors in Opera*, 2006/7, 1: 15–16). An apparently simple response to this is Walter Felsenstein's:

> In this era of the ascendancy of the stage director we unfortunately attach more importance to a director's interpretation of a work that to the desire to have the work itself perfectly realized. We must reject any interpretation whose primary aim is to produce an interesting performance but which does not carefully explore

Table 18.2 *Audience as condition of house policy and production style*

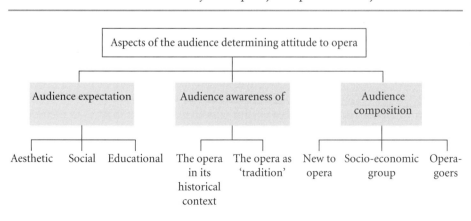

the intentions of the composer and the author and try to fulfil them as closely as possible.   (Brook, 1995: 366)

This sounds eminently sensible but, depending on the opera, the composer and the period, there are simply too many imponderables to be as confident as Felsenstein would like to suggest. The question can never be whether interpretation is needed, only of what kind, and for whom?

For a sophisticated audience who can be relied upon to know the piece, a radical staging will be a stimulating experience of something with which they thought they were familiar – perhaps too much so, as Niklaus Lehnhoff suggests: 'I'm not one for easy answers. I aim at an audience that is intelligent, unprejudiced and ready to explore new waters. Opera buffs who get carried away by high Cs are as unbearable as audiences who are content to see what they know' (Lehnhoff in *Directors in Opera*, 2006/7, 1: 92–3). However, for an audience new to the opera – perhaps to opera altogether – there are assumptions that it would be irresponsible to make. They may not know the story, understand the social conventions of the period, or the musical forms. This does not imply that a 'standard' production is required. On the contrary, such an audience may be much better placed to appreciate production innovations perhaps derived from film, circus, theatre, etc. which has implications for both production and the repertoire. Humphrey Burton thinks that: 'it is necessary, in considering the future of opera, to discuss what *kind* of opera has a future. Is there a future for revitalised performances of composers who had all stopped working by 1950, or in the case of Benjamin Britten, 1970? Or is it going to be an opera that at least mixes new works with old in a better combination that will not be dominated totally by yet another rethinking of *Madama Butterfly* or *Tosca*? (Graubard, 1986: 33).

The experience of other media will in any case affect an audience's expectations and make different, perhaps more sophisticated demands than those of the opera's original period. For Jonathan Miller, a major aspect of the director's work is: 'making the best of a bad job is what you spend a lot of time doing in opera, endlessly performing elaborate reconstructive surgery, grafting artificial hearts into things which haven't got them, or putting limbs on to things which have effective hearts but no locomotor ability at all' (Miller in *Directors in Opera*, 2006/7, 2: 11). There are many operas whose characterisation, motivation or action is weak and which need a director to create a stage presence within which its actual strengths – a melodious score or a strong central character – can flourish.

In other cases, as in the theatre, the world of the opera may be a block or distraction. Although it is possible for an educated audience to see through the neo-classical pretences of, say *La clemenza di Tito*, for many it can remain what it seems to be: an opera about ancient Rome. To get past this requires careful strategies if the result is to be consonant with the style of the score, the kinds of musical forms and behaviour of the characters. If not, then rather than creating an interesting tension between classical form and modern context, the piece may simply fall apart. For Nicholas Hytner: 'By and large . . . I've always tried to find a stage world for these old pieces which is suitable for the mode of expression of the play or opera I'm doing – which I think is very rarely a simple updating' (Hytner in *Directors in Opera*, 2006/7, 1: 73.

At the heart of these differing ideas there remains some idea of an 'authenticity' – an 'original' that carries its own justification within it. Jonathan Miller argues that:

> no writer, no author, no composer has total access to all his own meanings. This is surely evident in everyday life; at times everyone needs an objective perspective on his actions. The producer can provide this insight . . . in the process of modern theatre and modern opera [we see] successive amendments to a constitution inherited from the past. One constantly has to make allowances for modern sensibilities, for unforeseeable changes in the perception of the modern audience.
> (Graubard, 1986: 51–2)

This is, as he says, not a 'vandal's charter' but a formula for responsible engagement between text, tradition and the modern world. To achieve this requires a profound understanding of all three elements, and to realise them demands two major abilities.

The first is the 'professional' aspect of the director's work, as Felsenstein insisted: 'he must be able, by his own methods, to help appropriately cast singers, and also the conductor and designer, become profoundly familiar with the work, and to induce them to bring forth a highly personal interpretation, but one that is completely faithful to the work, according to the laws of the theatre' (Brook, 1995: 366). The ability to enable collaboration is essential and this has to be grounded in both professional skill and an 'authentic' vision of the work. The second is educative, for both those involved in a production and the audience. It applies equally, with different emphases, to both older and in particular modern operas. Ann Getty points to 'a gap between the development of the art form and the development of the audience; this gap is greater than in any other art form. If the gap becomes a chasm opera may well follow the epic and the pastoral to extinction' (Graubard, 1986: 2). This affects not only audiences but, perhaps most saliently, critics as well. Critics should be in a position to guide audiences towards new work and new productions. But to do so, there needs to be a contract between the makers, critics and audiences. Given the challenge of contemporary opera and production, the roles of all three need to be openly recognised and redefined. The problem is an international one, as Fedora Barbieri shows: 'The public, especially in Italy, does not arrive prepared to hear modern works; they need to be prepared for what they are going to listen to, but there are no facilities for preparation' (Grabaurd, 1986: 14).

Although many companies offer talks and encounters with the artists, the level is difficult to judge for something that has no general educational support. In Britain, for example, there are courses in art, theatre/drama and music at GCSE and A level, degree and adult education classes. Opera has no such infrastructure, which reinforces the impression that serious attention is unnecessary, so that Julius Rudel can ask: 'Are we moving away from the original plan that opera is to be, and I quote, "an entertainment of the highest order"? Do we really need the audience to learn more and more?' (Rudel, in Graubard, 1986: 15). Essentially there is no reliable way in which an audience can know what there is to know in the first place, so that opera has a number of problems to contend with:

- It is expensive, labelled as elitist, poorly represented in the broadcast media and usually at the most banal traditional level.
- Artistically there is a definitive gap between audiences for, and appreciation of, modern and most pre-nineteenth-century operas. This is increased by modernist dramaturgy and staging of new and older works.
- Because there is little or no educational grounding available, access depends upon happenstance which is unlikely to provide a systematic approach.

The future direction – perhaps existence – of opera therefore depends upon three things:

- Above all new work. This alone can genuinely engage with important contemporary ideas and concerns, the latest developments in music and production.
- The continuance of the older repertoire, both the traditional 'standard' operas and rediscoveries. There must always be room for productions that challenge or analyse old works, but this has to be carefully balanced against the need for accessibility.
- Dedicated education without which opera must increasingly be relegated either to its assumed elitism, supported by Johnson's misused 'irrational and exotic entertainment', or be an unthinking source of mere comfortable pleasure. No serious art form could survive either of these. This is precisely what Britten meant when he wrote that:

> Music demands more from a listener than simply the possession of a tape-machine or a transistor radio. It demands some preparation, some effort, a journey to a special place, saving up for a ticket, some homework on the programme perhaps, some clarification of the ears and sharpening of the instincts. It demands as much effort on the listener's part as the other two corners of the triangle, this holy triangle of composer, performer and listener.
>
> (Kildea, 2000: 261)

Motifs from *The Ring* used in Chapter 10

The motifs from *The Ring* used in the analysis of Wotan's monologue set out in Table 10.7b are listed below. The numbers attached to each theme refer to those in the 'Thematic Guide' in Spencer and Millington (2000). The motif names in this appendix and Table 10.7b are not Wagner's but interpretative names, albeit broadly agreed by most commentators.

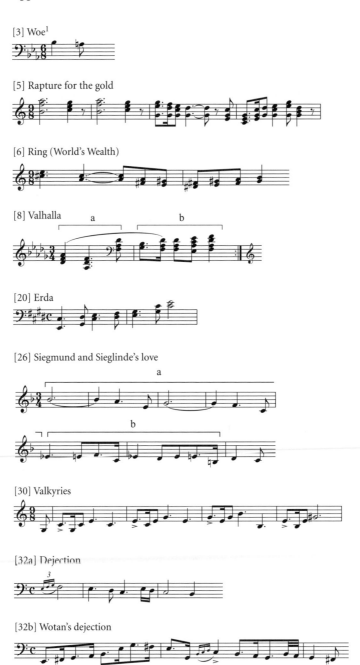

Figure A1.1 Motifs for *The Ring* analysis in Table 10.7b
Note: [1] This is in fact a minor verson of the Rhinemaidens' cry of exultation on the word 'Rheingold' – the root of *The Ring*'s problems and struggle.

The development of singing voices in opera

Each major period of opera has had its own musical and singing priorities so that technique, singing style and the register of voices has changed over time. The terms in general use now (soprano, tenor, baritone, bass) have meant and implied different things. In addition, in certain periods there have been far more precise subdivisions of the main types, with clear character implications and with singers specialising in them and audience expectation attuned to them. In the modern age the entire historic repertoire is available and most singers are expected to cope across a wide range of styles. The result is often to iron out niceties that were essential to the original composition. It is important, therefore, to be aware of this shifting vocal nexus as part of the aesthetic of periods and individual works (Table A2.1).

In all voices a decisive shift took place at the beginning of the nineteenth century, in part as the *castrato* was dropped which realigned both the starring role of the high female voice and the male voice, with the tenor coming into prominence for the first time.

Soprano

This term is usually applied in the seventeenth and eighteenth centuries to the male (*castrato*) voice. It was the last vocal type to enter into art music (via the madrigal). However the female soprano was also used: Vittoria Archilei performed in the Florentine *Intermedii* and Caterina Martinelli in Monteverdi's *Arianna*. The female vocal range in this period was generally closer to what would now be considered the mezzo-soprano. In the seventeenth century almost all female roles were written for this lower range. In France, which had its own terminology for all voices, the soprano voice was usually referred to as the 'dessus' the voice that was 'over' or 'above'.

At the beginning of the nineteenth century, as the female voice became the only high voice, a number of new categories and types developed, in particular the *coloratura* (coloured voice), which the French called *soprane à roulades* (soprano with flourishes). The *coloratura* voice was in particular the preferred type in Italy in the *bel canto* repertoire.

Table A2.1 *The development of singing voices*

	Seventeenth and eighteenth centuries	Early nineteenth century	Later nineteenth century	Twentieth century
Soprano	Term generally applied to the *castrato* voice	The *bel canto coloratura* soprano	Lyric soprano *Spinto* soprano	
	General term for the female voice		Lyric-dramatic soprano	
Mezzo-soprano Contralto	In general, a foil to the soprano character Comic, secondary or lower-class characters	Developed as a major voice by Rossini		Term *contralto* largely dropped
Tenor	Main male voice until about 1650 then superseded by the *castrati*.	*Tenore di grazia* (*Ténor leger*) *Tenore di forza* (*Fort-ténor*)	*Tenore robusto* Heldentenor	*Tenore altino* or *Contraltino*
	In France (no *castrati*) the tenor develops as the *Haute-ténor* and the *Taille* (tenor proper)			
Bass Baritone	Bass used as the general term for the lower male voice	Bass and bass-baritone increasingly distinguished. Baritone = (Fr.) *basse chantante* Bass = *basse noble* Basso profondo = *basse profonde*	Development of the Baritone as an important character and musical voice	
	Magisterial but rarely a major singing voice except in Handel. Comic old men			
Counter-tenor	English term, in France the *Haute-ténor*, not used in opera			Revived in 1950s (Alfred Deller) Used in *castrato* roles and inspires new roles
Castrato	Starring male voice from about 1650	Final role in Meyerbeer's 1824 *Il crociato in Egitto*		Replaced by female or or counter-tenor voices

In general, sopranos or soprano roles (as with the tenor voice) were divided between the lyric and the *spinto* voice. The distinction was between the easy, *legato* voice and one that required, and celebrated, *spinto* (effort), in itself an analogue for the heroic or urgent nature of the character. In France these types were named after two early exponents, Falcon (lyric) and Dugazon (*spinto*). The creation of larger opera houses and orchestras, the growing demands typified by Verdi and later *Verismo*, saw the development of a less delicate style, the lyric-dramatic voice. In Germany the equivalents were the dramatic and the heroic soprano. In the twentieth century the *coloratura* voice and repertoire has seen a revival, while some contemporary composers have written for extraordinarily high registers, making the voice something between an instrument and an actual role.

Mezzo-soprano and *contralto*

Originally the lower female voice was used for secondary roles such as companions and servants, and thus usually a foil to the soprano, especially in comedy. The vogue for the *castrato* and the use of a lower *castrato* voice additionally relegated the lower female voice to secondary status. Handel, however, wrote more sympathetic roles for the contralto as both female and male characters, while Rossini positively preferred the lower, mezzo voice and many of his major female roles are written for it.

The lower end of the range, identified as the contralto, became increasingly identified with less glamorous roles and since the 1950s there are few singers who describe themselves as contraltos. Quite simply, the term mezzo-soprano has seemed more alluring.

Tenor

The tenor – meaning the voice that 'held' the main line – was the most important voice up to the middle of the seventeenth century. It was then gradually replaced by the *castrato*. This obtained in Italy and was followed by countries that adopted the Italian opera. This did not apply in France which, instead preferred the high tenor, 'Haut-Contre'; the tenor itself was called the 'Taille'. In the early period, tenors were used, but the male heroic parts were almost always given to *castrati*. This ended with the abandonment of the *castrato* voice, whose last major role was Armando in Meyerbeer's *Il crociato in Egitto* (1824).

Even more than the soprano, the tenor voice and role developed as a major type in the nineteenth century and was subdivided according to style and kind of role. The *bel canto* tenor was described as the *tenore di grazia*, the French *ténor leger*.

Then, in parallel with the soprano, as musical style changed with Verdi and then *Verismo*, there developed the *tenore di forza*, in France the *fort-ténor*, and the more forceful *tenore robusto* for roles such as Otello. In Germany, this equated with the *Heldentenor*. A specialised high tenor, the *tenore altino* or *contraltino*, was used for roles such as the Astrologer in *Le Coq d'Or*. In addition, in France there were two kinds of specialised, comic, types, again named after specific singers: the *Laruette* for old men and the nasal *Trial* for simpletons.

Bass and baritone

In general the lower male voice was thought of as the 'bass'. The distinction between bass and baritone is still often unclear, with a major role such as Boris Godunov described as both; Hans Hotter, for example, throughout his career moved between high baritone, bass-baritone and bass.

In the seventeenth and earlier eighteenth centuries, the low male voice was used for impressive figures such as rulers and was rarely given significant arias, although Handel did, unusually, write major parts for them. The bass was generally also used for comic older men, like the Panatalone of the *Commedia dell'arte*. In France the voice was divided between the *basse* proper and the higher *basse taille* – equivalent to the Italian *baritono*.

Major changes, as with the other voices, took place in the mid-nineteenth century when the designations *bass* and *bass-baritone* became usual. In France, distinctions again in parallel with the other voices were made: between the lyrical *basse chantante*, the *basse noble*, equating with the older, impressive type but still less prominent musically, and the *basse profonde* – the modern *bass* proper. The baritone only developed in its own right in the mid nineteenth century, largely because of Verdi's interest in lyrical, often older (fatherly) characters.[1] Significantly, the 'Verdian' baritone came into prominence at the same time as the dramatic tenor.

Counter-tenor

This voice has become a major element since its revival in the 1950s, largely through the work of Alfred Deller who revived it in the English repertoire, above all for Purcell. Tippett wrote that 'It was quite clear to me that this was the voice which Purcell wrote for. I had at that time been drawn more and more to Purcell, and more and more to Purcell performances. I had wondered how on earth I would discover this voice which could do those florid vocalisations with the clarity which was obviously part of it' (Giles, 1993: 135). In fact the voice was not exclusively English. In France, where the *castrato* never really obtained, there was the *haute-contre*, which was either a naturally high tenor or a *falsetto*. In the opera house, the counter-tenor is now a major contender for the *castrato* roles (see above), but has also inspired modern roles for composers including Britten (Oberon in *A Midsummer Night's Dream*), Philip Glass (Akhnaten) and Aribert Reimann (the Fool in *Lear*).

The development of lyric theatre alternatives to 'opera'

While comic opera had always existed (*opera buffa* in Italy, one aspect of the *Zarzuela* in Spain) it is significant that it was in the Northern industrialising countries that this emphasis really developed. It was here, among the newly urbanised populations, that the desire for a music theatre freed from the constraints of the court and the demands of serious opera required a different approach (Table A3.1). It substantially began as the melody-centred *ballad opera*, *Singspiel* and lighter *Opéra-comique* of the eighteenth century. By the early nineteenth century this produced both opera of a traditional kind but, again, lightened and focused on melody as well as larger-scale comic works. By the middle of the century a new emphasis appeared as the dominant bourgeoisie wanted this kind of opera to be married to more or less robust satire.

Table A3.1 *The split in opera between serious art form and entertainment*

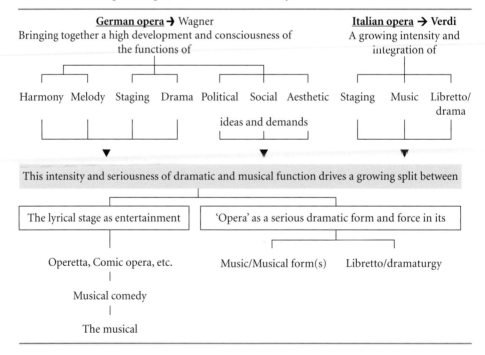

This took in political events, high culture and received morality: on the whole the satire was stronger and the mood more licentious in France (Hervé, Offenbach) than in Britain (Gilbert and Sullivan), Germany (Suppé, Johann Strauss) or the United States (de Koven, Herbert) (Table A3.2).

By the end of the century the mood changed and these works turned increasingly away from satire to a more sentimental, escapist mood accompanied by an even

Table A3.2 *The development of light operatic forms*

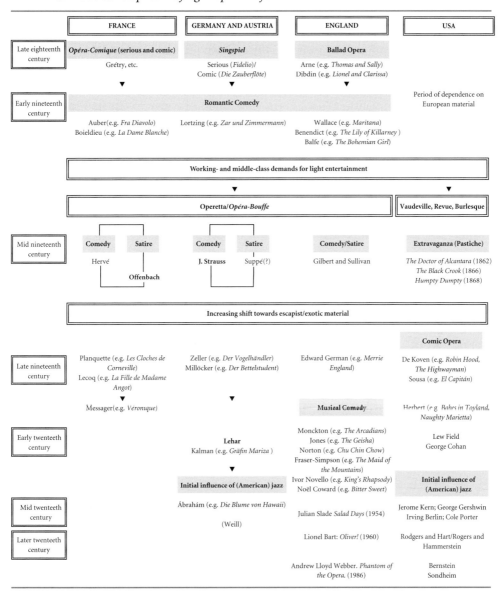

greater loosening of the dramatic structure. Even well-trained composers such as Lehár turned to sentimental romantic plots that made few demands on the audience and for which they provided a series of superb melodies in a variety of exotic styles.

This diminution of the dramatic purpose increased the emphasis on 'hit' numbers which increasingly dominated many of these works. By the end of the century, for example, Planquette's *Les Cloches de Corneville* shot to fame on the basis of a single number, as a result of which managements vied to buy it. Out of this grew the far looser musical comedy, essentially a play interspersed with songs. In England this became a major genre in the hands of Ivor Novello and Noël Coward. In America a shift in musical style, using aspects of jazz and popular song, but still acknowledging the Viennese operetta, developed into the modern musical (Table A3.1).

The musical did not necessarily avoid serious or at least significant subjects. The Rodgers and Hammerstein musicals all approached important subjects such as American colonialism (*South Pacific*), the kind of America GIs had fought for (*Oklahoma!*) and Nazi oppression (*The Sound of Music*); Bernstein's *West Side Story* used *Romeo and Juliet* to confront the perennial problems of ethnic violence and Sondheim has consistently dramatised important and often disturbing issues. At the same time the musical has been flippant (*The Boyfriend, Salad Days*), sentimental where it might have been trenchant (*Evita, Phantom of the Opera*), or simply a vehicle for commercial tunes (*Mamma Mia!, We Will Rock You*). The musical is an important subject in its own right. But it has remained conservative as a popular form of this kind almost inevitably must and almost always avoided the exploration of serious themes in a way that might disturb its audience.

One result has been that opera itself has been cut adrift from the world of entertainment. This has enabled it to develop musically and dramatically in a way that increases its serious purpose. But it has also increased the sense of opera as an elite form that has contributed to the decline in its broad appeal (Table A3.2).

Appendix 4

Some major operas and artistic and political events of the twentieth century, 1899–2008

These are set out in Table A4.1.

Table A4.1 *Chronology of selected events*

Date	Composer	Opera	Politics, etc.	Theatre and literature	Painting, etc.
1899			Freud: *The Interpretation of Dreams*		
1900	Puccini	*Tosca*			
	Charpentier	*Louise*			
	Dvořák	*Rusalka*			
1901				Chekhov: *Three Sisters*	Klimt: *Judith 1*
1902	Debussy	*Pelléas et Mélisande*			
	Cilea	*Adriana Lecouvreur*			Picasso: *La Vie*
1903	d'Albert	*Tiefland*			
1904	Janáček	*Jenůfa*		Chekhov: *The Cherry Orchard*	
	Puccini	*Madama Butterfly*			
1905	Strauss	*Salome*	1st Russian Revolution		Fauvism first shown. Die Brücke formed
1906	Smyth	*The Wreckers*			
1907	Delius	*A Village Romeo and Juliet*		Strindberg: *The Ghost Sonata*	Picasso: *Les Demoiselles d'Avignon*
	Dukas	*Ariane et Barbe-bleu*			
1909	Strauss	*Elektra*		Diaghliev/Ballets Russes in Paris	Futurism announced.
1910	Puccini	*La Fanciulla del West*			Birth of abstract art
	Bloch	*Macbeth*			
	Bloch	*Macbeth*			*(cont.)*

397

Table A4.1 (*cont.*)

Date	Composer	Opera	Politics, etc.	Theatre and literature	Painting, etc.
1911	Strauss	*Der Rosenkavalier*		Craig: *The Art of the Theatre*	
	Wolf-Ferrari	*Jewels of the Madonna*			
1912	Schreker	*Der ferne Klang*			
	Strauss	*Ariadné auf Naxos*			
1913	Faure	*Pénélope*		Stravinsky: *The Rite of Spring*	Duchamp: *The Large Glass*
	da Falla	*La Vida Breve*			
	Montemezzi	*L'amore de tre re*			
1914	Zandonai	*Francesca da Rimini*	1st World War		Vorticism created
	Stravinsky	*Le Rossignol*			
	Boughton	*The Immortal Hour*			
1915	Pizzetti	*Fedra*			
1916	Holst	*Sāvitri*			Dada founded
1917	Busoni	*Turandot*	Russian Revolution proper		De Stijl founded
	Pfitzner	*Palestrina*			
1918	Bartok	*Duke Blubeard's Castle*			Malevich: *White on White*
	Puccini	*Il trittico*			
	Stravinsky	*The Soldier's Tale*			
1919	Strauss	*Die Frau ohne Schatten*			Bauhaus opens in Weimar
	Delius	*Fennimore and Gerda*			
1920	Korngold	*Die tote Stadt*			
	Janáček	*The Adventures of Mr Brouček*			
1921	Hindemith	*Mörder, Hoffnung der Frauen*			
	Janáček	*Kát'a Kabanová*			
	Prokofiev	*The Love for Three Oranges*			
1922	Hindemith	*Sancta Susanna*		Joyce: *Ulysses*	
	Stravinsky	*Renard*		Eliot: *The Waste Land*	
	Stravinsky	*Mavra*			
1923	da Falla	*El retablo de Maese Pedro*			
	Hindemith	*Lehrstücke*			

Table A4.1 (*cont.*)

Date	Composer	Opera	Politics, etc.	Theatre and literature	Painting, etc.
1924	Schoenberg	*Erwartung*			1st Surrealist manifesto
	Schoenberg	*Die glückliche Hand*			
	Strauss	*Intermezzo*			
	Janáček	*The Cunning Little Vixen*			
1925	Ravel	*L'Enfant et les Sortilèges*		Eisenstein: *Battleship Potemkin*	
	Busoni	*Doktor Faust*		Kafka: *The Trial*	
	Berg	*Wozzeck*			
1926	Puccini	*Turandot*			
	Hindemith	*Cardillac*			
	Szymanowski	*King Roger*			
	Janáček	*Več Makropolos*			
1927	Krenek	*Jonny spielt auf*		*The Jazz Singer*	
	Stravinsky	*Oedipus Rex*			
1928	Weill	*Der Tsar Lass sich Photographieren*			
	Strauss	*Der ägyptishe Helena*			
	Weill	*Die Dreigroschenoper*			
1929	R. Vaughan Williams	*Sir John in Love*	Wall Street crash		
	Hindemith	*Neues vom Tage*			
	Weill	*Happy End*			
1930	Shostakovich	*The Nose*			
	Schoenberg	*Von Heute auf Morgen*			
	Weill	*Aufstieg und Fall der Stadt Mahagonny*			
	Janáček	*From the House of the Dead*			
	Weill	*Der Jasager*			
1931	Haba	*Matka*			Dali: *The Persistence of Memory*
1933	Weill	*Die sieben Todsünden*	Hitler made Chancellor		
	Strauss	*Arabella*			

(*cont.*)

Table A4.1 (*cont.*)

Date	Composer	Opera	Politics, etc.	Theatre and literature	Painting, etc.
1934	Shostakovich	*Lady Macbeth of the Mtsensk District*			
	Respighi	*La Fiamma*			
	Virgil Thomson	*Four Saints in Three Acts*			
1935	Strauss	*Die Schweigsame Frau*			
	Gershwin	*Porgy and Bess*			
1936	Enescu	*Oedipus*	Spanish Civil War (−1939)		International Surrealist exhibition
1937	Menotti	*Amelia al Ballo*			Picasso: *Guernica*
	Berg	*Lulu*			
	Orff	*Carmina Burana*			
	R. Vaughan Williams	*Riders to the Sea*			
1938	Hindemith	*Mathis der Maler*		Honegger: *Jeanne d'Arc au bûcher*	
	Strauss	*Friedenstag*			
	Strauss	*Daphne*			
1939	Orff	*Der Mond*	2nd World War (−1945)		
1940	Dallapiccola	*Volo di Notte*			
1942	Strauss	*Capriccio*			
1943					Mondrian: *Broadway Boogie Woogie*
1945	Britten	*Peter Grimes*	Atom bomb dropped on Japan		
1946	Menotti	*The Medium*			Start of Abstract Expressionism
	Britten	*Rape of Lucretia*			Minimalist art
	Prokofiev	*Betrothal in a Monastery*			
	Weill	*Street Scene*			
1947	Poulenc	*Les Mamelles de Tirésias*			
	Briten	*Albert Herring*			
	von Einem	*Dantons Tod*			

Table A4.1 (*cont.*)

Date	Composer	Opera	Politics, etc.	Theatre and literature	Painting, etc.
1948	Prokofiev	*The Story of a Real Man*	Communist extension into Eastern Europe		
1949	Orff	*Antigonae*	Apartheid introduced in South Africa		
	Dallapiccola	*Il Prigioniero*			
1950	Menotti	*The Consul*			Jackson Pollock: *Lavender-mist*
1951	Dessau	*Die Verurteilung des Lukullus*			(Action painting) named
	R. Vaunghan Williams	*The Pilgrim's Progress*			
	Stravinsky	*The Rake's Progress*			
	Britten	*Billy Budd*			
	Menotti	*Amahl and the Night Visitors*			
1952	Henze	*Boulevard Solitude*			
	Bernstein	*Trouble in Tahiti*			
1953	Britten	*Gloriana*		Beckett: *Waiting for Godot*	Matisse: *L'Escargot*
	von Einem	*Der Prozess*			
1954	Copland	*The Tender Land*			
	Britten	*The Turn of the Screw*			
1955	Tippett	*A Midsummer Marriage*	Vietnam War begun		
	Floyd	*Susannah*			
1956	Henze	*König Hirsch*	Hungarian uprising crushed		
	Moore	*The Ballad of Baby Doe*			
1957	Poulenc	*Dialogues des Carmélites*	Treaty of Rome	Bergman: *The Seventh Seal*	
	Hindemith	*Der Harmonie der Welt*			
	Schoenberg	*Moses und Aron* (staged)			
1958	Barber	*Vanessa*			
	Pizzetti	*Assassinio nella Cattedrale*			
	Menotti	*Maria Golovin*			

(*cont.*)

Table A4.1 (*cont.*)

Date	Composer	Opera	Politics, etc.	Theatre and literature	Painting, etc.
1959	Poulenc	*La Voix Humaine*			1st Happenings in New York
	Prokofiev	*War and Peace* (1st version)			
1960	Britten	*A Midsumer Night's Dream*		Fellini: *La dolce vita*	
1961	Nono	*Intolleranza 1960*			Berlin Wall built
	Martinů	*The Greek Passion*			
	Henze	*Elegy for Young Lovers*			
1962	Tippett	*King Priam*	Cuban missile crisis		Warhol: *Soup Can*
1963				Fellini: *Otto e Mezzo*	
1964				Pasokini: *Il Vangelo Secondo Matteo*	
1965	Zimmermann	*Soldaten*			
	R. Rodney Bennett	*The Mines of Sulphur*			
	Henze	*Der Junge Lord*			
1966	Henze	*The Bassarids*			
	Crosse	*Purgatory*			
1967					Hockney: *A Bigger Splash*
1968	Birtwistle	*Punch and Judy*			
1969	Penderecki	*The Devils of Loudun*	1st man on the moon	Pound: *Drafts and Fragments of Cantos CX–CXVII*	
1970	Tippett	*The Knot Garden*		Peter Brook's *A Midsummer Night's Dream*	
	Britten	*Owen Wingrave*			
1972	P. Maxwell Davies	*Taverner*	Watergate		
1973	Britten	*Death in Venice*			
1974				English National Opera	
	Nono	*Al gran sole carico d'amore*	End of the Vietnam War		
	Kokkonen	*The Last Temptation*			

Table A4.1 (*cont.*)

Date	Composer	Opera	Politics, etc.	Theatre and literature	Painting, etc.
1976	Henze	*We Come to the River*			Christo: *Running Fence*
	Glass	*Einstein on the Beach*			
1977	Tippett	*The Ice Break*			
	Musgrave	*Mary Queen of Scotts*			
	Blake	*Toussaint*			
1978	Ligeti	*Le Grand Macabre*			
	Reimann	*Lear*			
	Sallinen	*The Red Line*			
1979	Berg	*Lulu* (3rd act completion)			
1980	P. Maxwell Davies	*The Lighthouse*			
	Glass	*Satyagraha*			
1981	Stockhausen	*Donnerstag* aus *Licht*			
1983	Berio	*Un re in ascolto*			
	Sallinen	*The King Goes Forth to France*			
	Glass	*Akhnaten*			
1986	Birtwistle	*The Mask of Orpheus*			
1987	Weir	*A Night at the Chinese Opera*			
	Adams	*Nixon in China*			
1988	Stockhausen	*Montag* aus *Licht*			
	Turnage	*Greek*			
1989	Tippett	*New Year*	Fall of the Berlin Wall		
1991	Adams	*The Death of Klinghoffer*			
	Schnittke	*Life with an Idiot*	Maastricht Treaty		
1993	Stockhausen	*Dienstag* aus *Licht*			
1994	Birtwistle	*The Second Mrs Kong*	Free universal election in South Africa		
	Adès	*Powder Her Face*			

(*cont.*)

Table A4.1 (*cont.*)

Date	Composer	Opera	Politics, etc.	Theatre and literature	Painting, etc.
1996	Henze	*Venus and Adonis*			Liebeskind Berlin Jewish Museum
1997	Tan Dun	*Marco Polo*			Centre Pomipdou, Paris
1998	Dove	*Flight*	Good Friday Agreement		
1999	Ruders	*The Handmaid's Tale*			Gehry: Bilbao Museum (1997)
2000	Turnage	*The Silver Tassie*			
	Saariaho	*L'Amour du Loin*			
2001	Sawyer	*From Morning to Midnight*	9/11 attack on USA		
2003	Dusapin	*Perelà Uomo di Fumo*	Invasion of Iraq		
2004	Dillon	*Philomela*			
	Adès	*The Tempest*			
2005	Barry	*Bitter Tears of Petra von Kant*			
2007	Dove	*Pinocchio*			
	Henze	*Phaedra*			
2008	MacMillan	*The Sacrifice*	Lehman Brothers collapses		
2011	Turnage	*Anna Nicole*			

Glossary of key terms

* = A term defined elsewhere in this glossary.

Aria	(It. 'Air, song'). A self-standing solo, traditionally melody-centred, usually introduced by a *recitativo** setting its context.
Arioso	(It. 'Aria-like'). Something between *recitativo** *accompagnato* and *aria**, usually dramatic, often lyrical, but rarely with the kind of structured melody of the *aria* proper.
Atonal	Music that does not follow the principles of tonal harmony, described by Schoenberg as emancipating harmonies outside traditional key relationships.
Ballad-opera	The English equivalent of *Singspiel** and, to a lesser extent, *Opéra-comique**. Operas alternating sung and spoken passages, but often with a strong accent on popular, ballad-like melody.
Bel canto	(It. Beautiful song/singing) Writing where the beauty of the vocal line is the dominant feature and means of expression.
Da capo aria	(It. 'From the head', i.e. top). An aria* in three parts (a–b–a) in which at the end of the second (b) section the (a) section is repeated 'from the top', usually with some stylistic changes or embellishments.
Dialectical	('Double reading'). The reading of a situation or statement so as to expose both its apparent meaning and its meaning as the expression of a particular attitude.
Dramaturgy	The structuring of all the elements of a drama so as to make a particular experience for the audience.
Grand opéra	(Fr. 'Large-scale opera'). Developed in the early nineteenth century in France as a deliberate process of aggrandisement of French culture. Typified by quasi-historical subjects, large-scale scenography, use of crowds, scenic effects and often including ballet.
Intermezzo	(It. 'Placed between', also *Intermedio*). Initially a short comic opera performed between the acts of an *opera seria**, but later developed into longer pieces as the origins of the *opera buffa**.
Leitmotif	(Ger. 'Leading motif'). Initially associated with Wagner; a musical figure, usually attached to a character or idea that then recurs in the course of the opera with the character, etc. or as a reminiscence.

Minimalism	Composition whose dominant characteristic is the use of short, repeated, melodic or rhythmic cells (Adams, Reich, Glass).
Narrative	The basic story as distinct from how it is treated in the *dramaturgy**.
Naturalism	A philosophical belief in the purely material nature of human life. Operas of this sort are usually concerned with contemporary working-class society. See *Realism**.
Numbers opera	An opera made up of separate, numbered, elements (*aria, duet, ensemble*, etc.) rather than *through-composed**.
Opera buffa	(It. 'Buffoon/comic opera'). The standard Italian form of comic opera, usually involving non-aristocratic characters and always *through-composed**.
Opèra-Comique	(Fr. Actors' opera). Opera mixing song with speech; can be either properly comic (Offenbach) or dramatic/tragic (*Carmen*). See *Ballad-opera, Singspiel.*
Opera seria	(It. 'Serious opera'). The serious, heroic, but rarely tragic, operatic form of the eighteenth* and early nineteenth centuries. The structure is dominated by the principles of Zeno and Metastasio.
Plot	Aristotle's 'ordered arrangement of the incidents'. See *Dramaturgy**.
Realism	Staging that looks real but where the characterisation and themes are not those of real life but an idealised, romanticised or fantasised version. See *Naturalism**.
Recitativo	(It. 'Recitation'). Sung text whose rhythms and accents are close to normal speech; often used to provide the context for the following aria, duet, etc. Up to the early part of the nineteenth century *recitative* could be either (i) *Secco* ('dry') or *semplice* (plain): accompanied only by continuo instruments and almost always conversational; or (ii) *Accompagnato*: accompanied by full orchestral forces, usually for more dramatic scenes.
Ritornello	(It. 'Little return'). In early opera the orchestral introduction which then returns between the different verses.
Scena	(It. 'Scene'). A complete dramatic entity, usually for a single character, that can include orchestral music, *aria**, *arioso**, *recitativo**, etc.
Serialism	Schoenberg's system of composition using a 'row' that includes all twelve pitches in the chromatic scale.
Singspiel	(Ger. 'Sing-play'). Opera with musical passages interspersed with spoken ones. There is no necessary implication of comic or tragic content. (See *Ballad-opera**, *Opéra-comique**).
Sprechgesang	(Ger. 'Speech-song') also *Sprechstimme* ('Speech voice'). A notated vocal line in which speech is pitched.
Strophe/strophic	Where the text, and therefore its setting, is a sequence of verses that repeat the basic melody, etc.

Symphonic	Used loosely, to mean that there is a sense of musical organisation analogous to that of the symphony with its integrated thematic structuring.
Tessitura	(It. 'Texture'). The vocal range of a part; how it 'lies' for the voice.
Through-composed	Where there is a musical continuum uninterrupted by speech.
Tonal, tonality	Music which can be described as being in a recognisable 'tonic' key, even if it departs from that key for extended passages.
Verfremdungseffekt	(Ger. 'Distancing or alienation effect'). Associated with Brecht. A device used to make the audience stand outside the *narrative** so that they can achieve an objective, *dialectical** understanding.

Notes

1 Pre-operatic forms

1. An interesting recreation of the *Favola* [*sic*] was made in 1981 by Paul van Nevel and the Huelgas Ensemble, transferred to CD on Sony SB2K 60095.
2. So, *Intermedio I* is called *L'armonia delle sfere* with *Intermedio II* continuing the harmony/music theme with the *Contest between the Muses and the Pierians*. This is followed by Apollo and his defeat of the Pythian monster which brought peace to the state of Delphi as well as the institution of the Delphic Oracle. Apollo is the god most associated with music – as well as truth, light, prophecy and healing, all to the good of the Medici. *Intermedio IV* is a prophecy of the Golden Age and is set in the underworld, where the demons bewail their future loss of souls to torment. In *Intermedio V*, the sea goddess Amphitryte rises from the sea to hymn the newly weds and then the character of Arion shows the eternal nature of music. Finally in *Intermedio VI* Apollo and Bacchus – god here of revelry and rejoicing – descend to join the Medici with Harmony and Rhythm.
3. In fact they were so celebrated that the designs were published.
4. Philip Pickett and the Musicians of the Globe. *The Masque of Oberon* on Philips 446217–2

2 First operatic forms

1. This choric function only starts to change with the Romantic period, when the chorus becomes increasingly individualised and a genuine part of the action.
2. Landi's *La morte d'Orfeo* (1619), a rather wayward treatment of the myth, includes a scene where Charon waives his objection to ferrying a living man across the Styx but is tempted by alcohol and sings a drinking song while becoming thoroughly inebriated.
3. When Caterina Martinelli, Monteverdi's pupil, who was intended to sing the eponymous role in his *Arianna*, died, the part was taken by Isabella Andreini, the leading actress with the famous *Compagnia dei Gelosi*.
4. The initial operas had had a classical five-act structure, but only insofar as there was a dramaturgical idea of the five episodes with a chorus between each of them. With growing production values and a more developed social context, the operas needed real act units with breaks in between, and the notional five acts frequently gave way to a non-classical, but more practical three-act structure.

3 Formalisation

1. The literary and dramatic *Académie Française* in 1635, the *Académie de Danse* in 1661, and the *Académie de l'Opéra* in 1671.
2. The 'Prologue' to Lully's 1696 *Armide* is a dialogue in which La Gloire and La Sagesse vie in praising Louis, and opens: 'Tout doit céder dans l'Univers/A l'auguste héros que j'aime' (All the Universe must yield/To the august hero whom I love).
3. And by extension the *opera buffa* (comic opera), although this was rarely their main concern.
4. This is not mechanical, however, and there are exceptions as the drama requires. Act I, scene i consists of a *recitativo accompagnato* and a chorus; act II, scene i and act III, scene viii each begin with an aria; there are two duets (nos. 60 and 86), a quartet (no. 89) and an ensemble (no. 94). In some cases two or more recitatives follow one another (nos. 22 and 23; 25 and 26; 32 and 33; 64, 65 and 66; 92 and 93); two arias (nos. 13 and 57) are preceded by a *sinfonia* rather than a recitative.
5. Sometimes the repeat is not from the very beginning but a few bars in, where there is a sign, hence *dal segno*.
6. *Don Carlos*, iv.i (Modena, 1866 five-act version).
7. *Die Walküre*, ii.ii.
8. This is sometimes referred to as the *Affektenlehre* (Doctrine of the affections) although, while the matter was of great and widespread concern, there was no single 'doctrine' as such.
9. In the 1731 revision used here (Händel, 1996: xxiii). In the 1711 original an extra aria for Eustazio ended scene viii. In 1731 the role (and therefore the aria) were cut, resulting in a tighter structure.
10. *Siroe*, adapted by Haym, 1728; *Poro*, adapted from *Alessandro nell'Indie*, 1731; *Ezio* in an adaptation, 1732. He had also used two of Zeno's libretti: *Faramondo*, 1738; *Alessandro Severo*, 1738.
11. Five from *Lotario* and one each from *Partenope*, *Admeto* and *Giulio Cesare*.
12. *Alessandro* was adapted in 1731 as Handel's *Poro*.
13. Radice (1998: 103–4).
14. See Joseph Addison's essay of 6 March 1711 in *The Spectator* which describes, and mocks, the production – including the use of real birds (Strunk, 1998: 683–6).
15. And would remain so until the end of the nineteenth century when gas and then electricity enabled lighting to be controlled and lowered.
16. Other than the acts being divided between several locations, no doubt in order to emphasise the splendour of the premiere: i.i The port of Alexandria; i.vii An apartment in Ptolemy's palace; i.x A large courtyard: ii.i A vast plain outside the city; ii.vi Cleopatra's apartments; ii.x A vast plain with ruins; ii.xi A spacious courtyard; ii.xv A splendid temple; iii.i A large parade ground; iii.iii Cleopatra's apartments; iii.xi A great hall.

4 Reform: the reintegration of elements

1. Such as Handel's *pasticcii Elipidia, Ormisda* or *Venceslao*, from music by Hasse, Vinci, Poppora and Orlandini.
2. There were travellers and collectors who had gone to Greece at least from the mid sixteenth century, but they were isolated examples and without the desire or ability to undertake anything like scientific exploration of the antiquities.
3. The timings are those of the recording by Frieder Bernious on the *Orfeo* label, C 381 953 F, 1995.
4. An *opera seria*, two *intermezzi*, five *Singspiele* and an *operetta* for children.

5 Comedy and the 'real world'

1. See below.
2. The term 'comic opera' is used here to include all operas with a comic strain. It does not refer to the later French *opéra comique* which included works ranging from high tragedy to low comedy proper but always mixing the spoken and sung word.
3. There are examples of the serious or tragic *intermezzo*, really short operas that avoid the structure of the *opera seria*, such as Hasse's 1770 *Piramo e Tisbe* to a libretto by Coltellini. Hasse considered this as one of his finest works.
4. *Commedia dell'arte* players played a role in the earliest opera, including work with Monteverdi.

6 Authentic performance

1. The singer is the subject of Chapter 12. Here, we are only concerned with elements that derive from notions of 'authenticity'.
2. This raises questions that are the subject of Chapter 18.

7 Romanticism and Romantic opera in Germany

1. See Tables 3.3a and 3.3b.
2. *Fidelio* is in fact the fourth setting of the libretto:
   1790 Pierre Gaveaux. *Léonore, ou l'amour conjugal*, set in Spain
   1804 Ferdinando Paer: *Leonora, ossia l'amore conjugale*, set in Spain
   1805 Simon Mayr: *Amor coniugale*, set in Poland.
3. In particular, he worked with the theatrical experimenter and dramatist, Ludwig Tieck for whose festival *Midsummer Night's Dream* Mendelssohn wrote his incidental music and which was presented in one of the earliest attempts to recreate the Elizabethan stage.

8 Opera in nineteenth-century Italy

1. *The New Grove Dictionary of Opera* (*Grove*, 1997) has full articles on each, giving their historical developments and definitions.

2. The word probably implies something 'carved out' of the narrative text to enable the aria to take place.

3. The tripartite structure and its elements are examined in detail on p. 131, but what is apparent already is that its forward dynamic is quite different to the equally conventional three sections of the *da capo* aria with its return to the opening contemplation. It is instructive to look back at the way Handel needed a sequence of three *da capo* aria scenes to move Rinaldo from supine desolation to action (see Chapter 3, Tables 3.3a and 3.3b).

4. But not the traditional, hugely extended *cadenza* with flute solo. This was, almost certainly added at the end of the nineteenth century for Melba 'after Donizetti's death, and is stylistically distant from the kind of *cadenza* he would have written' (Dotto and Park, 2003, ii: 442).

9 *Grand opéra* and the visual language of opera

1. In this chapter 'Grand opera' will: (a) refer to the genre proper; (b) be used rather than the French '*Grand Opéra*'; the word 'Opéra' will refer to the 'principal opera company of Paris' with its various changes of title and venue since 1794 (see *Grove*, 1997, iii: 866).

2. E.g: act i: Antonio's 'La danse n'est pas ce que j'aime'; Laurette's 'Je crains de lui parler la nuit'; Blondel's 'O Richard; Blondel and Laurette's 'Un bandeau couvre les yeux'; the act iii trio 'Le gouverneur, pendant la danse'; the rondo 'Et zic et zic et zic'.

3. Grétry even shows early interest in mediaeval music, writing the strings to sound like antique instruments in the Blondel/Richard duet.

4. The bar-graph presentation does not pretend to be absolute or scientific. The table is intended to indicate how the overall structure can be approached and understood.

10 The Wagnerian revolution

1. The last example of complex plotting is in *Götterdämmerung* with its magic potion, changed and mistaken identities. This apparent throwback to earlier structures is because it was the first part of *The Ring* libretto to be written.

2. The legendary/historical *Nibelungenlied* has a rhymed strophic structure.

3. In this respect alone it is interesting to compare the opening Preludes of *Parsifal* and *Lohengrin*.

4. This is the subject of endless discussion, but for a fascinating gloss, see D. Cooke (1979), in particular the introductory section 'The unsolved problem'.

11 Nationalists: vernacular language and music

1. Two especially good studies of this complexity, show to what extent even the composers themselves made assumptions that actually contradicted or potentially invalidated their intentions (Tyrrell, 1988; Taruskin, 2000).

2. Despite his strong nationalism, Smetana was never able to completely master Czech either as speaker or in his word setting.
3. Available on Manchester Files CDMAN 179 (Classical Gallery).
4. These and other pieces of the period are available on *Music from the court of St Petersburg*, vols. II and VI (*OPUS111*, OPS 30–179, 1996 and OPS 30–231, 1998).
5. *The New Grove Dictionary of Opera* (*Grove*, 1997) lists more than one hundred operas based on Pushkin's works.
6. The main groups were the Union of Welfare and the Union of Salvation which then split into the Northern and Southern Groups in 1822.
7. The *Peredvizhniki* (The society for circulating art exhibitions), founded in 1870, whose work covered all aspects of Russian rural and urban life.

12 The role of the singer

1. The last of these is both fascinating and important but beyond the scope of this chapter. A model for pursuing the subject is provided by Rosselli (1995) and Potter (2000).

13 The turn of the century and the crisis in opera

1. See Chapter 9.
2. In fact, Mascagni and his librettists followed Verga's own dramatisation, although with knowledge of, and reference to, the original story.
3. Only the first two novels, depicting the lower levels of society, *I Malavoglia* and *Mastro-Don Gesualdo*, were completed.
4. The precedent to which Mascagni appealed was the Prelude to Rossini's *Ermione*.
5. Puccini famously responded positively to such modern composers as Debussy and Schoenberg, and scores such as *Il Tabarro*, *La Fanciulla del West* and *Turandot* show clear evidence of their influence.
6. He had been sent to Bayreuth by Ricordi in 1888 to prepare a cut version of *Die Meistersinger* for its first Italian performance.
7. At an earlier stage, Verdi had admired the subject.
8. The following were all written prior to *Salome*: *Aus Italien*, 1886; *Macbeth*, 1886–8; *Don Juan*, 1888–9; *Tod und Verklärung*, 1888–9; *Till Eulenspiegel*, 1894–5; *Also Sprach Zarathustra*, 1895–6; *Don Quixote*, 1896–7; *Ein Heldenleben*, 1897–8; *Symphonia Domestica*, 1902–3.
9. These examples all come from *Götterdämmerung* which, although the last to be composed, had the first text of the cycle to be written and retains the greatest resemblance to the standard libretto.

14 First modernism: Symbolist and Expressionist opera

1. He did, however, design and produce a number of other works including Gluck's *Orfeo ed Euridice*, *Hamlet* and *King Lear*,

2. See the comparative table in Jarman (1989: 12–15).
3. Perle (1980) lists and explores nineteen motifs.

15 The dramaturgy of opera: libretto – words and structures

1. The actual plots are not especially complicated. The difficulty arises because so much that has happened before the operas begins is left to be slowly revealed, leaving the audience in some bewilderment.
2. Morra (2007: 106).
3. 'Peripeteia' (reversal) and 'anagnorisis' (discovery) are straightforward. 'Pathos' is usually translated as 'suffering' or 'calamity' in this context, but literally means 'feeling' – in this respect the feeling appropriate to the tragic climax. See Aristotle (1965: 40–2) or (1970: 46–7).

16 Narrative opera: realistic and non-realistic

1. Translations are the singing version given in the score and not, therefore, literal as elsewhere.

18 Directors and the direction of opera

1. The words 'director' and producer' are used as synonyms in this chapter. Until recently 'director' was mainly used in the theatre and 'producer' in opera, but this has changed, especially with the increasing using of theatre directors in the opera house.
2. In Germany from the 1830s onwards there were moves by men such as Ludwig Tieck to investigate the staging of Elizabethan drama, which eventually fed into a radical new kind of production; but this was on the fringes of mainstream theatre and opera.

Appendix 2

1. Interestingly, it is just this quality that many reviewers have found lacking in Placido Domingo's upper register in *Simon Boccanegra* where he has assumed the central, baritone role.

Bibliography

Abbate, Carolyn, 1989. '*Opera as Symphony: A Wagnerian Myth*', in Carolyn Abbate and Roger Parker (eds.), University of California Press, Berkeley

Achten, Nicolas, 2008. Liner Notes in Caccini, *L'Euridice*, Scherzi Musicali, Ricercar 269

Adams, John, 2008. *Hallelujah Junction: Composing an American Life*, Faber & Faber, London

Adams, J.Q., 1924. 'Regularis Concordia of St Ethelwold', in *Chief Pre-Shakespearean Dramas*, Houghton Mifflin, Boston, MA

Adorno, Theodor, 1991. *Alban Berg: Master of the Smallest Link* (trans. J. Brand and C. Hailey), Cambridge University Press

2005. *In Search of Wagner* (trans. R. Livingstone), Verso, London

Ainsley, John Mark, 2007. Interview broadcast by BBC Radio 3, *Music Matters*, 16 January

Algarotti, Francesco, 1755. *Saggio sopra l'opera in musica* (trans. anon), in O. Strunk (ed.), *Source Readings in Music History*, rev. edn., W.W. Norton, New York and London, 1998

Allison, John, 2005. Review in *Gramophone Magazine*, September

Anderson, E. (trans.), 1990. *Mozart's Letters*, Barrie & Jenkins, London

Anderson, J.J. (ed.), 1977. *Patience*, Manchester University Press

Aristotle,1965. *Poetics*, Loeb Classical Library, William Heinemann, London and Harvard University Press, Cambridge, MA

1970. *Poetics*, in *Classical Literary Criticism* (trans. T. S. Dorsch), Penguin Books, London

Arni, Erkkii, 1987. 'The King's Story', in Royal Opera House Covent Garden programme for *The King Goes Forth to France*, April

Auden, W.H., 1956. *Metalogue to the Magic Flute*

1962. *The Dyer's Hand*, Faber & Faber, London

Auden, W.H. and Kallman, C., 1993. *Libretti and Other Dramatic Writings by W. H. Auden, 1939–1973* (ed. Edward Mendelson), Faber & Faber, London

Balthazar, Scott L. (ed.), 2004. *The Cambridge Companion to Verdi*, Cambridge University Press

Barbier, Patrick, 1995. *Opera in Paris, 1800–1850* (trans. R. Luoma), Amadeus Press, Portland, OR

Bardi, Pietro de', 1634. *Letter to Giovanni Battista Doni*, in O. Strunk (ed.), *Source Readings in Music History*, rev. edn., W.W. Norton, New York and London, 1998

414

Barth, Herbert, Dietrich Mack and Egan Voss, 1975. *Wagner: A Documentary Study*, Thames & Hudson, London

Bauman, Thomas, 1985. *Northern German Opera in the Age of Goethe*, Cambridge University Press

Becker, Heinz and Gudrun, 1993. *Giacomo Meyerbeer: A Life in Letters*, Christopher Helm, London

Belinsky, V.G., 1976. *Thoughts and Notes on Russian Literature, in Belinsky, Chernyshevsky and Dobrolyubov: Selected Criticism*, Ralph E. Maw (ed. and trans.), Indiana University Press, Bloomington and London

Benedetti, Jean Norman, 1988. *Stanislavski: A Biography*, Methuen Drama, London

Bentley, E. (ed.), 1968. *The Theory of the Modern Stage*, Penguin Books, London

Berio, Luciano, 2006. *Remembering the Future*, Harvard University Press, Cambridge, MA and London

Berlioz, Hector, 1970. *The Memoirs of Berlioz* (trans. D. Cairns), Panther, London

Biondi, Fabio, 2009. Interview in *BBC Music Magazine*, February

Birtwistle, Harrison, 1986. 'Composer and Producer Speak', in the programme for *The Mask of Orpheus*, English National Opera

Bowen, Meirion, 1997. *Michael Tippett*, Robson Books, London

Brecht Bertolt, 1948. *Antigonemodel*, trans., Gebrüder Weiss, Berlin
 1978. *Brecht on Theatre*, ed. and trans. John Willett. Eyre & Methuen, London

  (i) 'On Gestic Music'
  (ii) 'Notes to the Opera *Aufstieg und Fall der Stadt Mahagonny*

Brook, Stephen, 1995. *Opera: A Penguin Anthology*, Viking, New York

Brown, David, 1974. *Mikhail Glinka: A Biographical and Critical Study*, Oxford University Press, London
 1982. *Tchaikovsky: A Biographical and Critical Study*, 2 vols., Victor Gollanz, London

Bucarelli, Maura (ed.), 1992. *Rossini 1792–1992: mostro storico-documentario*, Electa, Perugia

Budden, Julian, 2002. *Puccini: His Life and Works*, Oxford University Press

Burke, Edmund, 2003. *A Philosophical Inquiry into the Origin of our Ideas of the Sublime and the Beautiful*, 1757, in C. Harrison, P. Wood and J. Gaiger, *Art in Theory 1648–1815*, Blackwell Publishing, Oxford

Burney, Charles, 1957. *A General History of Music*, 1799, 2 vols., Dover, London
 1981. *Memoirs of the Life and Writings of the Abate Metastasio*, 3 vols., 1796, in D. Kimbell, *Verdi in the Age of Italian Romanticism*, Cambridge University Press

Cairns, David. 1999. *Berlioz*, 2 vols., Penguin, London
 2006. *Mozart and his Operas*, Allen Lane, London

Carnegie, Patrick, 2006. *Wagner and the Art of the Theatre*, Yale University Press, New Haven and London

Carner, Mosco (ed.), 1974. *Letters of Puccini*, Harrap, London
 1992. *Puccini*, Duckworth, London

Caro, Roberto de, 1992. Liner Notes to Peri, *Euridice*, Ensemble Arpeggio, Arts 47276–2

Carter, Tim, 2008. 'Ah, Virtue hide yourself', in Glyndbourne Festival Opera programme, *Poppea*

Casati, Marisa di Gregorio and Marco Marica n.d. *Per amore di Verdi: vita, immagini, ritratti*, Grafiche Step, Parma

Cavalieri, Emilio de', 1970. *Rappresentatione di anima e di corpo*, Archiv 2708 016, 1970

Charlton, David (ed.), 2003. *The Cambridge Companion to Grand Opera*, Cambridge University Press

Clarke, M. and C. Crisp, 1973. *Ballet: An Illustrated History*, Hamish Hamilton, London

Clements, Andrew, 2000. *Mark-Anthony Turnage*, Faber & Faber, London

Cobban, Alfred, 1990. *A History of Modern France: 1715–1799*, vol. 1, Penguin, London

Cochrane, Peggy, 1970. Note before Finale of act II, in libretto booklet to Decca SET 460–3

Collins, Michael and Elise Kirk (eds.), 1984. *Opera and Vivaldi*, University of Texas, Austin

Conati, Marcello (ed.), 1986. *Encounters with Verdi* (trans R. Stokes), Cornell University Press, Ithaca

Conati, Marcello and Mario Medici, 1994. *The Verdi–Boito Correspondence*, trans. W. Weaver, University of Chicago Press

Cooké, Deryck, 1979. *I Saw the World End: A Study of Wagner's 'Ring'*, Clarendon Press, Oxford

Cooke, Mervyn, 1999. *The Cambridge Companion to Benjamin Britten*, Cambridge University Press 2005

  2005. *The Cambridge Companion to Twentieth-Century Opera*, Cambridge University Press

Cooper, Barry, 2000. *Beethoven*, Oxford University Press

Cooper, Martin, 1956. 'Christoph Willibald Gluck', *The Decca Book of Opera*, Werner Laurie, London

Corghi, A. (ed.), 1981. *Edizione critica delle opere di Gioachino Rossini: Sezione prima – opera teatrali, Volume II 'L'Italiana in Algeri'*, Fondazione Rossini, Pesaro

Cowart, Georgia J, 2008. *The Triumph of Pleasure: Louis XIV and the Politics of Spectacle*, University of Chicago Press

Cross, Eric, 1981. *The Late Operas of Antonio Vivaldi, 1727–1738*, 2 vols., UMI Research Press, Ann Arbor

Cross, Jonathan, 1997. Introduction to Birtwistle, *The Mask of Orpheus*, NMC D050

  2000. *Harrison Birtwistle: Man, Mind, Music*, Faber & Faber

  2003. *The Cambridge Companion to Stravinsky*, Cambridge University Press

Curtis, Alan (ed.), 1989. Monteverdi, *L'incoronazione di Poppea*, 'Preface', Novello, London

Dahlhaus, Carl, 1979. *Richard Wagner's Music Dramas* (trans. Mary Whittall), Cambridge University Press

  1987. *Schoenberg and the New Music* (trans. D. Puffett and A. Clayton), Cambridge University Press

Dean, Winton, 1970. *Handel and the Opera Seria*, Oxford University Press

  2006. *Handel's Operas 1726–1741*, Boydell Press, Woodbridge

Deathridge, John, 2008. *Wagner Beyond Good and Evil*, University of California Press, Berkeley

Debussy, Claude, 1902. *Musica*, in O. Strunk (ed.), *Source Readings in Music History*, rev. edn., W.W. Norton, New York and London, 1998

   1913. *La revue musicale S.I.M.*, in O. Strunk (ed.), *Source Readings in Music History*, rev. edn., W.W. Norton, New York and London, 1998

   1964. Libretto for *Pelléas et Mélisande*, Decca SET 277–9

Del Mar, Norman, 1962. *Richard Strauss: A Critical Commentary on his Life and Works*, 3 vols., Barrie & Rockliff, London

Dent, Edward J., 1965. *Foundations of English Opera*, Da Capo Press, New York

Diderot, Denis, 1760s/1770s. *Rameau's Nephew*, in O. Strunk (ed.), *Source Readings in Music History*, rev. edn., W.W. Norton, New York and London, 1998

Directors in Opera, 2 parts, 2006/7, Opera Magazine, London

Donizetti, Gaetone, n.d. *Lucia di Lammermoor*, Kalmus edn., Miami, Florida

Donnington, Robert, 1969. *Wagner's 'Ring' and Its Symbols*, Faber & Faber, London

Dotto, Gabrielle and Parker, Roger (eds.), 2003. *Donizetti: Lucia di Lammeer mor, Critical Edition*, Ricordi/Fondazione Donizetti di Bergamo, 2 vols.

Dove, Jonathan, 2007. *Programme for Pinocchio*, Opera North

Downey, Charles, 2007. *The Melancholy Dusapin, Ionarts*, March 3

Downing, A. Thomas, 2002. *Aesthetics of Opera in the Ancien Régime 1647–1785*, Cambridge University Press

Duggan, Christopher, 2008. *The Force of Destiny: A History of Italy since 1796*, Penguin Books, London

Dukore, Bernard, F. (ed.), 1974. *Dramatic Theory and Criticism: Greeks of Grotowski*, Harcourt, New York

Dusapin, Pascal, 2004. 'Interview with Pascal Dusapin' (A. Gindt), in Liner Notes for *Perelà, uomo di fumo*, Naïve MO 782168

Eliot, T.S, 1969. *The Sacred Wood*, Methuen, London

Evans, Peter, 1996. *The Music of Benjamin Britten*, Clarendon Press, Oxford

Fauré, Gabriel, 1907. Review of *Salome* in *Le Figaro*, 9 May

Filipski, Kevin, 1992. Amazon.com review of Richard Strauss, *Salome*. ROH Covent Garden

Friedrich, Caspar David, 2003. Letter to Professor Schultze, 8 February 1809, in C. Harrison, P. Wood and J. Gaiger, *Art in Theory 1648–1815*, Blackwell Publishing, Oxford

Galatopoulos, Stelios, 2002. *Bellini: Life, Times, Music*, Sanctuary Publishing, London

Gänzl, Kurt, 1987. *The British Musical Theatre*, 2 vols., Macmillan, London

   1997. *The Musical*, Northeastern University Press, Boston

Gardner, Edward, 2010. Interview in *Inside ENO*, Issue 17/Spring

Gerhard, Ansel, 1988 (trans. Mary Whittall), *The Urbanization of Opera*, University of Chicago Press, Chicago and London

Giles, Peter, 1993. *The History and Technique of the Counter-Tenor*, Scolar Press, Aldershot and Ashgate, Brookfield, VT

Gindt, Antoine, 1990. 'Synopsis', in section 'Texte', for Pascal Dusapin, *Romeo et Juliette*, Accord 201162

Girardi, Michele, 2000 (trans. Laura Basini). *Puccini: His International Art*, University of Chicago Press, Chicago and London

Glass, Philip, 1999 (ed. Richard Kostelanetz). *Writings on Glass: Essays, Interviews, Criticism*, University of California Press, Berkeley, Los Angeles and London

Glinka, Mikhail, 1965. *Ivan Susanin*, 3 vols., Yedatelstvo 'Moskva', Moscow (libretto in vol. I is of *A Life for the Tsar* and not as in the printed score).

Gluck, C.W.W., *Alceste* 1988. *Christoph Willibald Gluck. Sämtliche Werke.* 1.3.a. Ed. G. Croll. Bärenreiter, Kassel

Goethe, J.W., *Italian Journey* (trans. author)

Goldman, A. and E. Sprinchorn, 1970. *Wagner on Music and Drama*, Dutton, London

Goldoni, Carlo, 1992. *Mémoires de M. Goldoni* (1797), Aubier, Paris

Goodman, Alice, 2000. 'Forging Nixon', in *Nixon in China*, English National Opera programme, June

Gramophone, 2009a. *Gramophone Magazine*, August
    2009b. Interview with Cyndia Sieden, December

Graubard, Stephen, 1986. *The Future of Opera*, The Daedalus Library, Lanham and London

Grayson, D. A., 1986. *The Genesis of Debussy's 'Pelléas et Mélisande'*, UMI Research Press, Ann Arbor

Griffiths, Paul, 1982. *Igor Stravinsky: 'The Rake's Progress'*, Cambridge University Press
    1996. 'The Soldiers' Tales', in English National Opera programme, *Die Soldaten*

Grimm, Jakob, 1966. *Teutonic Mythology*, vol. III (trans J. S. Stallybrass), Dover, New York

Grimm, Jakob and Wilhelm, 2009. *Selected Tales* (trans. J. Crick), Oxford University Press

Grossman, Vassily, 2010. *Everthing Flows* (trans. R. and E. Chandler), Harvill Secner, London

Grout, Donald and Margaret, 2003. *A Short History of Opera*, Columbia University Press, New York

Grove, 1980. *New Grove Dictionary of Music and Musicians* (ed. S. Sadi, 20 vol., Macmillan, London, 1980
    1997. *New Grove Dictionary of Opera* (ed. S. Sadie), 4 vols., Macmillan, London

Gutman, Robert, 1971. *Richard Wagner: The Man, his Mind and his Music*, Pelican Books, London
    1999. *Mozart: A Cultural Biography*, Secker & Warburg, London

Hako, Pekka, 2006 'A Fairy-Tale for Grown-Ups', in liner booklet for *The King Goes Forth to France*, Ondine, ODE 1066–2D

Hall, Michael, 1984. *Harrison Birtwistle*, Robson Books, London
    1996. *Leaving Home*, Faber and Faber, London
    1998. *Harrison Birtwistle in Recent Years*, Robson Books, London

Händel, G.F. 1996. *Rinaldo*, 1731 rev. ed. David Kimbell, Bärenreiter, Kassel, etc.

Happé, Peter, 1975. *English Mystery Plays*. Penguin, London

Heartz, Daniel, 1990. *Mozart's Operas*, University of California Press, Berkeley

Heller, Karl, 1997. *Antonio Vivaldi: The Red Priest of Venice* (trans. D Marinelli), Amadeus Press, Portland, OR

Henze Hans Werner, 1974. '*The Bassarids*: Hans Werner Henze talks to Paul Griffith', *The Musical Times*, no. 580, vol. 115, October

    1982. *Music and Politics: Collected Writings 1953–81* (trans. P. Labanyi), Faber & Faber, London

    1996. 'Henze's New Opera', in *Opera*, vol. 17, no. 8, August

    1998. *Bohemian Fifths: An Autobiography* (trans. S. Spencer), Faber & Faber, London

Herbert, David, 1979. *The Operas of Benjamin Britten*, Hamish Hamilton, London

Hibberd, Sarah, 2009. *French Grand Opera and the Historical Imagination*, Cambridge University Press

Hill, Aaron, 1987. *Preface* to the *Rinaldo Wordbook*, 1711, in C. Hogwood, *Handel*, Thames & Hudson, London

Hofmannsthal, Hugo von, 1927. *Correspondence between Richard Strauss and Hugo von Hofmannsthal 1907–1918* (trans P. England), Martin Secker, London

Hogwood, C. 1984. *Handel*, Thames & Hudson, London

Hollander, H., 1963. *Leoš Janáček: His Life and Work* (trans. Paul Hamburger), John Calder, London

Hope-Wallace, Philip, 1959. *A Picture History of Opera*, Edward Hulton, London

Hosking, Geoffrey, 1998. *Russia: People and Empire 1552–1917*, Fontana, London

Howard, Patricia, 1969. *The Operas of Benjamin Britten: An Introduction*, Barrie & Rockliff, London

    1995. *Gluck: An Eighteenth-Century Portrait in Letters and Documents*, Clarendon Press, Oxford

Hugo Victor, 1827. 'Preface' to *Cromwell*, in Berhard F. Dukore (ed.), *Dramatic Theory and Criticism*, Harcourt, New York, 1994

    1963. *Hernani*, Les petits classiques Bordas, Paris

Hutchings, Arthur, 1964. 'Introduction', in Gluck, *Orfeo ed Euridice*, Decca SET 443–4

Ibsen Henrik, 1970. Review of Karl Gutzkow's *Zopf und Schwert*, 13 April 1851, in James McFarlane (ed.), *Henrik Ibsen: Penguin Critical Anthologies*, Penguin, London

Janáček Leoš, 1992 (?). *Kát'a Kabanová*, ed. Charles Mackerras, Universal Edition, New York

Jarman, Douglas, 1989. *Alban Berg: Wozzeck*, Cambridge University Press

Jarocinski, S., 1976. *Debussy: Impressionism and Symbolism* (trans. R. Meyers), Eulenburg Books, London

Jefferson, A., 1985. *Richard Strauss: Der Rosenkavalier*, Cambridge University Press

Johnson, Victoria, 2008. *Backstage at the Revolution: How the Royal Paris Opéra Survived the End of the Old Regime*, University of Chicago Press

Jordan, Ruth, 1994. *Fromental Halévy*, Kahn & Averill, London

Keefe, Simon (ed.), 2003. *The Cambridge Companion to Mozart*, Cambridge University Press

Kemp, Ian, 1987. *Tippett: The Composer and his Music*, Oxford University Press

Kennedy, Michael, 1999. *Richard Strauss: Man, Musician, Enigma*, Cambridge University Press

Kenny, Elizabeth, 2008. 'Introduction', in Purcell, *Dido and Aeneas*, Chandos 0757

Kerman, Joseph, 1956. *Opera as Drama*, Alfred A. Knopf, New York

Kesting, Jürgen, 1966. *Luciano Pavarotti: The Myth of the Tenor*, Robson Books, London
  1992. *Maria Callas* (trans. John Hunt), Quartet Books, London

Kildea, Paul, 2000. *Britten on Music*, Oxford University Press

Kimbell, David, 1981. *Verdi in the Age of Italian Romanticism*, Cambridge University Press
  1991. *Italian Opera*, Cambridge University Press
  1998. *Vincenzo Bellini: Norma*, Cambridge Opera Handbooks, Cambridge University Press

Kinderman, William, 1995. *Beethoven*, Oxford University Press

Koch, Heinrich, 1998. *Introductory Essay on Composition*, vol. ii., part 2, section 3, 1787, in O. Strunk (ed.), *Source Readings in Music History*, (rev. edn.), W.W. Norton, New York and London

Kurtz, Michael, 1988. *Stockhausen: A Biography*, Faber & Faber, London

Large, Brian, 1970. *Smetana*, Duckworth, London

Lawrence, Richard, 2008. *Danielle de Nise: Handel Arias*, in *Gramophone Magazine*, June

Leyda, Jay and Sergei Bertensson, 1947. *The Mussorgsky Reader: A Life of Modest Mussorgsky in Letters and Documents*, W.W. Norton, New York

Lockspeiser, E., 1963. *Debussy*, Dent, London

Machlis, Joseph, n.d. 'The Early Vocal Works of Arnold Schoenberg', in *The Music of Arnold Schoenberg*, vol. 4, Gould/Gramm/Vanni (LP), CBS 72459/70 [MET 2012]

Maes, Francis, 2000 (trans. A.J. and E. Pomerans). *A History of Russian Music*, University of California Press, Berkeley, Los Angeles and London

Maeterlinck, Maurice, 1896. *The Tragic in Daily Life*, 1896, in Berhard F. Dukore (ed.) *Dramatic Theory and Criticism*, Harcourt, New York, 1974
  1904. *The Modern Drama*, in Bernard F. Dukore, (ed.) *Dramatic Theory and Criticism*, Harcourt, New York, 1974

Magee, Bryan, 2000. *Wagner and Philosophy*, Allen Lane, London

Mahler, Alma, 1968. *Gustav Mahler: Memories and Letters* (ed. Donald Mitchell), John Murray, London

Mallarmé, Stéphane, 1994. *Stéphane Mallarmé: Collected Poems* (trans. Henry Weinfield), University of California Press, Berkeley, Los Angeles and London

Mann, William (trans.), 1970. *Der Ring des Nibelungen*, 2 vols., The Friends of Covent Garden, London

March, Ivan *et al.* (eds.), 2008. *The Penguin Guide to Recorded Classical Music 2008*, Penguin, London

Massenet, Jules, 1970. *My Recollections*, Greenwood Press, Westport

Matheopoulos, Helena, 1998. *Diva: The New Generation*, Little, Brown & Company, London

Matteson, Johann, *Der vollkommene Capellmeister*, part ii, 1739, in O. Strunk (ed.), *Source Readings in Music History*, rev. edn., W.W. Norton, New York and London, 1998

Matthews, Colin, 1997. 'Introduction' to Libretto of Birtwistle, *The Mask of Time*, NMC D050

Maw, Ralph, E. (ed. and trans.), 1976. *Belinsky, Chernyshevsky and Dobrolyubov: Selected Criticism*, Indiana University Press, Bloomington and London

May, Thomas, 2006. *The John Adams Reader: Essential Writings on an American Composer*, Amadeus Press, Portland, OR

McFarlane, James (ed.), 1970. *Henrik Ibsen*, Penguin, London

Mercadante, Saverio, 1831. Letter of 23 November 1831, catalogue reference XIII.7.21(100 in the library of S. Pietro a Majella, Naples Conservatorium of Music (trans. author)

   1838. Letter of 1 January 1838, catalogue reference XIII.7.21(100 in the library of S. Pietro a Majella, Naples Conservatorium of Music (trans. author)

Metastasio, Pietro, 1761. *Opere del Signore Abate Petro Metastasio Romano Poeta Cesareo*, vol. III, Rome, 1761

Meyer, Martin, 1983. *The Met: One Hundred Years of Grand Opera*, Thames & Hudson, London

Meyer, Stephen, 2003. *Carl Maria von Weber and the Search for German Opera*, Indiana University Press, Bloomington and Indianapolis

Meyerbeer, Giacomo, 1980. Les Huguenots, Philip Gosset and Charles Rosen (eds.), *The Garland Series of Early Romantic Opera*, Garland Publishing, New York and London

Miller, Richard, 1996. *On the Art of Singing*, Oxford University Press

Millington, Barry (ed.), 1992a. *The Wagner Companion*, Thames & Hudson, London

  1992b. *Wagner*, in *The Master Musicians* series, J.M. Dent, London

Milner, Anthony, 1956. 'George Frederick Handel', in *The Decca Book of Opera*, Werner Laurie, London

Monteverdi, Claudio, *Giulio Cesare, Explanation of the Letter Printed in the Fifth book of Madrigals* (1607) in O. Strunk (ed.), *Source Readings in Music History*, rev. edn., W.W. Norton, New York and London, 1998

Morra, Irene, 2007. *Twentieth-Century British Authors and the Rise of Opera in Britain*, Ashgate, Aldershot

Musorgsky, Modest, 1975. *Boris Godunov* (ed. David Lloyd-Jones), Oxford University Press

Newman, Ernest, 1968. *Wagner Nights*, Putnam & Co., London

Nichols, Roger, 1992. *Debussy Remembered*, Faber & Faber, London and Boston

Nichols, Roger and Richard Langham Smith, 1989. *Claude Debussy: Pelléas et Mélisande*, Cambridge University Press

Nietzsche, Friedrich, 1971. *Also sprach Zarathustra* (trans R.J. Hollindale), Penguin, London

Nono, Luigi, 1999a. In Jürg Stenzl, 'Stories: Luigi Nono's "Theatre of Consciousness"' (trans. A. Clayton), CD notes, Teldec Newline 8573–81059–2

  1999b. In 'Luigi Nono, *Al gran sole carico d'amore*' (trans. A. Clayton), CD notes, Teldec Newline 8573–81059–2

Oliver, Michael, 1996. *Benjamin Britten*, Phaidon Press., London

Orledge, R., 1982. *Debussy and the Theatre*, Cambridge University Press

Osborne, Charles (ed.), 1971. *Letters of Giuseppe Verdi*, Victor Gollancz, London

Osborne, Richard, 1993. *Rossini*, The Dent Master Musicians, J. M. Dent, London

Osmond-Smith, David, 1991. *Berio*, Oxford University Press

Pacini, Giovanni, 1875. *Le mie memorie artistiche*, Chapter xi (F. Magnani ed.), Florence (trans. author)

Pendle, Karin, 1979. *Eugène Scribe and French Opera of the Nineteenth Century*, UMI Research Press, Ann Arbor

Peri, Jacopo, 'Preface' to *The Music for Euridice* in O. Strunk (ed.), *Source Readings in Music History*', rev. edn., W.W. Norton, New York and London, 1998

Perle, George, 1980. *The Operas of Alban Berg, Volume One / Wozzekc*, University of California Press, Berkeley, Los Angeles and London

Phillips-Matz, Mary Jane, 1993. *Verdi: A Biography*, Oxford University Press

Pollard, Stephen, 2010. 'Mozart Gets Butchered', *Jewish Chronicle* 11 November

Pople, Anthony (ed.), 1997. *The Cambridge Companion to Berg*, Cambridge University Press

Porges, Henry, 1983. *Wagner Rehearsing the 'Ring'* (trans. Robert L Jacobs), Cambridge University Press

Potter, John (ed.), 2000. *The Cambridge Companion to Singing*, Cambridge University Press
    2009. *Tenor: The History of a Voice*, Yale University Press, New Haven

Puccini, Giacomo, n.d. *La Bohème*, G. Ricordi & c., Milano, 1953

Puffett, Derek, 1989. *Richard Strauss: Salome*, Cambridge University Press

Pushkin Alexander, 1997. *Alexander Pushkin* (A.D.P. Briggs trans. and ed.), Everyman, London

Radice, M.A. (ed.), 1998. *Opera in Context*, Amadeus Press, Portland, OR

Raguenet, François, 1702. *A Comparison between the French and Italian Music and Operas*. Paris; anonymous English trans., 1709, in O. Strunk (ed.), *Source Readings in Music History*, rev. edn., W.W. Norton, New York and London, 1998

Raskatov, Alexander, 2011. *A Dog's Heart*, English National Opera programme

Reich, Steve, 1998. *Writings about Music*: 'Music as a Gradual Process', in O. Strunk (ed.), *Source Readings in Music History*, rev. edn., W.W. Norton, New York and London, 1998

Reimann, Aribert, 1989. *Lear*, ENO Programme

Robbins Landon, H C., 1988 *Mozart's Last Year*, Thames & Hudson, London
    1991. *Mozart and Vienna*, Thames & Hudson, London
    1996. *The Mozart Compendium*, Thames & Hudson, London

Rognoni, Luigi, 1968. *Gioacchino Rossini*, Einaudi editore, Torino

Rolland, Romain, 1980. 'Beethoven the Creator', in Nicholas John, *Fidelio*, English National Opera Guide 4, John Calder, London

Ross, Alex, 2008. *The Rest is Noise*, Fourth Estate, London

Rosselli, John, 1995. *Singers of the Italian Opera: The History of a Profession*, Cambridge University Press

Rossini, Gioachino, 1981. *L'Italiana in Algeri* (ed. Azio Corghi), *Edizione critica delle opere di Gioachino Rossini: Sezione prima – opere teatrali*, vol. ii, Fondazione Rossini, Pesaro
    2004. 'Mosè in Egitto' (ed. Charles S. Brauneri), *Edizione critica delle opere di Gioachino Rossini: Sezione prima – opere teatrali*, vol. xxiv, Fondazione Rossini, Pesaro

Rousseau, Jean-Jacques, 1775. *Lettre sur la musique française*, in O. Strunk (ed.), *Source Readings in Music History*, rev. edn., W.W. Norton, New York and London, 1998

Rutherford, Susan, 2006. *The Prima Donna and Opera, 1815–1930*, Cambridge University Press

Schiele, Egon, 2003. '*SelfPortrait 2*' (trans. W. Stone and A. Vivis), in *Music while Drowning: German Expressionist Poems* (ed. David Miller and Stephen Watts), Tate Publishing, London

Schiller, Friedrich, 1973. Letter to Goethe of 4 April 1797, in John Prudoe, *The Theatre of Goethe and Schiller*, Basil Blackwell, Oxford

    1974. *On the Stage as a Moral Institution*, in Bernard F. Dukore (ed.), *Dramatic Theory and Criticism*, Harcourt, New York

Schlegel, Karl, 1809–11. *Lectures on Dramatic Art and Literature*. Cap. XXII, 'The Spirit of the Romantic Drama', in Bernard F. Dukore (ed.), *Dramatic Theory and Criticism*, Harcourt, New York, 1974

Schlosser, J.A., 1996. *Beethoven: The First Biography*, Amadeus Press, Portland, OR

Schmidt, H.-C., 1991. 'A Question Relating to Zimmermann's Opera "Die Soldaten"' (trans. C.R.Williams), in CD notes to *Die Soldaten*, Teldec 9031–72775–2

Schoenberg, A. 1984 (ed. Leonard Stein). *Arnold Schoenberg: Style and Idea*, Faber & Faber, London and Boston

Scholes, Percy, 1965. *The Oxford Companion to Music*, 9th edn., 'Opera', Oxford University Press

Schonberg, Harold, 1970. *The Lives of the Great Composers*, Davis-Poynter, London

Scott, Michael, 1977. *The Record of Singing to 1914*, Duckworth, London

Scott, Walter, 1841. [*Tales of my Landlord*]: *The Bride of Lammermoor*, Robert Cadell, Edinburgh

Senici, Emanuele, 2004. *The Cambridge Companion to Rossini*, Cambridge University Press

Servadio, Gaia, 2003. *Rossini*, Constable, London

Smith, J. A., 1986. *Schoenberg and his Circle: A Viennese Portrait*, Schirmer, New York

Solomon, Maynard, 1998. *Beethoven*. Schirmer, New York

Spaethling, Robert (ed.), 2000. *Mozart's Letters, Mozart's Life*, Faber & Faber, London

Spencer, Stewart, 2000. *Wagner Remembered*, Faber & Faber, London

Spencer, Stewart and Barry Millington (eds.), 2000. *Wagner's Ring of the Nikelung: A Companion*, Thames & Hudson, London

Stanislavski, Konstantin with Pavel Rumyantsev, 1998. *Stanislavski on Opera* (trans. Elizabeth Hapgood), Routledge, New York and London

    2008. *My Life in Art* (trans. Jean Norman Benedetti), Routledge, London

Stanley, Glenn (ed.), 2000. *The Cambridge Companion to Beethoven*, Cambridge University Press

Stasov, Valdimir, 1968. *Selected Essays on Music* (trans. F. Jonas), Barrie & Rockliff, London

Štědroň, B., 1955. *Leoš Janáček: Letters and Reminiscences* (trans. G. Thomsen), Artia, Prague

Stein, Erwin (ed.), 1964. *Arnold Schoenberg: Letters* (trans. E. Wilkins and E. Kaiser), Faber & Faber, London and Boston

Stendhal, 1985. *The Life of Rossini* (trans. Richard N. Coe). John Calder, London

Stevens, Maryanne, 2000. 'The Exposition Universelle', in Robert Rosenbaum, Maryanne Stevens and Ann Dumas (eds.), *1900: Art at the Crossroads*, Royal Academy of Arts, London

Stockhausen, Karlheinz, 2000. *Stockhausen on Music* (ed. Robin Maconie), Marion Boyars, London and New York

Stravinsky, Igor, 1998. *Poetics of Music*, 1946, O. Strunk (ed.), *Source Readings in Music History*, rev. edn., W.W. Norton, New York and London

Strohm, Reinhardt, 1997. *Dramma per musica*, Yale University Press, New Haven

Strunk, O. (ed..), 1998. *Source Readings in Music History*, rev. edn., W.W. Norton, New York and London

Taruskin, Richard, 2000. *Defining Russia Musically*, Princeton University Press, Princeton and Oxford

   2010. *Music in the Nineteenth Century: The Oxford History of Western Music* (5 vols.), vol. 3, Oxford University Press

Thompson, O., 1965. *Debussy: Man and Artist*, Dover, New York

Till, N., 1992. *Mozart and the Enlightenment*, Faber & Faber, London

Tippett, Michael, 1969. *The Knot Garden*, Schott & Co., London

   1974. *Moving into Aquarius*, Paladin, London

   1983. 'Preface' to *The Mask of Time*, EMI 0777 7 64711 2 9

Tommasini, Anthony, 2008. 'Second Date with a Little Black Dress', *New York Times*, June 11

Toye, Francis, 1962. *Giuseppe Verdi: His Life and Works*, Victor Gollancz, London

Trowell, Brian, 1966. 'Introduction' to Rameau, *Hippolyte et Aricie*, ed. Anthony Lewis, L'Oiseau-Lyre SOL286–7–8

Turnage, Mark-Anthony, 1990. *Living with 'Greek'*, ENO programme, *Greek*

   2001. *Turnage on Tassie: A Conversation with Jennifer Batchelor*, liner notes for *The Silver Tassie*, ENO Alive

Turner, J.M.W., 1974. *The Fallacies of Hope*, in *Turner 1775–1851*, Tate Gallery Publications, London

Tusa, Michael, 1991. *'Euryanthe' and Carl Maria von Weber's Dramaturgy of German Opera*, Clarendon Press, Oxford

   2000. 'Beethoven's Essay in Opera: Historical, Text-Critical and Interpretative Issues in *Fidelio*, in *The Cambridge Companion to Beethoven* (ed. Glenn Stanley), Cambridge University Press

Tyrrell, John (ed.), 1982. *Leoš Janáček: Kát'a Kabanová*, Cambridge University Press

   1988. *Czech Opera*, Cambridge University Press

   1992. *Janáček's Operas: A Documentary Account*, Faber & Faber, London and Boston

Upton, George, 1906. *The Standard Operas*, Hutchinson, London

Verga, Grovanni, 1998. *I malavoglia*, (1881), (trans. Eric Lane), Dedalus, Cambridge

Viéville, Jean Laurent Le Cerf de La, 1702. *Comparaison de la musique italienne, et de la musique françoise*, in O. Strunk (ed.), *Source Readings in Music History*, rev. edn., W.W. Norton, New York and London, 1998

Wagner, Richard, 1968. *Tristan und Isolde* (trans. William Mann), The Friends of Covent Garden, London

1994–5. *Richard Wagner's Prose Works* (trans. W.A. Ellis), London 1892–9, 8 vols., reprinted Bison Books, University of Nebraska

> Vol. i *The Art-Work of the Future and Other Works*
> Vol. ii *Opera and Drama*
> Vol. iv *Opera and Politics*
> Vol. v *Actors and Singers*
> Vol. vi *Religion and Art*
> Vol. vii *Pilgrimage to Beethoven and Other Writings*
> Vol. viii *Jesus of Nazareth and Other Writings*

1998. *Lohengrin*, in *Sämtliche Werke*, Band 7, ii, John Deathridge and Klaus Döge (eds.), Schott Musik, Mainz

2000. *Der fliegende Holländer*, in *Sämtliche Werke*, Band 4, iii, Egon Voss (ed.), Schott Musik, Mainz

2002. *Die Walküre*, in *Sämtliche Werke*, Band 11, Christa Jost (ed.), Schott Musik, Mainz

Walker, Lucy (ed.), 2009. *Benjamin Britten: New Perspectives on his Life and Work*, The Boydell Press, Woodbridge

Warrack, John, 1976. *Carl Maria von Weber*, Cambridge University Press

Weaver, William, 1977. *Verdi: A Documentary Study*, Thames & Hudson, London

1994. (trans), *The Verdi–Boito Correspondence*, University of Chicago Press

Weisstein, Ulrich (ed.), 1964. *The Essence of Opera*, W.W. Norton, New York

Weitzman, Ronald, 1987, 'Sallinen's Music: An Introduction and Appraisal', in Royal Opera House Covent Garden, programme for *The King Goes Forth to France*, April

Westerman, Gerhart von, 1973. *Opera Guide*, Sphere, London

Whenham, John, 1994. *Claudio Monteverdi: 'Orfeo'*, Cambridge Opera Handbook, Cambridge University Press

White, Eric Walter, 1979. *Tippett and his Operas*, Barrie & Jenkins, London

1983. *Benjamin Britten: His Life and Operas*, Faber & Faber, London and Boston

Whittall, Arnold, 1983. *The Music of Britten and Tippett: Studies in Themes and Techniques*, Cambridge University Press

Willett, John (ed.), 1977. *Brecht on Theatre*, Hill & Wang, New York/Eyre Methuen, London

Williams, Bernard, 2006. *On Opera*, Yale University Press, New Haven and London

Wilson, Alexandra, 2009. *The Puccini Problem*, Cambridge University Press

Winter, M.H., 1974. *The Pre-Romantic Ballet*, Pitman, London

Yeats, William Butler, 1965. 'Sailing to Byzantium', in *Collected Poems*, Macmillan, London

Zimmermann, Bernd Alois, 1996. 'Zu den "Soldaten"' (trans. J. Batchelor), in English National Opera programme, *Die Soldaten*

Zola, Émile, 1966–9. *Le drame lyrique*, 1893, in *Oeuvres complètes*, vol. 15, Henri Mitterrand (general ed.), Cercle du Livre Précieux, Paris

    1974. *Naturalism on the Stage*, in Bernard F. Dukore, *Dramatic Theory and Criticism*, Harcourt, New York

    2004. *Thérèse Raquin*, 'Preface' (trans. R. Buss), Penguin, London

Zoppelli, Luca, 1994. *L'opera come racconto*. Marsilio, Venice

Index

Operas are included under their composer's name. Tables have not been indexed.